SOCIOLOGICAL THOUGHT:

BEYOND EUROCENTRIC THEORY

edited by

Nahla Abdo

Canadian Scholars' Press Inc.   Toronto   1996

Sociological Thought: Beyond Eurocentric Theory

Edited by Nahla Abdo

First published in 1996 by
Canadian Scholars' Press Inc.
180 Bloor Street West, Suite 1202
Toronto, Ontario
M5S 2V6

Canadian Cataloguing in Publication Data

Main entry under title:

Sociological thought: beyond Eurocentric theory

Includes bibliographical references.
ISBN 1-55130-063-X ISBN: 978-1-55130-063-4

1. Sociology — Philosophy. 2. Sociology — History.
I. Abdo, Nahla, 1953–   .

HM24.S63   1996   301'.01   C95–931921–2

Page layout by Brad Horning

Printed and bound in Canada

 # Contents

 # Acknowledgements

Khaldûn, Ibn, *The Muqaddimah: An Introduction to History*. Translated by Franz Rosenthal and edited by N.J. Dawood. Copyright © 1967 by Princeton University Press. Reprinted by permission of Princeton University Press. Giddens, Anthony, (Ed.) *Emile Durkheim: Selected Writings*. Copyright © 1972 Cambridge University Press. Reproduced with the permission of Cambridge University Press. Max Weber, *Economy and Society*. 2 *vols.*, trans/ed. Roth and Wittich, University of California Press, reproduced with permission. Marx, K. and Engels, F. *The German Ideology*. Copyright © 1970 International Publishers Co. Reproduced with permission. Marx, K., selections from *Capital vol. 1*. Copyright © 1954. Progress Publishers. Luxemburg, Rosa. *The Accumulation of Capital*. Translated by Agnes Schwarzschild. Copyright © 1951 Routledge.

Introduction

Sociology is an international discipline that is not confined by nationality, race, gender or geographical space. This notwithstanding, in the West and particularly in North America, sociology has become defined as the exclusive and specific product of four founding fathers: Comte, Durkheim, Marx and Weber. Some sociological texts also include Saint Simon and/or Spencer either added to or in place of Comte and/or Durkheim. Yet Marx and his so-called shadow Weber — to use Zeitlin's words — remain the formidable pillars of Western sociology.

By confining itself to Western male founders alone, conventional sociology has managed to exclude the female half of Western society as well as all non-European societies and social scientists. This Eurocentric male character of sociology jeopardizes the very claim to objectivity and representation social science is required to exhibit.

This book is not about the male biases of sociology or its gender exclusionary practices. Since the emergence of the feminist movement in the 1960s, a number of feminists, including Sandra Harding and Dorothy Smith, have challenged social science disciplines in general for their male biases. Feminist sociologists have pointed out that even what is known as sociological methodology may be flawed as it has been predominantly, if not exclusively, written by, about and for men. Some feminists have gone so far as to assert the existence of a "Feminist Methodology" distinct from male, mainstream methodology. Whether one agrees or not with the claim of a distinct field called feminist methodology, it is important to realize that current sociological work, in both its theoretical and methodological aspects, can no longer ignore the significance and centrality of women in the creation and maintenance of their societies.

This work includes a chapter from Rosa Luxemburg's own writings. This inclusion does not claim to provide a feminist critique of social science (sociology) nor does it profess to present a gender perspective on society, let alone a feminist one. Rather, the aim of this chapter is to include the voice of a female social science theorist in the discipline. The inclusion of Luxemburg in a textbook on sociological theory aims at redressing the conventional exclusion of women in the field of theorizing.

The importance of the assigned excerpts from Luxemburg's *The Accumulation of Capital*, as Chapter One demonstrates, goes beyond the gender level. The chapter on imperialism provides the ultimate bridge necessary between East and West. The topic of imperialism has unfortunately attracted very little, if any, attention from the "four fathers" of sociological theory.

Moreover, available literature on Western epistemology provides compelling evidence for the Eurocentric prejudice of conventional social science in general and its inherent cultural and racial biases in particular. As Chapter One demonstrates, the exclusion of non-European theorists from conventional Western social science is a systematic attempt at presenting or representing Western civilization as a unique and self-contained development. As Bernal and Amin demonstrate, between the Renaissance and the Enlightenment, Western social philosophers have arbitrarily constructed a theory of civilization with imaginary roots in Greek philosophy. In the process they glossed over a period of over five centuries during which the West was seen to be in the Dark Ages. In contrast to existing textbooks on sociological theory, this edited volume represents classical sociology as an inclusive discipline that recognizes the contributions of non-European theorists and acknowledges those of women.

Chapter One introduces the textual framework for what I call *inclusive sociology*. "Orientalism, Eurocentrism and the Making of Theory" deals with the defining parameters of conventional sociology. A critique of conventional sociology in terms of both content and determination of who gets to be recognized as a sociologist is provided. This critique elaborates the limitations of the discipline and hopefully contributes to a fresh perspective on sociology.

Chapter Two includes excerpts from Ibn Khaldûn's famous work, *The Muqaddimah* or "The Introduction". This chapter, which contains excerpts from *The Muqaddimah: An Introduction to History*, provides a study of Arab/Muslim social history up until the 14th century. In addition to his contribution to non-European civilization, Ibn Khaldûn's social philosophy presents a challenge to Western epistemology. In this chapter the reader may discern a highly developed social science methodology, which employs concepts and techniques for data collection similar to those "discovered" 500 years later.

Chapter Three, which contains selections from *Emile Durkheim: Selected Writings* edited and translated by Anthony Giddens, explores the notion of "The Division of Labour" and Durkheim's thesis on mechanical solidarity and organic solidarity. As Giddens informs us these are Durkheim's most significant conceptual and methodological contributions to sociology.

Durkheim uses the concept of the "The Division of Labour" as a methodological tool to explain societal transition in human history. This transition from a primitive, traditional and collective society into a more developed professional, specialized and industrial/contractual society is what Durkheim calls transition from mechanical solidarity into organic solidarity. This transition, as the chapter shows, has implications for socio-economic change as well as for change in what the author calls morality, particularly individual morality, which he distinguishes from the primitive collective morality.

This chapter will be read from another — albeit unintended — dimension. On the one hand we will discern the threads of Eurocentrism in Durkheim's approach. On the other hand this chapter draws our attention to similarities in the methodological enquiry used by both Durkheim and Ibn Khaldûn. This is particularly true in the way both have laid down some "general laws governing the transformation of human societies". Similarity may also be detected in both theorists' use of dualist typologies, most importantly Durkheim's mechanical/organic solidarity society and Ibn Khaldûn's bedouin/sedentary society.

Chapter Four selects two pieces of writings from Max Weber. The first, entitled "Basic Sociological Terms" from Weber's *Economy and Society Vol. 1*, explains and defines a variety of sociological concepts. The second, entitled "Protestant Asceticism and the Spirit of Capitalism", taken from *Weber: Selections in Translation*, provides Weber's explanation of the origins and development of capitalism in the West. The latter piece is of particular significance to the context of this textbook as it addresses some of the major issues raised in the first chapter, for example, the role of religion, notably Christianity, in the development of Western civilization.

As Brian Turner (1994) and Maxime Rodinson (1987), among others, have observed, in Islam, as in Christianity, one can equally discern clear and explicit "roots" for the development of the capitalist mode of production. In other words, to distinguish Christianity over Islam or any other religion, as Weber does, by attributing superiority to the former, is not scientifically based. Weber's position on the issue of Christianity is, to say the least, Orientalist. By drawing a clear distinction between the West and its "religion" (Christianity) on the one hand, and the East and its religion(s), Islam among others, Weber confirms the Orientalist belief in the dichotomy; West is West and East is East and the two shall never meet (or never met).

Chapter Five provides an entry into the Marxist theory of social-human development with two excerpts. One is from Karl Marx and Frederick Engels, *The German Ideology,* and is entitled, "Feuerbach: Opposition of the Materialist and Idealist Outlook", and the other is from Karl Marx's *Capital Vol.1.* From the latter we include the following topics: "The Fetishism of Commodities and the Secret Thereof", "The Secret of Primitive Accumulation", "Expropriation of the Agricultural Population From the Land", "Bloody Legislation Against the Expropriated...", "Genesis of the Capitalist Farmer", and "Reaction of the Agricultural Revolution on Industry".

These selections address two major concerns in the discipline of sociology. From the piece on "Feuerbach" we learn about the age-old sociological debate between the materialist and the idealist conceptions of history. By tracing these concepts to their historical roots, albeit European roots, Marx and Engels help clarify some of the major contentious issues in Western epistemology. The excerpts from *Capital Vol.1*, take us from the realm of the general and abstract, as presented in "Feuerbach", to the realm of the specific and concrete. These deceptively short pieces provide a multitude of insights into the area of sociological research. In *Capital,* Marx explains that capitalism is a social and historical force for change which presents actual and concrete implications for human beings

In addition to the actualization and concretization of concepts provided in *Capital,* Marx manages to challenge one of sociology's major tenets with respect to research, namely, the conventional equation arbitrarily struck between objectivity and neutrality. This is particularly true with regard to the nature of capitalist change. While admitting the progressive and developmental character of capitalism, Marx is unequivocally critical of the devastating effects capitalism has on the social, economic, political and cultural relations and structures of people undergoing this form of transformation. His sympathy unmistakenly lies with the class(es) who tend to lose most in this process, the direct agricultural producers and the working class.

The final chapter in this textbook consists of Rosa Luxemburg's main thesis on imperialism. From *The Accumulation of Capital* we select "The Historical Conditions of Accumulation". The reasons for choosing this chapter are twofold: by addressing the concept of imperialism we fill in a gap created by conventional sociology; and the assigned excerpts on imperialism go beyond economic imperialism as they cover the social and historical setting for the expansion of capitalism in its high stage of accumulation.

It goes without saying that Luxemburg's theoretical contribution to the overall objectives of this textbook is quite significant. This chapter provides the missing link or the connecting bridge between East and West. This will be demonstrated by examining the author's account of the socio-economic and cultural impact of imperialism on a number of "Eastern" countries, notably India, Egypt and Algeria.

SELECTED BIBLIOGRAPHY

Rodinson, Maxim. (1987). *Europe and the Mystique of Islam* (translated by Roger Veinus). Seattle: University of Washington Press.

Turner, Bryan. (1994). *Orientalism, Postmodernism and Globalism*. London: Routledge.

 # Nahla Abdo

The Orient as "Object Other"

> Thus one ends up with a typology which makes of the studied "object" another being, with regard to whom the studying subject is transcendent: we will have a *homo Sinicus, a homo Arabicus, a homo Africanus,* the man — the "normal man"... — being the European man of the historical period, that is, since Greek antiquity. One sees how much, from the eighteenth to the twentieth century, hegemonism and anthropocentrism...are accompanied by europeocentrism in the area of human and social sciences, and more particularly in those in direct relationship with non-European peoples. [emphasis in original]
>
> Anwar Abdel-Malek

In his seminal work entitled "Orientalism in Crisis", published in 1963, Anwar Abdel-Malek lays down the foundations of the thesis/theory of Orientalism developed later by Edward Said (1978) and Bryan Turner (1974, 1983) among others. Broadly defined, Orientalism is an epistemological construct designed to study, describe, analyze and understand the Orient (e.g., India, China, Arab Near East, Egypt and North Africa). During the 19th century, Orientalism became a general phenomenon as it permeated all fields in the humanities and social sciences. Orientalism, Abdel-Malek observes was "built into the structure of the social science of the European countries in the period of imperialist penetration and implantation" (p.107). Research in the Orient during this epoch was compiled by an amalgam of university dons, businessmen, military men, colonial officials, missionaries, publicists and adventurers, whose only objective was "to gather intelligence information in the area to be occupied in order to better assure its enslavement to the European powers" (Abdel-Malek,1963:107).

Critics of Orientalism such as Said (1978), Turner (1974, 1980), Rodinson (1973, 1984) and Amin (1989) agree that the discipline was a part and parcel of the Western colonial enterprise in the East. Although some authors have tended to focus on the discursive character of the discipline, emphasizing the question of presentation and re-presentation particularly within the realm of literary and cultural studies, Abdel-Malek attributes to Orientalism a fundamental role in the propagation and promotion of colonialism. Orientalism is conceived as the political-philosophical foundations of colonialism. Ahmad Aijaz, while critiquing Said's emphasis on the literary manifestations of Orientalism, reaffirms Abdel-Malek's position on the strong relationship between Orientalism and colonialism (Aijaz, 1992).

Orientalism constructs specific concepts and methodologies, which are diametrically opposed to concepts and methodologies utilized in the analysis of Western culture and civilization. Until the Second World War, Europe had monopolized the field of Orientalism until its decline and eventual replacement with the US. The latter has since assumed hegemony over most fields of sciences, particularly social sciences and knowledge of the Orient.

The Orient is generally conceptualized as an object of study stamped with an "otherness". This "otherness" is constitutive of an essentialist character. In addition to its essentialist and essentializing approach to the Orient, Orientalism claims to be historical in that it deals with the history of the Orient. Yet the notion of history employed by Orientalists is synonymous to the notion of past. The past of the Orient is studied in a characteristically ahistorical manner. Orientalism transfixes the being, "the object" of study. The "other"/Orient is thought of as fixed and natural instead of evolutionary, dynamic and cultured.

Orientalism denies the object of study (being it the subject people, country, nation, society...etc.,) of its evolutionary and dynamic character. Instead, the Orient is conceived of as a glorified past with brilliant exotic essence, to use Said's words (1978), but without a present, let alone a future. Many Western theoretical accounts of the East/Orient, including those of Marx and Weber, attract this critique.

In so far as Western social sciences and especially sociology are concerned, the main characteristic feature of "present-time Europe" — that is Europe from the 18th to the 20th century — is the development of the capitalist system or mode of production. It is not surprising that all sociology is constructed around understanding the transition to and the development of capitalism. Capitalism has become the cornerstone for measuring development, change, progress, movement and modernization. All nations, countries, peoples and civilizations who were not part of capitalism were relegated to an outside world with the status of "other" and eventually excluded from sociology's conceptualization of society. An alternative conceptual framework was consequently constructed to project or study the Orient "other".

The assumption that capitalism is Western has been passed to us via two major approaches, the Marxist and the Weberian approaches. According to Marx, capitalism is the product of class contradictions and the consequent commoditization of land and labour which were characteristic of 18th and 19th century Europe and particularly England. The process of capitalist development is seen as internal to the dynamic changes within the feudal mode of production. In the Marxist literature, concepts such as "womb", "pregnancy" and "birth" were indicative of the Western character of capitalism. The other approach, which is associated with Weber, attributed to capitalism a Western character for various reasons. But, as we shall see later, a primary reason for such development in the West was attributed to the Western Christian/Protestant cultural ethics.

These approaches, as divergent as they are, appear to suffer from similar assumptions that where there was feudalism there is now capitalism; and hence where there was no feudalism there can be no capitalism. This assumption is faulty at both the factual and the historical levels. Neither Marx nor Weber allows that capitalism required both Western and non-Western forces to develop. Capitalism could not have developed nor accumulated on an expanded level had it not been for the natural and material wealth Europe obtained by force from virtually all the Third World. Third World colonies furnished capitalism both with human and natural resources, while being deprived of most of the benefits of capitalism.

The criticism of Marx's theory of the origins of capitalism must not be construed as a general criticism of classical Marxism. On the contrary, classical Marxists, including Lenin and Luxemburg, were not inattentive to the relationship of West/East or West and the Third World. Both have realized the importance of the Third World (Lenin) and the East (Luxemburg) in serving as primary sources for the so-called "primitive accumulation". Both realized the role played by opening up new consumer and labour markets, cheap raw material and cheap labour power in the further development of capitalism, whether in its extended accumulation form, to use Luxemburg's terms, or in its imperialist stage, to use Lenin's.

Orientalism is deficient not only in its conceptualization of self and other but also in its means and methods. Research methodologies, modes of enquiry and the selection of data are, in most disciplines of social sciences, dependent on, if not determined by, a general conceptual framework. The same is true with Orientalism as a discipline. Based on the specific imagery constructed about the Orient, namely, as the natural other and the ahistorical fixed object, data on the Orient have largely been concerned with the latter's past, its "mysterious" religion, "exotic" space and unchanging traditional history. Data gathered on the Orient in the late 19th and early 20th centuries were primarily individual accounts of Catholic and Protestant missionaries, travellers and colonial administrators. It is not surprising, therefore, that most of these reports were, if not exotic and paternalistic, then ethnicist and racist. As recent data from the Orient were not yet available to Western social scientists — archival data gathered by the colonial powers were not released as most of the Orient was still under European colonialism — the Orient as Jean Chesneaux observed was studied as "dead civilization" (in Abdel-Malek, 1963: 109-110).

The so-called dead civilization of the East and its incompatibility with scientific advance was loudly expressed by Renan's infamous statement that: "Anyone... who has been in the East or in Africa will have been struck by the hidebound spirit of the true believer, by this kind of iron circle which surrounds his head, rendering him absolutely closed to science, incapable of learning anything or of opening himself to a new idea" (in Hourani, 1980:12). In 1883, Renan, contrasting the Aryan race to the Semitic, declared that Islam "was a religion which prevented the use of reason and growth of science...". According to him: "there had never been and there could not be, such a thing as a Muslim scientist: science had indeed existed and been tolerated inside Islamic society, but the scientists and philosophers were not really Muslims...". Arabic philosophy and science, according to Renan, "were Arabic only in language, in spirit they were 'Greco-Sassanian'" (in Hourani, 1980:62).

When typologized/categorized as the other, the Orient began to acquire characteristics which distinguished it from those conventionally employed in studying the West. Weber's position that 'all what is not Occidental is Oriental' became a typical reflection of much of Western modern social science, not only in its conservative and liberal traditions, but also in terms of its radical tradition based on the works of Marx and Engels and the schools of thought which followed them. This polarity between West and East, as Bryan Turner observed, reproduces the world as Western/non-Western "by reference to a cluster of absences — the missing middle class, the missing city, the absence of political rights, the absence of revolutions..." (Turner, 1974:81).

The perspective of absences or lacks, to use Shohat and Stam's words (1994), became a convenient mechanism employed by Western scholars seeking to see the world in binary oppositional terms.

Although the propagation of Orientalism was heightened during the colonial era, the official death of colonialism brought about by consecutive Third World national liberation movements, particularly after the Second World War, did not diminish the West's interest in this form of scholarship. Quite to the contrary, renewed interest in Orientalism was seen, at least by England, as vital for rearranging its "responsibilities that remain in the colonies and strengthening the relations with the Dominions, the close neighbours of the peoples of Asia and Africa" (Abdel-Malek, 1963:121). It was later adopted by the US as the latter began to acquire a hegemonic role in world politics.

The shift in the centre of gravity from Europe to the US after the Second World War was accompanied by new ideologies; of which Orientalism occupied a major role as US interest in the Orient and particularly the Middle East began to assume a central role in the country's economic and geo-political interests. In 1946 the Middle East Institute was founded in Washington, followed in 1949 by the Council for Middle East Affairs in New York. Realizing the new place it occupied in world politics, the US began to look for more efficient means to control the Middle East. And with the emergence of the Middle East as a geo-political region with significant import to the US, studies by the US of the Orient began to focus on the Arab/ Muslim component of this area.

Our discussion of Orientalism will focus on Islam and the Arab Muslim region of the Orient. Of the various religions, nationalities and cultures which make up the Orient, Arab-Muslims have been most targeted by Western imperialist interests. Space precludes us from detailing the history of Western animosity and hostility towards Muslim-Arabs: suffice it to mention that unlike other Oriental/Eastern nations and religions, Arab-Muslim history was not confined to Asia (the Orient). In fact, the Arabs were present in Europe and exerted significant impact, politically and culturally, on European history during the expansion of Islam. Arab colonization of major parts of Europe presented a threat to the West. This is particularly true if one considers the expansion of the Umayyad dynasty over all of Spain where the Arabs controlled and ruled Spain for over 400 years, followed by other waves of Arab-Muslim colonization of the Ottoman Empire in parts of Eastern Europe.

It is in this context that Bryan Turner, Albert Hourani and Edward Said, among others, have suggested that the notion of Orientalism emerged as a discourse of power in the context of a geo-political struggle between Europe and the Middle East (Turner, 1983; Hourani, 1980). Elaborating on this, Albert Hourani, the renowned Arab/Middle Eastern historian, wrote:

> The idea that political encounter (enmity) between
> Christianity and Islam goes back to the beginning of the
> century. That encounter has been expressed in terms of holy
> war, of Crusade and Jihad. The first great Muslim expansion
> in Christian lands, Syria, Egypt and North Africa, Spain and
> Sicily; the first Christian reconquests, in Spain, Sicily and
> the Holy Land; the spread of Ottoman power in Asia Minor
> and the Balkans; and then the spread of European power in
> the last two centuries: all these processes have created and
> maintained an attitude of suspicion and hostility on both
> sides and still provide, if not a reason for enmity, at least a
> language in which it can express itself. (Hourani, 1980:4)

"Islam", Albert Hourani suggests, is seen with the eyes of inherited fear
and hostility. It is seen "not in itself but as the symbol of some enemy nearer
home" (Hourani, 1980:10).

This history has been used to legitimize the West's hatred, suspicion and
contempt for the Arabs. Most critics agree that this history of rivalry has not
been ruptured despite the disappearance of the old threat. The reason for the
survival of the claim for Western epistemological superiority over the Arab/
Muslim Middle East, Turner argues, is "closely tied to the crises of global
politics and, in particular, to the location of Islam with respect to the energy
requirements of industrial societies" (Turner, 1983:18-19).

The juxtaposing of notions like oil, Islam, Arabs and Middle East and
their usage as synonymous is common in various academic and popular
works in the West. I have often asked high school students to define the
Middle East. What comes to their mind when encountering the term? In
almost all occasions, the response follows these lines: the Middle East is
made up of oil, Islam, desert, Arabs, wealth and veiled and secluded women.
Outraged by these responses, I often found myself forced to deconstruct
Canadian students' Orientalist knowledge of the Middle East and re-construct
the history and cultures of Arabs, Muslims and Middle Easterners.

North American popular culture disseminated through various media
outlets — T.V. newspapers and commercials — feeds into the Western
constructs of Orientalism and Eurocentrism.

As an ideological discourse with a clear political agenda, as a project
constructed around more or less defined power relations, Orientalism is not
concerned with scientific or historical facts. Orientalism homogenizes Arabs,
Middle Easterners and Muslims and presents them as an undifferentiated
entity. In so doing, Orientalism constructs a mythical entity void of any
historical or factual foundations. The fact that not all Arabs are Muslims nor
all Muslims are Arabs, and the fact that the overwhelming majority of

Muslims reside outside of the Middle East appears to be of little or no import to the Orientalists. Orientalism does not only gloss over fundamental distinctions which exist between these different categories, it also ignores internal distinctions, conflicts and contradictions which exist within each of these entities, such as different ethnicities, religions and classes.

The homogenization process of Orientalism has the effect of flattening the Orient, in this case the Middle East, Islam and the Arabs, thus transforming these entities into undifferentiated Other void of culture and history. Through the process of Othering, a relationship of domination which involves the reconstruction of the powerful as a distinct subject has been established. In this relationship, the subject(s) involved in reconstructing the Other as inferior lay down the rules of this dichotomy by reasserting themselves as the sole agents of history.

Moreover, within the context of Orientalism, Orientals are rendered immutable, fixed objects of stagnation both in absolute as well as relative terms. Qualities and characteristics bestowed on them contrast with those of West/Occident, Turner's notion of cluster of absences and Shohat and Stam's thesis of lacks become the denominator of the Orientalist construct of the East. In this relational existence Occidentalism is reconstructed as a form of power difference and manifests itself as a form of Eurocentrism.

Although the term Orientalists can be used to denote different things including, for example, Western researchers who work on the Orient, the seemingly neutral qualities of the discipline have hardly existed. Orientalism is a form of racism. This is particularly so as the ideology is utilized in a constitutive manner, that is, as an institutionalized form of knowledge incorporated into the structure of power relations. Orientalism becomes a form of racism when put to use by the powerful forces of capitalism/colonialism or imperialism in subjugating the colonized. The Algerian and Palestinian histories of settler colonial subjugation furnish clear examples of Orientalist racism or racist Orientalism.

Feminist Responses to the Othering Paradigm

Othering as a form of power relations is not confined to the Orient or Orientalists. This process, to reassert what we have already said, is the product of social relations of domination and subordination. Othering has created a wide range of marginalized groups. These include all non-white-non-Europeans, such as natives, blacks and people of colour internal to the capitalist centres as well as Third World peoples in general. Othering is a process which also affects women, homosexuals and differently abled peoples. Feminist literature provides ample evidence on the Othering of women in

European male-sciences. Referring to the issue of woman-as-Other, Hartsock observed: "the Other is always seen as Not, as a lack, a void, as lacking in the valued qualities of the society, whatever those values may be" (Hartsock, 1987:86).

Similar to the Orientalist Othering, sexist Othering, namely, marginalizing women and turning them into Other, has created the same division: natured women and civilized men. This distortion, which is similar to the arbitrary construction of the Orient by Orientalism, Memmi observed, renders the Other fixed—without possibility of evolution (Memmi,1968: 71-72).

One of the major contributions of feminist scholarship is the attempt to revisit the history of modern sciences and disclose the inner biases on which they have been established. In the process of rewriting modern sciences, largely viewed as a white-male European construct, feminist scholars dispelled a major myth about the objectivity/neutrality of science. The methodologies adopted by most modern scientists, from Newton to Descartes to Bacon, feminists assert, are ideological constructs designed to capture, control and manipulate the Other. The Other here represents "earth/nature" and the different social/class groups affiliated with it. These include peasants and women: "women and peasants were/are defined as 'earth' or parts of the earth—as nature is identified with the earth and her plants—under early capitalism slaves were defined as 'cattle' and women as 'breeders' of these cattle" (Mies, Bennholdt-Thomsen and Von Werlhof, 1988:88).

The scientific revolution, feminists assert, has served as an ideological shield for capitalist pillage of nature and the exploitation of labour power. The capitalist drive to gain control over all that is non-capitalist was at the core of most sciences. The scientific revolution, Carolyn Storey observes, marks "an unprecedented juncture in Western history wherein the ancient dichotomies posited between mind and body, and particularly male and female, became a conscious social organizing principle" (Storey, 1989:54).

The relationship between capitalism and modern science is dialectical in that the former serves as a material basis for the latter, providing it with material and financial support. Sciences, including social sciences, serve as a strong mechanism for the promotion and expansion of capitalism. With this relationship in mind Maria Mies exposes the terms of civilized and progress promoted as European notions, in other words, notions attributed to the natural Other, such as "wild, savage, uncontrolled, and backward" (Mies, 1986: 74-75). The notion of progress, Mies adds, is not the product of hard labour or intelligence. Nor is it, one may add, the product of a particular religious belief such as the Protestant Ethic, as Weber wrote. The notion of progress is intrinsically linked to the oppression of Others and to the exploitation of natural resources (Mies, 1986:74).

Like Anwar Abdel-Malek, Samir Amin and Martin Bernal on development, feminists have also exposed the strong alliance between science and religion. Christianity, in its Catholic as well as Protestant forms, has permeated modern sciences. As the Other/nature/woman was seen as chaotic and unorderly, Christianity was evoked as a principle of Order deemed necessary to "tame a seemingly disordered and chaotic world" (Harding, 1986:116; Storey, 1989:76-77). It is not surprising, therefore, that Descartes saw mathematical laws as God-given laws (in Merchant, 1980: 205) and Newton believed that the "Laws of Gravity" were "imposed on creation by God" (Storey, 1989:80).

The legacy of Othering, not unlike that of colonial and imperial violence, still lingers on. The reconstruction of the Orient/woman/nature Other continues to permeate most mainstream, male-stream, writings in social sciences. Yet, one cannot fully understand the Orient as the Other unless we examine the construction of the Occident or Europe as distinct or different. For, the East in the Orientalist *epistime* is as imaginary as the West was rendered in the Eurocentric ideal. It is in this sense, Ella Shohat and Robert Stam conclude that, "the 'myth of the West' and 'the myth of the East' form the verso and recto of the same colonial sign" (Shohat and Stam, 1994:15).

Eurocentrism: Orientalism's Other Face

Science and technology, which accompanied the development of capitalism in Europe, justified the mythical construction of Europe as a civilizational oneness. Eurocentrism constructed the image of the new West as an uninterrupted continuum of Greek rationalism, science and secular philosophy. The need to present the West as different and distinguished from the rest parallels the drive for power and control Europe found itself preoccupied with during the Renaissance and early Modern period.

A note on the similarity between the two constructs, Eurocentrism and Orientalism, is worth mentioning here. Eurocentrism shares with Orientalism a vision of the world that is polar and oppositional, a vision which divides the world into a hierarchy of binarism; thus the creation of Us/the West vs. Them/the East is a relationship based on the cultural superiority of the former over the latter. The Eurocentric vision and construction of Western civilization as the natural extension of Greek civilization removes Ancient Greece from its Levantine context and Egyptian ancestors, the very milieu in which Greek civilization unfolded and developed. This removal, both Bernal (1987) and Amin (1989) argue, facilitates the annexation of Hellenism to Europe.

Like Orientalism, Eurocentrism constructs the West as an idealized entity in ways flattering to the European. As observed earlier, in this idealized construct science and technology are often seen as Western. The correlative of this attitude in the realm of theory as some critics observe "is to assume that all theory is 'Western', or that movements such as feminism and deconstruction, wherever they appear, are 'Western', a view that projects the West as 'mind' and theoretical refinement and the non-West as 'body' and unrefined raw material" (Shohat and Stam, 1994: 14).

In this case as well, Christianity has been often invoked, albeit arbitrarily, as a unifying principle for European culture. Seen as a cultural foundation for Europeanism, Christianity itself had to go through major alterations. Christianity, which as Amin (1989) observes was not born on the banks of the Loire or the Rhine, had to be assimilated and annexed to the West. Thus, the "Holy Family and the Egyptian and Syrian Church Fathers had to be made European." The Holy Family was stripped of its Middle Eastern dark complexion and dark hair and turned into white-skinned blond symbols. Non-Christian Ancient Greece also had to be assimilated into this lineage, by accentuating an alleged contrast between Greece and the ancient Orient and inventing commonalities between these civilized Greeks and the still barbaric Europeans (Amin, 1989: 100).

In his book subtitled *The Fabrication of Ancient Greece 1785-1985*, Martin Bernal (1987) demystifies the Greek Christian origin of the West and argues that ancient Greeks were quite conscious that they belonged to the cultural area of the ancient Orient. Not only did they recognize what they had learned from the Egyptians and the Phoenicians, but they also did not see themselves as the 'anti-Orient', which Eurocentrism portrays them as being. On the contrary, the Greeks claimed that they had Egyptian ancestors.

For Bernal, 19th-century "Hellenomania" was inspired by the racism of the Romantic movement, whose architects were often the same people whom Abdel-Malek (1962) and Said (1978) cite as the manufacturers of Orientalism. Bernal, for whom linguistics was central, illustrates how the impulse to remove Ancient Greece from its Levantine context has forced linguists into some "dubious acrobatics". Thus he asserts: "up to half of the Greek language was borrowed from the Egyptian and the phoenician tongues". But linguists invented a mysterious "Proto-Aryan" myth dear to Eurocentrism, that of the "Aryan purity" of Greece (Bernal, 1987:22).

Bryan Turner argues that "the Aristotelianism which became the major Christian framework for the philosophical formulation of Christian beliefs was transmitted by Islamic scholars — Averroes (or Ibn Rushd, the Arab philosopher of Spain, 1126-98), Avicenna (or Ibn Sina, d. 1037), al Kindi and al-Razi". As a result, he asserts, one must view this as "an area of common experience and historical development, where medieval Christian culture was dependent on Islam" (Turner, 1983:33). Responding to various Western authors, such as Bertrand Russell who dismisses the significance and originality of Arab thought and O'Leary who held that Muslim philosophers were 'only translators of Greek culture', Turner argues: "The great attraction of seeing our philosophical, cultural and scientific inheritance as based upon Greek culture and of seeing Islam as simply a neutral vehicle for the transmission of those values is that it allows us to connect scientific freedom of thought with political democracy" (1983:34). Political democracy and openness, which the West associates with Hellenism, have always been cherished as peculiar to Western capitalist societies. This association is false. "The problem with this emphasis on Hellenism and democratic inquiry", Turner writes, "is that it ignores the fact that Greek society was based on slavery and that the majority of the population was, therefore, precluded from these open debates between citizens" (Turner, 1983:34).

The dichotomy created by Eurocentrism, which divides the world into the West and the Rest, ignores the fact that much of the scientific and technological foundations of the West were borrowed from the Rest. Until recent centuries, Europe was a borrower of science and technology; the alphabet, algebra and astronomy all came from outside of Europe. Quoting a number of historians on this issue, Shohat and Stam suggest that "even the caravels used by Henry the Navigator were modeled after lateen-sailed Arab dhows. From China and East Asia Europe borrowed printing, gunpowder, the magnetic compass, mechanical clockwork, segmental-arch bridges, and quantitative cartography..." (Shohat and Stam, 1994:14). In fact, Martin Bernal goes as far as suggesting that civilization itself was first assembled in the East and more specifically around the Euphrates and Dejla (or Iraq today). On this, Bernal has the following to say:

> Few scholars would contest the idea that it was in Mesopotamia that what we call 'civilization' was first assembled. With the possible exception of writing, all the elements of which it was composed — cities, agricultural irrigation, metalworking, stone architecture and wheels for both vehicles and pot-making — had existed before and elsewhere. But this assemblage, when capped by writing, allowed a great economic and political accumulation that can usefully be seen as the beginning of civilization. (Bernal, 1987:12)

Essentialism is characteristic of Eurocentrism but is not confined to the West. In fact, nations, cultures or religions defined in ethnicist terms are prone to become essentialist. This is evident in most Eastern national, cultural or religious communities, including Hinduism, Buddhism and Islam. When reconstructed as culture, ethnicity or political ideology, instead of religion, Islam, or more properly Islamicism, acquires essentialist characteristics. The dichotomy East and West, at least since the 1980s, has been further entrenched not by the powerful West but by the de-empowered Muslim East. Some authors refuse to equate Islamic essentialism with other forms of essentialism claiming that Euro-North American essentialism comes out of a power position and that it is part of a hegemonic ideology, while the Muslim world lacks that power. Others contend that Muslim essentialism is itself a response or resistance to European hegemony and as such cannot share similar oppressive characteristics.

While there is some truth in both claims one must not be oblivious to the fact that Islamicists are quite selective in what they keep and what they cast away as Western. No where in any of these countries is the Western economic system of capitalism and its culture of individualism and class and gender exploitation resented, resisted or disdained. In fact, the main and perhaps only area which Islamicists try to control or safeguard from Western influence is the domain of women and the family. It is in this area that Islamicists feel threatened by Western culture. Thus ideas and practices which involve women's active participation in education, labour, political and other aspects of social building are either discouraged or actively fought by Islamicists.

There is nothing essentialist about being Muslim per se. However, by redefining women and the family in terms which suit their political agenda, Islamicists manage to essentialize Muslim women and create a dichotomy between Muslim women and non-Muslim women. This form of essentialism is neither more legitimate not less oppressive than other forms of essentialism. The dichotomizing impact of Muslim essentialism which aims at keeping women away from the achievements and contributions of their sisters in other cultures stalls the progress and development of Muslim society.

In their comprehensive and original study entitled *Unthinking Eurocentrism*, Ella Shohat and Robert Stam (1994) expand on the concept of Eurocentrism. By defining it as a mode of thought engaging a number of mutually reinforcing intellectual tendencies or operations, the authors go beyond the East/South, which resides outside the borders of the West/North, and maintain that Eurocentric Otherness has included peoples who reside in the borders of Western societies. These include the natives, blacks, Hispanics and other ethnic, racial and national groups who despite their differential sizes have been lumped together as "minorities". By reconceptualizing Eurocentrism as an exclusive ideology applied to a multitude of nationalities, races and ethnicities, the authors provide a politicized and inclusive definition of the concept. Eurocentrism is seen as a form of internal colonialism.

Similar to other critics of Eurocentrism, Shohat and Stam trace the history of the concept which is based on the projection of a linear historical trajectory leading from classical Greece to imperial Rome and then to the metropolitan capitals of Europe and the US. Yet, in an equally innovative and original way, they take the concept one step further and trace its movement in the more recent history between the West and particularly North America and the Third World. Eurocentrism, they argue, attributes to the West an inherent progress toward democratic institutions. While so doing, it supresses non-European democratic traditions, obscuring, in the process, the manipulations embedded in Western formal democracy and masking the West's part in subverting democracies abroad. This political ideology minimizes the West's oppressive practices by regarding them as contingent, accidental, exceptional, failing to recognize colonialism, slave-trade, and imperialism as fundamental catalysts of the West's disproportionate power.

The authors who are cultural critics place a special emphasis on what they see as Eurocentrism's appropriation of the cultural and material production of non-Europeans. Cultural appropriation, they maintain, is accomplished while denying the Other achievements and its own appropriation, thus consolidating its sense of self and glorifying its own cultural anthropophagy (Shohat and Stam, 1994: 2-3).

It is crucial to understand that our critique of Eurocentrism and Orientalism is not a vindication of individual Europeans. Victimology, to use Shohat's concept, is not our concern. The tremendous contributions of Western scholars notwithstanding, our concern with Eurocentrism and Orientalism is only in so far as these two are perceived as institutionalized norms and practices. The Eurocentric and Orientalist constructions concern us only in so far as they are seen as organizing principles and means of reinforcement used by the West to oppress the Others. The stance we take here is basically a critique of the assumed universalism of European norms and Western values. It is a critique of Europe's historical role of oppression of the internal and external others. It is a stance which confers with Aime Cesaire's words that "no race has monopoly on beauty, intelligence or strength".

Moreover by refuting the superiority of the West as an inborn or inherent quality we do not wish to suggest that the Orient or the Other is superior. Western universality and its claim for oneness and continuum from Greek civilization is rejected on the basis of its ahistorical non-factual claims. And on this very basis we do not consider the East as homogeneous or as one unit. In fact, as Sadeq Jalal Al-Azm has strongly suggested in his "Orientalism in Reverse" (1981), any critique of Orientalism will have to take into consideration the racial, ethnic, gender and class contradictions and inequalities which grip the Orient. The Orient must not be taken as passive recipient of

Western victimization. Regimes in the Orient, even prior to the advent of colonialism and imperialism have had their share in inflicting oppression and exploitation onto their own societies. Moreover, in his critique of Edward Said's thesis on Orientalism, Al-Azm refused to see Orientalism as an-all homogenizing theory spanning over many centuries as Said has constructed it. Al-Azm argues that the Orientalism, which corresponds to the racial and colonial practices of the West, is that which has its roots in the 19th-century Europe.

Our position in this chapter, not unlike that of most critics of Orientalism and Eurocentrism, is that the reality of the history of the relationship between East and West is one of interdependency and not of binarism and isolation. Europe and later North America could pride themselves for their scientific and technological achievements not because of the presence of a special "gene" or "intelligence" called European or Western, nor because of an inherent or in-built quality in Christianity or Europeanism, but rather because the East and what has become labelled as the Third World have historically furnished the grounds for Europe's scientific and technological take-off. It is only by recognizing the existence of a relationship of interdependency and a certain degree of mutuality within the world, as Bryan Turner once observed, can we move beyond Eurocentrism and Orientalism. It is only by rejecting polarity, hostility and dichotomy can one view the world as a polycentric universe.

Orientalism, Eurocentrism and Sociology

Since this text is concerned with classical sociology, it is only logical that we examine the works of the pillars of Western sociology, Karl Marx and Max Weber. However, this by no means suggests that Orientalism and Eurocentrism end with the death of these "classical" sociologists. The extent to which Orientalism and Eurocentrism have become entrenched in modern social sciences and particularly contemporary sociology is demonstrable in the work of Daniel Lerner and various other contemporary sociological schools. This is clear in Lerner's well known statement: "What the West is, the Middle East strives to become" (Lerner, 1964:47); it is evident in Rostow's economic stages and the take-off model; it is also embedded in the Modernization approach. There is a wide range of sociological modifications of the Weberian notion of patrimonialism, such as the Patron-Client model and the dichotomy-based approaches of sociological enquiry, most notable being that of traditionality-modernity contrast.

The following critical re-examination of the works of Marx and Weber, it is hoped, will facilitate the linkage between the classical and modern, and demonstrate the ideological continuum between the "old" and the "contemporary".

Marx and the Dark Alleys of the Orient

The strength of the Marxist theory lies in the theoretical and analytical tools Marx used to analyze Europe's transition from feudalism to capitalism. By examining the dynamics of Europe's pre-capitalist (feudal) mode of production, Marx has conceptually and analytically set the grounds for the emergence of capitalism's most dynamic social classes, the bourgeoisie and the proletariat. Placed in diametrically opposed positions, with the bourgeoisie owning the means of production and the proletariat owning only their labour power, the dynamics between the two provided the central organizing principle of the capitalist mode of production. This relationship is one of exploitation, surplus extraction and capitalist expansion. Marx's method is dynamic, historical, materialist and undoubtedly challenging.

The significance of historical materialism lies in the emphasis this method places on the relationship between theory/abstraction on the one hand, and social context/reality on the other. The social, economic, political and historical context make up the forces and source from which theories and categories are abstracted.

Responding to critics who try to reduce historical materialism to economic determinism, Engels, in a letter to Joseph Bloch of 21 September 1890, wrote:

> According to the materialist conception of history, the *ultimate* determining element in history is the production and reproduction of real life. Neither Marx nor I have ever asserted more than this. Therefore if somebody twists this into saying that the economic factor is the *only* determining one, he is transforming that proposition into a meaningless, abstract, absurd phrase. The economic situation is the basis, but the various components of the superstructure — political forms of the class struggle and its consequences, such as: constitutions drawn up by the victorious class after a successful battle, etc., juridical forms, and even the reflections of all these actual struggles in the minds of the participants, political, juristic, philosophical theories, religious views and their further development into systems of dogmas — also exercise their influence upon the course of the historical struggles and in many cases determine their *form* in particular. There is an interaction of all these elements in which, amid all the endless number of accidents...the economic movement is finally bound to assert itself. Otherwise the application of the theory to any period of history one chose would be easier than the solution of a simple equation of the first degree. (in Sayer, 1987: 6)

I took the liberty of presenting the above paragraph to further establish the historical roots of the concepts in Marx. Theoretical categories for Marx, as Sayer asserts, "were not free-floating analytic devices, innocent of historical content". Rather, for him "ideas, categories" are but "the abstract ideal expressions of...social relations. Indeed, the categories are not more eternal than the relations they express. They are historical and transitory products". For Marx, Sayer continues, "there is no theoretical Archimedean point, from which scientific analysis could commence, which lies outside the history and societies of which historical materialism tries to make sense. For Marx, our categories of analysis inescapably partake of the social reality they seek to depict; they 'bear the stamp of history'" (Sayer, 1987:126).

Recognizing the value of the method of historical materialism becomes all the more important in the face of the special treatment Marx and Engels rendered to analyzing non-European, particularly Eastern, economic structures. As we shall see shortly, unfortunately, none of the above features of Marx's conceptual and analytical faculties was used when he and Engels embarked on a brief, nonetheless important description of non-Western societies, particularly India and the Ottoman Empire. Instead of the dynamic, historical materialist approach, Marx constructed a new set of terms and categories with little or no historical context.

In his account on Asia (the Orient) Marx has lumped together all of Asia, including India and the Ottoman Empire, under one geographical unit and consequently homogenized them as one system of production called "the Asiatic Mode of Production". The characteristics of the Asiatic Mode of Production (hereafter AMP) as laid down by Marx were the absence of independent classes, the presence of an all empowering state which owns and controls the land, and the existence of masses of peasantry who cultivate the land and are totally dependent on the state for their livelihood.

A cluster of absences, as Bryan Turner observed, has thus been established to describe the Orient/East. The absence of classes he claimed to characterize the Orient/East, particularly the bourgeoisie, led Marx to envision the history of the Orient as stagnant and in fact as totally absent (Turner, 1983). Hence, for Marx, no improvement or development in the forces of production can emerge in the Orient since the class which initiates these developments is absent. Moreover, because of the alleged absolute control of the state, the Asiatic state was described as despotic. Marx makes several references to the Mongul emir as well as the Ottoman sultan. Furthermore, because of the despotic nature of rule in the AMP, the state can move the peasants from their land to other parts without any resistance from the peasantry. Therefore, the peasantry in the East were portrayed as passive and with little attachment to the land.

The assumed absence of classes or objective conditions capable of internally producing the bourgeois class led Marx to the logical conclusion that change in Asia is only possible if induced or imposed from the outside. This logic appears to advocate a developmental/progressive role for colonial capitalism. Although Marx was well aware of the misery and destruction the British colonial rule wrought on India, his theoretical construction could not avoid slipping into the colonial Orientalist discourse.

The Orientalist approach characteristic of the AMP, most critics suggest, is largely based on the fact that Marx's exercise was not founded on reliable information. Marx's sources of information were, in fact, based on the literature gathered by Britain's colonial administrators in the area. Moreover, this approach is Eurocentric in that it constructed a special and separate mode of existence in the East in contrast and opposition to that constructed by him about the West. Thus, the dynamic, progressive and developed West was contrasted with the stagnant, despotic and immovable East. At this point, one may add that in his *On Colonialism* Marx has gone as far as arguing that since the history of all societies is the history of struggles between classes, it followed that Asia "has no history at all, at least no known history" (1972:81).

The most substantive critiques of the AMP are those articulated by Marxist and neo-Marxist scholars who conducted theoretical and empirical work in various regions of Asia, particularly India and the Arab Middle East. Critics have pointed out a major contradiction in the concept of AMP, arguing that Marx's theory in general and his notion of the mode of production in particular are dynamic and that his approach is historical and dialectical in that it provides a framework to view the world in constant change and development. The notion of the AMP, on the other hand, constructs a static framework which portrays history in a static manner. Marxist scholars including Althusser (1969) have gone as far as suggesting that the concept of the AMP can be treated as a pre-scientific interest which Marx and Engels abandoned in their maturity. Others like Hindess and Hirst (1975) pointed out the incompatibility of the concept AMP with the central element of the Marxist theory of the state as the product of a society divided along class lines. If classes were absent in Asia, then it is difficult to explain the existence of a state, let alone a strong despotic state. In other words, Marxists have a difficult time explaining the AMP from a Marxist perspective.

Like Orientalism, which views the whole of the Orient as an undifferentiated homogeneous lump, the AMP lumps together a vast area called Asia, presents it as a homogeneous entity and fails to see differences between, among and within its different countries. Responding to this gross misrepresentation of Asian histories, many Third World scholars have pointed to a number of similarities between the feudal mode of production and the pre-capitalist, pre-colonial mode of production in India and other parts of Asia. Among other things they pointed to the role of the Zamindari class in India, the Latifundi class in Latin America and the Mullak classes in the case of many Middle Eastern countries.

Furthermore, studies based on case histories have found that differences in the way people produce and reproduce themselves differ not only between one country and the other but also within the same country from one region to the next. These studies (Chandra, 1981; Abdo, 1989, 1992; Singh, 1993; Rodinson, 1973, 1984) have demonstrated that, among other things, classes, particularly those mediating between peasantry and the state, were not absent. Quite to the contrary, commercial capitalism was quite vibrant in many Asian counties.

Historical evidence brought by those and other studies has also demonstrated the presence of multiple forms of peasant production and peasant relations to land and production. The notion of stagnation and peasant passivity was equally refuted as historical evidence documented the 1856 peasant uprising in India, and the 1858 peasant uprisings in Syria and Lebanon are just an example.

Marx's treatment of the Orient, it may be concluded, is not different from the Orientalist/Eurocentric ideological construction of a mythical Orient whose characteristics are treated as immutable traits defined in simple opposition to the characteristics of the "Occidental" world. This treatment, as Turner has correctly observed, uses an accounting scheme to demonstrate the presence of history in the West and its absence in the East. In so doing, the Orient is presented as a collection of gaps or a list of deficiencies — the absence of private property, the absence of social classes, the absence of historical changes in the mode of production (Turner, 1983: 24).

Before leaving this section on Marx, I would like to address the issue of the relationship between this form of Orientalism and racism. In the course of the past five years while teaching sociological theory from a historical perspective, I was often confronted by some of my students asking me: If Marx is Orientalist and if he advocates a positive role for colonialism in the Third World, what would make him different from other Eurocentric racists, and why do you still advocate his theory and methodology?

My answer is that as historical sociologists we need to appreciate that Marx was himself the product of a particular historical configuration in Europe, a history which was plagued with exploitation of the European masses as well as oppression and colonialism of the Third World. European culture at the time was one of imperialist and colonialist nature. Even Marx and Engels, despite their pungent criticism of the effects of British colonial rule, have reproduced the language of cultural dominance, which traditionally shaped views of other regions.

Yet, to justify one's ethnocentrism because of the mileu within which he or she operates is hardly an answer to such a concern. It is possible to provide a more intelligent response to these queries by addressing the difference between Marxist sociology and Marxism. This issue can be addressed at a number of levels. On the one hand, there is the realization that, unlike other social theorists, Marx was consistent in that his focus, even when discussing the Orient, remained on the material life conditions of people. It is the Asiatic social structure, the role of its social, political forces such as state, peasantry and absence of a middle class, which were at the centre of his analysis. For Marx, the stagnation of Asia, the despotism of its state and the passivity of its peasantry were not explained as the product of inner characteristics of the people of Asia. Marx did not seek to explain Asia's lack of capitalist development by delving into the former's religions, ethics or traditional beliefs. He did not seek to explain stagnation and passivity by going into the so-called Arab mind, as some social theorists, including Weber, have done. Although the AMP is totally different than the Feudal Mode of Production in Europe, his treatment of the former was still focused on the political economic structure in Asia. He still found the major contradictions to be between the state and peasantry.

Another level of analysis concerns the fact that Marx was among the first European social theorists to demonstrate the connection between theory and practice and dispel the myth about the neutrality/objectivity of both the natural and social sciences. As Marxism was a theory concerned not only with analyzing and understanding the world but also with changing it, Marx's position and biases alongside the oppressed and against the oppressors were integral to his theoretical formulations. Not surprisingly, therefore, as Aijaz Ahmad has suggested, Marxism provided the theoretical and practical framework for most liberation struggles in the Third World (Aijaz, 1992).

Weber And The Missing World-Transforming Ethic

Most sociologists acknowledge the significant and perhaps central role religion plays in Weber's sociology. Yet, as with other sociological phenomena discussed by Weber, they disagree on how and in what precise ways does the specific phenomenon manifests itself in human evolution. This disagreement is, in part, due to the highly complex methodology Weber employed in his sociological enquiry, a methodology which is often ambiguous and sometimes even contradictory.

In "Max Weber On Race", Ernst Manasse recognizes the contradictory positions on "race" uttered by Weber in different periods and stages of his intellectual career. This is particularly true with regard to Weber's position on the differences between the "Semitic/Slavic" and the "Aryan/German" races (Manasse: 1947:191-192). In an attempt to explain differences in attitudes towards labour between Polish and German workers, Weber has resorted to culture, standard of living and racial differences between the two races. In an attempt to explain the superiority of the German race over that of the Polish, Weber explained the inferiority of the latter in terms of the Slavic "low demands on material and ideal life" (Manasse, 1947:194). Weber, as Manasse informs us, "did not hesitate to make race responsible for national differences in a somewhat uncritical manner" (Manasse, 1947:194).

Weber's position on forming a causal relationship between race, ethnicity and religious traits, on the one hand, and people's attitudes and stage of development, on the other, is, to say the least, flimsy. In dealing with the phenomenon of the blacks in the United States, the Jewish religion and the Indian caste system, Weber was more inclined to use "objective" structural factors, such as economic (labour conditions) and political (status of the group in the power hierarchy), as determinants of attitudes instead of resorting to inner cultural or traditional traits used in his previous explanation. Shifts and alterations in Weber's position were also observed by Gerth and Mills who suggested that when Weber became disenchanted with German politics he began to place more weight on material factors to explain his sociology (Gerth and Mills, 1961: 502).

This inconsistent and often illusive approach to sociological phenomena assumes a particularly distinctive character when Weber deals with Islam, the prophet Mohammad and the Islamic civilization. Weber's treatment of Islam, as the following pages will demonstrate, is "inconsistent and at best obtuse" to use Bryan Turner's words, Weber does not only "change his approach to certain key sociological issues, develop different lines of argument during his life and holds to different positions without attempting any complete revision" (Turner, 1974:8). A close scrutiny of Weber's treatment of Islam suggests that the real problem lies in Weber's rather consistent position on Islam. A position exemplified in his insistence on presenting Islam as a "simplistic dervish faith" created by "a promiscuous sensual" Mohammad, ruled by an "irrational class of warriors" and motivated only by "booty and real estate gain" (Weber, 1978: 444-626).

Islam, in Weber's sociology, is treated as a part of his general thesis on contrasting the Orient with the Occident. It is part of his general interest in showing why the Orient (in this case Islam) has failed to develop along the lines of the West. Weber approached Islam at two different levels. One level of analysis is objective or quasi-structural where the author tries to examine the presence or rather absence of economic and political pre-requisites to capitalist development. The other is subjective, where he attempts to establish a relationship between the alleged lack of development and the attitudes, behaviour and other subjective characters he attributes to the personalities of Muslim leaders and particularly those of the prophet Mohammad.

Like Marx, Weber employed a cluster of absences which he sees as responsible for the lack of capitalism in the Orient. These absences, however, are established not only in contrast to the Western feudal prerequisites for capitalist development but also from characteristics to which capitalism has given birth. Hence, the Orient/Islam came to represent the lack of everything the West has: it lacked bureaucracy, competence based on impersonal rules, a rationally established hierarchy, free contract, technical training, fixed salaries (Weber, 1978: 229). The list of lacunae goes on to include absence of rational law, a free labour market, autonomous cities, a money economy and a developed bourgeois class.

One can argue that Weber, like Marx, has approached the Orient in a fundamentally ahistorical manner. Yet, economic characteristics did not play the central role in Weber's thesis of the Orient. The notion of "Patrimonialism", which Weber constructs as the framework for understanding the Orient, is applied to the Orient from the "traditional Orient" to the "modern Mohammedan world [*sic*]" (Weber, 1978: 228) — a period of over 13 centuries. It is an essentially political construct. Patrimonialism is more concerned with the political form of domination rather than the form of production.

Patrimonialism was postulated as the mode of governance characteristic of the Orient in general and Islam in particular. It refers to the absolute control of the ruler, the sultan. It is the domination of one ruler who requires a special loyal army to exercise his authority. The legitimacy of the control of the ruler is derived from the personal loyalty of his administrative staff. This staff is recruited either from "persons who are already related to the chief by traditional ties of royalty. These include kinsmen, slaves, clients, coloni" or persons in a relation of loyalty not based on kinship such as all sorts of favourites, persons standing in a relation of fealty to their lord (vassals), or finally, free men who voluntarily enter into a relation of personal loyalty as officials. To this long list of personalities who make up the structure of governance in the Muslim Orient, Weber adds the exotic "head eunuch, who was in charge of the harem" (Weber, 1978: 228).

Constructed as an ideal-type, patrimonialism involves a deliberate exaggeration and aggrandizement of the essential defining characteristics of the phenomenon under study. The properties of an ideal-type as Weber asserts are "*more or less present* and occasionally absent in some cases" (emphasis added).

Nowhere, however, does Weber inform us about which elements of his ideal-type construction of the notion of patrimonialism exist in the Muslim world and which elements are fabricated. It is, nonetheless, apparent that Weber has misread Muslim history. One needs not go into details critiquing Weber's list of absences in the Orient. Both Maxime Rodinson (1973;1984) and Bryan Turner (1974) have provided detailed historical analyses of the presence of developed cities and a highly developed merchant class in Islam, particularly in "early Islam". Other Middle Eastern scholars have refuted the Weberian construct in their case studies. In his "Tributary Mode of Production", developed to conceptualize Middle Eastern social formations, Samir Amin asserts that market exchange and wage labour were never absent, but they remain limited and have little social and economic scope. Furthermore, commenting on the notion of "rational" or "scientific laws" deemed by Weber absent in the Orient, Amin maintains that these "laws" were not needed in tributary formations since the economy is simple and transparent, unlike in capitalism where the worker has no knowledge or control over the destination of products (Amin, 1989: 30-31).

It is not necessary either to go into Weber's ideal-type construction of the notion of patrimonialism to prove its fallacy and irrelevance to various Middle Eastern social formations. Only in passing though, one may observe that the phenomenon of eunuchs Weber compiles among his collection of the components of patrimonialism is specifically Turkish and not Muslim. It is not sanctioned nor was practised by Muslims. It was introduced to the East during the Ottoman Empire.

The similarities alluded to earlier between Marx and Weber in terms of their approaches to the Orient, I must emphasize, stop at this objective level. Namely, in so far as both occupy themselves with the alleged absent characteristics deemed as prerequisite for capitalist development. However, whereas Marx's position on the Orient stops with his thesis on the AMP, Weber's concern goes far beyond an objective analysis. As the following pages will demonstrate, Weber can be described as an Orientalist par excellence. On the one hand, his sweeping generalization and homogenization of the Orient amounts to no more than a fabrication of the orientalist mind. This is the same kind of fabrication Martin Bernal spoke of when he criticized Eurocentrism. On the other, Weber's racially based utterances are inflated with contempt, hatred, ridicule and disparaging statements about Islam and Muslims, and go beyond an attempt to understand Islam.

Weber and Islamophobia

Marx's interest in the Orient and Islam stops at the level of demonstrating the alleged absence of pre-capitalist conditions. Marxism, as argued earlier, is primarily concerned with the dynamics and contradictions of capitalism.

Weber's sociology, by contrast, is comparative in approach. As Parsons has observed: "Weber's inductive study turns from the method of agreement to that of difference. This takes the form of an ambitious series of comparative studies all directed to the question why did modern rational bourgeois capitalism appear as a dominant phenomenon only in the modern West?" (Parsons, 1949:512). In his enterprise, Weber has sought to establish the rationality and consequently superiority of the Occident by alluding to its distinctiveness and difference from the Orient.

We expect a thorough analysis of Islam from an author like Weber whose sociology of religion deals with the Abrahamin religions. After all, Islam is among the three Abrahamin religions. Unfortunately however, this is not the case as Weber finds the parallels and compatibilities only between Christianity and Judaism — affirming the Orientalist adherence to the Judeo-Christian tradition — and refuses to recognize Islam as a member of the monotheistic trio.

Rejecting Islam as part of the monotheistic religions made it possible for Weber to reconstruct Islam as the site of missing ethos; it is missing all essential ethics which led the West in its Christian and Jewish religions to progress, development and modernity. Islam lacks what Weber considers as the world-transforming ethic, namely the Protestant puritan ethic, the Calvinist teachings towards the existing material world and the ascetic character of Christianity. Islam, according to Weber, "accepts a purely hedonist spirit especially towards women, luxuries and property" (in Turner,1974:12). The Quran, in his account, is based on accommodating ethics and finds no conflict between moral injunctions and the world, and it follows that no ascetic ethic of world-mastery could emerge in Islam (Turner, 1974:12).

Instead of involving ascetic ethics, Islam, according to Weber, is a "warrior's ethic". It is based primarily on land conquest and booty appropriation. The religion of the Prophet, Weber states,

> which is fundamentally political in its orientation, and his position in Medina, which was in between that of an Italian podesta and that of Calvin at Geneva, grew primarily out of his purely prophetic mission. A merchant, he was first a leader of pietistic conventicles in Mecca, until he realized more and more clearly that the organization of the interests of warrior clans in the acquisition of booty was the external basis provided for his missionizing. (Weber, 1965: 47)

Islam, in other words, is not a God-based mission as Muslims believe, but a Prophet-based mission aimed at enhancing the interests of a group of warriors seeking to expand their land acquisition and booty.

Mohammad's program, Weber insists, was oriented entirely to the unification of the faithful for the sake of fighting the infidels and of maintaining the largest possible number of warriors (Weber, 1978: 444). On the political and financial nature of Islam, Weber continues: "Mohammad constructed the commandment of the holy war involving the subjugation of the unbelievers to political authority and economic domination of the faithful. If the infidels were members of 'religions with a sacred book', their extermination was not enjoined; indeed, their survival was considered desirable because of the financial contribution they could make" (Weber, 1978: 474). Weber's insistence on considering Islam as an opportunist religion is emphasized time and again. In this reference he argues: "To an even greater degree than the Crusades, religious war for the Muslims was essentially an enterprise directed towards the acquisition of large holdings of real estate, because it was primarily oriented to securing feudal revenue" (Weber, 1978:474).

Islam, Weber contends, lacks the intellectualism of Christianity and Judaism. Sufism, which could have contributed in that direction, has failed to do so partly because its orientation was not along intellectual lines and partly because the "tendencies towards rationalism were completely lacking in the dervish faith" (Weber, 1978:512). Islam lacked the ascetic features of Protestantism and therefore it lacked rationalism. "Any rational system of ascetic control of everyday life was alien to this warrior religion from the outset" (1978:574). Islam is a religion of warriors and not of salvation. Its doctrine of predestination, he claims, "was simple, ritualistic, magical and therefore kept the religion without planned procedure for the control of the workaday world, as did the Puritan doctrine of predestination" (1978:574).

Attacked in Weber's campaign of contempt and disdain are the Muslim caliphs (Khalifeh) or the carriers/propagators of Islam. Described as "the simple warriors of the early Islamic faith", these "warriors", Weber insists, have made obligatory "the violent propagation of the true prophecy which consciously eschews universal conversion and enjoins the subjugation of unbelievers under the dominion of a ruling order dedicated to the religious war as one of the basic postulates of their faith, without recognising the salvation of the subjugated" (1978:594).

Weber does not only paint a distorted picture of Islam, or in his words, "the national Arabic warrior religion". In fact, he goes so far as describing Islam as a monster threatening to swallow up the world — i.e., Weber's world. Consider, for example, the following statement:

> The religious commandments of the holy war were not
> directed in the first instance to the purpose of conversion.
> Rather, the primary purpose was war until they (the followers

> of alien religions of the book) will humbly pay the tribute. i.e., until Islam should rise to the top of this world's social scale, by exacting tribute from other religions. (1978:624)

Nowhere, one may argue, has Weber been so obsessed with the relationship between religion, booty and wealth as he is with Islam. Describing Islam as "the religion of masters", Weber contends: "Military booty is important in the ordinances, in the promises, and above all in the expectations characterizing particularly the most ancient period of the religion... . The most pious adherents of the religion became the wealthiest, or more correctly, enriched themselves with military booty...". Moreover, "the role played by wealth accruing from spoils of war and from political aggrandizement in Islam is diametrically opposed to the role played by wealth in the Puritan religion. The Muslim tradition depicts with pleasure the luxurious raiment, perfume, and meticulous beard-coiffure of the pious [*sic*]". Muslim propagators, such as the Mahdi "used cosmetics...in order to be more successful with women" (1978:624).

Weber concludes his (re)presentation of Islam in the following statement:

> Islam was never really a religion of salvation; the ethical concept of salvation was actually alien to Islam... . An essentially political character marked all the chief ordinances of Islam: the elimination of private feuds in the interest of increasing the group's striking power against external foes; the proscription of illegitimate forms of sexual behaviour and the regulation of legitimate sexual relations along strongly patriarchal lines (actually creating sexual privileges only for the wealthy), in view of the facility of divorce and the maintenance of concubinage with female slaves.... (1978:625)

In fact, the list goes on to include Islam's "unquestioned acceptance of slavery, serfdom, and polygamy, the disesteem for and subjection of women; the essentially ritualistic character of religious obligations; and finally, the great simplicity of religious requirements and the even greater simplicity of the modest ethical requirements" (1978:626).

Finally, of all Muslim leaders, Weber's onslaught on the prophet Mohammad appears to occupy much of his energy. The Prophet, according to Weber, exhibits a nature of "strong sensual passions and... explosions of wrath over very small provocations" (1978:625).

A critique of Weber's thesis on Islam would have been possible had he kept his presentation at a reasonable level of objective, scientific or even quasi-scientific analysis. But with this essentially Islamophobic display, any critique, I believe, would amount to no more than a futile exercise. There is one issue, however, which deserves to be taken up, namely, Weber's reading of the position of women in Islam. There is nothing original in the thesis that Islam is a patriarchal religion. Patriarchy is not unique to Islam as it characterizes all religions. Had Weber, for whom comparative sociology is not an unfamiliar territory, compared Islam with other religions, his conclusions on Islam would have been fundamentally different.

As previous discussions have shown, Islam, for Weber, was to fit a special project with more or less clear ideological and political aims. Weber saw Islam as a threat to (his) Christian world and therefore, chose to re-present it as an inferior religion. It is within this context of Christian/Jewish superiority that Weber places Muslim women. According to Weber, Islam, unlike Christianity, treats women inhumanely as slaves and sex objects. Before we criticize Weber's re-construction of Muslim women, let's compare his thesis on Islam with that of Lord Cromer, the symbol of imperialism in the Middle East, Egypt in particular, who also held Islam as a barrier against progress.

In his *Modern Egypt*, Lord Cromer espoused the idea that "British rule is being used with conscious benevolence for the good of the Egyptians". For him, Islam as a religion is a "noble monotheism" but as a social system it "has been a complete failure". According to him:

> Islam keeps women in a position of inferiority, it crystallises religion and law into an inseparable and immutable whole, with the result that all elasticity is taken out of the social system; it permits slavery; its general tendency is towards intolerance of other faiths; it does not encourage the development of the power of logical thought. Thus Muslims can scarcely hope to rule themselves or reform their societies; and yet Islam can generate a mass of feeling which, in a moment, can break whatever brittle bonds the European reformer has been able to establish with those he is trying to help. (in Hourani, 1980:13)

It could be suggested that Weber's main thesis was taken from Lord Cromer's work, which was available at the time Weber was writing. Albert Hourani suggests that Weber has, in fact, borrowed from Medieval European thought on Islam.

"Medieval Europe", Hourani argues, thought of Muhammad as follows:

> At worst he was a 'fraudulent demoniac or magician', at best an impostor who claimed prophetic gifts in order to

obtain power, an oppressor when he had power, a man of
loose morals and a hypocrite, who used religious claims to
justify his immorality. (Hourani, 1980:24)

Both Medieval thought and that of Weber have judged Islam not for
being what it is but for being what it is not, namely, for not being Christian.
Weber, Hourani adds, has also borrowed from an earlier German philosopher,
Schlegel, who wrote that Islam was "'a religion of empty arrogance and
senseless pride', preached by a 'prophet of unbelief'. It missed the elements
of salvation, reconciliation, mercy love and happiness...therefore, it produced
no civilisation" (in Hourani, 1980:33).

Weber's description/distortion of Muslim women's lives and struggles
ignores a long history of their participation in the making of their histories. A
plethora of literature by Arab and Muslim feminists documents the relatively
advanced status of Muslim women over those in other religions. Authors
point to the important economic, political and social/literary role Muslim
women have historically played since the days of the Prophet, they also
emphasize the fact that only in Islam women can legally inherit property
(Ahmad, 1990; Mernissi, 1985; Saa'dawi, 1983). Finally, the Orientalist
depiction of women as passive, silent and placid victims suggested by Weber
and later adhered to by other Western scholars has received tremendous
attention by Muslim and Arab feminists. Keddie's and Baron's edited work
Women in Middle Eastern History (1991); Abu-Lughod's, *Writing Women's
World* (1993); Lazreg's *The Eloquence of Silence* (1994) and Badran's
"More than a Century of Egyptian Feminism" (1993) are just a few examples
from the body of literature on Arab, Muslim and Middle Eastern women.

Conclusion

Moving towards polycentric sociology requires our unlearning
Eurocentrism. It also entails unlearning Orientalism and the other forms of
ideological construction of Third World peoples, those of the East, of the
South as well as the other marginalized groups, ethnicities and cultures
residing within the confines of the industrial capitalist centres. The construction
of a polycentric vision of the globe involves the reconstruction of theory as
an expression of universal mutuality and interdependency among and between
cultures, nations and ethnicities.

Unlearning Orientalism and Eurocentrism, as Turner and Amin remind
us, must begin by recognizing the historical fallacies upon which both theses
are based. In the process of unlearning a 'fabricated' vision of the world, a
new and more representative world vision, based on a tradition of
interconnectedness and interdependency, must be reconstructed.

History testifies that the West has become what it is — wealthy, rich, technologically advanced and scientifically innovative — by rendering the rest as Third Worlds. Western science and technology must be seen as the cumulative historical product of the labour power of preceding cultures and civilizations. For the past two centuries the relationship between the West and the East has been mediated through colonialism and imperialism. The impact of colonialism on the indigenous populations of the Third World in general, including the East, has been grave if not unthinkable, regardless of the means used by the colonial power(s). Whether colonialism was imposed through capitalist investment, via settlerism, such as the cases of South Africa, Algeria, Rhodesia, Palestine and Canada, or through trading for natural resources such as in the British appropriation of cotton from Egypt, tea and cotton from India, the French wine grapes from Algeria, gold from Africa, fur from the native peoples in Canada, the impact of colonialism has been devastating.

Marxist, radical and feminist scholars have all emphasized the importance of taking colonialism and imperialism as a point of departure to understand differences between cultures and societies. The study of differences, they all agree, must be grounded historically and contextualized in their proper setting. While recognizing the oppressive role of the outsider is a necessary condition in the process of unlearning oppression, it is not sufficient. Internal oppression, or oppression from within one's own society, nation or culture must also be recognized and challenged. Oppression on the basis of gender, class, sexual orientation, ethnic and religious background is characteristic of all human societies. Unfortunately this world is replete with human tragedies caused by little more than ethnic, tribal and religious conflicts. In other words, one must look for both the "outside" and the "inside" for the source of oppression. Finally, recognizing this, one must move forward and begin to address and emphasize similarities between one and (an)other.

I agree with Turner and Amin, among others, who suggest that the move towards a polycentric approach to understanding the world must focus on the parallels and compatibilities between the different societies, cultures, countries and nations. Yet, it is one thing to assert the importance of changing an idea, a concept or a category, and another thing to actually change it. Therefore, unless this proposition is accompanied with precise and practical means of change, it is hard to imagine how desired changes would come about. Here are some ideas which deal with the practical aspects of polycentrism.

To begin with, polycentrism as an alternative inclusive/inclusionary world view or approach is not restricted to the discipline of sociology. It is applicable to all sciences and particularly social sciences. Moreover, as Shohat and Stam demonstrate, a polycentric approach can also be employed to critique state polices including multiculturalism. Shohat and Stam introduce the concept of "polycentric multiculturalism" as an alternative policy to North American liberal multiculturalism. "Polycentric multiculturalism" focuses on "empowering the disempowered", to use the authors' terminology. Thus, characteristic of polycentric multiculturalism is the rejection of a narrow political identification of the different ethnic and cultural entities. Polycentric multiculturalism allows a basis of shared social desires and identifications and rejects Western hierarchy of cultures.

In Shohat and Stam's definition, polycentric multiculturalism represents a way of globalizing multiculturalism. In this context, polycentric multiculturalism rejects the idea that any single community or part of the world is "epistemologically privileged". In other words, polycentric multiculturalism involves a "restructuring and reconceptualization of the power relations between communities", within and beyond the nation state, and seeks to transform subordinating institutions and discourses through dispersing power to the disempowered and acknowledging underrepresented groups as active participants (Shohat and Stam, 1994:47-49).

As precise and practical as Shohat and Stam's definition my seem, it remains partial in nature. As the historical materialist approach teaches us, concepts, categories and ideas are reflections or representations of actual social relations. These relations involve production relations in a highly developed capitalist system. To change the image or the perception of the different ethnic or cultural groups and communities, by changing political representation alone, does not guarantee a real change in the economic living conditions of the groups involved. Therefore, a restructuring of the concept/ policy multiculturalism involves a political, social and economic restructuring of relations within North American society. It follows that to introduce the concept of polycentrism as an approach to replacing differences and distinctions with similarities and compatibilities, one needs to re-think and re-examine the totality of relations involved in each historical conjunction.

At a more academic level, when dealing with social science disciplines, polycentrism entails a globalized inclusive approach to the discipline concerned. In sociology, for example, a polycentric approach will have to account for the contributions to the discipline of people with different cultural, ethnic, gender and historical backgrounds. It is to this end that the current book hopes to contribute.

SELECTED BIBLIOGRAPHY

Abdo, Nahla. (1987). *Family, Women and Social Change in the Middle East: The Palestinian Case.* Toronto: Canadian Scholars'Press.

Abdo, Nahla. (1989). "Colonial Capitalism and Rural Class Formation: An Analysis of the Processes of Social, Economic and Political Change in Palestine, 1920–1947" (Ph.D. diss., Department of Sociology, University of Toronto, 1989).

Abdo, Nahla. (1992). "Zionism and the Palestinian Working Class", *Studies in Political Economy* No. 37, Spring, pp. 59-93.

Abdo, Nahla. (1993). "Race, Gender and Politics: The Struggle of Arab Women in Canada", in Linda Carty (ed.) *And Still We Rise*, Toronto: Women's Press, pp. 71-98.

Abu-Lughod, Laila. (1993). *Writing Women's World: Bedouin Stories.* Berkeley: University of California Press.

Ahmed, Leila. (1992). *Women and Gender in Islam: Historical Roots of a Modern Debate.* New Haven, Connecticut:Yale University Press.

Aijaz, Ahmad. (1992). *In Theory: Classes, Nations and Literatures.* London:Verso.

Al-Azm, Sadeq Jalal. (1981). *Orientalism and Inverted Orientalism* (in Arabic). Beirut: Dar al-Farabi.

Alloula, Malek. (1986). *The Colonial Harem.* Minneapolis: University of Minnesota Press.

Althusser, L. (1969). *For Marx.* Harmondsworth.

Amin, Samir. (1989). *Eurocentrism.* New York: Monthly Review Press.

Badran, Margot. (1993). "More than a Century of Egyptian Feminism" in Judith E. Tucker, ed. *Arab Women: Old Boundaries New Frontiers.* Indiana University Press in association with the Centre for Contemporary Arab studies, Georgetown University.

Bernal, Martin. (1987). *Black Athena: The Afroasiatic Roots of Classical Civilization.* vol. 1 New Brunswick, NJ: Rutgers University Press.

Blaut, J.M. (1993). *The Colonizer's Model of the World: Geographical Diffusionism and Eurocentric History.* New York and London: Guilford Press.

Cesaire, Aime. (1972). *Discourse on Colonialism.* New York: Monthly Review Press.

Chandra, Bipan. (1981). "Karl Marx, His Theories of Asiatic Societies and Colonial Rule." *Review* Vol. 1 (Summer), pp. 13-91.

Chaudhuri, Nupur, and Margaret Strobel, eds. (1992). *Western Women and Imperialism: Complicity and Resistance.* Bloomington: Indiana University Press.

Gerth, H. and C. Wright Mills. (1961). *From Max Weber: Essays in Sociology.* New York: Oxford University Press.

Harding, S. (1986). *The Science Question in Feminism.* Ithace: Cornell University Press.

Hartsock, N. (1987). "False Universalities and Real differences: Reconstituting Marxism for the Eighties." *New Politics,* Vol 1, No. 2., Winter, 83-96.

Hindess, B and Paul Hirst, (1975). *Pre-Capitalist Modes of Production.* London and Boston.

Hourani, Albert. (1980). *Europe and the Middle East.* London: Macmillan.

Keddie, Nikki and Beth Baron, eds. (1991). *Women in Middle Eastern History: Shifting Boundaries in Sex and Gender.* Yale University Press.

Khater, Akram and Cynthia Nelson. (1987). "Al-Haraka al-Nissa'iyyah: The Women's Movement and Political Participation in Modern Egypt." *Women's Studies Int. Forum* 11 (5), pp. 465-483 (USA).

Lazreg, Marnia. (1994). *The Eloquence of Silence; Algerian Women in Question.* London: Routledge.

Lerner, Daniel. (1964). *The Passing of the Traditional Society: Modernizing the Middle East.* New York: The Free Press.

Manasse, Ernst M. (1947). "Max Weber on Race." *Social Research,* Vol 14 (pp. 191-221).

Marx, K. and Frederick Engels. (1972) *On Colonialism.* New York: International Publishers.

Memmi, Albert. (1968). *Dominated Man.* Boston:Beacon Press.

Merchant, Carolyn. (1980). *The Death of Nature: Women, Econolgy and the Scientific Revolution.* San Fransisco: Harper.

Merchant, Carolyn. (1989). *Ecological Revolutions: Nature, Gender and the Science in New England.* Chapel Hill: University of North Carolina.

Mies, Maria. (1986). *Patriarchy and Accumulation on a World Scale: Women in International Division of Labour.* London: Zed Books.

Mies, M. Bennholdt-Thomsen, V, and C Von Werlhof. (1988). *Women: The Last Colony.* London: Zed Book.

Mernissi, Fatima. (1991). *The Veil and the Male Elite: A Feminist Interpretation of Women's Rights in Islam.* Reading, Massachusetts: Addison Wesley Publishing Company.

Parsons, Talcott. (1949). *The Structure of Social Action.* Chicago: Fress Press.

Renan, E. (1896). *The Poetry of the Celtic Races and Other Studies.* London: Heinemann.

Rodinson Maxime. (1973). *Islam and Capitalism*. New York: Pantheon Books.

Rodinson Maxime. (1984). *Marxism and the Muslim World*. New York: Monthly Review Press.

Rodinson Maxime. (1987). *Europe and the Mystique of Islam* (translated by Roger Veinus). Seattle: University of Washington Press.

Rosaldo, Renato. (1989). *Culture and Truth: The Remaking of Social Analysis*. Boston: Beacon Press.

Saadawi, Nawal. (1983). *Women at Point Zero*. London:Zed Press.

Said, Edward. (1978). *Orientalism*. New York: Pantheon

Said, Edward. (1992). *Culture and Empire* . New York: Knoff

Sayer, Derek. (1987). *The Violence Of Abstraction: The Analytic Foundations Of Historical Materialism*. Oxford and London: Basil Blackwell.

Shohat, Ella and Robert Stam. (1994). *Unthinking Eurocentrism: Multiculturalism and the Media*. New York and London: Routledge.

Singh, Hira. (1993). "Classifying Non-European, Pre-Colonial Social Formations: More Than a Quarrel Over a Name." *Journal of Peasant Studies*, Vol. 20 No. 2, pp. 317-347.

Storey, C. (1987). *"Objective", "Neutral" and "Natural" Phallacies: Feminism (s) and the Epistemological Critique of Science and the "Pro-Family" Movement*. M.A. Thesis, Carleton University.

Strobel, Margaret. (1990). *European Women in British Africa and Asia*. Bloomington: Indiana University Press.

Turner, Bryan S. (1974). *Weber and Islam: A Critical Study*. London: Routledge & Kegan Paul.

Turner, Bryan S. (1981). *For Weber: Essays on the Sociology of Fate* London: Routledge & Kegan Paul.

Turner, Bryan S. (1983). *Religion and Social Theory: A Materialist Perspective* . London: Heinemann Educational Books.

Weber, Max. (1978). *Economy and Society* Vol. 1 (edited by Guenther Roth and Claus Wittich). Berkeley: University of California Press.

Weber, Max. (1965). *The Sociology Of Religion* (trans. Ephraim Fischocff). London.

West, Cornel. (1992) *Beyond Eurocentrism and Multiculturalism. Vols I and II*. Monroe. Maine: Common Courage Press.

Ibn Khaldûn

Ibn Khaldûn's (1332–1406) social thought, while largely ignored by most Western sociologists, has received some outstanding praise by the few who read him. Most critics knowledgeable of his theoretical and methodological contribution to the understanding of human history recognize the pioneering and profound value of his contribution. In evaluating *The Muqaddimah*, Yves Lacoste (1965) for example, affirms that "Ibn Khaldûn's articulate and systematic approach to the study of history and human civilisations has no parallel in the history of social thought of other societies and civilisations previous to his own time" (in Dhaouadi, 1990: 320). Mahmoud Dhaouadi (1990:319) considers Ibn Khaldûn as "the founding father of scientific thought on the dynamics of human societies"; and Mahdi A'mel sees him as a historical and dialectical materialist preceding Marx by almost five centuries (A'mel, 1985).

Before introducing Ibn Khaldûn's work, I would like to briefly touch upon some of the issues and debates surrounding the author, to help contextualize Ibn Khaldûn's work both historically and within social sciences. The first thing which comes to the mind of a Western student introduced to Ibn Khaldûn's work is why has he been absent from standard social science thought. To this query we have responded in detail in the previous chapter. Suffice it to recall here that the Eurocentric and exclusionist nature of Western social sciences precludes the inclusion of non-white, non-European thinkers in their midst.

Critics of Ibn Khaldûn (A'mel, 1985; Dhaouadi, 1990) have often occupied themselves with the question of whether Ibn Khaldûn was a sociologist, a social scientist, a historian or any number of these. To this debate one may point out that we only need to remember that the emergence of specialized sciences as separate and independent fields of enquiry (e.g., sociology, anthropology, history, philosophy, etc.) are late-eighteenth-century phenomenon. To try to fit a 14th-century social thinker into this division would be a futile exercise. Similarly, there is little value in trying to determine whether Ibn Khaldûn was a Marxist, a historical and dialectical materialist as A'mel (1985) suggests, or whether his work was a combination of the Weberian and Marxian approaches as Dhaouadi (1990) tries to affirm. Imposing 19th- or 20th-century concepts on social thought which is the product of the 14th century can be quite problematic, particularly when considering the historical and cultural specificity of 14th-century Muslim North Africa.

The following introduction will outline some of the most salient features of Ibn Khaldûn's conceptual and methodological articulations as presented in his seminal work *al-Muqaddimah*.

al-Muqaddimah: I'lm Al-U'mran

The following text by Ibn Khaldûn is taken from *al Muqaddimah*, which is one of the six-book volume containing his research and investigation of the history of the Arab Maghreb — the geopolitical zone that now comprises the countries of Algeria, Tunisia, Morocco, Mauritania and Libya.

In this volume of *al-Muqaddimah*, also known by Ibn Khaldûn as "I'lm al U'mran" (the new science) the author develops his theory of the development and demise of social organizations. Ibn Khaldûn identifies three phases of human social organizations or stages of historic developments. These include Badawa (literally Bedouins' life), which refers to Arab primitive form(s) of social organization; Tamaddun (literally city/town life) or urbanism; and Hadara (literally civilization) as the most developed form of social organization.

The book begins with an examination of people's physical environment and the impact it has on the forms of social organization and non-physical characteristics. This is then followed by a discussion of the development of primitive social organization, its forms of leadership, modes of sustenance and the relationship between and among primitive organizations. Characteristic of this simple epoch (form) is the solidarity, cohesion and cooperation that exists within the group.

The author then discusses the second level of development, namely, the transformation of primitive social organization into higher, urban forms of society. This stage is identified by him as Tamaddun (urbanism) — The Arabic origin of Tamaddun is *mudun* (plural) or *madina* (single), i.e., city/town. Tamaddun, therefore, represents transition or movement from tribal presence or village to the town. In this more complex epoch human cooperation takes a higher form and requires new forms of law and governance. Urbanism as a higher state of human social organization is analyzed at two different levels; the first deals with the societal level, examining the mode of people's survival in the city/town and the second concerns the state/government level. The development of the state is seen by Ibn Khaldûn as the highest form of human social organization. While the notion of the state/government is discussed by him in general, Ibn Khaldûn places a special emphasis on the development and demise of the Muslim form of rule, i.e., the caliphate.

The third stage of the development of social organization, Hadara or civilization, pertains to the development of higher forms of socio-economic organization, which feature the development of commerce, the crafts and sciences. These stages are seen as conditions and consequences of urban life and, as such, necessary and indispensable for the understanding of human history.

There is no fine line separating the three stages of development. The major transformation in social organization, however, is represented in the breakup of the material conditions and other characteristics that define the primitive stage of organization, Badawa, and its transformation into a higher level organized via the state. Therefore, Ibn Khaldûn's theory of social organization is largely about social transformation from Badawa to Hadara (from simple primitive organization into more complex urban civilization). The methodological resemblance with Marx's discussion of the development of human social history is quite evident. Such resemblance is even clearer if compared with the epochs of history presented by Engels in his *The Origin of the Family, Private Property and the State* (Engels, 1972).

The Methodology of Ibn Khaldûn

Ibn Khaldûn advances what he considers as a "new science" to the discussion and understanding of historical phenomena. He criticizes the descriptive — one may add empiricist — notion of history, which treats history as a sequence of events and happenings, each of which is explained by another previous event. According to him this form of interpretation is concerned with appearances and cannot evaluate critically the content or "facts" of the event. Such descriptive history was criticized by Ibn Khaldûn as deficient, problematic and even distortive of the facts. Instead he introduces a "scientific notion of history" based on objective examination of social phenomena (A'mel, 1985).

Ibn Khaldûn's research methodology into social organization begins with the *social phenomena*, which to him represent facts or realities. These phenomena are governed by certain *objective laws*, which, among other things, concern the groups' forms of cooperation, modes of survival and forms of governance. Distinguished from an individual subjective event, the social phenomenon is conceived by Ibn Khaldûn as a product of human social relations. The latter, in turn are themselves the product of social, economic and political conditions characteristic of the specific era under investigation. For this reason, Ibn Khaldûn affirms that the objective laws cannot be significantly influenced by isolated individuals. The laws of social organization can be formulated through the gathering of a large body of data. Data can be obtained either via recorded history or through observation of present events.

Ibn Khaldûn considers these laws as general laws applicable to all societies with similar structures. In his methodology, social organizations or human societies are perceived as dynamic and not static. They constantly change and transform into higher stages of development. According to a number of authors, Ibn Khaldûn's laws of history are not biologically or psychologically based but rather reflect the social, economic and political environment of the society under discussion (A'mel, 1985; Issawi, 1986).

A central concept in Ibn Khaldûn's theory of human history and social organization is the term *Asabiyyah*. The term denotes a number of things. While the term is originally pre-Islamic referring to tribal solidarity largely based on blood ties (*Asabiyyah Qabaliyyah*), Ibn Khaldûn used it to express a collective experience shared by a social group as a signifier of the group's status. Rosenthal, the introducer of *al-Muqaddimah*, shares the opinion of other authors who suggest that the term *Asabiyyah* refers to the form of cooperation and solidarity, which characterizes simple or primitive social organizations. Blood relations, which may be a factor, are not a necessary condition for the emergence of *Asabiyyah*. In this context *Asabiyyah* refers to long and close contact as members of a group brought together by proximity and common life experiences. In today's sociological terminology *Asabiyyah* is equivalent to the notion of social solidarity expressed by Durkheim.

The term is central to Ibn Khaldûn's theory of social organization and social change because it is the presence of *Asabiyyah* that keeps the group together and defines its status and power. And, conversely, the breakdown of *Asabiyyah* or social solidarity is the reason behind the demise of the simple social organizations and their transformation into higher more developed ones. While *Asabiyyah* is stronger in primitive social organizations it is also present in urban stage among states and governments. For Ibn Khaldûn, group *Asabiyyah* is present among the ordinary people as well as among the ruling elite. Therefore, the breakdown in *Asabiyyah* among the ruling quarters can also cause the demise, at least partial, of the state or ruling dynasty.

Finally, first-time readers of Ibn Khaldûn, particularly students in Western institutes, may find the author's frequent reference to "God" (at every beginning and end of a chapter) as unusual if not unscientific. Yet as a 14th-century (1332-1406) North African Muslim scholar, Ibn Khaldûn was first and foremost the product of his time. He basically followed the traditional style of writing of his time. This style of writing ought not to detract from the scientific basis of Ibn Khaldûn's theory. Quite to the contrary, as Mahdi A'mel observes, Ibn Khaldûn was the first social historian capable of freeing historical thinking (theory) from the control of religious thinking. He discovered in historical phenomena their materialist substance, and thus was able to replace God (the spirit, the ideal) used earlier as bases for explanations. He replaced these absolute realities with necessary social relations or necessary human development and established the materialist basis for knowledge without denying religion and religious laws or (Shari'a) (A'mel, 1985). To this one may add that four to five centuries later most Western social and natural scientists heavily based their theories on religious and spiritual grounds.

THE MUQADDIMAH: AN INTRODUCTION TO HISTORY

Foreword

History is a discipline widely cultivated among nations and races. It is eagerly sought after. The men in the street, the ordinary people, aspire to know it. Kings and leaders vie for it.

Both the learned and the ignorant are able to understand it. For on the surface history is no more than information about political events, dynasties, and occurrences of the remote past, elegantly presented and spiced with proverbs. It serves to entertain large, crowded gatherings and brings to us an understanding of human affairs. It shows how changing conditions affected (human affairs), how certain dynasties came to occupy an ever wider space in the world, and how they settled the earth until they heard the call and their time was up.

The inner meaning of history, on the other hand, involves speculation and an attempt to get at the truth, subtle explanation of the causes and origins of existing things, and deep knowledge of the how and why of events. History, therefore, is firmly rooted in philosophy. It deserves to be accounted a branch of it.

The outstanding Muslim historians made exhaustive collections of historical events and wrote them down in book form. But, then, persons who had no right to occupy themselves with history introduced into those books untrue gossip which they had thought up or freely invented, as well as false, discredited reports which they had made up or embellished. Many of their successors followed in their steps and passed the information on to us as they had heard it. They did not look for, or pay any attention to, the causes of events and conditions, nor did they eliminate or reject nonsensical stories.

Little effort is being made to get at the truth. The critical eye, as a rule, is not sharp. Errors and unfounded assumptions are closely allied and familiar elements in historical information. Blind trust in tradition is an inherited trait in human beings. Occupation with the (scholarly) disciplines on the part of those who have no genuine claim to them is widespread. But the pasture of stupidity is unwholesome for mankind. No one can stand up against the authority of truth, and the evil of falsehood is to be fought with enlightening speculation. The reporter merely dictates and passes on (the material). It takes critical insight to sort out the hidden truth; it takes knowledge to lay truth bare and polish it so that the critical insight may be applied to it.

Many systematic historical works have been composed, and the history of nations and dynasties in the world has been compiled and written down. But there are very few historians who have become so well known as to be recognized as authorities, and who have replaced the products of their predecessors by their own works. They can almost be counted on the fingers. There are, for instance, Ibn Ishâq;[1] at-Tabarî;[2] Ibn al-Kalbî;[3] Muhammad b. 'Umar al-Wâqidî;[4] Sayf b. 'Umar al-Asadi;[5] al-Mas'ûdî,[6] and other famous historians who are distinguished from the general run.

It is well known to competent persons and reliable experts that the works of al-Mas'ûdî and al-Waqudi are suspect and objectionable in certain respects. However, their works have been distinguished by universal acceptance of the information they contain and by adoption of their methods and their presentation of material. The discerning critic is his own judge as to which part of their material he finds spurious, and which he gives credence to. Civilization, in its different conditions, contains different elements to which historical information may be related and with which reports and historical material may be checked.

Most of the histories by these authors cover everything because of the universal geographical extension of the two earliest Islamic dynasties[7] and because of the very wide selection of sources of which they did or did not make use. Some of these authors, such as al-Mas'ûdî and historians of his type, gave an exhaustive history of pre-Islamic dynasties and nations and other affairs in general. Some later historians, on the other hand, showed a tendency towards greater restriction, hesitating to be so general and comprehensive. They brought together the happenings of their own period and gave exhaustive historical information about their own part of the world.

They restricted themselves to the history of their own dynasties and cities. This was done by Ibn Hayyân, the historian of Spain and the Spanish Umayyads,[8] and by Ibn ar-Raqîq, the historian of Ifrîqiyah[9] and the dynasty in Kairouan (al-Qayrawân).[10]

The later historians were all tradition-bound and dull of nature and intelligence, or did not try to avoid being dull. They merely copied their predecessors and followed their example. They disregarded the changes in conditions and in the customs of nations and races that the passing of time had brought about. Thus, they presented historical information about dynasties and stories of events from the earliest times as mere forms without substance, blades without scabbards; as knowledge that must be considered ignorance, because it is not known what of it is extraneous and what is genuine. It concerns happenings, the origins of which are not known. It concerns species, the genera of which are not taken into consideration, and whose specific differences are not verified. They neglected the importance of change over the generations in their treatment of (historical material), because they had no one who could interpret it for them. Their works, therefore, give no explanation for it. When they then turn to the description of a particular dynasty, they report the historical information parrot-like and take care to preserve it as it had been passed down to them, whether imaginary or true. They do not turn to the beginning of the dynasty. Nor do they tell why it unfurled its banner and was able to give prominence to its emblem, or what caused it to come to a stop when it had reached its term. The student, thus, has still to search for the beginnings of conditions and for (the principles of) organization adopted by the various dynasties. He must himself inquire why the various dynasties brought pressure to bear upon each other and why they succeeded each other. He must search for a convincing explanation of the elements that made for mutual separation or contact among the dynasties. All this will be dealt with in the Introduction to this work.

Other historians, then, came with too brief a presentation. They went to the extreme of being satisfied with the names of kings, without any genealogical or historical information, and with only a numerical indication of the length of their reigns. This was done by Ibn Rashîq in the *Mîzân al-'amal*,[11] and by those lost sheep who followed his method. No credence can be given to what they say. They are not considered trustworthy, nor is their material considered worthy of transmission, for they caused useful material to be lost and damaged the methods and customs acknowledged to be sound and practical by historians.

When I had read the works of others and probed into the recesses of yesterday and today, I shook myself out of that drowsy complacency and sleepiness. Although not much of a writer, I exhibited my own literary ability as well as I could, and, thus, composed a book on history. In this book I lifted the veil from conditions as they arose in the various generations. I arranged it methodically in chapters dealing with historical facts and reflections. In it I showed how and why dynasties and civilization originated. I based the work on the history of the two races that constitute the population of the Maghrib at this time and people its various regions and cities, and on that of their ruling houses, both long- and short-lived, including the rulers and allies they had in the past. These two races are the Arabs and the Berbers. They are the two races known to have resided in the Maghrib for such a long time that one can hardly imagine they ever lived elsewhere, for its inhabitants know no other human races.

I corrected the contents of the work carefully and presented it to the judgment of scholars and the elite. I followed an unusual method of arrangement and division into chapters. From the various possibilities, I chose a remarkable and original method. In the work, I commented on civilization, on urbanization, in a way that explains to the reader how and why things are as they are, and shows him how the men who constituted a dynasty first came upon the historical scene. As a result, he will wash his hands of any blind trust in tradition. He will become aware of the conditions of periods and races that were before his time and that will obtain thereafter.

I divided the work into an introduction and three books:

The Introduction deals with the great merit of historiography, offers an appreciation of its various methods, and cites historians' errors.

The First Book deals with civilization and its essential characteristics, namely, royal authority, government, gainful occupations, ways of making a living, crafts, and sciences, as well as with the causes and reasons thereof.

The Second Book deals with the history, races, and dynasties of the Arabs, from the beginning of creation down to this time. This will include references to such famous nations and dynasties contemporaneous with them, as the Nabataeans, the Syrians, the Persians, the Israelites, the Copts, the Greeks, the Byzantines, and the Turks.

The Third Book deals with the history of the Berbers and of the Zanâtah who are part of them; with their origins and races; and, in particular, with the royal houses and dynasties of the Maghrib.

Later on, there was my trip to the East, to seek the manifold illumination it offers and to fulfil the religious duty and custom of circumambulating the Ka'bah and visiting Medina, as well as to study the systematic works on history. As a result, I was able to fill the gaps in my historical information about the non-Arab (Persian) rulers of those lands, and about the Turkish dynasties in the region over which they ruled. I added this information to what I had written here. I inserted it into the treatment of the nations of the various districts and rulers of the various cities and regions that were contemporary with those races. In this connection I was brief and concise and preferred the easy goal to the difficult one. I proceeded from genealogical tables to detailed historical information.

Thus, this work contains an exhaustive history of the world. It forces stubborn stray wisdom to return to the fold. It gives causes and reasons for happenings in the various dynasties. It turns out to be a vessel for philosophy, a receptacle for historical knowledge. The work contains the history of the Arabs and the Berbers, both the sedentary groups and the nomads. It also contains references to the great dynasties that were contemporary with them, and, moreover, clearly points out memorable lessons to be learned from early conditions and from subsequent history. Therefore, I called the work 'Book of Lessons and Archive of Early and Subsequent History, Dealing with the Political Events concerning the Arabs, Non-Arabs, and Berbers, and the Supreme Rulers who were Contemporary with them.'

I omitted nothing concerning the origin of races and dynasties, the synchronism of the earliest nations, the reasons for change and variation in past periods and within religious groups; also concerning dynasties and religious groups, towns and hamlets, strength and humiliation, large numbers and small numbers, sciences and crafts, gains and losses, changing general conditions, nomadic and sedentary life, actual events and future events — all things expected to occur in civilization. I treated everything comprehensively and exhaustively and explained the arguments and reasons for its existence.

As a result, this book has become unique, as it contains unusual knowledge and familiar if hidden wisdom. Still, after all has been said, I am conscious of imperfections when I look at the work of scholars past and present. I confess my inability to penetrate so difficult a subject. I wish that men of scholarly competence and wide knowledge would look at the book with a critical, rather than a complacent eye, and silently correct and overlook the mistakes they come upon. The capital of knowledge that an individual scholar has to offer is small. Admission (of one's shortcomings) saves from censure. Kindness from colleagues is hoped for. It is God whom I ask to make our deeds acceptable in His sight. He is a good protector.

The Introduction

The excellence of historiography. An appreciation of the various approaches to history. A glimpse of the different kinds of errors to which historians are liable. Why these errors occur.

It should be known that history is a discipline that has a great number of approaches. Its useful aspects are very many. Its goal is distinguished.

History makes us acquainted with the conditions of past nations as they are reflected in their national character. It makes us acquainted with the biographies of the prophets and with the dynasties and policies of rulers. Whoever so desires may thus achieve the useful result of being able to imitate historical examples in religious and worldly matters.

The (writing of history) requires numerous sources and much varied knowledge. It also requires a good speculative mind and thoroughness, which lead the historian to the truth and keep him from slips and errors. If he trusts historical information in its plain transmitted form and has no clear knowledge of the principles resulting from custom, the fundamental facts of politics, the nature of civilization, or the conditions governing human social organization, and if, furthermore, he does not evaluate remote or ancient material through comparison with near or contemporary material, he often cannot avoid stumbling and slipping and deviating from the path of truth. Historians, Qur'ân commentators and leading transmitters have committed frequent errors in the stories and events they reported. They accepted them in the plain transmitted form, without regard for its value. The did not check them with the principles underlying such historical situations, nor did they compare them with similar material. Also, they did not probe with the yardstick of philosophy, with the help of knowledge of the nature of things, or with the help of speculations and historical insight. Therefore, they strayed from the truth and found themselves lost in the desert of baseless assumptions and errors.

This is especially the case with figures, either of sums of money or of soldiers, whenever they occur in stories. They offer a good opportunity for false information and constitute a vehicle for nonsensical statements. They must be controlled and checked with the help of known fundamental facts.

For example, al-Mas'ûdî and many other historians report that Moses counted the army of the Israelites in the desert. He had all those able to carry arms, especially those twenty years and older, pass muster. There turned out to be 600,000 or more. In this connection, al-Mas'ûdî forgets to take into consideration whether Egypt and Syria could possibly have held such a number of soldiers. Every realm may have as large a militia as it can hold and support, but no more. This fact is attested by well-known customs and familiar conditions. Moreover, an army of this size cannot march or fight as a unit. The whole available territory would be too small for it. If it were in battle formation, it would extend two, three, or more times beyond the field of vision. How, then, could two such parties fight with each other, or one battle formation gain the upper hand when one flank does not know what the other flank is doing! The situation at the present day testifies to the correctness of this statement. The past resembles the future more than one drop of water another.

Furthermore, the realm of the Persians was much greater than that of the Israelites. This fact is attested by Nebuchadnezzar's victory over them. He swallowed up their country and gained complete control over it. He also destroyed Jerusalem, their religious and political capital. And he was merely one of the officials of the province of Fârs. It is said that he was the governor of the western border region. The Persian provinces of the two 'Irâqs,[1] Khurâsân, Transoxania, and the region of Derbend on the Caspian Sea were much larger than the realm of the Israelites. Yet, the Persian army did not attain such a number or even approach it. The greater concentration of Persian troops, at al-Qâdisîyah, amounted to 120,000 men, all of whom had their retainers. This is according to Sayf, who said that with their retainers they amounted to over 200,000 persons. According to 'Â'ishah and az-Zuhrî, the troop concentration with which Rustum advanced against Sa'd at al'Qâdisîyah amounted to only 60,000 men, all of whom had their retainers.

Then, if the Israelites had really amounted to such a number, the extent of the area under their rule would have been larger, for the size of administrative units and provinces under a particular dynasty is in direct proportion to the size of its militia and the groups that support the dynasty. Now, it is well known that the territory of the Israelites did not comprise an area larger than the Jordan province and Palestine in Syria and the region of Medina and Khaybar in the Hijâz. Also, there were only three generations between Moses and Israel, according to the best-informed scholars. Moses was the son of Amram, the son of Kohath, the son of Levi, the son of Jacob who is Israel-Allâh. This is Moses' genealogy in the Torah.[2] The length of time between Israel and Moses was indicated by al-Mas'ûdî when he said: 'Israel entered Egypt with his children, the tribes, and their children, when they came to Joseph numbering seventy souls. The length of their stay in Egypt until they left with Moses for the desert was two hundred and twenty years. During those years, the kings of the Copts, the Pharaohs, passed them on (as their subjects) one to the other.' It is improbable that the descendants of one man could branch out into such a number within four generations.

It has been assumed that this number of soldiers applied to the time of Solomon and his successors. Again, this is improbable. Between Solomon and Israel, there were only eleven generations, that is: Solomon, the son of David, the son of Jesse, the son of Obed, the son of Boaz, the son of Salmon, the son of Nahshon, the son of Amminadab, the son of Ram, the son of Hezron, the son of Perex, the son of Judah, the son of Jacob. The descendants of one man in eleven generations would not branch out into such a number, as has been assumed. They might, indeed, reach hundreds or thousands. This often happens. But an increase beyond that to higher figures is improbable. Comparison with observable present-day and well-known nearby facts proves that assumption and report to be untrue. According to the definite statement of the Israelite stories,[3] Solomon's army amounted to 12,000 men, and his horses numbered 1,400, which were stabled at his palace. This is the correct information. No attention should be paid to nonsensical statements by the common run of informants. In the days of Solomon, the Israelite state saw its greatest flourishing and their realm its widest extension.

Whenever contemporaries speak about the dynastic armies of their own or recent times, and whenever they engage in discussions about Muslim or Christian soldiers, or when they get to figuring the tax revenues and the money spent by the government, the outlays of extravagant spenders, and the goods that rich and prosperous men have in stock, they are quite generally found to exaggerate, to go beyond the bounds of the ordinary, and to succumb to the temptation of sensationalism. When the officials in charge are questioned about their armies, when the goods and assets of wealthy people are assessed, and when the outlays of extravagant spenders are looked at in ordinary light, the figures will be found to amount to a tenth of what those people have said. The reason is simple. It is the common desire for sensationalism, the ease with which one may just mention a higher figure, and the disregard of reviewers and critics. This leads to failure to exercise self-criticism about one's errors and intentions, to demand from oneself moderation and fairness in reporting, to reapply oneself to study and research. Such historians let themselves go and made a feast of untrue statements. 'They procure for themselves entertaining stories in order to lead others away from the path of God.'[4] This is a bad enough business.

It may be said that the increase of descendants to such a number would be prevented under ordinary conditions which, however, do not apply to the Israelites. The increase in their case would be a miracle in accordance with the tradition which said that one of the things revealed to their forefathers, the prophets Abraham, Isaac, and Jacob, was that God would cause their descendants to increase until they were more numerous than the stars in heaven and the pebbles of the earth. God fulfilled this promise to them as an act of divine grace bestowed upon them and as an extraordinary miracle in their favour. Thus, ordinary conditions could not hinder it and nobody should speak against it.

Someone might come out against this tradition with the argument that it occurs only in the Torah which, as is well known, was altered by the Jews. The reply to this argument would be that the statement concerning the alteration of the Torah by the Jews is unacceptable to thorough scholars and cannot be understood in its plain meaning, since custom prevents people who have a revealed religion from dealing with their divine scriptures in such a manner. Thus, the great increase in numbers in the case of the Israelites would be an extraordinary miracle. Custom, in the proper meaning of the word, would prevent anything of the sort from happening to other peoples.

It is true that a movement of (such a large group) would hardly be possible, but none took place, and there was no need for one. It is also true that each realm has only its particular number of militia. But the Israelites at first were no militiamen and had no dynasty. Their numbers increased that much, so that they could gain power over the land of Canaan which God had promised them and the territory of which He had purified for them. All these things are miracles. God guides to the truth.

The history of the Tubba's, the kings of the Yemen and of the Arabian Peninsula, as it is generally transmitted, is another example of silly statements by historians. It is said that from their home in the Yemen, the Tubba's used to raid Ifrîqiyah and the Berbers of the Maghrib. Afrîqus b. Qays b. Sayfî, one of their great early kings who lived in the time of Moses or somewhat earlier, is said to have raided Ifrîqiyah. He caused a great slaughter among the Berbers. He gave then the name of Berbers when he heard their jargon and asked what that *barbarah* was. This gave them the name which has remained with them since that time. When he left the Maghrib, he is said to have concentrated some Himyar tribes there. They remained there and mixed with the native population. Their descendants are the Sinhâjah and the Kutâmah. This led at-Tabarî, al-Mas'ûdî, and others to make the statement that the Sinhâjah and the Kutâmah belong to the Himyar. The Berber genealogists do not admit this, and they are right. Al-Mas'ûdî also mentioned that one of the Himyar kings after Afrîqus, Dhû l-Adh'âr, who lived in the time of Solomon, raided the Maghrib and forced it into submission. Something similar is mentioned by al-Mas'ûdî concerning his son and successor, Yâsir. He is said to have reached the Sand River in the Maghrib and to have been unable to find the passage through it because of the great mass of sand. Therefore, he returned.

Likewise, it is said that the last Tubba', As'ad Abû Karib, who lived in the time of the Persian Kayyanid king Yastâsb, ruled over Mosul and Azerbaijan. He is said to have met and routed the Turks and to have caused a great slaughter among them. Then he raided them again a second and a third time. After that, he is said to have sent three of his sons on raids, (one) against the country of Fârs, one against the country of the Soghdians, one of the Turkish nations of Transoxania, and one against the country of the Rûm (Byzantines). The first brother took possession of the country up to Samarkand and crossed the desert into China. There, he found his second brother who had raided the Soghdians and had arrived in China before him. The two together caused a great slaughter in China and returned together with their booty. They left some Himyar tribes in Tibet. They have been there down to this time. The third brother is said to have reached Constantinople. He laid siege to it and forced the country of the Rûm into submission. Then, he returned.

All this information is remote from the truth. It is rooted in baseless and erroneous assumptions. It is more like the fiction of storytellers. The realms of the Tubba's was restricted to the Arabian Peninsula. Their home and seat was San'â' in the Yemen. The Arabian Peninsula is surrounded by the ocean on three sides: the Indian Ocean on the south, the Persian Gulf jutting out of the Indian Ocean to Basrah on the east, and the Red Sea jutting out of the Indian Ocean to Suez in Egypt on the west. This can be seen on the map. There is no way from the Yemen to the Maghrib except via Suez. The distance between the Red Sea and the Mediterranean is two days' journey or less. It is unlikely that the distance could be traversed by a great ruler with a large army unless he controlled that region. This, as a rule, is impossible. In that region there were the Amalekites and Canaan in Syria, and, in Egypt, the Copts. Later on, the Amalekites took possession of Egypt, and the Israelites of Syria. There is, however, no report that the Tubba's ever fought against one of these nations or that they had possession of any part of this region. Furthermore, the distance from the Yemen to the Maghrib is great, and an army requires much food and fodder. Soldiers travelling in regions other than their own have to requisition grain and livestock and to plunder the countries they pass through. As a rule, such a procedure does not yield enough food and fodder. On the other hand, if they attempted to take along enough provisions from their own region, they would not have enough animals for transportation. So, their whole line of march necessarily takes them through regions they must take possession of and force into submission in order to obtain provisions from them. Again, it would be a most unlikely and impossible assumption that such an army could pass through all those nations without disturbing them, obtaining its provisions by peaceful negotiation. This shows that all such information is silly or fictitious.

Mention of the allegedly impassable Sand River has never been heard in the Maghrib, although the Maghrib has often been crossed and its roads have been explored by travellers and raiders at all times and in every direction. Because of the unusual character of the story, there is much eagerness to pass it on.

With regard to the supposed raid of the Tubba's against the countries of the East and the land of the Turks, it must be admitted that the line of march in this case is wider than the (narrow) passage at Suez. The distance, however, is greater, and the Persian and Byzantine nations are interposed on the way to the Turks. There is no report that the Tubba's ever took possession of the countries of the Persians and Byzantines. They merely fought the Persians on the borders of the 'Irâq and of the Arab countries between al-Bahrayn and al-Hîrah, which were border regions common to both nations.[5] It would, however, ordinarily have been impossible for the Tubba's to traverse the land of the Persians on their way to raid the countries of the Turks and Tibet, because of the nations that are interposed on the way to the Turks, because of the need for food and fodder, as well as the great distance, mentioned before. All information to this effect is silly and fictitious. Even if the way this information is transmitted were sound, the points mentioned would cast suspicion upon it. All the more then must the information be suspect since the manner in which it has been transmitted is not sound. In connection with Yathrib (Median) and the Aws and Khazraj, Ibn Ishâq says that the last Tubba' travelled eastward to the 'Irâq and Persian, but a raid by the Tubba's against the countries of the Turks and Tibet is in no way confirmed by the established facts. Assertions to this effect should not be trusted; all such information should be investigated and checked with sound norms. The result will be that it will most beautifully be demolished.

Even more unlikely and more deeply rooted in baseless assumptions is the common interpretation of the following verse of the *Sûrat al-Fajr*: 'Did you not see what your Lord did with 'Âd — Iram, that of the pillars?'[6]

The commentators consider the word Iram the name of a city which is described as having pillars, that is, columns. They report that 'Âd b. 'Ûs b. Iram had two sons, Shadîd and Shaddâd, who ruled after him. Shadîd perished. Shaddâd became the sole ruler of the realm, and the kings there submitted to his authority. When Shaddâd heard a description of Paradise, he said: 'I shall build something like it.' And he built the city of Iram in the desert of Aden over a period of three hundred years. He himself lived nine hundred years. Iram is said to have been a large city, with castles of gold and silver and columns of emerald and hyacinth, containing all kinds of trees and freely-flowing rivers. When the construction of the city was completed, Shaddâd went there with the people of his realm. But when he was the distance of only one day and night away from it, God sent a clamour from heaven, and all of them perished. This is reported by at-Tabarî, ath-That'âlibî, az-Zamakhsharî, and other Qur'ân commentators. They transmit the following story on the authority of one of the men around Muhammad, 'Abdallâh b. Qilâbah. When he went out in search of some of his camels, he came upon the city and took away from it as much as he could carry. His story reached Mu'âwiyah, who had him brought to him, and he told the story. Mu'âwiyah sent for Ka'b al-ahbâr and asked him about it. Ka'b said, 'It is Iram, that of the pillars. Iram will be entered in your time by a Muslim who is of a reddish, ruddy colour, and short, with a mole at his eyebrow and one on his neck, who goes out in search of some of his camels.' He then turned around and, seeing Ibn Qilâbah, he said: 'Indeed, he is that man.'

No information about this city has since become available anywhere on earth. The desert of Aden where the city is supposed to have been built lies in the middle of the Yemen. It has been inhabited continuously, and travellers and guides have explored its roads in every direction. Yet, no information about the city has been reported. No antiquarian, no nation has mentioned it. If (the Qur'ân commentators) said that it had disappeared like other antiquities, the story would be more likely, but they expressly say that it still exists. Some identify it with Damascus, because Damascus was in the position of the people of 'Âd. Others go so far in their crazy talk as to maintain that the city lies hidden from sensual perception and can be discovered only by trained magicians and sorcerers. All these are assumptions that would better be termed nonsense.

All these suggestions proffered by Qur'ân commentators were the result of grammatical considerations, for Arabic grammar requires the expression, 'that of the pillars', to be an attribute of Iram. The word 'pillars' was understood to mean columns. Thus, Iram was narrowed down in its meaning to some sort of building. (The commentators) were influenced in their interpretation by the reading of Ibn az-Zubayr who read a genitive construction: 'Âd of Iram. They then adopted these stories, which are better called fictitious fables.

In fact, however, the 'pillars' are tent poles. If 'columns' were intended by the word, it would not be far-fetched, as the power of (the people of 'Âd) was well known, and they could be described as people with buildings and columns in the general way. But it would be far-fetched to say that a special building in one or another specific city (was intended). If it is a genitive construction, as would be the case according to the reading of Ibn az-Zubayr, it would be a genitive construction used to express tribal relationships, such as, for instance, the Quraysh of Kinânah, or the Ilyâs of Mudar, or the Rabî'ah of Nîzar. There is no need for such an implausible interpretation which uses for its starting point silly stories of the sort mentioned, which cannot be imputed to the Qur'ân because they are so implausible.

Another fictitious story of the historians, which they all report, concerns the reason for ar-Rashîd's destruction of the Barmecides. It is the story of al-'Abbâsah, ar-Rashîd's sister, and J'far b. Yahyâ b. Khâlid, his minister. Ar-Rashîd is said to have worried about where to place them when he was drinking wine with them. He wanted to receive them together in his company. Therefore, he permitted them to conclude a marriage that was not consummated. Al-'Abbâsah then tricked Ja'far in her desire to be alone with him, for she had fallen in love with him. Ja'far finally had intercourse with her — it is assumed, when he was drunk — and she became pregnant. The story was reported to ar-Rashîd who flew into a rage.

This story is irreconcilable with al-'Abbâsah's position, her religiousness, her parentage, and her exalted rank. She was a descendant of 'Abdallâh b. 'Abbâs and separated from him by only four generations, and they were the most distinguished and greatest men in Islam after him. Al-'Abbâsah was the daughter of Muhammad al-Mahdî, the son of Abû Ja'far 'Abdallâh al-Mansûr, the son of Muhammad as-Sajjâd, the son of the Father of the Caliphs 'Alî. 'Alî was the son of 'Abdallâh, the Interpreter of the Qur'ân, the son of the Prophet's uncle, Al-'Abbâs. Al-'Abbâsah was the daughter of a caliph and the sister of a caliph. She was born to royal power into the prophetical succession (the caliphate), and was descended from the men around Muhammad and his uncles. She was connected by birth with the leadership of Islam, the light of the revelation, and the place where the angels descended to bring the revelation. She was close in time to the desert attitude of true Arabism, to that simple state of Islam still far from the habits of luxury and lush pastures of sin. Where should one look for chastity and modesty, if she did not possess them? Where could cleanliness and purity be found, if they no longer existed in her house? How could she link her pedigree with that of Ja'far b. Yahyä and stain her Arab nobility with a Persian client? His Persian ancestor had been acquired as a slave, or taken as a client, by one of her ancestors, an uncle of the Prophet and noble Qurashite, and all Ja'far did was that he together with his father was drawn along (by the growing fame of) the 'Abbâsid dynasty and thus prepared for and elevated to a position of nobility. And how could it be that ar-Rashîd, with his high-mindedness and great pride, permit himself to become related by marriage to Persian clients. If a critical person looks at this story in all fairness and compares al-'Abbâsah with the daughter of a great ruler of his own time, he must find it disgusting and unbelievable that she could have done such a thing with one of the clients of her dynasty and while her family was in power. He would insist that the story be considered untrue. And who could compare with al-'Abbâsah and ar-Rashîd in dignity.

The reason for the destruction of the Barmecides was their attempt to gain control over the dynasty and their retention of the tax revenues. This went so far that when ar-Rashîd wanted even a little money, he could not get it. They took his affairs out of his hands and shared with him in his authority. He had no say with them in the affairs of his realm. Their influence grew, and their fame spread. They filled the positions and ranks of the government with their own children and creatures who became high officials, and thus barred all others from the positions of wazir, secretary, army commander, doorkeeper, and from the military and civilian administration. It is said that in the palace of ar-Rashîd, there were twenty-five high officials, both military and civilian, all children of Yahyâ b. Khâlid. There, they crowded the people of the dynasty and pushed them out by force. They could do that because of the position of their father, Yahyâ, mentor to Hârûn both as crown prince and as caliph. Hârûn practically grew up in his lap and got all his education from him. Hârûn let him handle his affairs and used to call him 'father'. As a result, the Barmecides, and not the government, wielded all the influence. Their presumption grew. Their position became more and more influential. They became the centre of attention. All obeyed them. All hopes were addressed to them. From the farthest borders, presents and gifts of rulers and amirs were sent to them. The tax money found its way into their treasury, to serve as an introduction to them and to procure their favour. They gave gifts to and bestowed favours upon the men of the Shî'ah and upon important relatives of the Prophet. They gave the poor from the noble families related to the Prophet something to earn. They freed the captives. Thus, they were given praise as was not given to their caliph. They showered privileges and gifts upon those who came to ask favours from them. They gained control over villages and estates in the open country and near the main cities in every province.

Eventually, the Barmecides irritated the inner circle. They caused resentment among the elite and aroused the displeasure of high officials. Jealousy and envy of all sorts began to show themselves, and the scorpions of intrigue crept into their soft beds in the government. The Qahtabah family, Ja'far's maternal uncles, led the intrigues against them. Feelings for blood ties and relationship could not move or sway the Qahtabahs from the envy which was so heavy on their hearts. This joined with their master's incipient jealousy, with his dislike of restrictions and high-handedness, and with his latent resentment aroused by small acts of presumptuousness on the part of the Barmecides. When they continued to flourish, as they did, they were led to gross insubordination.

Ja'far himself paved the way for his own and his family's undoing, which ended with the collapse of their exalted positions, with the heavens falling in upon them and the earth's sinking with them and their house. Their days of glory became a thing of the past, an example to later generations.

Close examination of their story, scrutinizing the ways of government and their own conduct, discloses that all this was natural and is easily explained. One understands that it was only jealousy and struggle for control on the part of the caliph and his subordinates that killed them. Another factor was the verses that enemies of the Barmecides among the inner circle surreptitiously gave the singers to recite, with the intention that the caliph should hear them and his stored-up animosity against them be aroused.

These are the verses:

Would that Hind could fulfil her promise to us
And deliver us from our predicament,
And for once act on her own.
The impotent person is he who never acts on his own.[7]

When ar-Rashîd heard these verses, he exclaimed: 'Indeed, I am just such an impotent person.' By this and similar methods, the enemies of the Barmecides eventually succeeded in arousing ar-Rashîd's latent jealousy and in bringing his terrible vengeance upon them. God is our refuge from men's desire for power and from misfortune.

The stupid story of ar-Rashîd's winebibbing and his getting drunk in the company of boon companions is really abominable. It does not in the least agree with ar-Rashîd's attitude toward the fulfilment of the requirements of religion and justice incumbent upon caliphs. He consorted with religious scholars and saints. He wept when he heard their sermons. Then, there is his prayer in Mecca when he circumambulated the Ka'bah. He was pious, observed the times of prayer, and attended the morning prayer at its earliest hour. He used to go on raids (against unbelievers) one year and to make the pilgrimage to Mecca the next. He once rebuked his jester, Ibn Abî Maryam, who made an unseemly remark to him during prayer. When Ibn Abî Maryam heard ar-Rashîd recite: 'How is it that I should not worship Him who created me?'[8] he said: 'Indeed, I do not know why.' 'Jokes even at prayer?' he said. 'Beware, beware of the Quar'ân and Islam. Apart from that, you may do whatever you wish.'

Furthermore, ar-Rashîd possessed a good deal of learning and simplicity, because his epoch was close to that of his forebears who had those qualities. The time between him and his grandfather, al-Mansûr, was not a long one. He was a young lad when al-Mansûr died. Al-Mansûr possessed a good deal of learning and religion.

His son, al-Mahdî, ar-Rashîd's father, experienced the austerity of al-Mansûr, who would not use public funds to provide new clothes for his family. One day, al-Mahdî came to him when he was at his office discussing with the tailors the patching of this family's worn garments. Al-Mahdî did not relish that and said: 'O Commander of the Faithful, this year I shall pay for the family's clothes from my own income.' Al-Mansûr's reply was: 'Do that.' He did not prevent him from paying himself but would not permit any public Muslim money to be spent for that purpose.

Ar-Rashîd was very close in time to that caliph and to his forebears. He was reared under the influence of such and similar conduct in his own family, so that it became his own nature. How could such a man have been a winebibber and have drunk wine openly? It is well known that noble pre-Islamic Arabs avoided wine. The vine was not one of the plants cultivated by them. Most of them considered it reprehensible to drink wine. Ar-Rashîd and his forebears were very successful in avoiding anything reprehensible in their religious or worldly affairs and in making all praiseworthy actions and qualities of perfection, as well as the aspirations of the Arabs, their own nature....

It is a well-established fact that ar-Rashid had consented to keep Abû Nuwâs[9] imprisoned until he repented and gave up his ways, because he had heard of the latter's excessive winebibbing. Ar-Rashîd used to drink a date liquor, according to the 'Iraqî legal school whose *responsa* (concerning the permissibility of that drink) are well known. But he cannot be suspected of having drunk pure wine. Silly reports to this effect cannot be credited. He was not the man to do something that is forbidden and considered by Muslims as one of the greatest of capital sins. Not one of (the early 'Abbâsids) had anything to do with effeminate prodigality or luxury in matters of clothing, jewellery, or the kind of food they took. They still retained the tough desert attitude and the simple state of Islam. Could it be assumed they would do something that would lead from the lawful to the unlawful and from the licit to the illicit? Historians such as at-Tabarî, al-Mas'ûdî, and others are agreed that all the early Umayyad and 'Abbâsid caliphs used to ride out with only light silver ornamentation on their belts, swords, bridles, and saddles, and that the first caliph to originate riding out in golden apparel was al-Mu'tazz b. al-Mutawakkil, the eighth caliph after ar-Rashîd. The same applied to their clothing. Could one, then, assume any differently with regard to what they drank? This will become still clearer when the nature of dynastic beginnings in desert life and modest circumstances is understood....

A current story explains how al-Ma'mûn came to be al-Hasan b. Sahl's son-in-law by marrying his daughter Bûrân. One night, on his rambles through the streets of Baghdad, al-Ma'mûn is said to have come upon a basket that was being let down from one of the roofs by means of pulleys and twisted cords of silk thread. He seated himself in the basket and grabbed the pulley, which started moving. He was taken up into a chamber of extraordinary magnificence. Then, a woman of uncommonly seductive beauty is said to have come out from behind curtains. She greeted al-Ma'mûn and invited him to keep her company. He drank wine with her the whole night long. In the morning he returned to his companions at the place where they had been awaiting him. He had fallen so much in love with the woman that he asked her father for her hand. How does all this accord with al-Ma'mûn's well-known religiosity and learning, his emulation of the way of life of his forefathers, the right-guided ('Abbâsid) caliphs, his adoption of the way of life of those pillars of Islam, the first four caliphs, his respect for religious scholars, or his observance in his prayers and legal practice of the norms established by God! How could it be correct that he would act like one of those wicked scoundrels who amuse themselves by rambling about at night, entering strange houses in the dark, and engaging in nocturnal trysts in the manner of Bedouin lovers! And how does that story fit with the position and noble character of al-Hasan b. Sahl's daughter, and with the firm morality and chastity that reigned in her father's house!

There are many such stories. They are always cropping up in the works of the historians. The incentive for inventing and reporting them shows a tendency to forbidden pleasures and for smearing the reputation of others. People justify their own subservience to pleasure by citing the supposed doings of men and women of the past. Therefore, they often appear very eager for such information and are alert to find it when they go through the pages of published works.

I once criticized a royal prince for being so eager to learn to sing and play the strings. I told him it was not a matter that should concern him and that it did not befit his position. He referred me to Ibrâhîm b. al-Mahdi[10] who was the leading musician and best singer of his time. I replied: 'For heaven's sake, why do you not rather follow the example of his father or his brother? Do you not see how that pursuit prevented Ibrâhîm from attaining their position?' The prince, however, was deaf to my criticism and turned away.

Further silly information is accepted by many historians. They do not care to consider the factual proofs and circumstantial evidence that require us to recognize that the contrary is true....

Dynasty and government serve as the world's market-place, attracting to it the products of scholarship and craftsmanship alike. Wayward wisdom and forgotten lore turn up there. In this market stories are told and items of historical information are delivered. Whatever is in demand on this market is in general demand everywhere else. Now, whenever the established dynasty avoids injustice, prejudice, weakness, and double-dealing, with determination keeping to the right path and never swerving from it, the wares on its market are as pure silver and fine gold. However, when it is influenced by selfish interests and rivalries, or swayed by vendors of tyranny and dishonesty, the wares of its market-place become as dross and debased metals. The intelligent critic must judge for himself as he looks around, examining this, admiring that, and choosing the other....

Lengthy discussion of these mistakes has taken us rather far from the purpose of his work. However, many competent persons and expert historians slipped in connection with such stories and assertions, and they stuck in their minds. Many weak-minded and uncritical men learned these things from them, and even (competent historians) accepted them without critical investigation, and thus (strange stories) crept into their material. In consequence, historiography became nonsensical and confused, and its students fumbled around. Historiography came to be considered a domain of the common people. Therefore, today, the scholar in this field needs to know the principles of politics, the nature of things, and the differences among nations, places, and periods with regard to ways of life, character qualities, customs, sects, schools, and everything else. He further needs a comprehensive knowledge of present conditions in all these respects. He must compare similarities or differences between present and past conditions. He must know the causes of the similarities in certain cases and of the differences in others. He must be aware of the differing origins and beginnings of dynasties and religious groups, as well as of the reasons and incentives that brought them into being and the circumstances and history of the persons who supported them. His goal must be to have complete knowledge of the reasons for every happening, and to be acquainted with the origin of every event. Then, he must check transmitted information with the basic principles he knows. If it fulfils their requirements, it is sound. Otherwise, the historian must consider it as spurious and dispense with it. It was for this reason alone that historiography was highly esteemed by the ancients, so much so that at-Tabarî, al-Bukhârî, and before the, Ibn Ishâq and other Muslim religious scholars, chose to occupy themselves with it. Most scholars, however, forgot this, the secret of historiography, with the result that it became a stupid occupation. Ordinary people as well as scholars who had no firm foundation of knowledge, considered it a simple matter to study and know history, to delve into it and sponge on it. Strays got into the flock, bits of shell were mixed with the nut, truth was adulterated with lies.

'The final outcome of things is up to God.'[11]

A hidden pitfall in historiography is disregard for the fact that conditions within nations and races change with the change of periods and the passage of time. This is a sore affliction and is deeply hidden, becoming noticeable only after a long time, so that rarely do more than a few individuals become aware of it.

This is as follows. The condition of the world and of nations, their customs and sects, does not persist in the same form or in a constant manner. There are differences according to days and periods, and changes from one condition to another. Such is the case with individuals, times, and cities, and it likewise happens in connection with regions and districts, periods and dynasties.

The old Persian nations, the Syrians, the Nabataeans, the Tubba's, the Israelites, and the Copts, all once existed. They all had their own particular institutions in respect of dynastic and territorial arrangements, their own politics, crafts, languages, technical terminologies, as well as their own ways of dealing with their fellow men and handling their cultural institutions. Their historical relics testify to that. They were succeeded by the later Persians, the Byzantines, and the Arabs. The old institutions changed and former customs were transformed, either into something very similar, or into something distinct and altogether different. Then, there came Islam. Again, all institutions underwent another change, and for the most part assumed the forms that are still familiar at the present time as the result of their transmission from one generation to the next.

Then, the days of Arab rule were over. The early generations who had cemented Arab might and founded the realm of the Arabs were gone. Power was seized by others, by non-Arabs like the Turks in the east, the Berbers in the west, and the European Christians in the north. With their passing, entire nations ceased to exist, and institutions and customs changed. Their glory was forgotten, and their power no longer heeded.

The widely accepted reason for changes in institutions and customs is the fact that the customs of each race depend on the customs of its ruler. As the proverb says: 'The common people follow the religion of the ruler.'[12]

When politically ambitious men overcome the ruling dynasty and seize power, they inevitably have recourse to the customs of their predecessors and adopt most of them. At the same time, they do not neglect the customs of their own race. This leads to some discrepancies between the customs of the new ruling dynasty and the customs of the old race.

The new power, in turn, is taken over by another dynasty, and customs are further mixed with those of the new dynasty. More discrepancies come in, so that the contrast between the new dynasty and the first one is much greater than that between the second and the first one. Gradual increase in the degree of discrepancy continues. The eventual result is an altogether distinct (set of customs and institutions). As long as there is this continued succession of different races to royal authority and government, changes in customs and institutions will not cease to occur.

Analogical reasoning and comparison are well known to human nature. They are not safe from error. Together with forgetfulness and negligence, they sway man from his purpose and divert him from his goal. Often, someone who has learned a good deal of past history remains unaware of the changes that conditions have undergone. Without a moment's hesitation, he applies his knowledge (of the present) to historical information, and measures such information by the things he has observed with his own eyes, although the difference between the two is great. Consequently, he falls into an abyss of error.

This may be illustrated by what the historians report concerning al-Hajjâj.[13] They state that his father was a schoolteacher. At the present time, teaching is a craft and serves to make a living. It is a far cry from the pride of group feeling. Teachers are weak, indigent, and rootless. Many weak professional men and artisans who work for a living aspire to positions for which they are not fit but which they believe to be within their reach. They are misled by their desires, a rope which often slips from their hands and precipitates them into the abyss of ruinous perdition. They do not realize that what they desire is impossible for men like them to attain. They do not realize that they are professional men and artisans who work for a living. And they do not know that at the beginning of Islam and under the (Umayyad and 'Abbâsid) dynasties, teaching was something different. Scholarship, in general, was not a craft in that period. Scholarship consisted of transmitting statements that people had heard the Lawgiver (Muhammad) make. It was the teaching of religious matters that were not known, by way of oral transmission. Persons of noble descent and people who shared in the group feeling and directed the affairs of Islam were the ones who taught the Book of God and the Law of the Prophet, (and they did so) as one transmits traditions, not as one gives professional instruction. The Qur'ân was their Scripture, revealed to the Prophet in their midst. It constituted their guidance, and Islam was their religion, and for it they fought and died. It distinguished them from the other nations and ennobled them. They wished to teach it and make it understandable to the Muslims. They were not deterred by censure coming from pride, nor were they restrained by criticism coming from arrogance. This is attested by the fact that the Prophet sent the most important of the men around him with his embassies to the Arabs, in order to teach them the norms of Islam and the religious laws he brought. He sent his ten Companions[14] and others after them on this mission.

Then, Islam became firmly established and securely rooted. Far-off nations accepted Islam at the hands of the Muslims. With the passing of time, the situation of Islam changed. Many new laws were evolved from the (basic) texts as the result of numerous and unending developments. A fixed norm was required to keep (the process) free from error. Scholarship came to be a habit. For its acquisition, study was required. Thus, scholarship developed into a craft and profession.

The men who controlled the group feeling now occupied themselves with directing the affairs of royal and governmental authority. The cultivation of scholarship was entrusted to others. Thus, scholarship became a profession that served to make a living. Men who lived in luxury and were in control of the government were too proud to do any teaching. Teaching came to be an occupation restricted to weak individuals. As a result, its practitioners came to be despised by the men who controlled the group feeling and the government.

Now, Yûsuf, the father of al-Hajjâj, was one of the lords and nobles of the Thaqîf, well known for their share in the Arab group feeling and for their rivalry with the nobility of the Quraysh. Al-Hajjâj's teaching of the Qur'ân was not the same as the teaching of the Qur'ân is at this time, namely, a profession that serves to make a living. His teaching was the kind practised at the beginning of Islam, and as we have just described.

Another illustration of the same (kind of error) is the baseless conclusion critical readers of historical works draw when they hear about the position of judges, leadership in war, and the command of armies that judges exercised. Their misguided thinking leads them to aspire to similar positions. They think that the office of judge at the present time is as important as it was formerly. When they hear that the father of Ibn Abî'Âmir, who had complete control over Hishâm, and that the father of Ibn 'Abbâd, one of the rulers of Sevilla, were judges, they assume that they were like present-day judges. They are not aware of the change in customs that has affected the office of judge. Ibn Abî'Âmir and Ibn 'Abbâd belonged to Arab tribes that supported the Umayyad dynasty in Spain and represented the group feeling of the Umayyads, and it is known how important their positions were. The leadership and royal authority they attained did not derive from the rank of the judgeship as such. In the ancient administrative organization, the office of judge was given by the dynasty and its clients to men who shared in the group feeling (of the dynasty), as is done in our age with the wazirate in the Maghrib. One has only to consider the fact that (in those days judges) accompanied the army on its summer campaigns and were entrusted with the most important affairs, such as are entrusted only to men who can command the group feeling needed for their execution.

Hearing such things, some people are misled and get the wrong idea about conditions. At the present time, weak-minded Spaniards are especially given to errors in this respect. The group feeling has been lost in their country for many years, as the result of the annihilation of the Arab dynasty in Spain and the emancipation of the Spaniards from the control of Berber group feeling. The Arab descent has been remembered, but the ability to gain power through group feeling and mutual co-operation has been lost. In fact, the (Spaniards) came to be like (passive) subjects, without any feeling for the obligation of mutual support. They were enslaved by tyranny and had become fond of humiliation, thinking that their descent, together with their share in the ruling dynasty, was the source of power and authority. Therefore, among them, professional men and artisans are to be found pursuing power and authority and eager to obtain them. On the other hand, those who have experience with tribal conditions, group feeling, and dynasties along the western shore, and who know how superiority is achieved among nations and tribal groups, will rarely make mistakes or give erroneous interpretations in this respect.

Another illustration of the same kind of error is the procedure historians follow when they mention the various dynasties and enumerate the rulers belonging to them. They mention the name of each ruler, his ancestors, his mother and father, his wives, his surname, his seal ring, his judge, doorkeeper, and wazir. In this respect, they blindly follow the tradition of the historians of the Umayyad and 'Abbâsid dynasties, without being aware of the purpose of those historians. Their predecessors wrote their histories for members of the ruling dynasty, whose children wanted to learn about the lives and circumstances of their ancestors, so that they might be able to follow in their steps and to do what they did, even down to such details as obtaining servants from among those who were left over from the previous dynasty and giving ranks and positions to the descendants of its servants and retainers. Judges, too, shared in the group feeling of the dynasty and enjoyed the same importance as wazirs, as we have just mentioned. Therefore, the historians of that time had to mention all these details.

Later on, however, various distinct dynasties made their appearance. The time intervals became longer and longer. Historical interest now was concentrated on the rulers themselves and on the mutual relationships of the various dynasties in respect to power and predominance. (The problem now was) which nations could stand up (to the ruling dynasty) and which were too weak to do so. Therefore, it is pointless for an author of the present time to mention that sons and wives, the engraving on the seal ring, the surname, judge, wazir, and doorkeeper of an ancient dynasty, when he does not know the origin, descent, or circumstances of its members. Present-day authors mention all these things in mere blind imitation of former authors. They disregard the intentions of the former authors and forget to pay attention to historiography's purpose.

An exception are the wazirs who were very influential and whose historical importance overshadowed that of the rulers. Such wazirs as, for instance, al-Hajjâj, the Banû Muhallab, the Barmecides, the Banû Sahl b. Nawbakht, Kâfûr al-Ikhshîdî, Ibn Abî 'Âmir, and others should be mentioned. There is no objection to dealing with their lives or referring to their conditions for in importance they rank with the rulers.

An additional note to end this discussion may find its place here.

History refers to events that are peculiar to a particular age or race. Discussion of the general conditions of regions, races and periods constitutes the historian's foundation. Most of his problems rest upon that foundation, and his historical information derives clarity from it. It forms the topic of special works, such as the *Murûj adh-dhahab* of al-Mas'ûdî. In this work, al-Mas'ûdî commented upon the conditions of nations and regions in the West and in the East during his period, the three hundred and thirties [the nine hundred and forties]. He mentioned their sects and customs. He described the various countries, mountains, oceans, provinces, and dynasties. He distinguished between Arab and non-Arab groups. His book, thus, became the basic reference work for historians, their principal source for verifying historical information.

Al-Mas'ûdî was succeeded by al-Bakrî,[15] who did something similar for routes and provinces, to the exclusion of everything else, because in his time, not many transformations or great changes had occurred among the nations and races. However, at the present time — that is at the end of the eighth [fourteenth] century — the situation in the Maghrib, as we can observe, has taken a turn and changed entirely. The Berbers, the original population of the Maghrib, have been replaced by an influx of Arabs (that began in) the fifth [eleventh] century. The Arabs outnumbered and overpowered the Berbers, stripped them of most of their lands, and also obtained a share of those that remained in their possession. This was the situation until, in the middle of the eighth [fourteenth] century, civilization both in the East and the West was visited by a destructive plague which devastated nations and caused populations to vanish. It swallowed up many of the good things of civilization and wiped them out. It overtook dynasties at the time of their senility, when they had reached the limit of their duration. It lessened their power and curtailed their influence. It weakened their authority. Their situation approached the point of annihilation and dissolution. Civilization decreased with the decrease of mankind. Cities and buildings were laid waste, roads and way signs were obliterated, settlements and mansions became empty, dynasties and tribes grew weak. The entire inhabited world changed. The East, it seems, was similarly visited, though in accordance with and in proportion to (its more affluent) civilization. It was as if the voice of existence in the world had called out for oblivion and restriction, and the world had responded to its call. God inherits the earth and all who dwell upon it.

When there is a general change of conditions, it is as if the entire creation had changed and the whole world been altered, as if it were a new and repeated creation, a world brought into existence anew. Therefore, there is need at this time that someone should systematically set down the situation of the world among all regions and races, as well as the customs and sectarian beliefs that have changed for their adherents, doing for this age what al-Mas'ûdî did for his. This should be a model for future historians to follow. In this book of mine, I shall discuss as much of that as will be possible for me here in the Maghrib. I shall do so either explicitly or implicitly in connection with the history of the Maghrib, in conformity with my intention to restrict myself in this work to the Maghrib, the circumstances of its races and actions, and its subjects and dynasties, to the exclusion of any other region.[16] (This restriction is necessitated) by my lack of knowledge of conditions in the East and among its nations, and by the fact that secondhand information would not give the essential facts I am after. Al-Mas'ûdî's extensive travels in various countries enabled him to give a complete picture, as he mentioned in his work. Nevertheless, his discussion of conditions in the Maghrib is incomplete. God is the ultimate repository of all knowledge. Man is weak and deficient. Admission (of one's ignorance) is a specific religious duty. He whom God helps finds his way made easy and his efforts and quests successful. We seek God's help for the goal to which we aspire in this work. God gives guidance and help. He may be trusted.

It remains for us to explain the method of transcribing non-Arabic sounds whenever they occur in this book of ours:

It should be known that the letters (sounds)[17] of speech are modifications of sounds that come from the larynx. These modifications result from the fact that the sounds are broken up in contact with the uvula and the sides of the tongue in the throat, against the palate or the teeth, and also through contact with the lips. The sound is modified by the different ways in which such contact takes place. As a result, the sounds become distinct. Their combination constitutes the word that expresses what is in the mind.

Not all nations have the same sounds in their speech. One nation has sounds different from those of another. The sounds of the Arabic alphabet are twenty-eight, as is known. The Hebrews have sounds that are not to be found in our language. In our language, in turn, there are (sounds) that are not in theirs. The same applies to the European Christians, the Turks, the Berbers, and other non-Arabs.

In order to express their audible sounds, literate Arabs chose to use conventional letters written individually separate, such as ', *b*, *j*, *r*, *t*, and so forth through all the twenty-eight letters. When they come upon a letter for which there is no phonetic equivalent in their language, it is not indicated in writing and not clearly expressed. Scribes sometimes express it by means of the letter which is closest to it in our language, the one either preceding or following it. This is not a satisfactory way of indicating a sound but a complete replacement of it.

Our book contains the history of the Berbers and other non-Arabs. In their names and in some of their words, we came across (sounds) that have no equivalents in our written language and conventional orthography. Therefore, we were forced to indicate such sounds (by special signs). As we said, we did not find it satisfactory to use the letters closest to them, because in our opinion this is not a satisfactory indication. In my book, therefore, I have chosen to represent such non-Arabic (sounds) in such a way as to indicate the two (sounds) closest to it, so that the reader may be able to pronounce it somewhere in the middle between the sounds represented by the two letters and thus reproduce it correctly.

I derived this idea from the way the Qur'ân scholars write sounds that are not sharply defined, such as occur, for instance, in *as-sirât* according to Khalaf's reading. The *s* is to be pronounced somehow between *s* and *z*. In this case, they spell the word with *s* and write a *z* into it. They thus indicate a pronunciation somewhere in the middle between the two sounds.

In the same way, I have indicated every letter that is to be pronounced somehow in the middle between two of our letters. The Berber *k*, for instance, which is pronounced midway between our clear *k* and *g* or *q*, as, for instance, in the name Buluggîn, is spelled by me with a *k* with the addition of one dot — from the *g* — below, or one dot or two — from the *q* on top of it. This indicates that the sound is to be pronounced midway between *k* and *g* or *q*. This sound occurs most frequently in the Berber language. In the other cases, I have spelled each sound that is to be pronounced midway between two sounds of our language, with a similar combination of two letters. The reader will thus know that it is an intermediate sound and pronounce it accordingly. In this way, we have indicated it satisfactorily.

God gives success.

BOOK ONE OF THE *KITAB ÂL-'IBAR*
The nature of civilization. Bedouin and settled life, the achievement of superiority, gainful occupations, ways of making a living, sciences, crafts, and all the other things that affect civilization. The causes and reasons thereof.

It should be known that history, in matter of fact, is informative about human social organization, which itself is identical with world civilization. It deals with such conditions affecting the nature of civilization as, for instance, savagery and sociability, group feelings, and the different ways by which one group of human beings achieves superiority over another. It deals with royal authority and the dynasties that result in this manner and with the various ranks that exist within them. Also with the different kinds of gainful occupations and ways of making a living, with the sciences and crafts that human beings pursue as part of their activities and efforts, and with all the other institutions that originate in civilization through its very nature.

Untruth naturally afflicts historical information. There are various reasons that make this unavoidable. One of them is partisanship for opinions and schools. If the soul is impartial in receiving information, it devotes to that information the share of critical investigation the information deserves, and its truth or untruth thus becomes clear. However, if the soul is infected with partisanship for a particular opinion or sect, it accepts without a moment's hesitation the information that is agreeable to it. Prejudice and partisanship obscure the critical faculty and preclude critical investigation. The result is that falsehoods are accepted and transmitted.

Another reason making untruth unavoidable in historical information is reliance upon transmitters. Investigation of this subject belongs to (the discipline) of personality criticism.[1]

Another reason is unawareness of the purpose of an event. Many a transmitter does not know the real significance of his observations or of the things he has learned about orally. He transmits the information, attributing to it the significance he assumes or imagines it to have. The result is falsehood.

Another reason is unfounded assumption as to the truth of a thing. This is frequent. It results mostly from reliance upon transmitters.

Another reason is ignorance of how conditions conform with reality. Conditions are affected by ambiguities and artificial distortions. The informant reports the conditions as he saw them, but on account of artificial distortions he himself has no true picture of them.

Another reason is the fact that people as a rule approach great and high-ranking persons with praise and encomiums. They embellish conditions and spread their fame. The information made public in such cases is not truthful. Human souls long for praise, and people pay great attention to this world and the positions and wealth it offers. As a rule, they feel no desire for virtue and have no special interest in virtuous people.

Another reason making untruth unavoidable — and this one is more powerful than all the reasons previously mentioned — is ignorance of the nature of the various conditions arising in civilization. Every event (or phenomenon), whether (it comes about in connection with some) essence or (as the result of) action, must inevitably possess a nature peculiar to its essence as well as to the accidental conditions that may attach themselves to it. If the student knows that nature of events and the circumstances and requirements in the world of existence, it will help him to distinguish truth from untruth in investigating the historical information critically. This is more effective in critical investigation than any other aspect that may be brought up in connection with it.

Students often happen to accept and transmit absurd information that, in turn, is believed on their authority. Al-Mas'ûdî, for instance, reports such a story about Alexander. Sea monsters prevented Alexander from building Alexandria. He took a wooden container in which a glass box was inserted, and dived in it to the bottom of the sea. There he drew pictures of the devilish monsters he saw. He then had metal effigies of these animals made and set them up opposite the place where building was going on. When the monsters came out and saw the effigies, they fled. Alexander was thus able to complete the building of Alexandria.

It is a long story, made up of nonsensical elements which are absurd for various reasons. Thus, (Alexander is said) to have taken a glass box and braved the sea and its waves in person. Now, rulers would not take such a risk. Any ruler who would attempt such a thing would work his own undoing and provoke the outbreak of revolt against himself, and be replaced by the people with someone else. That would be his end. People would not wait one moment for him to return from the risk he is taking.

Furthermore, the jinn are not known to have specific forms and effigies. They are able to take on various forms. The story of the many heads they have is intended to indicate ugliness and frightfulness. It is not meant to be taken literally.

All this throws suspicion upon the story. Yet, the element in it that makes the story absurd for reasons based on the facts of existence is more convincing than all the other arguments. Were one to go down deep into the water, even in a box, one would have too little air for natural breathing. Because of that, one's spirit[2] would quickly become hot. Such a man would lack the cold air necessary to maintain a well-balanced humour of the lung and the vital spirit. He would perish on the spot. This is the reason why people perish in hot baths when cold air is denied to them. It also is the reason why people who go down into deep wells and dungeons perish when the air there becomes hot through putrefaction, and no winds enter those places to stir the air up. Those who go down there perish immediately. This also is why fish die when they leave the water, for the air is not sufficient for a fish to balance its lung. The fish is extremely hot, and the water to balance its humour is cold. The air into which the fish now comes is hot. Heat, thus, gains power over its animal spirit, and it perishes at once. This also is the reason for sudden death, and similar things.

Al-Mas'ûdî reports another absurd story, that of the Statue of the Starling in Rome. On a fixed day of the year, starlings gather at that statue bringing olives from which the inhabitants of Rome get their oil. How little this has to do with the natural procedure of getting oil!

Another absurd story is reported by al-Bakrî. It concerns the way the so-called 'Gate City' was built. That city had a circumference of more than a thirty days' journey and had ten thousand gates. Now, cities are used for security and protection. Such a city, however, could not be controlled and would offer no security or protection.

Then, there is also al-Mas'ûdî's story for the 'Copper City'. This is said to be a city build wholly of copper in the desert of Sijilmâsah which Mûsâ b. Nusayr[3] crossed on his raid against the Maghrib. The gates of this city are said to be closed. When the person who climbs its walls, in order to enter it, reaches the top, he claps his hands and throws himself down and never returns. All this is an absurd story. It belongs to the idle talk of storytellers. The desert of Sijilmâsah has been crossed by travellers and guides. They have not come across any information about such a city. All the details mentioned about it are absurd. They contradict the natural facts that apply to the building and planning of cities. Metal exists at best in quantities sufficient for utensils and furnishings. It is clearly absurd and unlikely that there would be enough to cover a city with it.

There are many similar things. Only knowledge of the nature of civilization makes critical investigation of them possible. It is the best and most reliable way to investigate historical information critically and to distinguish truth from falsehood. It is superior to investigations that rely upon criticism of the personalities of transmitters. Such personality criticism should not be resorted to until it has been ascertained whether a specific piece of information is in itself possible, or not. If it is absurd, there is no use engaging in personality criticism. Critical scholars consider absurdity inherent in the literal meaning of historical information, or an interpretation not acceptable to the intellect, as something that makes such information suspect. Personality criticism is taken into consideration only in connection with the soundness (or lack of soundness) of Muslim religious information, because this religious information mostly concerns injunctions in accordance with which the Lawgiver (Muhamad) enjoined Muslims to act whenever it can be presumed that the information is genuine. The way to achieve presumptive soundness is to ascertain the probity (*'adâlah*) and exactness of the transmitters.

On the other hand, to establish the truth and soundness of information about factual happenings, a requirement to consider is the conformity (or lack of conformity of the reported information with general conditions).

Therefore, it is necessary to investigate whether if it possible that the (reported facts) could have happened. This is more important than, and has priority over, personality criticism. For the correct notion about something that ought to be can be derived only from (personality criticism), while the correct notion about something that was can be derived from (personality criticism) and external (evidence) by (checking) the conformity (of the historical report with general conditions).

If this is so, the normative method for distinguishing right from wrong in historical information on the grounds of inherent possibility or absurdity is to investigate human social organization, which is identical with civilization. We must distinguish the conditions that attach themselves to the essence of civilization as required by its very nature; the things that are accidental and cannot be counted on; and the things that cannot possibly attach themselves to it. If we do that, we shall have a normative method for distinguishing right from wrong and truth from falsehood in historical information by means of a logical demonstration that admits of no doubts. Then, whenever we hear about certain conditions occurring in civilization, we shall know what to accept and what to declare spurious. We shall have a sound yardstick with the help of which historians may find the path of truth and correctness where their reports are concerned.

Such is the purpose of this first book of our work. (The subject) is in a way an independent science with its own peculiar object — that is, human civilization and social organization. It also has its own peculiar problems — that is, explaining in turn the conditions that attach themselves to the essence of civilization. Thus, the situation is the same with this science as it is with any other science, whether it be a conventional or an intellectual one.

It should be known that the discussion of this topic is something new, extraordinary, and highly useful. Penetrating research has shown the way to it. It does not belong to rhetoric, one of the logical disciplines (represented in Aristotle's *Organon*), which are concerned with convincing words whereby the mass is moved to accept or reject a particular opinion. It is also not politics, because politics is concerned with the administration of home or city in accordance with ethical and philosophical requirements, for the purpose of directing the mass toward a behaviour that will result in the preservation and permanence of the species.

The subject here is different from those two disciplines which, however, are often similar to it. In a way, it is an entirely original science. In fact, I have not come across a discussion along these lines by anyone. I do not know if this is because people have been unaware of it, but there is no reason to suspect them of having been unaware of it. Perhaps they have written exhaustively on this topic, and their work did not reach us. There are many sciences. There have been numerous sages among the nations of mankind. The knowledge that has not come down to us is larger than the knowledge that has. Where are the sciences of the Persians that 'Umar ordered to be wiped out at the time of the conquest? Where are the sciences of the Chaldaeans, the Syrians, and the Babylonians, and the scholarly products and results that were theirs? Where are the sciences of the Copts, their predecessors? The sciences of only one nation, the Greeks, have come down to us, because they were translated through al-Ma'mûn's efforts. He was successful in this direction because he had many translators at his disposal and spent much money in this connection. Of the sciences of others, nothing has come to our attention.

The accidents involved in every manifestation of nature and intellect deserve study. Any topic that is understandable and real requires its own special science. In this connection, scholars seem to have been interested in the results (of the individual sciences). As far as the subject under discussion is concerned, the result, as we have seen, is just historical information. Although the problems it raises are important, both essentially and specifically, (exclusive concerns for it) leads to one result only: the mere verification of historical information. This is not much. Therefore, scholars might have avoided the subject.

God knows better. 'And you were given but little knowledge.'[4]

In the field under consideration here, we encounter certain problems, treated incidentally by scholars among the arguments applicable to their particular sciences, but that in object and approach are of the same type as the problems we are discussing. In connection with the arguments for prophecy, for instance, scholars mention that human beings co-operate with each other for their existence and, therefore, need men to arbitrate among them and exercise a restraining influence. Or, in the science of the principles of jurisprudence, in the chapter of arguments for the necessity of languages, mention is made of the fact that people need means to express their intentions because by their very nature, co-operation and social organization are made easier by proper expressions. Or, in connection with the explanation that laws have their reason in the purposes they are to serve, the jurists mention that adultery confuses pedigrees and destroys the species; that murder, too, destroys the human species; that injustice invites the destruction of civilization with the necessary consequence that the species will be destroyed. Other similar things are stated in connection with the purposes embedded in laws, which are based upon the effort to preserve civilization. Therefore they apply to things that belong to civilization. This is obvious from our references to these problems which are mentioned as representative of the general situation.

We also find a few of the problems of the subject under discussion treated in scattered statements by the sages of mankind. However, they did not exhaust the subject. For instance, we have the speech of the Môbedhân[5] before Bahrâm b. Bahrâm in the story of the owl reported by al-Mas'ûdî. It runs: 'O king, the might of royal authority materializes only through the religious law, obedience toward God, and compliance with His commands and prohibitions. The religious law persists only through royal authority. Mighty royal authority is accomplished only through men. Men persist only with the help of property. The only way to property is through cultivation. The only way to cultivation is through justice. Justice is a balance set up among mankind. The Lord set it up and appointed an overseer for it, and that overseer is the ruler.'

There also is a statement by Anôsharwân[6] to the same effect: 'Royal authority exists through the army, the army through money, money through taxes, taxes through cultivation, cultivation through justice, justice through the improvement of officials, the improvement of officials through the forthrightness of wazirs, and the whole thing in the first place through the ruler's personal supervision of his subjects' condition and his ability to educate them, so that he may rule them, and not they him.'

In the *Book on Politics* that is ascribed to Aristotle and has wide circulation, we find a good deal about our subject. The treatment, however, is not exhaustive, nor is the topic provided with all the arguments it deserves, and it is mixed with other things. In the book, the author referred to such general ideas as we have reported on the authority of the Môbedhân and Anôsharwân. He arranged his statements in a remarkable circle that he discusses at length. It runs as follows: 'The world is a garden the fence of which is the dynasty. The dynasty is an authority through which life is given to proper behaviour. Proper behaviour is a policy directed by the ruler. The ruler is an institution supported by the soldiers. The soldiers are helpers who are maintained by money. Money is sustenance brought together by the subjects. The subjects are servants who are protected by justice. Justice is something familiar,[7] and through it, the world persists. The world is a garden...' — and then it begins again from the beginning. These are eight sentences of political wisdom. They are connected with each other, the end of each one leading into the beginning of the next. They are held together in a circle with no definite beginning or end. The author was proud of what he had hit upon and made much of the significance of the sentences.

When our discussion in the section on royal authority and dynasties has been studied and due critical attention given to it, it will be found to constitute an exhaustive, very clear, fully substantiated interpretation and detailed exposition of these sentences. We became aware of these things with God's help and without the instruction of Aristotle or the teaching of the Môbedhân.

The statements of Ibn al-Muqaffa'[8] and the excursions on political subjects in his treatises also touch upon many of the problems of our work. However, he did not substantiate his statements with arguments as we have done. He merely mentioned them in passing in the flowing prose style and eloquent verbiage of the rhetorician.

Judge Abû Bakr at-Turtûshi[9] also had the same idea in the *Kitâb Sirâj al-Mulûk*. He divided the work into chapters that come close to the chapters and problems of our work. However, he did not achieve his aim or realize his intention. He did not exhaust the problems and did not bring clear proofs. He sets aside a special chapter for a particular problem, but then he tells a great number of stories and traditions and he reports scattered remarks by Persian sages such as Buzurjmihr[10] and the Môbedhân, and by Indian sages, as well as material transmitted on the authority of Daniel, Hermes, and other great men. He does not verify his statements or clarify them with the help of natural arguments. The work is merely a compilation of transmitted material similar to sermons in its inspirational purpose. In a way, at-Turtûshî aimed at the right idea, but did not hit it. He did not realize his intention or exhaust his problems.

We, on the other hand, were inspired by God. He led us to a science whose truth we ruthlessly set forth. If I have succeeded in presenting the problems of this science exhaustively and in showing how it differs in its various aspects and characteristics from all other crafts, this is due to divine guidance. If, on the other hand, I have omitted some point, or if the problems have got confused with something else, the task of correcting remains for the discerning critic, but the merit is mine since I cleared and marked the way.

God guides with His light whom He will.[11]

In this book, now, we are going to explain such various aspects of civilization that affect human beings in their social organization, as royal authority, gainful occupation, sciences, and crafts, all in the light of various arguments that will show the true nature of the varied knowledge of the elite and the common people, repel misgivings, and remove doubts.

We say that man is distinguished from the other living beings by certain qualities peculiar to him, namely: (1) The sciences and crafts which result from that ability to think which distinguishes man from the other animals and exalts him as a thinking being over all creatures. (2) The need for restraining influence and strong authority, since man, alone of all the animals, cannot exist without them. It is true, something has been said in this connection about bees and locusts. However, if they have something similar, it comes to them through inspiration,[12] not through thinking or reflection. (3) Man's efforts to make a living and his concern with the various ways of obtaining and acquiring the means of life. This is the result of man's need for food to keep him alive and subsist, which God instilled in him, guiding him to desire and seek a livelihood. God said: 'He gave every thing its natural characteristics, and then guided it.'[13] (4) Civilization. This means that human beings have to dwell in common and settle together in cities and hamlets for the comforts of companionship and for the satisfaction of human needs, as a result of the natural disposition of human beings toward co-operation in order to be able to make a living, as we shall explain. Civilization may be either desert (Bedouin) civilization as found in outlying regions and mountains, in hamlets (near) pastures in waste regions, and on the fringes of sandy deserts; or it may be sedentary civilization as found in cities, villages, towns, and small communities that serve the purpose of protection and fortification by means of walls. In all these different conditions, there are things that affect civilization essentially in as far as it is social organization.

Consequently, the discussion in this work falls naturally under six chapter headings:

(1) On human civilization in general, its various kinds, and the portion of the earth that is civilized.

(2) On desert civilization, including a report on the tribes and savage nations.

(3) On dynasties, the caliphate, and royal authority, including a discussion of government ranks.

(4) On sedentary civilization, countries, and cities.

(5) On crafts, ways of making a living, gainful occupations, and their various aspects. And

(6) On the sciences, their acquisition and study.

I have discussed desert civilization first, because it is prior to everything else, as will become clear later on. The discussion of royal authority was placed before that of countries and cities for the same reason. The discussion of ways of making a living was placed before that of the sciences, because making a living is necessary and natural, whereas the study of science is a luxury or convenience. Anything natural has precedence over luxury. I lumped the crafts together with gainful occupations, because they belong to the latter in some respects as far as civilization is concerned, as will become clear later.

God gives success and support.

CHAPTER 1
Human civilization in general

First Prefatory Discussion

Human social organization is something necessary. The philosophers expressed this fact by saying: 'Man is "political" by nature.' That is, he cannot do without the social organization for which the philosophers use the technical term 'town' (*polis*).

This is what civilization means. (The necessary character of human social organization or civilization) is explained by the fact that God created and fashioned man in a form that can live and subsist only with the help of food. He guided man to a natural desire for food and instilled in him the power that enables him to obtain it.

However, the power of the individual human being is not sufficient for him to obtain (the food) he needs, and does not provide him with as much food as he requires to live. Even if we assume an absolute minimum of food — that is, food enough for one day, (a little) wheat, for instance — that amount of food could be obtained only after much preparations such as grinding, kneading, and baking. Each of these three operations requires utensils and tools that can be provided only with the help of several crafts, such as the crafts of the blacksmith, the carpenter, and the potter. Assuming that a man could eat unprepared grain, an even greater number of operations would be necessary in order to obtain the grain: sowing and reaping, and threshing to separate it from the husks of the ear. Each of these operations requires a number of tools and many more crafts than those just mentioned. It is beyond the power of one man alone to do all that, or part of it, by himself. Thus, he cannot do without a combination of many powers from among his fellow beings, if he is to obtain food for himself and for them. Through co-operation, the needs of a number of persons, many times greater than their own number, can be satisfied.

Likewise, each individual needs the help of his fellow beings for his defence. When God fashioned the natures of all living beings and divided the various powers among them, many dumb animals were given more perfect powers than God gave to man. The power of a horse, for instance, is much greater than the power of a man, and so is the power of a donkey or an ox. The power of a lion or an elephant is many times greater than the power of man.

Aggressiveness is natural in living beings. Therefore, God gave each of them a special limb for defence against aggression. To man, instead, He gave the ability to think, and the hand. With the help of the ability to think, the hand is able to prepare the ground for the crafts. The crafts, in turn, procure for man the instruments that serve him instead of limbs, which other animals possess for their defence. Lances, for instance, take the place of horns for goring, swords the place of claws to inflict wounds, shields the place of thick skins, and so on. There are other such things. They were all mentioned by Galen in *De usu partium*.[1]

The power of one individual human being cannot withstand the power of any one dumb animal, especially the power of the predatory animals. Man is generally unable to defend himself against them by himself. Nor is his unaided power sufficient to make use of the existing instruments of defence, because there are so many of them and they require so many crafts and things. It is absolutely necessary for man to have the co-operation of his fellow men. As long as there is no such co-operation, he cannot obtain any food or nourishment, and life cannot materialize for him, because God fashioned him so that he must have food if he is to live. Nor, lacking weapons, can he defend himself. Thus, he falls prey to animals and dies much before his time. Under such circumstances, the human species would vanish. When, however, mutual co-operation exists, man obtains food for his nourishment and weapons for his defence. God's wise plan that mankind should subsist and the human species be preserved will be fulfilled.

Consequently, social organization is necessary to the human species. Without it, the existence of human beings would be incomplete. God's desire to settle the world with human beings and to leave them as His representatives on earth[2] would not materialize. This is the meaning of civilization, the object of the science under discussion.

The aforementioned remarks have been in the nature of establishing the existence of the object in this particular field. A scholar in a particular discipline is not obliged to do this, since it is accepted in logic that a scholar in a particular science does not have to establish the existence of the object of that science.[3] On the other hand, logicians do not consider it forbidden to do so. Thus, it is a voluntary contribution.

God, in His grace, gives success.

When mankind has achieved social organization, as we have stated, and when civilization in the world has thus become a fact, people need someone to exercise a restraining influence and keep them apart, for aggressiveness and injustice are in the animal nature of man. The weapons made for the defence of human beings against the aggressiveness of dumb animals do not suffice against the aggressiveness of man to man, because all of them possess those weapons. Thus, something else is needed for defence against the aggressiveness of human beings toward each other. It could not come from outside, because all the other animals fall short of human perceptions and inspiration. The person who exercises a restraining influence, therefore, must be one of themselves. He must dominate them and have power and authority over them, so that no one of them will be able to attack another. This is the meaning of royal authority.

It has thus become clear that royal authority is a natural quality of man which is absolutely necessary to mankind. The philosophers mention that it also exists among certain dumb animals, such as the bees and the locusts. One discerns among them the existence of authority and obedience to a leader. They follow one who is distinguished as their leader by his natural characteristics and body. However, outside of human beings, these things exist as the result of natural disposition and divine guidance, and not as the result of an ability to think or to administrate.

The philosophers go further. They attempt to give logical proof of the existence of prophecy and to show that prophecy is a natural quality of man. In this connection, they carry the argument to its ultimate consequences and say that human beings absolutely require some authority to exercise a restraining influence. They go on to say that such restraining influence exists through the religious law ordained by God and revealed to mankind by a human being. He is distinguished from the rest of mankind by special qualities of divine guidance that God gave him, in order that he might find the others submissive to him and ready to accept what he says. Eventually, the existence of an authority among them and over them becomes a fact that is accepted without the slightest disapproval or dissent.

This proposition of the philosophers is not logical, as one can see. Existence and human life can materialize without (the existence of prophecy) through injunctions a person in authority may devise on his own or with the help of a group feeling that enables him to force the others to follow him wherever he wants to go. People who have a (divinely revealed) book and who follow the prophets are few in number in comparison with the Magians⁴ who have none. The latter constitute the majority of the world's inhabitants. Still, they have possessed dynasties and monuments, not to mention life itself. They still possess these things at this time in the intemperate zones to the north and the south. This is in contrast with human life in the state of anarchy, with no one to exercise a restraining influence. That would be impossible.

This shows that the philosophers are wrong when they assume that prophecy exists by necessity. The existence of prophecy is not required by logic. Its (necessary character) is indicated by the religious law, as was the belief of the early Muslims.

God gives success and guidance.

CHAPTER 2
Bedouin civilization, savage nations and tribes and their conditions of life, including several basic and explanatory statements

1 Both Bedouins and sedentary people are natural groups
It should be known that differences of condition among people are the result

of the different ways in which they make their living. Social organization enables them to co-operate toward that end and to start with the simple necessities of life, before they get to conveniences and luxuries.

Some people live by agriculture, the cultivation of vegetables and grains; others by animal husbandry, the use of sheep, cattle, goats, bees, and silkworms, for breeding and for their products. Those who live by agriculture or animal husbandry cannot avoid the call of the desert, because it alone offers the wide fields, pastures for animals, and other things that the settled areas do not offer. It is therefore necessary for them to restrict themselves to the desert. Their social organization and co-operation for the needs of life and civilization, such as food, shelter, and warmth, do not take them beyond the bare subsistence level, because of their inability (to provide) for anything beyond those (things). Subsequent improvement of their conditions and acquisition of more wealth and comfort than they need, cause them to rest and take it easy. Then, they co-operate for things beyond the bare necessities. They use more food and clothes, and take pride in them. They build large houses, and lay out towns and cities for protection. This is followed by an increase in comfort and ease, which leads to formation of the most developed luxury customs. They take the greatest pride in the preparation of food and a fine cuisine, in the use of varied splendid clothes of silk and brocade and other (fine materials), in the construction of ever higher buildings and towers, in elaborate furnishings for the buildings, and the most intensive cultivation of crafts in actuality. They build castles and mansions, provide them with running water, build their towers higher and higher, and compete in furnishing them (most elaborately). They differ in the quality of the clothes, the beds, the vessels, and the utensils they employ for their purposes. 'Sedentary people' means the inhabitants of cities and countries, some of whom adopt the crafts as their way of making a living, while others adopt commerce. They earn more and live more comfortably than Bedouins, because they live on a level beyond the level of bare necessity, and their way of making a living corresponds to their wealth.

It has thus become clear that Bedouins and sedentary people are natural groups which exist by necessity, as we have stated.

2 The Bedouins are a natural group in the world

We have mentioned in the previous section that the inhabitants of the desert adopt the natural manner of making a living, namely, agriculture and animal husbandry. They restrict themselves to the necessary in food, clothing, and mode of dwelling, and to the other necessary conditions and customs. They do not possess conveniences and luxuries. They use tents of hair and wool, or houses of wood, or of clay and stone, which are not furnished (elaborately). The purpose is to have shade and shelter, and nothing beyond that. They also take shelter in caverns and caves. The food they take is either little prepared or not prepared at all, save that it may have been touched by fire.

For those who make their living through the cultivation of grain and through agriculture, it is better to be stationary than to travel around. Such, therefore, are the inhabitants of small communities, villages, and mountain regions. These people make up the large mass of the Berbers and non-Bedouins.

Those who make their living from animals requiring pasturage, such as sheep and cattle, usually travel around in order to find pasture and water for their animals, since it is better for them to move around in the land. They are called 'sheepmen', that is, men who live on sheep and cattle. They do not go deep into the desert, because they would not find good pastures there. Such people include the Berbers, the Turks, the Turkomans and the Slavs, for instance.

Those who make their living by raising camels move around more. They wander deeper into the desert, because the hilly pastures with their plants and shrubs do not furnish enough subsistence for camels. They must feed on the desert shrubs and drink the salty desert water. They must move around the desert regions during the winter, in flight from the harmful cold to the warm desert air. In the desert sands, camels can find places to give birth to their young ones. Of all animals, camels have the hardest delivery and the greatest need for warmth in connection with it. (Camel nomads) are therefore forced to make excursions deep (into the desert). Frequently, too, they are driven from the hills by the militia, and they penetrate farther into the desert, because they do not want the militia to mete out justice to them or to punish them for their hostile acts. As a result, they are the most savage human beings that exist. Compared with sedentary people, they are on a level with wild, untamable animals and dumb beasts of prey. Such people are the Bedouins. In the West, the nomadic Berbers and the Zanâtah are their counterparts, and in the East, the Kurds, the Turkomans, and the Turks. The Bedouins, however, make deeper excursions into the desert and are more rooted in desert life because they live exclusively on camels, while the other groups live on sheep and cattle, as well as camels.

It has thus become clear that the Bedouins are a natural group which by necessity exists in civilization.

3 Bedouins are prior to sedentary people. The desert is the basis and reservoir of civilization and cities

We have mentioned that the Bedouins restrict themselves to the bare necessities in their way of life and are unable to go beyond them, while sedentary people concern themselves with conveniences and luxuries in their conditions and customs. The bare necessities are no doubt prior to the conveniences and luxuries. Bare necessities, in a way, are basic, and luxuries secondary. Bedouins, thus, are the basis of, and prior to, cities and sedentary people. Man seeks first the bare necessities. Only after he has obtained the bare necessities does he get to comforts and luxuries. The toughness of desert life precedes the softness of sedentary life. Therefore, urbanization is found to be the goal to which the Bedouin aspires. Through his own efforts, he achieves what he proposes to achieve in this respect. When he has obtained enough to be ready for the conditions and customs of luxury, he enters upon a life of ease and submits himself to the yoke of the city. This is the case with all Bedouin tribes. Sedentary people, on the other hand, have no desire for desert conditions, unless they are motivated by some urgent necessity or they cannot keep up with their fellow city dwellers.

Evidence for the fact that Bedouins are the basis of, and prior to, sedentary people is furnished by investigating the inhabitants of any given city. We shall find that most of its inhabitants originated among Bedouins dwelling in the country and villages of the vicinity. Such Bedouins became wealthy, settled in the city, and adopted a life of ease and luxury, such as exists in the sedentary environment.

All Bedouins and sedentary people differ also among themselves in their conditions of life. Many a clan is greater than another, many a tribe greater than another, many a city larger than another, and many a town more populous than another....

4 Bedouins are closer to being good than sedentary people

The reason for this is that the soul in its first natural state of creation is ready to accept whatever good or evil may arrive and leave an imprint upon it. Muhammad said: 'Every infant is born in the natural state. It is his parents who make him a Jew or a Christian or a heathen.' To the degree the soul is first affected by one of the two qualities, it moves away from the other and finds it difficult to acquire it. When customs proper to goodness have been first to enter the soul of a good person, and his (soul) has thus acquired the habit of (goodness, that person) moves away from evil and finds it difficult to do anything evil. The same applies to the evil person.

Sedentary people are much concerned with all kinds of pleasures. They are accustomed to luxury and success in worldly occupation and to indulgence in worldly desires. Therefore, their souls are coloured with all kinds of blameworthy and evil qualities. The more of them they possess, the more remote do the ways and means of goodness become to them. Eventually they lose all sense of restraint. Many of them are found to use improper language in their gatherings as well as in the presence of their superiors and womenfolk. They are not deterred by any sense of restraint, because the bad custom of behaving openly in an improper manner in both words and deeds has taken hold of them. Bedouins may be as concerned with worldly affairs as (sedentary people are). However, such concern would touch only the necessities of life and not luxuries or anything causing, or calling for, desires and pleasures. The customs they follow in their mutual dealings are, therefore, appropriate. As compared with those of sedentary people, their evil ways and blameworthy qualities are much less numerous. They are closer to the first natural state and more remote from the evil habits that have been impressed upon the souls (of sedentary people) through numerous and ugly, blameworthy customs. Thus, they can more easily be cured than sedentary people. This is obvious. It will later on become clear that sedentary life constitutes the last stage of civilization and the point where it begins to decay. It also constitutes the last stage of evil and of remoteness from goodness. Clearly, the Bedouins are closer to being good than sedentary people....

5 Bedouins are more disposed to courage than sedentary people

The reason for this is that sedentary people have become used to laziness and ease. They are sunk in well-being and luxury. They have entrusted the defence of their property and their lives to the governor and ruler who rules them, and to the militia which has the task of guarding them. They find full assurance of safety in the walls that surround them, and the fortifications that protect them. No noise disturbs them, and no hunting occupies their time. They are carefree and trusting, and have ceased to carry weapons. Successive generations have grown up in this way of life. They have become like women and children, who depend upon the master of the house. Eventually, this has come to be a quality of character that replaces natural disposition.

The Bedouins, on the other hand, live apart from the community. They are alone in the country and remote from militias. They have no walls or gates. Therefore, they provide their own defence and do not entrust it to, or rely upon others for it. They always carry weapons. They watch carefully all sides of the road. They take hurried naps only when they are together in company or when they are in the saddle. They pay attention to the most distant barking or noise. They go alone into the desert, guided by their fortitude, putting their trust in themselves. Fortitude has become a character quality of theirs, and courage their nature. They use it whenever they are called upon or roused by an alarm. When sedentary people mix with them in the desert or associate with them on a journey, they depend on them. They cannot do anything for themselves without them. This is an observed fact. (Their dependence extends) even to knowledge of the country, the directions, watering places, and crossroads. Man is a child of the customs and the things he has become used to. He is not the product of his natural disposition and temperament. The conditions to which he has become accustomed, until they have become for him a quality of character and matters of habit and custom, have replaced his natural disposition. If one studies this in human beings, one will find much of it, and it will be found to be a correct observation.

6 The reliance of sedentary people upon laws destroys their fortitude and power of resistance

Not everyone is master of his own affairs. Chiefs and leaders who are masters of the affairs of men are few in comparison with the rest. As a rule, man must by necessity be dominated by someone else. If the domination is kind and just and the people under it are not oppressed by its laws and restrictions, they are guided by the courage or cowardice that they possess in themselves. They are satisfied with the absence of any restraining power. Self-reliance eventually becomes a quality natural to them. They would not know anything else. If, however, the domination with its laws is one of brute force and intimidation, it breaks their fortitude and deprives them of their power of resistance as a result of the inertness that develops in the souls of the oppressed, as we shall explain.

When laws are (enforced) by means of punishment, they completely destroy fortitude, because the use of punishment against someone who cannot defend himself generates in that person a feeling of humiliation that, no doubt, must break his fortitude.

When laws are (intended to serve the purposes of) education and instruction and are applied from childhood on, they have to some degree the same effect, because people then grow up in fear and docility and consequently do not rely on their own fortitude.

Thus, greater fortitude is found among the savage Arab Bedouins than among people who are subject to laws. Furthermore, those who rely on laws and are dominated by them from the very beginning of their education and instruction in the crafts, sciences, and religious matters, are thereby deprived of much of their own fortitude. They can scarcely defend themselves at all against hostile acts. This is the case with students, whose occupation it is to study and to learn from teachers and religious leaders, and who constantly apply themselves to instruction and education in very dignified gatherings. This situation and the fact that it destroys the power of resistance and fortitude must be understood.

It is no argument that the men around Muhammad observed the religious laws, and yet did not experience any diminution of their fortitude, but possessed the greatest possible fortitude. When the Muslims got their religion from Muhammad, the restraining influence came from themselves, as a result of the encouragement and discouragement he gave them in the Qur'ân. It was not a result of technical instruction or scientific education. The laws were the laws and precepts of the religion that they received orally and which their firmly rooted belief in the truth of the articles of faith caused them to observe. Their fortitude remained unabated, and it was not corroded by education or authority. 'Umar said, 'Those who are not (disciplined) by the religious law are not educated by God.' 'Umar's desire was that everyone should have his restraining influence in himself. His certainty was that Muhammad knew best what is good for mankind.

(The influence of) religion, then, decreased among men, and they came to use restraining laws. The religious law became a branch of learning and a craft to be acquired through instruction and education. People turned to sedentary life and assumed the character trait of submissiveness to law. This led to a decrease in their fortitude.

Clearly, then, governmental and educational laws destroy fortitude, because their restraining influence is something that comes from outside. The religious laws, on the other hand, do not destroy fortitude, because their restraining influence is something inherent. Therefore, governmental and educational laws influence sedentary people, in that they weaken their souls and diminish their stamina, because they have to suffer them both as children and as adults. The bedouins, on the other hand, are not in the same position, because they live far away from the laws of government, instruction, and education....

7 Only tribes held together by group feeling can live in the desert

It should be known that God put good and evil into the nature of man. Thus, He says in the Qur'ân: 'We led him along the two paths.'[1] He further says: 'And inspired the soul with wickedness as well as fear of God.'[2]

Evil is the quality that is closest to man when he fails to improve his customs and when religion is not used as the model to improve him. The great mass of mankind is in that condition, with the exception of those to whom God gives success. Evil qualities in man are injustice and mutual aggression. He who casts his eye upon the property of his brother will lay his hand upon it to take it, unless there is a restraining influence to hold him back. The poet thus says:

> *Injustice is a human trait. If you find*
> *A moral man, there is some reason why he is not unjust*

Mutual aggression of people in towns and cities is averted by the authorities and the government, which hold back the masses under their control from attacks and aggression upon each other. They are thus prevented by the influence of force and governmental authority from mutual injustice, save such injustice as comes from the ruler himself.

Aggression against a city from outside may be averted by walls, in the event of unpreparedness, a surprise attack at night, or inability (of the inhabitants) to withstand the enemy during the day. Or it may be averted with the help of government auxiliary troops, if (the inhabitants are) prepared and ready to offer resistance.

The restraining influence among Bedouin tribes comes from their *shaykhs* and leaders. It results from the great respect and veneration they generally enjoy among the people. The hamlets of the Bedouins are defended against outside enemies by a tribal militia composed of noble youths of the tribe who are known for their courage. Their defence and protection are successful only if they are a closely knit group of common descent. This strengthens their stamina and makes them feared, since everybody's affection for his family and his group is more important (than anything else). Compassion and affection for one's blood relations and relatives exist in human nature as something God put into the hearts of men. It makes for mutual support and aid, and increases the fear felt by the enemy.

Those who have no one of their own lineage (to care for) rarely feel affection for their fellows. If danger is in the air on the day of battle, such a man slinks away and seeks to save himself, because he is afraid of being left without support. Such people, therefore, cannot live in the desert, because they would fall prey to any nation that might want to swallow them up.

If this is true with regard to the place where one lives, which is in constant need of defence and military protection, it is equally true with regard to every other human activity, such as prophecy, the establishment of royal authority, or propaganda. Nothing can be achieved in these matters without fighting for it, since man has the natural urge to offer resistance. And for fighting one cannot do without group feeling, as we mentioned at the beginning.

8 Group feeling results only from blood relationship or something corresponding to it

(Respect for) blood ties is something natural among men, with the rarest exceptions. It leads to affection for one's relations and blood relatives, (the feeling that) no harm ought to befall them nor any destruction come upon them. One feels shame when one's relatives are treated unjustly or attacked, and one wishes to intervene between them and whatever peril or destruction threatens them. This is a natural urge in man, for as long as there have been human beings. If the direct relationship between persons who help each other is very close, so that it leads to close contact and unity, the ties are obvious and clearly require the (existence of a feeling of solidarity) without any outside (prodding). If, however, the relationship is somewhat distant, it is often forgotten in part. However, some knowledge of it remains and this causes a person to help his relatives for the known motive, in order to escape the shame he would feel in his soul were a person to whom he is somehow related treated unjustly.

Clients and allies belong in the same category. The affection everybody has for his clients and allies results from the feeling of shame that comes to a person when one of his neighbours, relatives, or a blood relation in any degree is humiliated. The reason for it is that a client (-master) relationship leads to close contact exactly, or approximately in the same way, as does common descent. It is in that sense that one must understand Muhammad's remark, 'Learn as much of your pedigrees as is necessary to establish your ties of kindred.' It means that pedigrees are useful only in so far as they imply the close contact that is a consequence of blood ties and that eventually leads to mutual help and affection. Anything beyond that is superfluous. For a pedigree is something imaginary and devoid of reality. Its usefulness consists only in the resulting connection and close contact. If the fact of (common descent) is obvious and clear, it evokes in man a natural affection, as we have said. If, however, its existence is known only from remote history, it moves the imagination but faintly. Its usefulness is gone, and preoccupation with it becomes gratuitous, a kind of game, and as such is not permissible. In this sense, one must understand the remark, 'Genealogy is something which is of no use to know and which it does no harm not to know.' This means that when common descent is no longer clear and has become a matter of scientific knowledge, it can no longer move the imagination and is denied the affection caused by group feeling. It has become useless.

9 Purity of lineage is found only among the savage Arabs of the desert and other such people

This is because of the poor life, hard conditions, and bad habitats that are peculiar to the Bedouins. They are the result of necessity, inasmuch as their subsistence depends on camels and camel breeding and pasturage. The camels are the cause of the Bedouins' savage life in the desert, since they feed on desert shrubs and give birth in the desert sands. The desert is a place of hardship and starvation, but to them it has become familiar and accustomed. Generations of Bedouins grew up in the desert. Eventually, they became confirmed in their character and natural qualities. No member of any other nation was disposed to share their conditions. No member of any other race felt attracted to them. But if one of them were to find ways and means of fleeing from these conditions, he would not give them up. Therefore, their pedigrees can be trusted not to have been mixed up and corrupted. They have been preserved pure in unbroken lines. This is the case, for instance, with Mudar tribes such as the Quraysh, the Kinânah, the Thaqîf, the Banû Asad, the Hudhayl, and their Khuzâ'ah neighbours. They lived a hard life in places where there was no agriculture or animal husbandry. They lived far from the fertile fields of Syria and the 'Irâq, far from the sources of seasonings and grains. How pure have they kept their lineages! These are unmixed in every way, and are known to be unsullied.

Other Arabs lived in the hills and at the sources of fertile pastures and plentiful living. Among these Arabs were the Himyar and the Kahlân, such as the Lakhm, the Judhâm, the Ghassân, the Tayy, the Qudâ'ah, and the Iyâd. Their lineages were mixed up, and their groups intermingled. It is known that (genealogists) differ with respect to each one of these families. This came about as the result of intermixture with non-Arabs. They did not pay any attention to preserving the (purity of) lineage of their families and groups. This was done only by (true) Arabs. Furthermore, the Arabs of the fertile fields were affected by the general human trend toward competition for the fat soil and the good pastures. This resulted in intermingling and much mixture of lineages. Even at the beginning of Islam, people occasionally referred to themselves by their places of residence. They referred to the Districts of Qinnasrîn, of Damascus, or of the 'Awâsim (the border region of northern Syria). This custom was then transferred to Spain. It happened not because the Arabs rejected genealogical considerations, but because they acquired particular places of residence after the conquest. They eventually became known by their places of residence. These became a distinguishing mark, in addition to the pedigree, used by the Arabs to identify themselves in the presence of their amirs. Later on, sedentary Arabs mixed with Persians and other non-Arabs. Purity of lineage was completely lost, and its fruit, the group feeling, was lost and rejected. The tribes, then, disappeared and were wiped out, and with them, group feeling was wiped out. But (the earlier situation) remained unchanged among the Bedouins.

God inherits the earth and all that is upon it.

10 How lineages become confused

It is clear that a person of a certain descent may become attached to people of another descent, either because he feels well-disposed toward them, or because there exists an alliance or client (-master) relationship, or yet because he had to flee from his own people by reason of some crime he committed. Such a person comes to be known as having the same descent as those to whom he is attached and is counted one of them with respect to the things that result from (common descent), such as affection, the rights and obligations concerning talion and blood money, and so on. When the things resulting from common descent are there, it is as if (common descent) itself were there, because the only meaning of belonging to one or another group is that one is subject to its laws and conditions, as if one had come into close contact with it. In the course of time, the original descent is almost forgotten. Those who knew about it have passed away, and it is no longer known to most people. Family lines in this manner continually changed from one tribal group to another, and some people developed close contact with others (of a different descent). This happened both in pre-Islamic and in Islamic times, and between both Arabs and non-Arabs....

11 Leadership over people who share in a given group feeling cannot be vested in those not of the same descent

This is because leadership exists only through superiority, and superiority only through group feeling. Leadership over people, therefore, must, of necessity, derive from a group feeling that is superior to each individual group feeling. Each individual group feeling that becomes aware of the superiority of the group feeling of the leader is ready to obey and follow him.

Now, a person who has become attached to people of a common descent usually does not share the group feeling that derives from their common descent. He is merely attached to them. The firmest connection he has with the group is as client and ally. This in no way guarantees him superiority over them. Assuming that he has developed close contact with them, that he has mixed with them, that the fact that he was originally merely attached to them has been forgotten, and that he has become one of their kin and is addressed as one having the same descent as they, how could he, or one of his forebears, have acquired leadership before that process had taken place, since leadership is transmitted in one particular branch that has been marked for superiority through group feeling? The fact that he was merely attached to the tribe was no doubt known at an earlier stage, and at that time prevented him (or rather, his forebears) from assuming leadership. Thus, it could not have been passed on by a man who was still merely attached (to the tribe). Leadership must of necessity be inherited from the person who is entitled to it, in accordance with the fact, which we have stated, that superiority results from group feeling.

Many leaders of tribes or groups are eager to acquire certain pedigrees. They desire them because persons of that particular descent possessed some special virtue, such as bravery, or nobility, or fame, however this may have come about. They go after such a family and involve themselves in claims to belong to a branch of it. They do not realize that they thus bring suspicion upon themselves with regard to their leadership and nobility....

These pedigrees are invented by people to get into the good graces of rulers, through (sycophantic) behaviour and through the opinions they express. Their (fabrications) eventually become so well known as to be irrefutable....

12 Only those who share in a group feeling can have a 'house' and nobility in the basic sense and in reality, while others have it only in a metaphorical and figurative sense

This is because nobility and prestige are the result of (personal) qualities. A 'house' means that a man counts noble and famous men among his forebears. The fact that he is their progeny and descendant gives him great standing among his fellows, for his fellows respect the great standing and nobility that his ancestors acquired through their qualities.

We have explained that the advantage of a (common) descent consists in the group feeling that derives from it and that leads to affection and mutual help. Wherever the group feeling is truly formidable and its soil kept pure, the advantage of a common descent is most evident, and the (group feeling) is more effective. It is an additional advantage to have a number of noble ancestors. Thus, prestige and nobility become firmly grounded in those who share in the group feeling (of a tribe), because there exists the result of (common) descent. The nobility of a 'house' is in direct proportion to the different degrees of group feeling, because (nobility) is the secret of (group feeling).

Isolated inhabitants of cities can have a 'house' only in a metaphorical sense. The assumption that they possess one is a specious claim. Seen in its proper light, prestige means to the inhabitants of cities that some of them count among their forefathers men who had good (personal) qualities and who mingled with good people, and (that, in addition, they) try to be as decent as possible. This is different from the real meaning of group feeling, as group feeling derives from descent and a number of forefathers. The terms 'prestige' and 'house' are used metaphorically in this connection, because there exists in this case a number of successive ancestors who consistently performed good deeds. This is not true and unqualified prestige.

A 'house' possesses an original nobility through group feeling and personal qualities. Later on, the people (who have a 'house') divest themselves of that nobility when group feeling disappears as the result of sedentary life, and they mingle with the common people. A certain delusion as to their former prestige remains in their souls and leads them to consider themselves members of the most noble houses. They are, however, far from that (status), because their group feeling has completely disappeared. Many inhabitants of cities who had their origins in noble Arab or non-Arab 'houses' share such delusions.

The Israelites are the most firmly misled in this delusion. They originally had one of the greatest 'houses' in the world, first, because of the great number of prophets and messengers born among their ancestors, extending from Abraham to Moses, the founder of their religious group and law, and next, because of their group feeling and the royal authority that God had promised and granted them by means of that group feeling. Then, they were divested of all that, and they suffered humiliation and indigence. They were destined to live as exiles on earth. For thousands of years, they knew only enslavement and unbelief. Still, the delusion of (nobility) has not left them. They can be found saying: 'He is an Aaronite'; 'He is a descendant of Joshua'; 'He is one of Caleb's progeny'; 'He is from the tribe of Judah.' This in spite of the fact that their group feeling has disappeared and that for many long years they have been exposed to humiliation. Many other inhabitants of cities who hold (noble) pedigrees but no longer share in any group feeling are inclined to similar nonsense.

Abû l-Walîd b. Rushd (Averroës) erred in this respect, He mentioned prestige in the *Rhetoric*, 'Prestige', he states, 'belongs to people who are ancient settlers in a town.' He did not consider the things we have just mentioned. I should like to know how long residence in a town can help (anyone to gain prestige), if he does not belong to a group that makes him feared and causes others to obey him. Averroës considers prestige as depending exclusively on the number of forefathers. Yet, rhetoric means to sway the opinions of those whose opinions count, that is, the men in command. It takes no notice of those who have no power. They cannot sway anyone's opinions, and their own opinions are not sought. The sedentary inhabitants of cities fall into that category. It is true that Averroës grew up in a generation and a place where people had no experience of group feeling and were not familiar with the conditions governing it. Therefore, he did not progress beyond his well-known (definition of) 'house' and prestige as something depending merely on the number of one's ancestors, and did not refer to the reality of group feeling and its influence among men.

13 *'House' and nobility come to clients and followers only through their masters and not through their own descent*

This is because, as we have mentioned before, only those who share in a group feeling have basic and true nobility. When such people take people of another descent as followers, or when they take slaves and clients into servitude, and enter into close contact with them, as we have said, the clients and followers share in the group feeling of their masters and take it on as if it were their own group feeling. By taking their special place within the group feeling, they participate to some extent in the descent to which that particular group feeling belongs.

His own descent and birth are of no help as regards the group feeling of (the master), since that group feeling has nothing to do with his own descent. The group feeling that belonged to his own family is lost, because its influence disappeared when he entered into close contact with that other family and lost contact with the men whose group feeling he had formerly shared. He thus becomes one of the others and takes his place among them. If a number of his ancestors also shared the group feeling of these people, he comes to enjoy among (these other people) a certain nobility and 'house', in keeping with his position as their client and follower. However, he does not come to be as noble as they are, but remains inferior to them.

This is the case with clients of dynasties and with all servants. They acquire nobility by being firmly rooted in their client relationship, and by their service to their particular dynasty, and by having a large number of ancestors who had been under its protection. One knows that the Turkish clients of the 'Abbâsids and, before them, the Barmecides, as well as the Banû Nawbakht, thus achieved 'house' and nobility and created glory and importance for themselves by being firmly rooted in their relationship to the ('Abbâsid) dynasty. Ja'far b. Yahyâ b. Khâlid had the greatest possible 'house' and nobility. This was the result of his position as a client of ar-Rashîd and his family. It was not the result of his own (noble) descent among the Persians. The same is the case with clients and servants under any dynasty. They have 'house' and prestige by being firmly rooted in their client relationship with a particular dynasty and by being its faithful followers. Their original descent disappears if it is not that of (the dynasty). It remains under cover and is not considered in connection with their importance and glory. The thing that is considered is their position as clients and followers, because this accords with that secret of group feeling which produces 'house' and nobility.

The nobility of (a client) is, in a way, derived from the nobility of his masters, and his 'house' is derived from what they have built. His own descent and birth do not help him. His glory is built upon his relationship as client to a particular dynasty, and upon his close contact with it as a follower and product of its education. His own original descent may have implied close contact with some group feeling and dynasty. If that (close contact) is gone and the person in question has become a client and follower of another (dynasty), his original (descent) is no longer of any use to him, because its group feeling has disappeared. The new (relationship) becomes useful to him, because (its group feeling) exists.

This applies to the Barmecides. It has been reported that they belonged to a Persian 'house', the members of which had been guardians of the Persian fire temples. When they became clients of the 'Abbâsids, their original (descent) was not taken into consideration. Their nobility resulted from their position as clients and followers of the ('Abbâsid) dynasty.

All other notions are unsupported and unrealistic delusions prompted by undisciplined souls. The facts of existence confirm our remarks.

14 Prestige lasts at best four generations in one lineage

The world of the elements and all it contains comes into being and decays. Minerals, plants, all the animals including man, and the other created things come into being and decay, as one can see with one's own eyes. The same applies to the conditions that affect created things, and especially the conditions that affect man. Sciences grow up and then are wiped out. The same applies to crafts, and to similar things.

Prestige is an accident that affects human beings. It comes into being and decays inevitably. No human being exists who possesses an unbroken pedigree of nobility from Adam down to himself. The only exception was made in the case of the Prophet, as a special act of divine grace to him, and as a measure designed to safeguard his true character.

Nobility originates in the state of being outside. That is, being outside of leadership and nobility and being in a base, humble station, devoid of prestige. This means that all nobility and prestige is preceded by the non-existence of nobility and prestige, as is the case with every created thing.

It reaches its end in a single family within four successive generations. This is as follows: The builder of the family's glory knows what it cost him to do the work, and he keeps the qualities that created his glory and made it last. The son who comes after him had personal contact with his father and thus learned those things from him. However, he is inferior to him in this respect, inasmuch as a person who learns things through study is inferior to a person who knows them from practical application. The third generation must be content with imitation and, in particular, with reliance upon tradition. This member is inferior to him of the second generation, inasmuch as a person who relies upon tradition is inferior to a person who exercises independent judgment.

The fourth generation, then, is inferior to the preceding ones in every respect. Its member has lost the qualities that preserved the edifice of its glory. He despises (those qualities). He imagines that the edifice was not built through application and effort. He thinks that it was something due his people from the very beginning by virtue of the mere fact of their descent, and not something that resulted from group (effort) and (individual) qualities. For he sees the great respect in which he is held by the people, but he does not know how that respect originated and what the reason for it was. He imagines that it is due to his descent and nothing else. He keeps away from those in whose group feeling he shares, thinking that he is better than they. He trusts that (they will obey him because) he was brought up to take their obedience for granted, and he does not know the qualities that made obedience necessary. Such qualities are humility (in dealing) with (such men) and respect for their feelings. Therefore, he considers them despicable, and they, in turn, revolt against him and despise him. They transfer leadership from him and his direct lineage to some other related branch, in obedience to their group feeling, after they have convinced themselves that the qualities of the (new leader) are satisfactory to them. His family then grows, whereas the family of the original (leader) decays and the edifice of his 'house' collapses.

That is the case with rulers who have royal authority. It also is the case with all the 'houses' of tribes, of amirs, and of everybody else who shares in a group feeling, and then also with the 'houses' among the urban population. When one 'house' goes down, another one rises in another group of the same descent.

The rule of four (generations) with respect to prestige usually holds true. It may happen that a 'house' is wiped out, disappears, and collapses in fewer than four, or it may continue unto the fifth and sixth generations, though in a state of decline and decay. The four generations can be defined as the builder, the one who has personal contact with the builder, the one who relies on tradition, and the destroyer.

Muhammad said: 'The noble son of the noble father of the noble grandfather of the noble great-grandfather: Joseph, the son of Jacob, the son of Isaac, the son of Abraham.' This indicates that Joseph had reached the limit in glory.

In the Torah, there is the following passage: 'God, your Lord, is powerful[3] and jealous, visiting the sins of the fathers upon the children unto the third and the fourth generations.' This shows that four generations in one lineage are the limit in extent of ancestral prestige....

15 Savage nations are better able to achieve superiority than others

Since desert life no doubt is the source of bravery, savage groups are braver than others. They are, therefore, better able to achieve superiority and to take away the things that are in the hands of other nations. The situation of one and the same group changes, in this respect, with the change of time. Whenever people settle in fertile plains and amass luxuries and become accustomed to a life of abundance and refinement, their bravery decreases to the degree that their wildness and desert habits decrease.

This is exemplified by dumb animals, such as gazelles, wild buffaloes, and donkeys, that are domesticated. When they cease to be wild as the result of contact with human beings, and when they have a life of abundance, their vigour and violence undergo change. This affects even their movements and the beauty of their coat. The same applies to savage human beings who become sociable and friendly.

The reason is that familiar customs determine human nature and character. Superiority comes to nations through enterprise and courage. The more firmly rooted in desert habits and the wilder a group is, the closer does it come to achieving superiority over others, if both (parties) are approximately equal in number, strength, and group feeling.

In this connection, one may compare the Mudar with the Himyar and the Kahlân before them, who preceded them in royal authority and in the life of luxury, and also with the Rabî'ah who settled in the fertile fields of the 'Irâq. The Mudar retained their desert habits, and the others embarked upon a life of abundance and great luxury before they did. Desert life prepared the Mudar most effectively for achieving superiority. They took away and appropriated what the other groups had in their hands....

16 The goal to which group feeling leads is royal authority

This is because group feeling gives protection and makes possible mutual defence, the pressing of claims, and every other kind of social activity. By dint of their nature, human beings need someone to act as a restraining influence and mediator in every social organization, in order to keep its members from (fighting) with each other. That person must, by necessity, have superiority over the others in the matter of group feeling. If not, his power cannot be effective. Such superiority is royal authority. It is more than leadership. Leadership means being a chieftain, and the leader is obeyed, but he has no power to force others to accept his rulings. Royal authority means superiority and the power to rule by force.

When a person sharing in the group feeling has reached the rank of chieftain and commands obedience, and when he then finds the way open toward superiority and the use of force, he follows that way, because it is something desirable. He cannot completely achieve his (goal) except with the help of the group feeling, which causes (the others) to obey him. Thus, royal superiority is a goal to which group feeling leads, as one can see.

Even if an individual tribe has different 'houses' and many diverse group feelings, still, there must exist a group feeling that is stronger than all the other group feelings combined, that is superior to them all and makes them subservient, and in which all the diverse group feelings coalesce, as it were, to become one greater group feeling. Otherwise, splits would occur and lead to dissension and strife.

Once group feeling has established superiority over the people who share in it, it will, by its very nature, seek superiority over people who have other group feelings unrelated to the first. If the one (group feeling) is the equal of the other or is able to stave off (its challenge), the (competing people) are even with and equal to each other. Each group feeling maintains its sway over its own domain and people, as is the case with tribes and nations all over the earth. However, if the one group feeling overpowers the other and makes it subservient to itself, the two group feelings enter into close contact, and the (defeated) group feeling gives added power to the (victorious) group feeling, which, as a result, sets its goal of superiority and domination higher than before. In this way, it goes on until the power of that particular group feeling equals the power of the ruling dynasty. Then, when the ruling dynasty grows senile and no defender arises from among its friends who share in its group feeling, the (new group feeling) takes over and deprives the ruling dynasty of its power, and, thus, obtains complete royal authority.

The power of (a given group feeling) may reach its peak when the ruling dynasty has not yet reached senility. (This stage) may coincide with the stage at which (the ruling dynasty) needs to have recourse to the people who represent the various group feelings (in order to master the situation). In such a case, the ruling dynasty includes (the people who enjoy the powerful group feeling) among those of its clients whom it uses for the execution of its various projects. This, then, means (the formation of) another royal authority, inferior to that of the controlling royal authority. This was the case with the Turks under the 'Abbâsids.

It is thus evident that royal authority is the goal of group feeling. When it attains that goal, the tribe (representing that particular group feeling) obtains royal authority, either by seizing actual control or by giving assistance (to the ruling dynasty) according to the circumstances prevailing. If the group feeling encounters obstacles on its way to the goal, it stops where it is, until God decides its fate.

17 Obstacles on the way toward royal authority are luxury and the submergence of the tribe in a life of prosperity

This is because, when a tribe has achieved a certain measure of superiority with the help of its group feeling, it gains control over a corresponding amount of wealth and comes to share prosperity and abundance with those who have been in possession of these things. It shares in them to the degree of its power and usefulness to the ruling dynasty. If the ruling dynasty is so strong that no one thinks of depriving it of its power or of sharing with it, the tribe in question submits to its rule and is satisfied with whatever share in the dynasty's wealth and tax revenue it is permitted to enjoy. Hopes would not go so high as to think of royal prerogatives or ways to obtain (royal authority). (Members of the tribe) are merely concerned with prosperity, gain, and a life of abundance. (They are satisfied) to lead an easy, restful life in the shadow of the ruling dynasty, and to adopt royal habits in building and dress, a matter they stress and in which they take more and more pride, the more luxuries and plenty they acquire, as well as all the other things that go with luxury and plenty.

As a result, the toughness of desert life is lost. Group feeling and courage weaken. Members of the tribe revel in the well-being that God has given them. Their children and offspring grow up too proud to look after themselves or to attend to their own needs. They have disdain also for all the other things that are necessary in connection with group feeling. This finally becomes a character trait and natural characteristic of theirs. Their group feeling and courage decrease in the next generations. Eventually, group feeling is altogether destroyed. They thus invite their own destruction. The greater their luxury and the easier the life they enjoy, the closer they are to extinction, not to mention (their lost chance of securing) royal authority. The things that go with luxury and submergence in a life of ease break the vigour of the group feeling, which alone produces superiority. When group feeling is destroyed, the tribe is no longer able to protect itself, let alone press any claims. It will be swallowed up by other nations.

18 Meekness and docility to outsiders that may come to be found in a tribe are obstacles on the way toward royal authority

This is because meekness and docility break the vigour of group feeling. If people are meek and docile (their group feeling) is lost. They do not become fond of meekness until they are too weak to defend themselves. Those who are too weak to defend themselves are all the more weak when it comes to withstanding their enemies and pressing their claims.

The Israelites are a good example. Moses urged them to go and become rulers of Syria. He informed them that God had made this their destiny. But the Israelites were too weak for that. They said: 'There are giants in that country, and we shall not enter it until the giants have departed.'[4] That is, until God has driven them out by manifesting His power, without the application of our group feeling, and that will be one of your miracles, O Moses. And when Moses urged them on, they persisted and became rebellious, and said: 'Go yourself and your Lord, and fight.'[5]

They had become used to being too weak to offer opposition and to press claims. The verse must be interpreted in that manner. (This situation) was the result of the quality of docility and the longing to be subservient to the Egyptians, which the Israelites had acquired through many long years and which led eventually to the complete loss of their group feeling. In addition, they did not really believe what Moses told them, namely, that Syria would be theirs and that the Amalekites who were in Jericho would fall prey to them, by virtue of the divine decree that God had made in favour of the Israelites. They were unable to do (what they were asked to do) and felt too weak to do it. They realized that they were too weak to press any claims, because they had acquired the quality of meekness. They suspected the story their prophet told them and the command he gave them. For that, God punished them by obliging them to remain in the desert. They stayed in the desert between Syria and Egypt for forty years. They had no contact with civilization nor did they settle in any city,[6] as it is told in the Qur'ân. This was because of the harshness the Amalekites in Syria and the Copts in Egypt had practised against them. From the context and meaning of the verse, it evidently refers to the implication of such a sojourn in the desert, namely, the disappearance of the generation whose character had been formed and whose group feeling had been destroyed by the humiliation, oppression, and force from which it had escaped, and the eventual appearance in the desert of another powerful generation that knew neither laws nor oppression and did not have the stigma of meekness. Thus, a new group feeling could grow up, and that enabled them to press their claims and to achieve superiority. This makes it evident that forty years is the shortest period in which one generation can disappear and a new generation can arise. Praised be the Wise, all-knowing One.

This shows most clearly what group feeling means. Group feeling produces the ability to defend oneself, to offer opposition, to protect oneself, and to press one's claims. Whoever loses it is too weak to do any of these things.

The subject of imposts and taxes belongs to this discussion of the things that force meekness upon a tribe.

A tribe paying imposts did not do that until it became resigned to meek submission with respect to paying them. Imposts and taxes are a sign of oppression and meekness that proud souls do not tolerate, unless they consider (paying them) easier than being killed and destroyed. In such a case, the group feeling (of a tribe) is too weak for its own defence and protection. People whose group feeling cannot defend them against oppression certainly cannot offer any opposition or press any claims. They have submitted to meekness, and, as we have mentioned before, meekness is an obstacle. When one sees a tribe humiliated by the payment of imposts, one cannot hope that it will ever achieve royal authority....

19 A sign of royal authority is a person's eager desire to acquire praiseworthy qualities, and vice versa

Royal authority is something natural to human beings, because of its social implications. In view of his natural disposition and his power of logical reasoning, man is more inclined toward good qualities than toward bad qualities, because the evil in him is the result of the animal powers in him, and inasmuch as he is a human being, he is more inclined toward goodness and good qualities. Now, royal and political authority come to man *qua* man, because it is something peculiar to man and is not found among animals. Thus, the good qualities in man are appropriate to political and royal authority since goodness is appropriate to political authority.

We have already noted that glory has a basis upon which it is built and through which it achieves its reality: group feeling and the tribal group.

Glory also depends upon a detail that completes and perfects its existence: (an individual's personal) qualities. Royal authority is a goal of group feeling. Thus, it is likewise a goal of the perfecting details, namely, the personal qualities. The existence of (royal authority without the perfecting details would be like the existence of a person with his limbs cut off, or it would be like appearing naked before people.

The existence of group feeling without the practice of praiseworthy qualities would be a defect among people who possess a 'house' and prestige. All the more so would it be a defect in men who are invested with royal authority, the greatest possible kind of glory and prestige. Furthermore, political and royal authority are God's guarantee to mankind and serve as a representation of God among men with respect to His laws. Now, divine laws affecting men are all for their good and envisage their interests. This is attested by the religious law. Bad laws, on the other hand, all result from stupidity and from Satan, in opposition to the predestination and power of God. He makes both good and evil and predetermines them, for there is no maker except Him.

He who thus obtained group feeling guaranteeing power, and who is known to have good qualities appropriate for the execution of God's laws concerning His creatures, is ready to act as His substitute and guarantor among mankind. He has the qualifications for that. This proof is more reliable and solid than the first one.

It has thus become clear that good qualities attest the (potential) existence of royal authority in a person who possesses group feeling. Whenever we observe people who possess group feeling and who have gained control over many lands and nations, we find in them an eager desire for goodness and good qualities, such as generosity, the forgiveness of error, tolerance toward the weak, hospitality toward guests, the support of dependents, maintenance of the indigent, patience in adverse circumstances, faithful fulfilment of obligations, liberality with money for the preservation of honour, respect for the religious law and for the scholars who are learned in it, observation of the things to be done or not to be done that those scholars prescribe for them, thinking highly of religious scholarship, belief in and veneration for men of religion and a desire to receive their prayers, great respect for old men and teachers, acceptance of the truth in response to those who call to it, fairness to and care for those who are too weak to take care of themselves, humility toward the poor, attentiveness to the complaints of supplicants, fulfilment of the duties of the religious law and divine worship in all details, avoidance of fraud, cunning, deceit, and shirking of obligations, and similar things. Thus, we know that these are the qualities of leadership, which (persons qualified for royal authority) have obtained and which have made them deserving of being the leaders of the people under their control, or to be leaders in general. It is something good that God has given them, corresponding to their group feeling and superiority.

Vice versa, when God wants a nation to be deprived of royal authority, He causes (its members) to commit blameworthy deeds and to practise all sorts of vices. This will lead to the complete loss of their political virtues, which will continue to be destroyed until they no longer exercise royal authority. Someone else will exercise it in their stead. This is to constitute an insult to them, in that the royal authority God has given them and the good things He has placed at their disposal are taken away from them. Upon close investigation, many such instances will be found among the nations of the past.

It should be known that a quality belonging to perfection, which tribes possessing group feeling are eager to cultivate and which attests to their (right to) royal authority, is respect for scholars, pious men, noble (relatives of the Prophet), well-born persons, and the different kinds of merchants and foreigners, as well as the ability to assign everybody to his proper station. The respect shown by tribes and persons (in control) of group feelings and families, for men of comparable nobility, tribal position, group feeling, and rank, is something natural. It mostly results from the desire for rank, or from fear of the people of the person to whom respect is paid, or from a wish for reciprocal treatment. However, in the case of people who have no group feeling to make themselves feared, and who have no rank (to bestow) for which one might hope, there can be no doubt as to why they are respected, and it is quite clear what one seeks through them, namely, glory, perfection in personal qualities, and total progress toward political leadership. Respect for one's rivals and equals must exist in connection with the special political leadership that concerns one's tribe and its competitors (and equals). Respect for excellent and particularly qualified strangers means perfection in general political leadership. The pious are thus respected for their religion; scholars, because they are needed for establishing the statutes of the religious law; merchants, in order to give encouragement (to their profession), so that their usefulness may be as widespread as possible. Strangers are respected out of generosity and in order to encourage them to undertake certain kinds (of activity). Assigning everybody to his proper station is done out of fairness, and fairness means justice. When people who possess group feeling have that, one knows that they are ready for general political leadership, which means royal authority. God permits (political leadership) to exist among them, because the sign of (political leadership) exists among them. Therefore, the first thing to disappear in a tribe that exercises royal authority, when God wants to deprive its members of their royal and governmental authority, is respect for such people. When a nation is observed to have lost it, it should be realized that its virtues have begun to go, and it can be expected that royal authority will cease to exist in it.

20 While a nation is savage, its royal authority extends farther

This is because such a nation is better able to achieve superiority and full control, and to subdue other groups. The members of such a nation have the strength to fight other nations, and they are among human beings what beasts of prey are among dumb animals. The Bedouins and the Zanâtah and similar groups, for instance, are such nations, as are the Kurds, the Turkomans, and the Veiled Sinhâjah.

These savage peoples, furthermore, have no homelands that they might use as fertile (pasture), and no fixed place to which they might repair. All regions and places are the same to them. Therefore, they do not restrict themselves to possession of their own and neighbouring regions. They do not stop at the borders of their horizon. They swarm across distant zones and achieve superiority over faraway nations....

21 As long as a nation retains its group feeling, royal authority that disappears in one branch will, of necessity, pass to some other branch of the same nation

The reason for this is that (the members of a particular nation) acquire royal authority only after (proving their) forcefulness and finding other nations obedient to them. A (few) are singled out to become the actual rulers and to be directly connected with the throne. It could not be all of them, because there is not enough room for all to compete, and because the existence of jealousy cuts short the aspirations of many of those who aspire to high office.

Those who are singled out to support the dynasty indulge in a life of ease and sink into luxury and plenty. They make servants of their fellows and contemporaries and use them to further the various interests and enterprises of the dynasty. Those who are far away from the government and who are thus prevented from having a share in it, remain in the shadow of the dynastic power. They share in it by virtue of their descent; they are not affected by senility, because they remain far from the life of luxury and the things that produce luxury.

Time gets the upper hand over the original group (in power). Their prowess disappears as the result of senility. (The duties of) the dynasty saps their energy. Time feasts on them, as their energy is exhausted by well-being and their vigour drained by the nature of luxury. They reach their limit, the limit that is set by the nature of human urbanization and political superiority. At that moment, the group feeling of other people (within the same nation) is strong. Their force cannot be broken. Their emblem is recognized to be victorious. As a result, their hopes of achieving royal authority, from which they had been kept until now by a superior power within their own group, are high. Their superiority is recognized, and, therefore, no one disputes their claim to royal authority. They seize power. They then have the same experience as (their predecessors) at the hands of those other groups within the nation that remain away from (the government). Royal authority thus continues in a particular nation until the force of its group feeling is broken and gone, or until all its groups have ceased to exist. That is how God proceeds with regard to life in this world.

This can be illustrated by what happened among the nations. When the royal authority of 'Âd was wiped out, their brethren, the Thamûd, took over. They were succeeded, in turn, by the Amalekites; the Amalekites were succeeded by the Himyar; the Himyar by the Tubba's, who belonged to the Himyar. They, likewise, were succeeded by the Adhwâ'. Then, the Mudar came to power.

The same was the case with the Persians. When the Kayyanid rule was wiped out, the Sassanians ruled after them. Eventually, God permitted them all to be destroyed by the Muslims.

The same was also the case with the Greeks. Their rule was wiped out and transferred to the Rûm (Romans).

This is how God proceeds with His servants and creatures.

All this has its origin in group feeling, which differs in different groups. Luxury wears out royal authority and overthrows it. When a dynasty is wiped out, power is taken away from that dynasty by those whose group feeling has a share in the (established) group feeling, since it is recognized that people submit and are subservient to (the established group feeling) and since people are used to the fact that this has superiority over all other group feelings. (The same group feeling), now, exists only in those people who are closely related (to the outgoing dynasty), because group feeling is proportionate to the degree of relationship. Eventually, a great change takes place in the world, such as the transformation of a religion, or the disappearance of a civilization, or something else willed by the power of God. Then, royal authority is transferred from one group to another—to the one that God permits to effect that change.

22 *The vanquished always want to imitate the victor in his distinctive characteristics, his dress, his occupation, and all his other conditions and customs*

The reason for this is that the soul always sees perfection in the person who is superior to it and to whom it is subservient. It considers him perfect, either because it is impressed by the respect it has for him, or because it erroneously assumes that its own subservience to him is not due to the nature of defeat but to the perfection of the victor. If that erroneous assumption fixes itself in the soul, it becomes a firm belief. The soul, then, adopts all the manners of the victor and assimilates itself to him. This, then, is imitation.

Or, the soul may possibly think that the superiority of the victor is not the result of his group feeling or great fortitude, but of his customs and manners. This also would be an erroneous concept of superiority, and (the consequences) would be the same as in the former case.

Therefore, the vanquished can always be observed to assimilate themselves to the victor in the use and style of dress, mounts, and weapons; indeed, in everything.

In this connection, one may compare how children constantly imitate their fathers. They do that only because they see perfection in them. One may also compare how almost everywhere people are dominated (in fashion) by the dress of the militia and the government forces, because they are ruled by them.

This goes so far that a nation dominated by another, neighbouring nation will show a great deal of assimilation and imitation. At this time, this is the case in Spain. The Spaniards are found to assimilate themselves to the Galician nations in their dress, their emblems, and most of their customs and conditions. This goes so far that they even draw pictures on the walls and have them in buildings and houses. The intelligent observer will draw from this the conclusion that it is a sign of being dominated by others.

In this light, one should understand the secret of the saying, 'The common people follow the religion of the ruler.' (This saying) belongs to the subject under discussion. The ruler dominates those under him. His subjects imitate him, because they see perfection in him, exactly as children imitate their parents, or students their teachers.

God is wise and all-knowing.

23 A nation that has been defeated and has come under the rule of another nation will quickly perish

The reason for this may possibly lie in the apathy that comes over people when they lose control of their own affairs and, through enslavement, become the instrument of others and dependent upon them. Hope diminishes and weakens. Now, propagation and an increase in civilization (population) take place only as the result of strong hope and of the energy that hope creates in the animal powers (of man). When hope and the things it stimulates are gone through apathy, and when group feeling has disappeared under the impact of defeat, civilization decreases and business and other activities stop. With their strength dwindling under the impact of defeat, people become unable to defend themselves. They become the victims of anyone who tries to dominate them, and a prey to anyone who has the appetite. It makes no difference whether they have already reached the limit of their royal authority or not.

Here, we possibly learn another secret, namely, that man is a natural leader by virtue of the fact that he has been made a representative (of God on earth). When a leader is deprived of his leadership and prevented from exercising all his powers, he becomes apathetic, even down to such matters as food and drink. This is in the human character. A similar observation may be made with regard to beasts of prey. They do not cohabit when they are in human captivity. The group that has lost control of its own affairs thus continues to weaken and to disintegrate until it perishes. God alone endures.

This may be illustrated by the Persian nation. In the past, the Persians filled the world with their great numbers. When their military force was annihilated by the Arabs, they were still very numerous. It is said that Sa'd b. Abî Waqqâs counted (the population) beyond Ctesiphon. It numbered 137,000, including 37,000 heads of families. But when the Persians came under the rule of the Arabs and were subjugated, they lasted only a short while and were wiped out as if they had never been. One should not think that this was the result of some persecution or aggression perpetrated against them. The rule of Islam is known for its justice. Such (disintegration) is in human nature. It happens when people lose control of their own affairs and become the instrument of someone else.

Therefore, the Negro nations are, as a rule, submissive to slavery, because (Negroes) have little that is (essentially) human and possess attributes that are quite similar to those of dumb animals, as we have stated.

24 Bedouins can gain control only over flat territory

On account of their savage nature, the Bedouins are people who plunder and cause damage. They plunder whatever they are able to lay their hands on without having to fight or to expose themselves to danger. They then retreat to their pastures in the desert. They do not attack or fight except in self-defence. Every stronghold or (locality) that seems difficult to attack, they by-pass in favour of some less difficult (enterprise). Tribes that are protected by inaccessible mountains are safe from their mischief and destructiveness. The Bedouins would not cross hills or undergo hardship and danger in order to get to them.

Flat territory, on the other hand, falls victim to their looting and prey to their appetite whenever they can gain power over it, when there is no militia, or when the dynasty is weak. Then they raid, plunder, and attack that territory repeatedly, because it is easily (accessible) to them. Eventually, its inhabitants succumb utterly to the Bedouins and then are pushed around by them in accordance with changes of control and shifts in leadership. Eventually, their civilization is wiped out. God has power over His creatures.

25 Places that succumb to the Bedouins are quickly ruined

The reason for this is that the Bedouins are a savage nation, fully accustomed to savagery and the things that cause it. Savagery has become their character and nature. They enjoy it, because it means freedom from authority and no subservience to leadership. Such a natural disposition is the negation and antithesis of civilization. All the customary activities of the Bedouins lead to wandering and movement. This is the antithesis and negation of stationariness, which produces civilization. For instance, they need stones to set them up as supports for their cooking-pots. So, they take them from buildings which they tear down to get the stones, and use them for that purpose. Wood, too, is needed by them for props for their tents and for use as tent poles for their dwellings. So, they tear down roofs to get the wood for that purpose. The very nature of their existence is the negation of building, which is the basis of civilization. This is the case with them quite generally.

Furthermore, it is their nature to plunder whatever other people possess. Their sustenance lies wherever the shadow of their lances falls. They recognize no limit in taking the possessions of other people. Whenever their eyes fall upon some property, furnishings, or utensils, they take them. When they acquire superiority and royal authority, they have complete power to plunder (as they please). There no longer exists any political (power) to protect property, and civilization is ruined.

Furthermore, since they use force to make craftsmen and professional workers do their work, they do not see any value in it and do not pay them for it. Now, labour is the real basis of profit. When labour is not appreciated and is done for nothing, the hope for profit vanishes, and no (productive) work is done. The sedentary population disperses, and civilization decays.

Furthermore, the Bedouins are not concerned with laws, or with deterring people from misdeeds or with protecting some against others. They care only for the property that they might take away from people through looting and imposts. When they have obtained that, they have no interest in anything further, such as taking care of people, looking after their interests, or forcing them not to commit misdeeds. They often impose fines on property, because they want to get some advantage, some tax, or profit out of it. This is their custom. It does not help to prevent misdeeds or to deter those who undertake to commit them. On the contrary, it increases (misdeeds), because as compared to getting what one wants, the possible financial loss through fines is insignificant.

Under the rule of Bedouins, their subjects live as in a state of anarchy, without law. Anarchy destroys mankind and ruins civilization, since, as we have stated, the existence of royal authority is a natural quality of man. It alone guarantees their existence and social organization.

Furthermore, every Bedouin is eager to be the leader. There is scarcely one among them who would cede his power to another, even to his father, his brother, or the eldest member of his family. That happens only in rare cases and under pressure of considerations of decency. There are numerous authorities and amirs among them. The subjects have to obey many masters in connection with the control of taxation and law. Civilization decays and is wiped out.

It is noteworthy how civilization always collapsed in places the Bedouins took over and conquered, and how such settlements were depopulated and laid in ruin. The Yemen where Bedouins live is in ruins, except for a few cities. Persian civilization in the Arab 'Irâq is likewise completely ruined. The same applies to contemporary Syria. Formerly, the whole region between the Sudan and the Mediterranean was settled. This is attested to by the relics of civilization there, such as monuments, architectural sculpture, and the visible remains of villages and hamlets.

26 Bedouins can acquire royal authority only by making use of some religious colouring, such as prophethood, or sainthood, or some great religious event in general

The reason for this is that because of their savagery, the Bedouins are the least willing of nations to subordinate themselves to each other, as they are rude, proud, ambitious, and eager to be the leaders. Their individual aspirations rarely coincide. But when there is religion (among them) through prophethood or sainthood, then they have some restraining influence in themselves. The qualities of haughtiness and jealousy leave them. It is, then, easy for them to subordinate themselves and to unite (as a social organization). This is achieved by the common religion they now have. It causes rudeness and pride to disappear and exercises a restraining influence on their mutual envy and jealousy. When there is a prophet or saint among them, who calls upon them to fulfil the commands of God, rids them of blameworthy qualities, and causes them to adopt praiseworthy ones, and who prompts them to concentrate all their strength in order to make the truth prevail, they become fully united and acquire superiority and royal authority. Besides, no people are as quick to accept (religious) truth and right guidance, because their natures have been preserved free from distorted habits and uncontaminated by base qualities. The only (difficulty) lies in the quality of savagery, which, however, is easily taken care of and which is ready to admit good (qualities), as it has remained in its first natural state, remote from the ugly customs and bad habits that leave their impress upon the soul.

27 The Bedouins are of all nations the one most remote from royal leadership

The reason for this is that the Bedouins are more rooted in desert life and penetrate deeper into the desert than any other nation. They have less need of the products and grain of the hills, because they are used to a tough, hard life.

Therefore, they can dispense with other people. It is difficult for them to subordinate themselves to each other, because they are not used to (any control) and because they are in a state of savagery. Their leader needs them mostly for the group spirit that is necessary for purposes of defence. He is, therefore, forced to rule them kindly and to avoid antagonizing them. Otherwise, he would have trouble with the group spirit, resulting in his undoing and theirs. Royal leadership and government, on the other hand, require the leader to exercise a restraining influence by force. If not, his leadership would not last.

Furthermore, it is the nature of the Bedouins not only to appropriate the possessions of other people but, beyond that, to refrain from arbitrating among them and to fail to keep them from (fighting) each other. When they have taken possession of a nation, they make it the goal of their rule to profit (from their position) by taking away the property of the members of that nation. They often punish crimes by fines on property, in their desire to increase the tax revenues and to obtain some (pecuniary) advantage. That is no deterrent. It is often an incentive to it, in view of the fact that incentives to commit misdeeds (may be very strong) and that, in the opinion of (the criminal), payment of a fine is insignificant, weighed against getting what he wants. Thus, misdeeds increase, and civilization is ruined. A nation dominated by the Bedouins is in a state no different from anarchy, where everybody is set against the others. Such a civilization cannot last and goes quickly to ruin, as would be the case in a state of anarchy, as we have mentioned before.

The Bedouins are by nature remote from royal leadership. They attain it once their nature has undergone a complete transformation under the influence of some religious colouring that wipes out all such (qualities) and causes the Bedouins to have a restraining influence on themselves and to keep people apart from each other.

This is illustrated by the Arab dynasty in Islam. Religion cemented their leadership with the religious law and its ordinances, which, explicitly and implicitly, are concerned with what is good for civilization. The caliphs succeeded one another. As a result, the royal authority and government of the Arabs became great and strong.

Later on, the Arabs were cut off from the dynasty for generations. They neglected religion. Thus, they forgot political leadership and returned to their desert. They were ignorant of the connection of their group feeling with the people of the ruling dynasty, because subservience and lawful (government) had become strange to them. They became once again as savage as they had been before. The epithet 'royal' was no longer applicable to them, except in so far as it applied to the caliphs who were (Arab) by race. When the caliphate disappeared and was wiped out, governmental power passed altogether out of their hands. Non-Arabs took over their power, and they remained as Bedouins in the desert, ignorant of royal authority and political leadership. Most Arabs do not even know that they possessed royal authority in the past, or that no nation had ever exercised such (sweeping) royal authority as had their race. The dynasties of 'Ād and Thamûd, the Amalekites, the Himyar, and the Tubba's testify to that statement, and then, there was the Mudar dynasty in Islam, the Umayyads and the 'Abbâsids. But when the Arabs forgot their religion, they no longer had any connection with political leadership, and they returned to their desert origins. At times, they achieve superiority over weak dynasties, as is the case in the contemporary Maghrib. But their domination leads only to the ruin of the civilization they conquer, as we have stated before.

28 Desert tribes and groups are dominated by the urban population

We have said before that desert civilization is inferior to urban civilization, because not all the necessities of civilization are to be found among the people of the desert. They do have some agriculture at home but do not possess the materials that belong to it, most of which (depend on) crafts. They do not have any carpenters, tailors, blacksmiths, or others (who) would provide them with the necessities required for making a living in agriculture and other things.

Likewise, they do not have (coined) money. They have the equivalent of it in harvested grain, in animals, and in animal products such as milk, wool, (camel's) hair, and hides, which the urban population needs and pays the Bedouins money for. However, while (the Bedouins) need the cities for their necessities of life, the urban population needs (the Bedouins) for conveniences and luxuries. Thus, as long as they live in the desert and have not acquired royal authority and control of the cities, the Bedouins need the inhabitants (of the latter). They must be active in behalf of their interests and obey them whenever (the cities) ask and demand obedience from them.

When there is a ruler in the city, the submissiveness and obedience of (the Bedouins) is the result of the ruler's superiority. When there is no ruler in the city, some political leadership and control by some of the inhabitants over the remainder must, of necessity, exist there. If not, the civilization of the city would be wiped out. Such a leader makes (the Bedouins) obey him and exert themselves in behalf of his interests. He does so either by persuasion, in that he distributes money among them and lets them have the necessities they need from his city, which enables their civilization to subsist; or, if he has the power to do so, he forces them to obey him, even if he has to cause discord among them so as to get the support of one party, with the help of which he will then be able to overcome the remainder and thus force the others to obey him, since they fear the decay of their civilization as the result of (the unstable situation). (These Bedouins) often cannot leave particular districts (and go) to other regions, because all of them are (already) inhabited by (other) Bedouins who usurped them and kept others out of them. They have, therefore, no hope of survival except by being obedient to the city. Thus, they are of necessity dominated by the urban population.

ENDNOTES

Foreword

1 Muhammad b. Ishâq, author of the famous biography (sîrah) of Muhammad. He died in 150 or 151 [A.D. 767/68].

2 Muhammad b. Jarir, author of the Annals, 224/25-310 [839-923].

3 Hisham b. Muhammad, d. 204 or 206 [819/20 or 821/22].

4 The biographer of Muhammad and historian of early Islam, 130-207 [747-823].

5 He died in 180 [796/97].

6 'Ali b. al-Husayn, d. 345 or 346 [956-957].

7 The Umayyads and the 'Abbasids.

8 Hayyan b. Khalaf, 377-469 [987/88-1076].

9 Ifirqiyah reflects the name of the Roman province of Africa. This geographical term is commonly used by Ibn Khaldun and has been retained in the translation.

10 Ibrahim b. al-Qasim, who lived ca. A.D. 1000

11 Hasan b. Recheck, 390 to 456 or 463 [1000 to 1064 or 170/71].

The Introduction

1 That is, Mesopotamia and north-western Persia adjacent to it.

2 Exod. 6: 16 ff.

3 Cf. Kings 10:26. As a rule, Muslim scholars gave an unpleasant connotation to the term 'Israelite stories', as mere fiction presented as history.

4 Qur'ân 31, 6 (5).

5 Al-Hirah on the Euphrates was the capital of the Lakhmid buffer state under Persian control. Al-Bahrayn (Bahrain) included the country on the north-western shore of the Persian Gulf, and not only the islands today known under that name.

6 Qur'ân 89. 6-7 (5-6).

7 The verses are by 'Umar b. Aba Rabi'ah who lived ca. A.D. 700.

8 Qur'ân 36.22 (21).

9 Poet (d. A.D. 810).

10   The son of the caliph al-Mahdi, who was for a short time considered by some groups as caliph. 162-224 [779-839].

11   Qur'ân 31. 22 (21).

12   *Dîn* 'religion' is here used in the more general sense of 'way of doing things'.

13   Al-Hajjaj b. Yusuf, the great governor of 'Iraq (*ca.* 660-714).

14   The *'asharah al-mubashsharah*, the ten early Muslims to whom Paradise was guaranteed.

15   The geographer, 'Abdallah b. Muchmmad, 432-487 [1040/41-1094]. He is repeatedly quoted by Ibn Khaldun. A new edition of al-Bakri's geographical dictionary, *Mu'jam ma sta'jam*, appeared in Cairo in 1945-51. *His Routes and Provinces (al-Masalik wa-l-mamalik)* is still unpublished except for some sections.

16   Ibn Khaldun soon changed his mind and added the history of the East to his work at a very early stage in its preparation.

17   The written symbol is considered to be identical with the sound indicated by it.

Book One of the Kitâb al-'Ibar

1   'Personality criticism' (*al-jarh wa-t-ta'dil*) is concerned with investigating the reliability or unreliability of the transmitters of traditions. Ibn Khaldun often has occasion to refer to it.

2   The 'vital spirit' which, according to Galenic and Muslim medicine, was believed to originate in the left cavity of the heart.

3   The great general (A.D. 640-716/17) who completed the conquest of the Muslim West.

4   Qur'ân 17. 85 (87).

5   Mobedh (<*magupat*) is the title of the Zoroastrian priest. Mobedhan actually is the Persian plural of the word.

6   Anosharwan is the celebrated Sassanian ruler Khosraw I, A.D. 531-579.

7   *Ma'luf* 'familiar' may here possibly mean 'harmonious'. Arabic *ta'lif* translates Greek **.

8   'Abdalla b. al-Muqaffa', d. 142 [759/60]

9   Muhammad b. al-Walid, *ca.* 451 to 520 or 525 [1059 to 1126 or 1131].

10   The wazir of Khosraw I Anosharwan who appears in Arabic literature and is the chief representative of Persian wisdom.

11   Cf. Qur'ân 24. 35 (35).

12   Arabic uses the same word (*wahy*) for Prophetical 'inspiration' and for what we would translate in this context as 'instinct'. The 'inspiration' of bees is mentioned in Qur'ân 16. 68 (70).

13   Qur'ân 20. 50 (52).

Chapter 1

1 At the beginning of the work, ed. C. G. Kuhn (Leipzig, 1821-33), III, 2.

2 Cf. Qur'ân 2. 30 (28).

3 The 'object' (*mawdû'*) of a science is the fundamental elements at its basis, such as quantities (measurements) in geometry, numbers in arithmetic, substances in physics, and so on. The object of Ibn Khaldûn's new science is human social organization, or civilization.

4 'Magians' originally meant the Zoroastrians. In later Islam they were considered as people who followed a kind of prophet but did not have Scriptures like the Christians and the Jews. Thus, they occupied a position somewhere between the latter and polytheists. The term was eventually used to denote the general idea of pagans.

Chapter 2

1 Qur'ân 90. 10 (10).

2 Qur'ân 91. 8 (8).

3 De Slane makes the important observation that the addition of 'powerful' in Exod. 20: 5 is found only in the Vulgate, which, therefore, must have been the ultimate source of Ibn Khaldûn's quotation.

4 Qur'ân 5. 22 (25).

5 Qur'ân 5. 24 (27).

6 Qur'ân 5. 26 (29).

EDITOR'S SELECTED BIBLIOGRAPHY

Editor's Introduction

A'mel, Mahdi. (1985) *fi Ilmiyyat al-fikr al-Khaldouni*, (Beirut: Dar al-Farabi).

Dhaouadi, Mahmoud. (1990) "Ibn Khaldun: The Founding Father of Eastern Sociology", in *International Sociology* Vol. 5 pp. 319-335, September 1990.

Engels, Frederick. (1972). *The Origin of the Family, Private Property and the State.* London: Lawrence.

Issawi, Charles (1986) *An Arab Philosophy of History: Selection From Ibn Khaldun's Prolegomena.* Princeton, N.J.: The Darwin Press.

Lacoste, Yves. (1965) *Ibn Khaldun.* Paris: François Maspero.

𝄞 Emile Durkheim

The following texts by Durkheim represent some of the author's most important contributions to the sociology of human-social organization. Here the author articulates his ideas about the transformation of human society from a primitive, simple and traditional stage into the more complex industrial one. He identifies the components of and rules that govern the primitive-traditional society and explains how, in the process, the breaking down of some of the characteristics of the traditional society, a new and more developed form of society emerges. The transition is explained in terms of a combination of both internal and external conditions and factors. While the internal refer to the fading away of some of the characteristic features of the primitive-traditional society (e.g., mutual trust and communal forms of survival), the external express the changing economic needs and priorities and the consequent development of the division of labour.

Central to Durkheim's theory of human development is the concept of the division of labour. It is the means by which human social organization transforms into a higher stage of development. Durkheim does not accept primitive social organizations or societies as given; instead, he seeks to explain them in terms of the values, norms and rules that kept these societies together for many years. Characteristic of primitive/simple societies, according to him, are a number of norms and values accepted collectively or commonly by the group. Among these are the collective or common means of survival, collective property ownership or more precisely possession of source of livelihood and a primitive form of solidarity, to which he refers, as mechanical solidarity.

In a society ruled by mechanical solidarity, decisions and rules are made by the community and not the individual. The individual is counted only in so far as he or she is in full consensus with the group/collective. What binds the group together is a feeling of a collective solidarity that derives its legitimation from a spiritual/religious conviction. Therefore, a breach of any of the values or mores of the collective can be severely sanctioned. Coercion and repression are used against any individual who steps outside the confines of the group's consensus. A generalized conformity or conscience collective is characteristic of mechanical solidarity. Conscience collective is perceived as the collective moral code that sustains and keeps the group as such. This is the set of morals and values upon which the social continuation of the community/group is dependent.

The primitive stage, however, does not stay as is. Gradually the sense of unity and conscience collective that binds the group/society begins to slacken. Instead there emerges a system of cooperative relations based on the division of labour and characterized by higher and more developed forms of rule and order. As the division of labour develops and becomes more complex, differentiations in occupations, specializations and opportunities also grow and become more complex. The moral sense of collectivism and the need for the group solidarity expressed in the mechanical form dissipates and begins to give way to a new form, organic solidarity. Instead of the moral authority of the conscience collective, the absolutist state in the early stages of the development of more complex society takes over these forms of coercion.

Commenting on Durkheim's work, Robert Bella and Anthony Giddens have both suggested that Durkheim's concern with the concept of the division of labour goes beyond its economic implications. And that it serves more than just as a means to explain the differences and contradictions between the traditional and industrialized/modern capitalist societies. It is also concerned with a moral code (a form of social justice), he feels is necessary to replace the collective morality that was lost with the dissolution of the primitive society. Thus, Durkheim writes: "Just as ancient peoples needed, above all, a common faith to live by, so we need justice, and we can be sure that this need will become ever more exacting, if, as every fact presages, the conditions dominating social evolution remain the same" (quoted in Giddens, 1972: xxv).

Durkheim uses the concept of "moral individualism" to refer to the new form of morality identified with the industrialized capitalist society. Moral individualism that was essential in the composition of early societies, particularly in its "cult" or group form, is not totally destroyed. Instead, it reappears in the new industrial society under the division of labour. In some sense, moral individualism appears to replace the conscience collective as the moral core of a society. While it is not clear what exactly moral individualism means, the religious reference or more exactly Christianity is invoked as a source for the notion of moral individualism. It is at this juncture where Durkheim establishes a relationship between Christianity, morality and industrialism and distinguishes the industrial Christian West from the East, whose religion is not Christianity and therefore lacks moral individualism and fails to modernize/ industrialize.

It is useful here to see the parallels between Durkheim's doctrine of social transformation, particularly his notion of conscience collective or mechanical solidarity with that of Ibn Khaldûn's theory of human-social organization and the notion of *Asabiyyah*. Both represent the core foundation of early/primitive societies. The main difference lies in the emphasis each author places on the origin of this solidarity. Durkheim appears to place a great deal of emphasis on the spiritual/religious meaning of mechanical solidarity. Ibn Khaldûn, on the other hand, provides a number of possibilities for the formation of *Asabiyyah*, such as blood relation, kin-ties, common residence and interest shared under the same environment. Also characteristic of primitive societies in both Ibn Khaldûn's and Durkheim's theories is the absence of state and the low level of social differentiation and division of labour among group members. The parallels in fact can be extended to include Durkheim's general paradigm based on the dualistic notion of traditionality viz modernity/industrialization. Ibn Khaldûn, it can be said, has also worked within a similar paradigm of Badawa (primitiveness) and Hadara (modernity/ civilization).

FORMS OF SOCIAL SOLIDARITY

Repressive Sanctions and Mechanical Solidarity

The link of social solidarity to which repressive law corresponds is one whose break constitutes a crime; we give this name to every act which, in any degree whatever, evokes against its author the characteristic reaction which we term 'punishment'. To seek the nature of this link is thus to ask what is the cause of punishment, or, more precisely what crime essentially consists in...

...an act is criminal when it offends strong and defined states of the *conscience collective*. The statement of this proposition is rarely disputed, but it is ordinarily given a sense very different from that which it ought to have. We take it as if it expressed, not the essential property of crime, but one of its repercussions. We well know that crime violates very general and intense sentiments; but we believe that this generality and intensity derive from the criminal character of the act, which consequently remains to be defined. We do not deny that every delict is universally condemned, but we take as agreed that the condemnation to which it is subjected results from its delinquent character. Then, however, we are hard put to say in what its delinquent character consists. Is it to be found in an especially serious transgression? Perhaps so; but that is simply to restate the question by putting one word in place of another, for it is precisely the problem to understand what this transgression is, and particularly this specific transgression which society reproves by means of organised punishment and which constitutes criminality. It can evidently come only from one or several characteristics common to all criminological types. The only one which satisfies this condition is the very opposition between a crime, whatever it may be, and certain collective sentiments. It is, accordingly, this opposition which forms the crime, rather than being a derivation of crime. In other words, we must not say that an action shocks the *conscience collective* because it is criminal, but rather that it is criminal because it shocks the *conscience collective*. We do not condemn it because it is a crime, but it is a crime because we condemn it. As for the intrinsic nature of these sentiments, it is impossible to specify them; they have the most diverse objects and cannot be encompassed in a single formula. We cannot say that they relate to the vital interests of society, or to a minimum of justice: all such definitions are inadequate. By this alone can we recognise it: a sentiment, whatever its origin and end, is found in all minds with a certain degree of strength and clarity, and every action which violates it is a crime...

Punishment is, first and foremost, an emotional reaction. This character is especially apparent in less developed societies. Primitive peoples punish for the sake of punishing, making the guilty party suffer solely for the sake of making him suffer and without seeking any advantage for themselves from the suffering which they impose. The proof of this is that they seek neither to strike back justly nor to strike back usefully, but merely to strike back. Thus they punish animals which have committed a wrong-doing and even inanimate objects which were it passive instrument. When punishment is applied only to people, it often extends further than the guilty party and reaches the innocent, his wife, his children, his neighbours, etc. That is because the passion which is the spirit of punishment ceases only when it is exhausted. If, therefore, after it has destroyed the one who immediately called it forth, it still remains strong, it expands in a quite mechanical fashion. Even when it is fairly mild, and relates only to the guilty party, it makes its presence felt by the tendency to surpass in severity the action against which it is reacting. That is the origin of the refinements of suffering added to capital punishment. Even in Rome the thief not only had to return the stolen object, but also pay retribution of double and quadruple the amount. Moreover, is not the very common punishment of the *lex talionis* a mode of satisfying the passion for vengeance?

But today, it is said, punishment has changed its character; it is no longer to avenge itself that society punishes, it is to defend itself. The suffering which it inflicts is in its hands no longer anything but a methodical means of protection. It punishes, not because chastisement offers it any intrinsic satisfaction, but so that the fear of punishment may paralyse those who contemplate evil. It is no longer anger, but a well thought-out precaution which determines repression. The preceding observations could not then be generalised; they would refer only to the primitive form of punishment and would not extend to the modern form.

But to justify such a radical distinction between these two sorts of punishment, it is not enough to state that they are employed with different ends in view. The nature of a practice does not necessarily change because the conscious intentions of those who apply it are modified. It might, in fact, still play the same role as before, but without this being perceived. In this case, why should it only become changed in that we are more aware of the effects which it produces? It adapts itself to new conditions of existence without any essential changes. This is the case with punishment. In fact, it is a mistake to believe that vengeance is simply useless cruelty. It is very possible that, in itself, it consists of a mechanical and aimless reaction, an emotional and unthinking action, an irrational need to destroy; but, in reality, it does tend to destroy that which is a threat to us. It consists, then, in a true act of defence, although an instinctive and unreflective one. We avenge ourselves only upon what has harmed us, and what has harmed us is always a threat. The instinct of vengeance is, in sum, only the instinct of conservation heightened by peril. Thus, vengeance is far from having had the negative and sterile role in the history of mankind which is attributed to it. It is a defensive weapon which has a definite value, although it is a crude weapon. Since it is not informed with an awareness of the end it serves, but functions automatically, it cannot, consequently, regulate itself, but responds rather haphazardly to the blind causes which urge it on, without anything moderating its responses. Today, as we understand more clearly the end to be attained, we know better how to utilise the means at our disposal; we protect ourselves more systematically and, accordingly, more efficiently. But this result was also obtained previously, although in a rather imperfect manner. There is no radical division between the punishment of today and yesterday, and consequently it was not necessary for the latter to change its nature in order to accommodate itself to the role that it plays in our civilised societies. The whole difference derives from the fact that it now produces its effects with a heightened awareness of what it does. But, although the individual or social consciousness may not be without influence upon the reality that it clarifies, it has not the power to change its nature. The internal structure of the phenomenon remains the same, whether men be conscious of it or not. We may thus conclude that the essential elements of punishment are the same as of old.

And in fact, punishment has remained, at least in part, a work of vengeance. It is said that we do not make the guilty party suffer for the sake of suffering; it is nonetheless true that we find it right that he should suffer. Perhaps we are wrong, but that is not the question. We seek, at the moment, to define punishment as it is or has been, not as it ought to be. It is certain that this expression of public prosecution which finds its way again and again into the language of the courts is not a mere expression. In supposing that punishment can really serve to protect us in the future, we think that it must be above all an *expiation* of the past. This is shown by the minute precautions we take to allot punishment as exactly as possible in relation to the severity of the crime; this would be inexplicable if we did not believe that the guilty party ought to suffer because of his wrongdoing, and in the same degree. This gradation is not necessary if punishment is only a means of defence. No doubt, there would be danger for society if the most serious offences were treated as simple transgressions; but it would be greater, in the majority of cases, if the latter were treated in the same way as the former. Against an enemy, we cannot take too much precaution. Shall we say that the authors of the smallest misdeeds have less perverse natures, and that to neutralise their criminal instincts less stringent punishments will suffice? But if their inclinations are less vicious they are not on that account less intense. Robbers are as strongly inclined to rob as murderers are to murder; the resistance offered by the former is not less than that of the latter, and consequently, to control it, we would have recourse to the same means. If, as has been said, it was solely a question of putting down a noxious force by an opposing force, the intensity of the second would be measured solely by the intensity of the first, without the quality of the latter entering into the consideration. The penal scale would then encompass only a small number of gradations. Punishment would vary only as the criminal is more or less hardened, and not according to the nature of the criminal act. An incorrigible robber would be treated in the same was as an incorrigible murderer. But, in fact, if it were shown that a misdoer was completely incurable, we would still not feel bound to punish him excessively. This is proof that we are faithful to the talion principle, although we apply it in a more refined sense than previously. We no longer measure in so material and gross a manner either the extent of the deed or of the punishment; but we still think there ought to be an equation between the two terms, whether or not we benefit from this balance.

Punishment thus remains for us what it was for our forefathers. It is still an act of vengeance since it is an expiation. What we avenge, what the criminal expiates, is the outrage to morality...

As for the social character of this reaction, it comes from the social nature of the offended sentiments. Because they are found in the consciousness of every individual, the infraction which has been committed arouses the same indignation in those who witness it or who learn of its existence. Everybody is attacked; consequently, everybody opposes the attack. Not only is the reaction general, but it is collective, which is not the same thing. It is not produced in an isolated manner in each individual, but is a total, unified response, even if this varies according to the case. In fact, in the same way as contrary sentiments repel each other, similar sentiments attract each other, and they attract as strongly as they themselves are intense. As contradiction is a threat which stirs them, it adds to their force of attraction. Never do we feel the need of the company of our compatriots so greatly as when we are in a foreign country; never does the believer feel so strongly attracted to his fellow believers as during periods of persecution. Of course, we always love the company of those who feel and think as we do, but it is with passion, and no longer solely with pleasure, that we seek immediately after discussions where our common beliefs have been directly attacked. Crime brings together honest men and concentrates them. We have only to notice what happens, particularly in a small town, when some moral scandal has just occurred. Men stop each other on the street, they visit each other, they seek to come together to talk of the event and to wax indignant in common. From all the similar impressions which are exchanged, and the anger that is expressed, there emerges a unique emotion, more or less determinate according to the circumstances, which emanates from no specific person, but from everyone. This is the public wrath.

Moreover, this is what gives it its functions: the sentiments in question derive all their force from the fact that they are common to everyone. They are strong because they are unquestioned. It is the fact that they are universally respected which gives them the specific respect which they are accorded. Now, crime is possible only if this respect is not truly universal; consequently, it implies that they are not absolutely collective, and thus damages this unanimity which is the source of their authority. If, then, when a crime takes place, the individuals whom it offends do not unite to manifest what they share in common, and to affirm that the case is anomalous, they would be permanently shaken. They must fortify themselves by the mutual assurance that they are still in unison. The only means for this is action in common. In short, since it is the *conscience collective* which is attacked, it must be that which resists, and accordingly the resistance must be collective...

Thus, the analysis of punishment has confirmed our definition of crime. We began by establishing inductively that crime consisted essentially in an act contrary to strong and defined states of the *conscience collective*. We have just seen that all the qualities of punishment ultimately derive from this nature of crime. That is because the rules that it sanctions express the most essential social likenesses.

Thus we see what type of solidarity penal law symbolises. It is well known, indeed, that there is a form of social cohesion whose cause lies in a certain conformity of all specific individuals to a common type which is none other than the mental type of the society. In these conditions, not only are all the members of the group individually attracted to one-another because they resemble one-another, but also because they are joined to that which is the condition of existence of this collective type: that is to say, to the society that they form by their union. Not only do citizens love each other and seek each other out in preference to strangers but they love their country. They want for it what they want for themselves, and wish it to prosper and endure, because without it, a great part of their psychological life would be hampered in its functioning. Conversely, society demands that they present these fundamental resemblances, because that is a condition of its cohesion. There are in us two forms of consciousness: one contains states which are personal to the character of each of us, while the states which comprise the other are common to the whole society. The first represent only our individual personality and constitute it; the second represent the collective type and, consequently, society, without which it would not exist. When it is one of the elements of this latter which determines our conduct, we do not act in our personal interest; we pursue collective ends. Although distinct, these two forms of consciousness are linked one to the other, since in the end they are only one, having one and the same organic substratum. They are thus interdependent. From this results a solidarity *sui generis*, based upon mutual resemblance, and directly linking individual to society.

DTS, pp. 35, 47-8, 52-6, 70-1 and 73-4

Restitutive Sanctions and the Relationship between Mechanical and Organic Solidarity

What distinguishes [the restitutive] sanction is that it is not expiatory but consists of a simple return in state. The person who violates or disregards the law is not made to suffer in relation to his wrongdoing; he is simply sentenced to comply. If certain things have already been done, the judge reinstates them as they should have been. He speaks of law; he says nothing of punishment.

Damage payments have no penal character; they are only a means of reviewing the past in order to reinstate it, as far as possible, in its normal form...

Neglect of these rules is not even punished diffusely. The defendant who has lost in litigation is not disgraced, his honour is not smirched. We can even imagine these rules differing from how they are now without any feeling of distaste. The idea of tolerating murder makes us indignant, but we quite easily accept modification of the law of inheritance, and can even conceive of its possible abolition. It is at least a question which we do not refuse to discuss. In the same way, we readily accept that the law of easements or that of usufructs may be organised differently, that the obligations of vendor and purchaser may be determined in another way, or that administrative functions may be distributed according to different principles. As these prescriptions do not correspond to any sentiment in us, and as we generally do not know scientifically the reasons for their existence, since this science does not exist, they have no roots in the majority of us. Of course, there are exceptions. We do not tolerate the idea that a contract, contrary to custom or obtained either through force or fraud, can bind the contracting parties. Thus, when public opinion finds itself in the presence of a case of this sort, it shows itself less indifferent than we have previously said, and it increases the legal sanction by its censure. The different domains of moral life are not radically separated one from another; on the contrary, they are continuous, and accordingly they contain marginal regions where these different characteristics are found at the same time. However, the preceding proposition remains true in the great majority of cases. It is proof that rules with a restitutive sanction either do not at all derive from the *conscience collective*, or are only feeble states of it. Repressive law corresponds to the heart, the centre of the common conscience; purely moral rules are already a less central part; finally, restitutive law originates in very marginal regions, spreading well beyond. The more it becomes truly itself, the more removed it becomes.

This characteristic is, moreover, manifest in the manner of its functioning. While repressive law tends to remain diffuse within society, restitutive law creates organs which are increasingly specialised: commercial courts, councils of arbitration, administrative courts of many kinds. Even in its most general part, that which pertains to civil law, it is exercised only through particular functionaries: magistrates, lawyers, etc., who are able to fill this role in virtue of very specialised training.

But, although these rules are to some degree outside the *conscience collective*, they do not refer only to individuals. If this were so, restitutive law would have nothing in common with social solidarity, for the relations that it regulates would bind individuals to one-another without binding them to society. These would simply be happenings in private life, as friendly relations are. But it is necessarily the case that society is far from being absent in this sphere of legal life. It is true that, generally, it does not intervene directly and actively; it must be solicited by the interested parties. But in being called forth, its intervention is nonetheless the essential cog in the machine, since it alone makes it function. It propounds the law through the organ of its representatives.

It has been contended, however, that this role has nothing properly social about it, but reduces itself to that of a conciliator of private interests; that, consequently, any individual can fill it, and that, if society is in charge of it, it is only for reasons of convenience. But nothing is more incorrect than to consider society as a sort of third-party arbitrator. When it is led to intervene, it is not to rectify individual interests. It does not seek to discover what may be the most advantageous solution for the adversaries and does not propose a compromise for them. Rather it applies to the particular case which is submitted to its general and traditional rules of law. Now law is, above all, a social thing, the objective of which is something other than the interest of the litigants. The judge who examines a request for divorce is not concerned with knowing whether this separation is truly desirable for the married parties, but rather whether the causes which are adduced come under one of the categories embodied in the law...

Since rules with restitutive sanctions are foreign to the *conscience collective*, the ties that they determine are not those which relate indiscriminately to everyone. That is to say, they are established, not between the individual and society, but between restricted, specific parts of society, whom they link to one-another. But, on the other hand, since society is not absent, it must be more or less directly interested, and it must feel the repercussions. Thus, according to the force with which society feels them, it intervenes more or less directly and actively, through the intermediary of special organs charged with representing it. These relations are, then, quite different from those which repressive law regulates, for the latter attach the particular individual to the *conscience collective* directly and without mediation: that is, the individual to society...

To sum up: the relations governed by co-operative law with restitutive sanctions, and the solidarity which they express, result from the division of social labour. We have explained, moreover, that, in general, co-operative relations do not convey other sanctions. In fact, it is in the nature of specialised tasks to escape the action of the *conscience collective*, for, in order for a thing to be the object of common sentiments, it must necessarily be shared: that is to say, it must be present in all minds such that everyone can represent it in one and the same manner. To be sure, in so far as functions have a certain generality, everybody can have some idea of them. But the more specialised they are, the more restricted the number of individuals who know each of them; consequently, the more marginal they are to the *conscience collective*. The rules which determine them cannot have that dominating force and transcendent authority which, when offended, demands expiation. It is also from public opinion that their authority derives, as with penal rules, but from such opinion localised in restricted regions of society.

Moreover, even in the special circles where they apply and where, consequently, they are represented in man's minds, they do not correspond to very active sentiments, nor even very often to any type of emotional state. For, as they fix the manner in which the different functions ought to concur in diverse combinations of circumstances which can arise, the objects to which they are connected are not always present in consciousness. We are not constantly called upon to administer guardianship, trusteeship, or exercise the rights of creditor or buyer, etc., or, more important, to exercise them in such and such a situation. Now, states of consciousness are strong only in so far as they are permanent. The violation of these rules reaches neither the common spirit of society, nor even, generally speaking, that of special groups, and consequently it can stimulate only a very moderate reaction. All that is necessary is that the functions concur in a regular manner. If this regularity is disrupted, it is sufficient for us to re-establish it. Assuredly, this is not to say that the development of the division of labour cannot influence penal law. There are, as we already know, administrative and governmental functions in which certain relations are regulated by repressive law, because of the particular character of this agency of the *conscience collective* and everything connected with it. In still other cases, the links of solidarity which unite certain social functions can be such that their breach stimulates repercussions which are sufficiently extensive to provoke a penal reaction. But, for the reason we have given, these reactions are exceptional...[thus] we recognise only two kinds of positive solidarity, which are distinguishable by the following qualities:

1. The first ties the individual directly to society without any intermediary. In the second, he depends upon society, because he depends upon the parts which compose it.

2. Society is not seen in the same aspect in the two cases. In the first, what we call 'society' is a more or less closely organised totality of beliefs and sentiments common to all the members of the group: it is the collective type. By contrast, the society to which we are bound in the second instance is a system of differentiated and specialised functions which are united in definite relationships. These two societies really make up only one. They are two aspects one and the same reality, but nonetheless they must be distinguished.

3. From this second difference there arises another which helps us to characterise and name the two kinds of solidarity.

The first can be strong only to the degree that the ideas and tendencies common to all the members of the society are greater in number and intensity than those which pertain to each individual member. Its strength is determined by the degree to which this is the case. But what makes our personality is how many particular characteristics we possess which distinguish us from others. This solidarity thus can grow only in inverse ratio to personality. There are in each of us, as we have said, two forms of consciousness: one which is common to our group as a whole, which, consequently, is not ourself, but society living and acting within us; the other, on the other hand, represents that in us which is personal and distinct, that which makes us an individual. Solidarity which comes from resemblance is at is *maximum* when the *conscience collective* completely envelopes our whole consciousness and coincides in all points with it. But, at that moment, our individuality is nil. It can develop only if the community takes a lesser part of us. There are, here, two contrary forces, one centripetal, the other centrifugal, which cannot flourish at the same time. We cannot, at one and the same time, develop ourselves in two opposite senses. If we have a strong inclination to think and act for ourselves, we cannot be as strongly inclined to think and act as others do. If our ideal is to present a unique and personal appearance, we cannot resemble everybody else. Moreover, at the moment when this latter solidarity exercises its force, our personality banishes, by definition, one might say, for we are no longer ourselves, but the collective being.

The social molecules which cohere in this way can act together only in so far as they have no action of their own, as with the molecules of inorganic bodies. That is why we propose to call this form of solidarity 'mechanical'. The term does not signify that it is produced by mechanical and artificial means. We call it that only by analogy to the cohesion which unites the elements of an inorganic body, as contrasted to that which forms a unity out of the elements of a living body. What finally justifies this term is that the link which thus unites the individual to society is wholly comparable to that which attaches a thing to a person. The individual consciousness, considered in this light, is a simple appendage of the collective type and follows all of its actions, as the possessed object follows those of its owner. In societies where this type of solidarity is highly developed, the individual is not his own master, as we shall see later; solidarity is, literally something which the society possesses. Thus, in these types of society, personal rights are not yet distinguished from real rights.

It is quite different with the solidarity which the division of labour produces. Whereas the previous type implies that individuals resemble each other, this latter presumes that they differ. The former is possible only in so far as the individual personality is absorbed into the collective personality; the latter is possible only if each one has a sphere of action which is peculiar to him — that is, if he possesses a personality. It is necessary, then, that the *conscience collective* leave open a part of the individual consciousness in order that the special functions may be established there, functions which it cannot regulate. The more this region is extended, the stronger is the cohesion which results from this solidarity. In fact, one the one hand, every individual depends more directly on society as labour becomes more divided; and, on the other, the activity of every individual becomes more personalised to the degree that it is more specialised. No doubt, as circumscribed as it is, it is never completely original; even in the exercise of our occupation, we conform to conventions and practices which are common to our whole occupational group. But, in this instance, the yoke that we submit to is much less heavy than when society completely controls us, and it leaves much more place open for the free play of our initiative. Here, then, the individuality of all grows at the same time as that of its parts. Society becomes more capable of collective action, at the same time that each of its elements has more freedom of action. This solidarity resembles that which we observe among the higher animals. Each organ, in effect, has its special character and autonomy; and yet the unity of the organism is as great as the individuation of the parts is more marked. Because of this analogy, we propose to call the solidarity which is due to the division of labour, 'organic'.

DTS, pp. 79, 80-2, 83, 96-101

6. THE DIVISION OF LABOUR AND SOCIAL DIFFERENTIATION

The Growth of Structural Differentiation in Social Development

Thus, it is an historical law that mechanical solidarity, which first stands alone, or nearly so, progressively loses ground, and that organic solidarity gradually becomes preponderant. But when the mode of solidarity becomes changed, the structure of societies cannot but change. The form of a body is necessarily transformed when the molecular relationships are no longer the same. Consequently, if the preceding proposition is correct, these must be two social types which correspond to these two types of solidarity.

If we try to construct hypothetically the ideal type of a society whose cohesion were exclusively the result of resemblance, we should have to conceive it as an absolutely homogeneous mass whose parts were not distinguished from one another, and which consequently had no structure. In short, it would be devoid of all definite form and all organization. It would be the actual social protoplasm, the germ out of which all social types would develop. We propose to call the aggregate thus characterised, a *horde*.

It is true that we have not yet, in any completely authenticated fashion, observed societies which complied in all respects with this definition. What gives us the right to postulate their existence, however, is that the lower societies, those which are closest to this primitive stage, are formed by a simple repetition of aggregates of this kind. We find an almost perfectly pure example of this social organization among the Indians of North America. Each Iroquois tribe, for example, is composed of a certain number of partial societies (the largest ones comprise eight) which present all the characteristics we have just mentioned. The adults of both sexes are equal to each other. The *sachems* and chiefs, who are at the head of each of these groups and by whose council the common affairs of the tribe are administered, do not enjoy any superiority. Kinship itself is not organized, for we cannot give this name to the distribution of the population in layers of generations. In the late epoch in which these peoples have been studied, there were, indeed, some special obligations which bound the child to its maternal relatives, but these are of little consequence, and are not perceptibly distinct from those which link the child to other members of society...

We give the name *clan* to the horde which has ceased to be independent by becoming an element in a more extensive group, and that of *segmental societies with a clan-base* to societies which are formed by an association of clans. We call societies 'segmental' in order to indicate that they are characterised by the repetition of similar groupings, rather like the rings of an earthworm, and we call this fundamental element a 'clan', because this word well expresses its mixed nature, at once familial and political. It is a family in the sense that all the members who compose it consider themselves relatives, and they are, in fact, for the most part consanguineous. The affinities that are created by these blood-ties are those which principally keep them united. In addition, they sustain relationships which we can term domestic, since we also find them in societies whose familial character is indisputable: I am referring to collective punishment, collective responsibility, and, as soon as private property makes its appearance, common inheritance. But, on the other hand, it is not a family in the proper sense of the word, for in order to belong to it, it is not necessary to have any definite relations of consanguinity with other members of the clan. It is enough to possess an external quality, which generally consists in having the same name. Although this sign is thought to denote a common origin, such a civil status really constitutes very inconclusive proof, and is very easy to copy. Thus, the clan contains a great many strangers, and this permits it to attain dimensions such as a family, properly speaking, never has. It often comprises several thousand persons.

Moreover, it is the fundamental political unit; the heads of clans are the only social authorities.

We can thus label this organisation 'politico-familial'. Not only has the clan consanguinity as its basis, but different clans within the same society are often considered as kin to one-another...

This organisation, just like the horde, of which it is only an extension, evidently carries with it no other solidarity than that derived from resemblance, since the society is formed of similar segments, and these in their turn enclose only homogeneous elements. No doubt, each clan has its own character and is thereby distinguished from others; but the solidarity is proportionally weaker as they are more heterogeneous, and vice versa. For segmental organisation to be possible, the segments must resemble one another: without that, they would not be united. And they must differ; without this, they would lose themselves in each other and be effaced. These two contrasting prerequisites are found in varying ratio in different societies, but the type of society remains the same...

The structure of societies where organic solidarity is preponderant is quite different.

These are formed, not by the repetition of similar, homogeneous segments, but by a system of different organs each of which has a special role, and which are themselves formed of differentiated parts. Not only are social elements not of the same nature, but they are not distributed in the same way. They are not juxtaposed in a linear fashion as the rings of an earthworm, nor entwined one with another, but co-ordinated and subordinated one to another around the same central organ which exercises a moderating action over the rest of the organism. This organ itself no longer has the same character as in the preceding case, for, if the other depend upon it, it, in its turn, depends upon them. No doubt, it still enjoys a special situation, a privileged position, but that is due to the nature of the role that it fills and not to some cause foreign to its functions, to some force communicated to it externally. Thus, there is no longer anything about it that is not temporal and human; between it and other organs, there is no longer anything but differences in degree. This is comparable to the way in which, in the animal, the dominance of the nervous system over other systems is reduced to the right, if one may speak thus, of obtaining the best food and of having its fill before the others. But it needs them, just as they have need of it.

This social type rests on principles so different from the preceding that it can develop only in proportion to the effacement of that type. In this type, individuals are no longer grouped according to their relations of lineage, but according to the particular nature of the social activity to which they devote themselves. Their nature and necessary milieu is no longer that given by birth, but that given by occupation. It is no longer real or fictitious blood-ties which mark the place of each one, but the function which he fills. No doubt, when this new form of organisation begins to appear, it tries to utilise and to take over the existing one. The way in which functions are divided thus follows, as faithfully as possible, the way in which society is already divided. The segments, or at least the groups of segments united by special affinities, become organs. It is thus that the clans which together formed the tribe of the Levites appropriated priestly functions for themselves among the Hebrew people. In a general way, classes and castes probably derive their origin and their character in this way; they arise from the numerous occupational organisations which spring up within the pre-existing familial organisation. But this mixed arrangement cannot endure, for between the two conditions that it attempts to reconcile, there is an antagonism which necessarily ends in a break. It is only a very rudimentary division of labour which can adapt itself to those rigid, defined moulds which were not made for it. It can grow only by freeing itself from the framework which encloses it. As soon as it has passed a certain stage of development, there is no longer any connection either between the given number of segments and the steady growth of functions which are becoming specialised, or between the hereditarily fixed properties of the first and the aptitudes that the second calls forth. The substance of social life must enter into entirely new combinations in order to organise itself upon completely different foundations. But the old structure, so far as it persists, is opposed to this. That is why it must disappear.

DTS, pp. 148-51, 152 and 157-9

The Decline of Mechanical Solidarity and Emergence of Moral Individualism

Not only, in a general way, does mechanical solidarity link men less strongly than organic solidarity, but also, as we advance in the scale of social evolution, it becomes increasingly weak.

The strength of the social ties which have this origin differ in relation to the three following conditions:

1. The relation between the volume of the *conscience collective* and that of the individual mind. The links are stronger the more the first completely envelops the second.

2. The average intensity of the states of the *conscience collective*. The relation between volumes being equal, it has as much power over the individual as it has vitality. If, on the other hand, it consists of only weak forces, it can

move the individual only weakly in the collective direction. He will the more easily be able to pursue his own course, and solidarity will thus be less.

3. The greater or lesser the fixity of these same states the more defined are beliefs and practices which exist, and the less place they leave for individual differences. They are uniform moulds within which all our ideas and actions are formed. Consensus is then as perfect as possible; all minds move in unison. Conversely, the more abstract and indeterminate the rules of conduct and thought, the more conscious direction must intervene to apply them to particular cases. But the latter cannot awaken without dissensions occurring, for as it varies from one man to another in quality and quantity, it inevitably leads to this result. Centrifugal tendencies thus multiply at the expense of social cohesion and the harmony of actions.

On the other hand, strong and defined states of the *conscience collective* are the basis of penal law. But we shall see that the number of these is less today than previously, and that it diminishes progressively as societies approach our social type. Thus it is the case that the average intensity and degree of fixity of collective states have themselves diminished. From this fact, it is true, we cannot conclude that the total extent of the *conscience collective* has narrowed, for it may be that the region to which penal law corresponds has contracted, and that the remainder, by contrast, has expanded. It may manifest fewer strong and defined states, but compensate with a greater number of others. But this growth, if it is real, is at most equivalent to that which is produced in the individual mind, for the latter has, at least, grown in the same proportions. If there are more things common to all, there are far more that are personal to each. There is, indeed, every reason to believe that the latter have increased more than the former, for the differences between men become more pronounced in so far as they are more educated. We have just seen that specialised activities have developed more than the *conscience collective*. It is, therefore, at least probable that, in each individual mind, the personal sphere has grown more than the other. In any case, the relation between them has at most remained the same. Consequently, from this point of view, mechanical solidarity has gained nothing, even if it has not lost anything. If therefore, from another aspect, we discover that the *conscience collective* has become weaker and more ill-defined, we can rest assured that the three conditions upon which its power of action rests, two, at least, are losing their intensity, while the third remains unchanged...

This is not to say, however, that the *conscience collective* is likely to disappear completely. Rather it increasingly comes to consist of very general and indeterminate ways of thought and sentiment, which leaves room open for a growing variety of individual differences. There is even a place where it is strengthened and made precise: this is, in the way in which it regards the individual. As all the other beliefs and all the other practices take on a less and less religious character, the individual becomes the object of a sort of religion. We have a cult of personal dignity which, as with every strong cult, already has its superstitions. It is, thus, we may say, a common faith but it is possible only by the ruin of all others and, consequently, cannot produce the same effects as this mass of extinguished beliefs. There is no compensation for these. Moreover, if it is common in so far as it is shared by the community, it is individual in its object. It if turns all wills towards the same end, this end is not social. It thus occupies a completely exceptional place in the *conscience collective*. It is still from society that it takes all its force, but it is not to society that it attaches us; it is to ourselves. Hence, it does not constitute a true social bond. That is why we have been justly able to criticise the theorists who have made this sentiment the only fundamental element in their moral doctrine with the ensuing dissolution of society. We can then conclude by saying that all social links which result from likeness progressively slacken.

DTS, 124-6 and 146-7

***

The condemnation of individualism has been facilitated by its confusion with the narrow utilitarianism and utilitarian egoism of Spencer and the economists. But this is very facile. It is not hard, to be sure, to denounce as a shallow ideal that narrow commercialism which reduces society to nothing more than a vast apparatus of production and exchange; and it is perfectly clear that all social life would be impossible if there did not exist interests superior to the interests of individuals. It is wholly correct that such doctrines should be treated as anarchical, and we fully agree with this view. But what is unacceptable is that this individualism should be presented as the only one that there is, or even could be. Quite the contrary; it is becoming increasingly rare and exceptional. The practical philosophy of Spencer is of such moral poverty that it now has hardly any supporters. As for the economists, even if they once allowed themselves to be seduced by the simplicity of this theory, they have for a long time now felt the need to modify the severity of their primitive orthodoxy and to open their minds to more generous sentiments. M. de Molinari is almost alone, in France, in remaining intractable and I am not aware that he has exercised a significant influence on the ideas of our time. Indeed, if individualism had not other representatives, it would be quite pointless to move heaven and earth in this way to combat an enemy who is in the process of quietly dying a natural death.

However, there exists another individualism over which it is less easy to triumph. It has been upheld for a century by the great majority of thinkers: it is the individualism of Kant and Rousseau and the spiritualists, that which the Declaration of the Rights of Man sought, more or less successfully, to translate into formulae, which is now taught in our schools and which has become the basis of our moral catechism. It is true that it has been thought possible to attack this individualism by reference to the first type; but the two are fundamentally different, and the criticisms which apply to the one could not be appropriate to the other. It is so far from making personal interest the aim of human conduct that it sees personal motives as the very source of evil. According to Kant, I am only certain of acting properly if the motives that influence me relate, not to the particular circumstances in which I am placed, but to my equality as a man *in abstracto.* Conversely, my action is wrong when it cannot be justified logically except by reference to the situation I happen to be in and my social condition, class or castes interests, my emotions, etc. Hence immoral conduct is to be recognised by the sign that it is closely linked to the individuality of the agent and cannot be universalised without manifest absurdity. Similarly, if Rousseau sees the general will, which is the basis of the social contract, as infallible, as the authentic expression of perfect justice, this is because it is a resultant of the totality of particular wills; consequently it constitutes a kind of impersonal average from which all individual considerations have been eliminated, since, being distinct from and even antagonistic to one-another, they are neutralised and cancel each other out. Thus, for both these thinkers, the only modes of conduct that are moral are those which are applicable to all men equally: that is to say, which are implied in the notion of man in general.

This is indeed far removed from that apotheosis of pleasure and private interest, the egoistic cult of the self for which utilitarian individualism has validly been criticised. Quite the contrary: according to these moralists, duty consists in turning our attention from what concerns us personally, from all that relates to our empirical individuality, so as to pursue solely that which is demanded by our human condition, that which we hold in common with all our fellow men. This ideal goes so far beyond the limit of utilitarian ends that it appears to those who aspire to it as having a religious character. The human person, by reference to the definition of which good must be distinguished from evil, is considered as sacred, in what can be called the ritual sense of the word. It has something of that transcendental majesty which the churches of all times have accorded to their gods. It is conceived as being invested with that mysterious property which creates a vacuum about holy objects, which keeps them away from profane contacts and which separates them from ordinary life. And it is exactly this characteristic which confers the respect of which it is the object. Whoever makes an attempt on a man's life, on a man's liberty, on a man's honour, inspires us with a feeling of revulsion, in every way comparable to that which the believer experiences when he sees his idol profaned. Such a morality is therefore not simply a hygienic discipline or a wise principle of economy. It is a religion of which man is, at the same time, both believer and god.

But this religion is individualistic, since it has man as its object; whose individualism is more uncompromising. Nowhere are the rights of man affirmed more energetically, since the individual is here placed on the level of sacrosanct objects; nowhere is he more jealously protected from external encroachments, whatever their source.

A verbal similarity has made possible the belief that *individualism* necessarily resulted from *individual*, and thus egoistic, sentiments. In reality, the religion of the individual is a social institution like all known religions. It is society which provides us with this ideal as the only common end which is today able to offer a focus for men's wills. To remove this ideal, without replacing it with any other, it therefore to plunge us into that very moral anarchy which it is sought to avoid.

Nonetheless we must not consider as perfect and definitive the formula with which the eighteenth century gave expression to individualism, a formula which we have made the mistake of maintaining in an almost unchanged form. Although it was adequate a century ago, it today needs to be enlarged and completed. It presented individualism only in its most negative aspect. Our forerunners were concerned solely with freeing the individual from the political shackles which hampered his development. Thus they regarded freedom of thought, freedom to write, and freedom to vote as the primary values that it was necessary to achieve — and this emancipation was indeed the precondition of all subsequent progress. However, carried away by the enthusiasm of the struggle, and concerned only with the objective they pursued, in the end they no longer saw beyond it, and made into something of an ultimate goal what was merely the next stage in their efforts. Now, political freedom is a means, not an end. It is worth no more than the manner in which it is put to use. If it does not serve something which exists beyond it, it is not merely fruitless, it becomes dangerous. If those who handle this weapon do not know how to use it in productive struggles, they will not be slow in turning it against themselves.

It is precisely for this reason that is has fallen today into a certain discredit. Men of my generation recall how great our enthusiasm was when, twenty years ago, we finally succeeded in toppling the last barriers which we impatiently confronted. But alas! disenchantment came quickly; for we soon had to admit that no one knew what use should be made of this freedom that had been so laboriously achieved. Those to whom we owed it only made use of it in internecine conflicts. And it was from that moment that one felt the growth in the country of this current of gloom and despondency, which became stronger with each day that passed, the ultimate result of which must inevitably be to break the spirit of those least able to resist.

Thus, we can no longer subscribe to this negative ideal. We must go beyond what has been achieved, if only to preserve it. Indeed, if we do not learn to put to use the means of action that we have in our hands, it is inevitable that they will become less effective. Let us therefore use our freedoms to discover what must be done and in order to do it. Let us use them in order to soften the functioning of the social machine, still so harsh to individuals, so as to put at their disposal all possible means for the free development of their faculties in order finally to progress towards making a reality of the famous precept: to each according to his works!

RB, 1898, pp. 7-8 and 12-13

The Causes of the Development of the Division of Labour

We have seen that the organised structure, and thus the division of labour, develop correspondingly as the segmental structure disappears. Thus either this disappearance is the cause of the development, or the development is the cause of the disappearance. The latter hypothesis is unacceptable, for we know that the segmental arrangement is an unsurmountable obstacle to the division of labour, and must at least partially have become dissolved for the division of labour to emerge. The latter can only develop in so far as the former ceases to exist. To be sure, once the division of labour appears, it can contribute towards the hastening of the other's regression, but it only comes into being once this regression has begun. The effect reacts upon the cause, but never loses its quality of effect; its action, consequently, is secondary. The growth of the division of labour is thus brought about by the social segments losing their individuality, as the boundaries between them become less marked. In short, a merging takes place which makes it possible for social life to enter into new combinations.

But the disappearance of this type can have this consequence for only one reason. That is because it produces a coming together between individuals who were separated — or, at least, a closer relationship than existed previously. Consequently, there is an interchange of action between parts of the social mass which, until then, had no effect upon one another. The more pronounced the segmental system, the more are our relations enclosed within the limits of the segment to which we belong. There are, as it were, moral gaps between the different segments. By contrast, these gaps are filled in as the system becomes levelled out. Social life, instead of being concentrated in a large number of separate, small centres, each of which resembles the other, is generalised. Social relations — or more correctly, intra-social relations — consequently become more numerous, since they extend, on all sides, beyond their original limits. The division of labour develops, therefore, as there are more individuals sufficiently in contact to be able to act and react upon one-another. If we agree to call this coming together, and the active commerce resulting from it, 'dynamic' or 'formal' density, we can say that the progress of the division of labour is in direct ratio to the moral or dynamic density of society.

But this moral relationship can only produce its effect if the real distance between individuals has itself diminished in some way. Moral density cannot grow unless material density grows at the same time, and the latter can be used to measure the former. It is useless, moreover, to try to find out which has determined the other; it is enough to state that they are inseparable.

The progressive condensation of societies in the course of historical development is produced in three principal ways:

1. Whereas lower societies are spread over immense areas relative to the size of their populations, among more advanced peoples population tends to become more and more concentrated... The changes brought about in the industrial life of nations prove the universality of this transformation. The productive activity of nomads, hunters, or shepherds implies the absence of all concentration, dispersion over the largest possible surface. Agriculture, since it necessitates a life in a fixed territory, presupposes a certain tightening of the social tissues, but is still incomplete, for there are stretches of land between each family. In the city, although the condensation was greater, the houses were contiguous, for joint property was no part of the Roman law. It grew up on our soil, and demonstrates that the social web has become tighter. On the other hand, from their origins, the European societies have witnessed a continuous growth in their density, short-lived regressions notwithstanding.

2. The formation of towns and their development is an even more characteristic symptom of the same phenomenon. The increase in average density may be due to the material increase of the birth-rate, and, consequently, can be reconciled with a very weak concentration, whereby the segmental type remains prevalent. But towns always result from the need of individuals to put themselves constantly in the closest possible contact with each other. There are so many points where the social mass is contracted more strongly than elsewhere. Thus when they multiply and expand the moral density must become raised. We shall see, moreover, that they receive a source of recruitment from immigration, something which is only possible when the fusion of social segments is advanced.

As long as social organisation is essentially segmental, towns do not exist. There are none in lower societies. They did not exist among the

Iroquois, nor among the ancient Germans. It was the same with the primitive populations of Italy... But towns did not take long to appear. Athens and Rome are or become towns, and the same transformation occurred throughout Italy. In our Christian societies, the town is in evidence from the beginning, for those left by the Roman empire did not disappear with it. Since then, they have increased and multiplied. The tendency of the country to stream into the town, so general in the civilised world, is only a consequence of this movement. It is not of recent origin; from the seventeenth century, statesmen have been preoccupied with it.

Because societies generally begin with an agricultural period, there has sometimes been the temptation to regard the development of urban centres as a sign of old age and decadence. But we must not lose sight of the fact that the length of this agricultural phase is shorter the more advanced the society. Whereas in Germany, among the Indians of America, and with all primitive peoples, it lasts for the duration of their existence, in Rome and Athens, it ends fairly quickly; and, with us, we can say that it never existed in pure form. On the other hand, urban life begins earlier and consequently expands further. The constantly increasing acceleration of this development proves that, far from constituting a sort of pathological phenomenon, it comes from the very nature of higher social types. The supposition that this movement has attained alarming proportions in our societies today, which perhaps are no longer flexible enough to adapt themselves to it, will not prevent this movement from continuing either within our societies, or after them; and the social types which will be formed after ours will probably be distinguished by a still more complete and raped contraction of rural life.

3. Finally, there are the number and rapidity of the means of communication and transportation. By suppressing or diminishing the gaps which separate social segments, they increase the density of society. It is not necessary, however, to prove that they become more numerous and perfected in societies of a more developed type.

Since this visible and measurable symbol reflects the variations of what we have called 'moral density' we can substitute it for this latter in the formula we have proposed. Moreover, we must repeat here what we said before. If society, in concentrating, determines the development of the division of labour, the latter in its turn, increases the concentration of society. But this is not important, for the division of labour remains the derived fact, and, consequently, the advances which it has made are due to parallel advances of social density, whatever may be the causes of the latter. That is all we wished to prove...

If work becomes progressively divided as societies become more voluminous and dense, it is not because external circumstances are more varied, but because struggle for existence is more acute.

Darwin quite correctly observed that the struggle between two organisms is as active as they are similar. Having the same needs and pursuing the same aims, they are in rivalry everywhere. So long as they have more resources than they need, they can still live side by side, but if their number increases to such proportions that their needs can no longer all be adequately satisfied, war breaks out, and it is the more violent the more marked this scarcity; that is to say, as the number of participants increase. It is quite otherwise if the co-existing individuals are of different species or varieties. As they do not feed in the same manner, and do not lead the same kind of life, they do not disturb each other. What is advantageous to one is without value to the others. The occasions for conflict thus diminish with occasions of confrontation, and this happens increasingly as the species or varieties become more distant from one-another...

Men obey the same law. In the same city, different occupations can co-exist without being obliged mutually to destroy one another, for they pursue different objectives. The soldier seeks military glory, the priest moral authority, the statesman power, the businessman riches, and the scholar scientific renown. Each of them can attain his end without preventing the others from attaining theirs. It is still the same even when the functions are less separated from one another. The occultist does not compete with the psychiatrist, the shoemaker with the hatter, the mason with the cabinet maker, the physicist with the chemist, etc. Since they perform different services, they can perform them together.

The closer functions approach one-another, however, the more points of contact they have; the more, consequently, they are exposed to conflict. As in this case they satisfy similar needs by different means, they inevitably seek to curtail the other's development. The judge never is in competition with the businessman, but the brewer and the wine-grower, the clothier and the manufacturer of silks, the poet and the musician, often try to supplant each other. As for those who have exactly the same function, each can prosper only to the detriment of the others. If, then, these different functions are pictured as a series of branches issuing from a common trunk, the struggle is at its minimum between the extreme points, whereas it increases steadily as we approach the centre. It is so, not only inside each city, but in all society. Similar occupations located at different points are as competitive as they are alike, provided the difficulty of communication and transport does not restrict the circle of their action.

This having been said, it is easy to understand that any condensation of the social mass, especially if it is accompanied by an increase in population, necessarily stimulates an advance in the division of labour.

DTS, pp. 273-8, 239-41 and 248-50

8. ANOMIE AND THE MORAL STRUCTURE OF INDUSTRY

The Problem of Anomie

The totality of moral rules truly forms about each person an imaginary wall, at the foot of which the flood of human passions simply dies without being able to go further. For the same reason — that they are contained — it becomes possible to satisfy them. But if it any point this barrier weakens, these previously restrained human forces pour tumultuously through the open breach; once loosed they find no limits where they can stop. They can only devote themselves, without hope of satisfaction, to the pursuit of an end that always eludes them. For example, if the rules of the conjugal morality lose their authority, and the mutual obligations of husband and wife become less respected, the emotions and appetites ruled by this sector of morality will become unrestricted and uncontained, and accentuated by this very release; powerless to fulfil themselves because they have been freed from all limitations, these emotions will produce a disillusionment which manifests itself visibly in the statistics of suicide. In the same way, should the morality governing economic life be shaken, and the search for gain become excited and inflamed beyond bounds, then one would observe a rise in the annual quota of suicides. One could multiply such examples. Furthermore, it is because morality has the function of limiting and containing that too much wealth so easily becomes a source of immorality. Through the power wealth confers on us, it actually diminishes the power of things to oppose us. Consequently, it lends strength to our desires and makes it harder to hold them in check. Under such conditions, moral equilibrium is unstable: it requires but a slight blow to disrupt it. Thus, we can understand the nature and source of this malady of infiniteness which torments our age. For man to see before him boundless, free, and open space, he must have lost sight of the moral barrier which under normal conditions would cut off his view. He no longer feels those moral forces that restrain him and limit his horizon. But if he no longer feels them it is because they no longer carry their normal degree of authority, because they are weakened and no longer as they should be. The notion of the infinite, then, appears only at those times when moral discipline has lost its ascendancy over wants; it is a sign of the attrition that occurs during periods when the moral system which has prevailed for centuries is shaken, and fails to respond to new conditions of human life, without any new system having yet been formed to replace that which has disappeared.

EM, 47-9

No living being can be happy, or even exist, unless his needs are adequately related to his means. In other words, if his needs require more than can be allocated to them, or even merely something of a different sort, they will be under continual friction and can only function painfully. Now an action which cannot be effected without suffering tends not to be reproduced. Unsatisfied tendencies atrophy, and as the impulse to live is merely the result of all other motivations, it is bound to weaken as the others lose their hold.

In the animal, at least in the normal state, this equilibrium is established with automatic spontaneity because the animal depends on purely material conditions. All the organism needs is that the supplies of substance and energy constantly employed in the process of living should be periodically renewed by equivalent quantities; that the replacement be equivalent to what is used up. When the gap created by the exigencies of life is filled, the animal, satisfied, asks nothing further. Its powers of thought are not sufficiently developed to imagine other ends than those implicit in its physical nature. Moreover, as the work demanded of each particular organ depends on the general state of vital energy and the needs of organic equilibrium, what is used up is in turn replaced and the balance is automatic. The limits of one are also those of the other; both are fundamental to the constitution of the existence in question, which cannot exceed them.

This is not the case with man, because most of his needs are not dependent on his body, or not to the same extent. Strictly speaking, we may consider that the quantity of material supplies necessary to the physical maintenance of a human life can be calculated, though this be less precise than in the preceding case, with a wider margin left for the free combinations of the will; for beyond the indispensable minimum which satisfies nature when instinctive, a more developed intelligence creates a wider range of conditions and desired ends demanding fulfilment. Such appetites, however, admittedly sooner or later reach a limit which they cannot pass. But how can we specify the quantity of a well-being, comfort or luxury legitimately to be desired by a human being? Nothing appears in man's organic nor in his psychological constitution which sets a limit to such tendencies. The functioning of individual life does not require them to cease at one point rather than at another; this is shown by the fact that they have constantly increased since the beginnings of history, becoming satisfied more and more, without any weakening of average health. Above all, how can we establish their proper variation with different conditions of life, occupations, relative importance of services, etc.? In no society are they equally developed at the different levels of the social hierarchy. Yet human nature is substantially the same among all men, in its essential qualities. It is not human nature which can assign the variable limit necessary to our needs. These are thus unlimited so far as they depend on the individual alone. Irrespective of any external regulatory force, our capacity for feeling is in itself an insatiable and bottomless abyss.

But if nothing external can restrain this capacity, it can only be a source of torment to itself. Unlimited desires are insatiable by definition and insatiability is rightly considered a sign of morbidity. Being unlimited, they constantly and infinitely surpass the means at their command; they cannot be quenched. Inextinguishable thirst is constantly renewed torture. It has been claimed, it is true, that human activity naturally aspires beyond assignable limits and sets itself unattainable goals. But how can such an indeterminate state be any more reconciled with the conditions of mental life than with the demands of physical life? All man's pleasure in acting, moving and exerting himself implies the sense that his efforts are not in vain and that by walking he advances. However, one does not advance when one proceeds toward no goal, or — which is the same thing — when the goal is in infinity. Since the distance between us and it is always the same, whatever road we take, it is just as if we have not moved. Even our feeling of pride looking back at the distance covered can only give a deceptive satisfaction, since the remaining distance is not proportionately reduced. To pursue a goal which is by definition unattainable is to condemn oneself to a state of perpetual unhappiness. Of course, a man may hope contrary to all reason, and hope has its pleasures even when irrational. It may sustain him for a time; but it cannot indefinitely survive the repeated disappointments of experience. What more can the future offer him than the past, since he can never reach an acceptable position nor even approach the glimpsed ideal? Thus, the more one has, the more one wants, and satisfactions received only stimulate instead of filling needs. Shall action as such be considered pleasurable? First only on condition that we are blind to its uselessness. Secondly, for this pleasure to be felt and to temper and partly veil the disquiet and distress which goes with it, such unending motion must at least always be easy and unhampered. If it is frustrated, only restlessness is left, with the unhappiness which it brings in tow. Now it would be a miracle if no insurmountable obstacle were ever encountered. In this situation, one is held to life only by a very thin thread, which can be broken at any moment.

To achieve any other result, the passions first must be limited. Only then can they be harmonised with capacities and satisfied. But since the individual has no way of limiting them, this must necessarily be accomplished by some force outside him. A regulative force must play the same role for moral needs which the organism plays for physical needs. This means that the force can only be moral.

Su, pp. 272-5

To [socialists] it appears that the way to realise social peace is to free economic appetites of all restraint on the one hand, and on the other to satisfy them by fulfilling them. But such an undertaking is contradictory. For these appetites cannot be appeased unless they are limited, and they cannot be limited except by something other than themselves. They cannot be regarded as the only purpose of society since they must be subordinated to some end which surpasses them, and it is only on this condition that they are capable of being really satisfied. Imagine the most productive economic organisation possible, and a distribution of wealth which assures abundance even for the most humble: perhaps such a transformation, at the very moment it was effected, would produce a measure of gratification. But this gratification could be no more than transitory. For although they may be temporarily assuaged, these demands will quickly make themselves felt again. Unless it is admitted that each individual should be equally compensated — and such levelling, if it conforms to the communist ideal, is completely opposed to the Saint-Simon doctrine, as to every socialist theory — there will always be some workers who will receive more and others less. So it is inevitable that at the end of a short time, the latter find their share inadequate compared with what others receive, and as a result new demands arise, at all levels of the social scale. Moreover, quite apart from any feelings of envy, desires will tend naturally to keep outstripping their goals, for the very reason that there will be nothing before them which stops them. Thus new satisfactions will be demanded, even more imperiously, since those already secured will have given them more strength and vitality. This is why those at the very top of the hierarchy, who consequently would have nothing above them to stimulate their ambition, could nevertheless not be held at the point they had reached, but would continue to be plagued by the same restlessness that torments them today. What is needed if social order is to reign is that the mass of men be content with their lot. But what is needed for them to be content, is not that they have more or less but that they be convinced they have no right to more. And for this, it is absolutely essential that there be an authority whose superiority they acknowledge and which tells them what is right. For an individual committed only to the pressure of his needs will never admit he has reached the extreme limits of his rightful portion. If he is not conscious of a force above him which he respects, which stops him and tells him authoritatively he has received his just due, then inevitably he will expect everything his needs demand. And since in our hypothesis these needs are limitless, their demands are necessarily without limit. For it to be otherwise, a moral power is required who superiority he recognises, and which cries out 'you must go no further'.

This is precisely the role played in ancient society by the powers whose progressive dethronement Saint-Simon notes. Religion instructed the humble to be content with their situation, and, at the same time it taught them that the social order is providential: that it is God himself who has determined each one's share. Religion gave men a perception of a world beyond this earth where everything would be rectified; this prospect made inequalities less noticeable, it stopped men from feeling aggrieved. Secular power, too, precisely because it held economic functions under its domination, contained and limited them. But even *a priori* it is impossible to suppose that, while for centuries it was in the nature of economic interests to be subordinated, in the future the roles will become completely reversed. This would be to admit that the nature of things could be completely transformed in the course of evolution. Undoubtedly one can be certain that this regulating function can no longer be fulfilled by the old forces, since nothing appears likely to stop their decline. Undoubtedly, too, this same function could not be exercised today in the same manner or spirit as formerly. Industry is now more highly developed and more essential to the social organism; thus it can no longer be contained within the same narrow bounds, subjected to a system as heavily repressive, and regulated to such a subordinate position. But it does not follow that it should be freed of all regulation, liberated from all limitations.

The problem is to know, under the present conditions of social life, what moderating functions are necessary and what forces are capable of executing them.

Soc., pp. 290-3

The preceding has removed one of the most serious charges which has been made against the division of labour.

It has often been accused of degrading the individual by reducing him to a mere machine. And if he does not know what the significance is of the operations he is called upon to perform, if he relates them to no end, he must indeed become wedded to routine. Every day he repeats the same movements with monotonous regularity, without being interested in them and without understanding them. He is no longer a living cell of a living organism which unceasingly interacts with neighbouring cells, which influences them, responds to their actions, and transforms itself in relation to changing circumstances and needs. He is no longer anything but an inert cog in the machinery, set in motion by an external force, and always moving in the same direction and in the same way. Obviously, no matter how one may represent the moral ideal, one cannot remain indifferent to such a debasement of human nature. If morality has individual perfection as its goal, it cannot permit such a degradation of the individual, and if it has society as its goal, it cannot let the very source of social life be drained; for the evil does not threaten only economic functions, but all social functions, however elevated they may be...

As a remedy, it has sometimes been proposed that in, addition to technical and specialised training, workers should be given a general education. But even if we can thus relieve some of the deleterious effects attributed to the division of labour, this is not a way of preventing them. The division of labour does not change its nature because it has been preceded by a general education. No doubt, it is good for the worker to be interested in art, literature, etc.; but it is still wrong that he should be treated as a machine all day long. Who cannot see, moreover, that two such forms of existence are too opposed to be reconciled, and cannot be followed by the same individual! If a man has become accustomed to vast horizons, total views, and fine abstractions, he cannot be confined within the strict limits of a specialised task without becoming frustrated. Such a remedy would make specialisation unobjectionable by making it intolerable and, consequently, more or less impossible.

What solves the contradiction is that, contrary to what is often said, the division of labour does not produce these consequences because of a necessity of its own nature, but only in exceptional and abnormal circumstances. In order for it to develop without having such a disastrous influence on the human mind, it is not necessary to temper it with its opposite. It is necessary and it is sufficient for it to be itself, for nothing to come from without to rob it of its specific character. For, normally, the role of each special function does not require that the individual close himself in, but that he keep himself in constant relations with neighbouring functions, take heed of their needs, of the changes which these needs undergo, etc. The division of labour presumes that the worker, far from being hemmed in by his task, does not lose sight of his collaborators, that he acts upon them and reacts to them. Then he is not a machine which repeats its actions without knowing their meaning, but he knows that they tend, in some way, towards an end that he can see fairly distinctly. He feels that he is of some use. For that, he need not embrace vast portions of the social horizon; it is sufficient that he perceive enough of it to understand that his actions have an aim beyond themselves. From that time on, as specialised and uniform as his activity may be, it is that of an intelligent being, for it has direction, and he knows it. The economists would not have allowed this intrinsic characteristic of the division of labour to remain obscured and consequently exposed to this unwarranted criticism, if they had not reduced it to being merely a means of increasing social productivity; if they had seen that it is above all a source of solidarity.

DTS, pp. 363 and 364-5

The Forced Division of Labour

It is not enough for there to be rules, however, for sometimes the rules themselves are what is at fault. That is what occurs in class-wars. The institution of classes or of castes constitutes an organisation of the division of labour, and it is a strictly regulated organisation; but it is often a source of conflict. The lower classes not being, or no longer being, satisfied with the role which is theirs by custom or law, aspire to functions which are closed to them and seek to dispossess those who are exercising them. Thus civil wars arise which are due to the manner in which labour is distributed.

Nothing comparable to this can be observed in the organism. No doubt, during periods of crisis, the different tissues war against one another and nourish themselves at the expense of others. But a cell or organ never seeks to usurp a role different from the one which it possesses. The reason for this is that each anatomical element automatically executes its purpose. Its structure and its place in the organism determines its task; its function is a consequence of its nature. It can acquit itself poorly, but it cannot assume another's task unless the latter abandons it, as happens in rare cases of substitution... It is not so in societies. Here the possibility is greater: there is a wider gulf between the hereditary dispositions of the individual and the social functions he will fill. The first do not imply the second with such immediate necessity. The field which is thus open to striving and resolution is also subject to many factors which can make the individual nature deviate from its normal direction, and create a pathological condition. Because this organisation is more flexible, it is also more delicate and more open to change. No doubt we are not from birth predestined to some specific position; but we do have tastes and aptitudes which limit our choice. If no heed is given to them, and they are constantly contradicted by our daily occupation, we shall suffer and seek a way out of our suffering. Now there is no other way out than to change the established order and to set up a new one. For the division of labour to produce solidarity, it is not sufficient, then, for every individual to be given a task to perform; he has also to be suited to his task.

But this precondition is not realised in the example we are examining. If the institution of classes or castes sometimes gives rise to unfortunate frictions instead of producing solidarity, this is because the distribution of social functions on which it rests does not correspond, or rather no longer corresponds to the distribution of natural talents... For wants to spread from one class to another, the differences which originally separated these classes must have diminished or disappeared. As a consequence of changes produced in society, some must have become capable of functions which were at first beyond them, while others have lost their original superiority. When the Plebeians aimed to dispute the right to religious and administrative functions with the Patricians, it was not only in imitation of the latter, but because they had become more intelligent, richer, more numerous, and their tastes and ambitions had developed correspondingly. As a consequence of such changes, the correspondence between the aptitudes of individuals and the kind of activity assigned to them is broken in a whole large area of society; constraint alone, more or less violent and direct in character, ties them to their functions. Hence the solidarity which results is defective and strained.

This consequence is thus not a necessary characteristic of the division of labour. It comes about not only under specific circumstances, that is, as the effect of external constraint. It is quite different when the division of labour is established in virtue of purely internal spontaneity, and where nothing hampers individual initiative. In this situation, harmony between individual natures and social functions is necessarily produced, at least in the majority of cases. For, if there is nothing which either unduly hinders or favours the chances of those competing for occupations, it is inevitable that only those who are most capable at each type of activity will move into it. The only factor which then determines the manner in which work is divided is the diversity of capacities; it comes about, inevitably, on the basis of aptitude, since this is the only determining element. Thus, the congruence between the constitution of each individual and his position is brought about of its own accord. It might be argued that this is still not enough to make men content, since there are some men whose aspirations outstrip their faculties. This is true, but these are exceptional and, one may say, morbid cases. Normally, man finds happiness in realising his nature; his needs are relative to his means. Thus, in the organism, each organ demands only as much food as it requires. The 'forced division of labour' is, then, the second abnormal type that we meet. But the meaning of the word 'forced' must not be misunderstood. Not every form of regulation is the same as constraint, since, as we have seen, the division of labour cannot operate without regulation. Even when functions are divided in accordance with pre-established rules, this is not necessarily the result of constraint. Such is the case even in a caste system, as long as it is founded in the nature of the society. This institution is never completely and wholly arbitrary. When it functions in a society in a regular way, and without opposition, it expresses, at least in a general way, the fixed manner in which occupation capacities are distributed. That is why, although tasks are, in certain measure, assigned by law, each organ executes its own function spontaneously. Constraint only begins when regulation, no longer corresponding to the real character of existence and, accordingly, no longer having any basis in customs, is only maintained by force.

Conversely, we may say that the division of labour produces solidarity only if, and in so far as, it is spontaneous. But by 'spontaneity' we should understand not simply the absence of all express and manifest violence, but also of everything that can even indirectly shackle the free unfolding of the social force that each carries in himself. It supposes, not only that individuals are not forcibly assigned to specific tasks, but also that no obstacle, of whatever nature, prevents them from occupying the place in the social framework which is compatible with their faculties. In short, labour is divided spontaneously only if society is constituted in such a way that social inequalities exactly express natural inequalities...

It is, moreover, easy to understand what makes this levelling process necessary. We have just seen that all external inequality compromises organic solidarity. There is nothing disturbing in this for less developed societies, where solidarity is determined primarily by common beliefs and sentiments. However strained the ties which come from the division of labour, since they are not the ones which most strongly attach the individual to society, social cohesion is not placed in jeopardy. The unhappiness which results from frustrated aspirations is not enough to turn men against the social order which creates them; they cling to this social order, not because they find it the necessary field for the development of their occupational activity, but because in their eyes it expresses the sum total of the beliefs and practices by which they live. They cling to it because their whole internal life is linked with it. All their convictions presuppose the existence of this order, because, serving as a basis for the moral and religious system, it appears to them as sacred. Personal, and temporal, frustrations are obviously too insignificant to upset states of consciousness which derive such an exceptional force from this origin. Moreover, since occupational life is not highly developed, these clashes occur only infrequently. For all these reasons, they have only a slight impact; they are accepted without difficulty. Men find these inequalities not only tolerable but even natural.

It is quite the opposite which occurs when organic solidarity becomes predominant; whatever undermines it attacks the social tie in its most essential form. In the first place, since in these conditions specialised activities are pursued almost continuously, they cannot be opposed without producing protracted discontent. Secondly, since the *conscience collective* is weaker, the frictions which are thus created can no longer be so completely nullified. Common sentiments no longer have the same capacity to keep the individual attached to the group under any circumstances. Subversive tendencies, no longer having the same counterweight, occur more frequently. Since it increasingly loses the transcendent character which placed it in a sphere above human interests, social organisation no longer has the same force of resistance, and at the same time becomes more subject to attack. As a purely human construction, it can no longer so directly oppose human demands. At the very moment at which the flood becomes more violent, the dam which holds it in is broken down; it thus becomes a greater threat. This is why, in organised societies, the division of labour must be increasingly placed in harmony with this ideal of spontaneity that we have just defined. If such societies direct, and must direct, their energies to abolishing external inequalities as far as possible, this is not only because enterprise is intrinsically worthwhile, but because their very existence is bound up with this problem. For these societies can survive only if there is solidarity between the elements of which they are composed; solidarity is possible only given this situation. Thus we may predict that this work of justice will become ever more complete, as the organised type develops. No matter how important the progress already made in this direction, in all probability it only gives a small idea of what will be achieved in the future.

DTS, pp. 367-70 and 373-4

9. POLITICAL SOCIOLOGY

Definition of Political Society and the State

An essential element that enters into any notion of a 'political' group is the opposition between governing and governed, between authority and those subject to it. It is quite possible that in the initial stages of social development this distinction may not have existed; such an hypothesis is all the more likely since we do find societies in which the distance between the two is barely perceptible. But in any case, the societies where it is found must not be confused with those where it does not occur. The former differ from the latter in type, and require different terms of description: we should keep the word 'political' for the first category. For if this expression has any meaning, it implies primarily the existence of some kind of organisation, however rudimentary; it implies an established power — which may be stable or fluctuating, weak or strong — to whose action individuals are subject, whatever it may be.

But a power of this type is not found solely in political societies. The family may have a head, with powers which are sometimes absolute in character, and sometimes restrained by those of a family council. The patriarchal family of the Romans has often been compared to a state in miniature. Although, as we shall see below, this expression is not justified, we could not object to it if the only distinguishing feature of the political society were the existence of a governmental structure. So we must look for some further characteristic.

This has sometimes been sought in the closeness of the ties which bind the political society to its territory. There is said to be a permanent connection between any nation and a given territory... But the family, at least in many countries, is no less bound to the land, i.e., to some defined area. The family, too, has its domain from which it is inseparable, since that domain is inalienable. We have seen that the patrimony of landed estate was sometimes the very core of the family; it is this which gave it its unity and continuity, and it was about this focus that domestic life revolved. Nowhere in political societies has territory had a more important role than this. We may add, moreover, that where prime importance attaches to national territory, it is of comparatively recent date. First, it seems rather arbitrary to deny any political character to the great nomad societies whose structure was sometimes very elaborate. Secondly, in the past it was the number of citizens and not the territory that was considered to be the primary element of the state. To annex a state was not to annex the country, but its inhabitants and to incorporate them within the conquering state. Conversely, a conquering people may settle down in the country which they have vanquished, without thereby losing their own cohesion or their political identity. During the whole early period of our history, the capital, that is, the territorial centre of gravity of the society, was extremely mobile. It is only recently that peoples became so identified with the territories they inhabit; that is, with what we should call the geographical expression of those peoples. Today, France is not only a mass of people consisting in the main of individuals speaking a certain language and who observe certain laws etc.; it is essentially a certain defined part of Europe. If indeed all the Alsatians had opted for French nationality in 1870, we might still be justified in considering France as mutilated or diminished, by the sole fact that she had abandoned a specific part of her soil to a foreign power. But this identification of the society with its territory has only occurred in the most advanced societies. This is undoubtedly the result of many factors: of the higher social value that the land has acquired, perhaps also of the relatively greater importance that the geographical bond has assumed since other social ties of a more moral kind have lost their force. We see the society of which we are members more as a defined territory because it is no longer perceived as essentially religious, or identified with its own unique set of traditions or with the support of a particular dynasty.

Leaving territory aside, perhaps we can find a criterion of the political

142 / Sociological Thought

society in the numerical size of the population. Certainly we should not ordinarily give this name to social groups comprising a very small number of individuals. Even so, a dividing line of the kind would be extremely ambiguous: when does a concentration of people become large enough to be classified as a political group? According to Rousseau, it entails at least ten thousand people; Bluntschli rates this as too low. Both estimates are equally arbitrary. A French *département* sometimes has more inhabitants than many of the city states of Greece and Italy. Any one of these, however, constitutes a state, whilst a *département* has no claim to such a name.

Nevertheless, we touch here upon a distinctive feature. To be sure, we cannot say that a political society differs from family groups or from professional groups because it is larger: for the numerical strength of a state may be very small. But it must be recognised that there is no political society which does not comprise numerous different families or professional groups, or both at once. If it were confined to a domestic society or family, it would be identical with it and hence be a domestic society. But from the moment that it becomes composed of a number of domestic societies, the resulting combination is something more than each of its elements. It is something new, which has to be designated by a different term. Thus the political society should not be confused with professional groups, or with classes if these exist; but it is always an aggregate of various professions or classes as it is of different families. We may conclude that when a society is made up of a number of different forms of secondary group, without itself being a secondary group in relation to a larger society, then it constitutes a social entity of a specific type. We may then define a political society as one formed by the coming together of a fairly large number of secondary social groups, which is subject to the same one authority, where this is not itself subject to any other permanently constituted superior authority...

Now that we know the distinguishing features of a political society, let us see what the morals are that relate to it. From the very definition which has just been given, it follows that these consist essentially in rules which specify the relation of individuals to this sovereign authority, to whose control they are subject. Since we need a word to indicate the particular group of officials entrusted with representing this authority, it is convenient to reserve the term 'state' for this. It is true that very often we apply the word not to the instrument of government but to the political society as a whole, or to the people governed and its government taken as one, and we ourselves have often used the term in this sense. It is in this way that we speak of the 'European states' or that we call France a 'state'. But since it is as well to have separate terms for phenomena as different as the society, and one of its organs, we apply the term 'state' more specifically to the agents of the sovereign authority, and 'political society' to the complex group of which the state is the highest organ...

The state may thus be defined as a group of officials *sui generis*, within which ideas and policies involving the collectivity are formulated, although they are not the product of collectivity. It is not accurate to say that the state embodies the *conscience collective*, for the latter goes beyond the state at every point. It is primarily diffuse in character: there is always a vast number of different social sentiments and social conditions which escape the purview of the state. The state is the centre only of a particular kind of consciousness; one which is circumscribed, but which is higher, clearer and with a more vivid sense of itself. There is nothing more obscure and ambiguous than the collective representations that are diffused in every society — myths, religious or moral tales, etc. We do not know either where they originate of where they are tending; they are not the product of deliberated thought. The representations that derive from the state are always more self-conscious, aware of their causes and their aims; they are arrived at in a less obscure fashion. The collective agency which plans them is more fully aware of what it is attempting to do. This is not to say that there is not often obscurity here also. The state, like the individual, is often mistaken as to the motives underlying its decisions, but whether this is so or not, they are in some degree consciously motivated. There is always, or at least usually, some sort of deliberation, and an understanding of the circumstances as a whole that make the decision necessary; and it is precisely this inner organ, the state, that is called upon to conduct these debates. Thus we have the councils, assemblies, debates and rulings which control the pace at which ideas are formulated. We may say, in summary: the state is a specialised agency whose responsibility it is to work out certain ideas which apply to the collectivity. These ideas are distinguished from the other collective representations by their more conscious and deliberate character.

LS, pp. 52-5, 58-9 and 61-2

State Power and Individual Liberties

...the place of the individual becomes greater...[as] the governmental power becomes *less absolute*. But there is no contradiction in the fact that the sphere of individual action grows at the same time as that of the state; or in the fact that functions which are not directly dependent upon the central regulative agency develop at the same time as the latter. Power can be at once absolute, and very elementary. The despotic government of a barbarian chief is very simple in structure: the functions he carries out are rudimentary and not very numerous. That is because the directive agency of social life can have absorbed all these in itself, without on that account being very highly developed, if social life itself is not very highly developed. This agency then holds exceptional power over the rest of society, because there is nothing to hold it in check or to neutralise it. But it is quite possible for it to expand at the same time as other agencies develop which form a counterweight to it. All that has to occur is for the total volume of the society to be increased. Undoubtedly the action that it exerts under these conditions is no longer of the same nature; the points at which it exercises its power have multiplied, and if it is less violent, it still imposes itself quite as strictly. Acts of disobedience to the commands of constituted authority are no longer treated as sacrilegious, or, consequently, repressed with the same severity. But they are not tolerated any more than before, although these commands are more numerous and govern a greater range of different conditions.

DTS, p. 199

...the degree of absolutism in government does not vary directly with the type of society. Since absolutism is found both in cases where collective life is extremely simple as well as in cases where it is very complex, it is not characteristic exclusively of less developed societies any more than it is of the others. One might consider, it is true, that the concentration of governmental powers always goes hand in hand with the concentration of the social mass, either because the first is a consequence of the latter, or because it contributes to forming it. But this is not the case. The Roman city, particularly after the fall of the Kings, was completely free from absolutism until the last century of the Republic: and the different segments or partial societies (*gentes*) of which it was composed reached a high degree of concentration and fusion precisely under the Republic. And in fact we find forms of government which deserve to be called absolute in the most different social types: in France in the seventeenth century, at the end of the Roman Empire, and in many primitive monarchies. Conversely, according to the circumstances, the same society may pass from being an absolute government into a quite different form; but a single society can no more change its type during the course of its evolution than an animal can change it species during its individual existence. France of the seventeenth century and France of the nineteenth century belong to the same type, in spite of the fact that the regulative agency was transformed. It is impossible to hold that, from Napoleon I to Louis-Philippe, French society changed from one social type to another, only then to undergo the reverse transformation from Louis-Philippe to Napoleon III. Such transmutations are incompatible with the notion of social type.

This specific form of political organisation thus does not depend upon the basic constitution of society, but upon particular, transitory, and contingent circumstances...the nature of the social type and that of the governmental type must be carefully distinguished, since as they are independent, they act independently of one-another, and sometimes even in opposite ways.

AS, 1900, pp. 69-70

There is no doubt what was the real nature of the aims pursued by the state in many societies. To keep on expanding its power and to add lustre to its fame — this was the sole or the main object of public activity. Individual interests and needs did not come into the reckoning. The religious character which permeated the political system of these societies explains this indifference of the state for what concerns the individual. The density of a state was closely bound up with that of the gods worshipped at its altars. If a state suffered reverses, then the prestige of its gods declined in the same measure, and vice versa. Public religion and civic morals were fused: they were merely different aspects of a single reality. To bring glory to the city was the same as enhancing the glory of the city gods: the relation was reciprocal. Now, the characteristic of religious phenomena is that they are wholly unlike those of the human order. They belong to a world apart. The individual as such is part of the profane world, whilst the gods are the very core of the religious world; and between these two worlds there is a gulf. The gods are made of a different substance to men: they have different ideas, needs, and live an existence completely distinct from that of men. To say that the aims of the political system were religious and religious aims political, is to say that there was a cleavage between the aims of the state on the ends pursued by individuals as such. How was it, therefore, that the individual could thus occupy himself with the pursuit of aims which were to such a degree foreign to his own private concerns? The answer is this: his private concerns were relatively unimportant to him and his personality and everything dependent upon it had only a low moral value. His personal views, his private beliefs and various individual aspirations seemed insignificant factors. What were valued by everyone were the beliefs held in common, the collective aspirations, the popular traditions and the symbols that expressed them. In these circumstances, the individual yielded spontaneously and without resistance to the instrument by which aims were realised which did not relate directly to himself. Absorbed by society, he meekly followed its imperatives and subordinated his own lot to the destinies of collective existence without any sense of sacrifice. This is because his particular fate had in his own eyes nothing of the meaning and high importance that we attribute to it today. If things were so, this is because they had to be so; societies could only exist at that time by virtue of this dependence.

But the further one advances in history, the more one is aware of the process of change. The individual personality at first is lost in the depths of the social mass, and only later begins to emerge from it. At first limited in scope and of small regard, the circle of individual activity expands and becomes the primary object of moral respect. The individual comes to acquire ever wider rights over his own person and over the possessions to which he has title; he also comes to form ideas about the world that seem to him most fitting and to freely develop his own nature. War fetters his activity, diminishes his stature and so becomes the supreme evil. Because it inflicts undeserved suffering on him, he sees in it more and more the supreme form of moral offence. In these conditions it is quite contradictory to expect him to submit to the same subordination as before. One cannot make of him a god, a god above all others, and at the same time an instrument in the hands of the gods. One cannot make him the supreme end and reduce him to the roles of means. If he is the moral reality, then it is he who must serve as the axis of public as well as private conduct. It should be the role of the state to help him to realise his superstition of which we ought to rid ourselves. But this would be to go against all the lessons of history: for the further we look, the more we find the human person tending to gain in dignity. There is no law more soundly established. Thus any attempt to base social institutions on an opposing principle is not feasible and could be convincing only for a moment. We cannot force things to be other than they are. We cannot stop the individual having become what he is — an autonomous centre of activity, an imposing system of personal forces whose energy can no more be destroyed than that of cosmic forces. It would be just as impossible to transform the physical atmosphere in the midst of which we breathe.

But then we seem to reach a contradiction that cannot be resolved. On the one hand we establish that the state goes on developing more and more: on the other, that the rights of the individual, which appear to be antagonistic to those of the state have a parallel development. The government organ takes on an even greater scale, because its function goes on growing in importance and because the aims that demand its intervention, increase in number; and yet we deny that it can pursue aims other than those that concern the individual. But these aims seems to belong to the individual alone. If, as is often supposed, the rights of the individual are given in the individual, the state does not have to intervene to establish them; they depend only upon the individual. But if this is so, and these rights are outside its sphere of action, how can this sphere of action go on expanding, if on the other hand it must avoid things which compromise the interests of the individual?

The only way of disposing of this difficulty is to reject the postulate that the rights of the individual are given in the individual, and to admit that the institution of these rights is in fact precisely the task of the state. Then, in fact, everything becomes clear. We can understand that the functions of the state may expand, without any diminishing of the individual. We can see too that the individual may develop without causing any decline of the state, since he would be in some respects himself the product of the state, and since the activity of the state would be essentially one of the individual liberation.

LS, pp. 68-71

The Nature of Democratic Government

...the state is nothing if it is not an agency distinct from the rest of society. If the state is everywhere, it is nowhere. The states comes into existence by a process of concentration that detaches a certain group of individuals from the collective mass. In that group, social thought is subjected to elaboration of a special kind and reaches an exceptional degree of clarity. Where there is no such concentration and where social thought remains entirely diffuse, it also remains obscure and the distinctive feature of the political society will be lacking. However, contact between this special agency and other social organs may vary in its degree of closeness and constancy. Certainly in this respect there can only be differences of degree. There is no state with such absolute power that those governing will sever all contact with the mass of its subjects. But differences of degree can be important: these increase externally in relation to the presence or absence of definite institutions designed to establish this contact, and how far they are developed or merely rudimentary. These are institutions that enable the people to follow the working of government (national assembly, official journals, education intended to equip the citizen to one day fulfil his functions, etc.), and also to communicate their views to the organs of government, directly or indirectly (i.e. electoral machinery). What we must reject above all is that conception which, by eliminating the state entirely, is a facile source of criticism. 'Democracy' thus understood, only exists in the early phases of the development of society. If everyone governs, it means in fact that there is no government. Collective sentiments, diffused, ambiguous and obscure as they may be, sway the people. The life of such peoples is in no way guided by deliberate policies. Societies of this description are like individuals whose actions are directed solely by routine and prejudice. They cannot be looked to as an example towards which we should progress: rather, they are a starting point. If we agree to reserve the name 'democracy' for political societies, it must not be applied to amorphous tribes which do not possess a state, and which are not political societies. The difference between this form

and democracy, is thus very wide, in spite of certain similarities. It is true
that in both cases — and this is what offers the resemblance — the whole
society participates in public life; but this occurs in very different ways. The
difference lies in the fact that in one case there is a state and in the other this
is lacking.

This initial characteristic, the existence of a state, is only one of the
necessary features of democracy; there is a second one, related to the first. In
societies where the governmental consciousness is restricted within narrow
limits, it comprises only a limited range of objectives. Since this clarified
sector of the *conscience collective* is limited to a small group of individuals,
it does not possess much range. There are all sorts of customs, traditions and
conventions which work automatically without the state itself being aware of
them, and which therefore are beyond its action. In a society such as the
monarchy of the seventeenth century the number of things on which
government deliberations had any bearing was very small. The whole sphere
of religion was outside its province, and along with religion, every kind of
collective prejudice: any absolute power would soon have come to grief if it
had attempted to destroy them. Today, on the other hand, we do not admit
there is anything in the realm of public life which cannot become subject to
the action of the state. In principle, we hold that everything should be
constantly open to question, that everything may be discussed, and that in so
far as decisions have to be taken, we are not tied to the past. The state has
really a far greater sphere of influence today than in other times, because the
sphere of this clarified consciousness has widened. Those obscure sentiments
change precisely because they are obscure. What cannot be seen is not easily
modified. All such forms escape the grasp, precisely because they are in the
shadows. On the other hand, the more the depths of social life become
illuminated, the more can changes be introduced. This is why the educated
man, who is a self-conscious being, can change more easily and radically
than the uneducated. The same is true of democratic societies. They are more
malleable and more flexible, and this advantage they owe to the fact that the
governmental consciousness has expanded in such a way as to include a
much broader range of objects. This contrasts sharply with those societies
that have been unorganised from the start, the pseudo-democracies. They
have wholly yielded to the yoke of tradition. Switzerland, and the Scandinavian
countries, too, are a good example of this.

To sum up, there is not, strictly speaking, a difference in nature between
the various forms of government; but they lie between two contrasting poles.
At one extreme, the governmental consciousness is almost completely isolated
from the rest of the society, and has a minimum range.

Aristocratic or monarchical societies, between which it is perhaps difficult to distinguish, fall into this category. The greater the degree to which there is direct communication between the governmental consciousness and the rest of society, the broader the range and comprehensiveness of this consciousness, the more democratic the society becomes. The concept of 'democracy' is thus defined in terms of a maximal extension of this consciousness, which determines this communication...

...[Thus] to arrive at a fairly definite idea of what a democracy is, we must begin by getting away from a number of current conceptions which simply confuse matters. The number of those governing must be left out of account and, even more important, their official titles. Neither must we believe that a democracy is necessarily a society in which the power of the state is weak. A state may be democratic and still have a strong organisation. The true characteristics of democracy are twofold: (1) a greater range of the governmental consciousness, and (2) closer communications between this consciousness and the mass of individuals. The confusions that have occurred can be understood to some extent by the fact that, in societies where government power is with the rest of society, because it is not distinct from it. It has no existence, so to speak, outside the mass of the people, and must therefore of necessity be in communication with that mass. In a small primitive tribe, the political leaders are only delegates, and always provisional, without any clearly defined functions. They live the same life as everyone else, and the decisions they make form a separate and definite agency. Also we find here nothing resembling the second feature already mentioned — the plasticity deriving from the range of governmental consciousness, that is, from the formulation of clarified collective ideas. Societies such as these are the victims of traditional routine. The second feature is perhaps even more distinctive than the first. The first criterion can still be very useful providing it is employed with care: we must guard against identifying the diffuse situation in which the state is not yet detached from society, and separately organised, with the communications that may exist between a clearly defined state and the society it governs.

Seen from this standpoint, a democracy thus appears as the political system by which the society can achieve a consciousness of itself in its purest form.

LS, pp. 99-102 and 106-7

Every society is despotic, at least if nothing external intervenes to restrain its despotism. Still, I would not say that there is anything artificial in this despotism: it is natural because it is necessary, and also because, in certain conditions, societies cannot endure without it. Nor do I wish to argue that there is anything intolerable about it: on the contrary, the individual does not feel it any more than we feel the atmosphere that weighs on our shoulders. From the moment the individual has been raised in this way by the collectivity, he will naturally desire what it desires and accept without difficulty the state of subjection to which he finds himself reduced. If he is to be conscious of this and to resist it, individualist aspirations must develop, and they cannot develop in these conditions.

But for it to be otherwise, we may say, is it not enough for the society to be on a fairly large scale? There is no doubt that when society is small, when it surrounds every individual on all sides and at every moment, it does not allow him to develop in freedom. If it is always present and always operating, it leaves no room to his initiative. But it is no longer the same when society has reached sufficient dimensions. When it is made up of a vast number of individuals, a society cannot exercise over each one a control which is as close, vigilant or effective as when it is concerned only with a small number. A man is far more free in a crowd than in a small group. Hence it follows that individual diversities can develop more easily; collective tyranny declines and individualism establishes itself as a reality — and in time, the reality becomes a right. But this can only happen on one condition: that is, that within this society, there must be no secondary groups formed that enjoy enough autonomy for each to become a small society within the larger one. For in this situation each would act towards its members as if it stood alone, and everything would happen as if the total society did not exist. Each group, tightly enclosing its component individuals, would block their development; the collective will would impose itself on conditions applying to the individual. A society made up of juxtaposed clans, or of more or less independent towns or villages, or of numerous professional groups, each autonomous in relation to the others, would have the effect of being almost as completely repressive of individuality as if it were made up of a single clan or town or corporation. The formation of secondary groups of this kind is bound to occur, for in a large-scale society there are always particular local or professional interests which tend naturally to bring together the people concerned. Hence we have the material for particular associations, corporations and groups of all kinds; and if there is nothing to offset or neutralise their activity, each of them will tend to absorb its members. In any case, there is always domestic society: we know how absorbing this is if left to itself — how it confines within its own circle and keeps in a state of dependence all who belong to it. (Even if secondary groups of this sort were not formed, a collective force would still establish itself at the head of the society to govern it. And if this collective force itself stands alone, if it has only individuals to deal with, the same necessary law will make those individuals fall under its domination.)

In order to prevent this happening, and to provide a sphere for individual development, it is not enough for a society to be large; the individual must be able to move with some degree of freedom over a broad field of action. He must not be curbed and dominated by secondary groups, and these groups must not be able to acquire a mastery over their members and mould them at will. There must therefore exist above these local, domestic — in a word, secondary — authorities, some overall authority which makes the law for them all: this overall authority must remind each of them that it is but a part, and not the whole, and that it must not monopolise what rightly belongs to the whole. The only means of averting this collective particularism, and the consequences which it implies for the individual, is to have a specialised agency with the duty of representing the overall collectivity, its rights and its interests, in relation to these individual collectivities. These rights and these interests merge with those of the individual. Thus the main function of the state is to liberate individual personalities. Since it holds its constituent societies in check, it prevents them from exerting the repressive influences over the individual which they would otherwise exert. So there is nothing inherently tyrannical about state intervention in the different spheres of social life; on the contrary, it has the objective and the effect of alleviating tyrannies that do exist. But could it not be argued that the state in turn might become despotic? This is undoubtedly the case, if there is nothing to counter-balance it. In this situation, as the only existing collective force, it produces the same effects upon individuals as any other collective force not neutralised by a counter-force. The state itself then becomes a levelling and repressive agency. And its repressive character is harder to endure than that of small groups, because it is more artificial. The state in our large-scale societies is so removed from individual interests that it cannot take into account the special, local conditions etc., in which they exist. Therefore when it attempts to control them, it succeeds only at the cost of contravening and distorting them. Moreover, it is too distant from the mass of the population to be able to mould them inwardly so that they voluntarily accept its influence. The individual eludes the state to some extent, since the state can only be effective in the context of a large-scale society, and individual diversity may not come to light. Hence, all kinds of resistance and distressing conflicts arise. Small groups do not have this disadvantage: they are close enough to the objects which provide their reason for existence to be able to adapt their actions as required; and they envelop the individuals fully enough to shape them in their own image. The conclusion to be drawn from this observation, however, is simply that if that collective force, the state, is to be the liberator of the individual, it has itself need of some counter-balance. It must be restrained by other collective forces, that is, by the secondary groups... While it is not desirable for these groups to stand alone, their existence is necessary.

And it is out of this conflict of social forces that individual freedoms are born. Here again we see the significance of these groups. Their usefulness is not merely to regulate and administer the interests under their supervision. They have a more general role; they form one of the conditions essential to the emancipation of the individual.

LS, pp. 74-8

EDITOR'S SELECTED BIBLIOGRAPHY

Editor's Introduction

Giddens, Anthony. (1972) *Emile Durkheim: Selected Writings* Cambridge U.P. (edited and translated by Anthony Giddens).

⚄④ Max Weber

To introduce Weber's work with the somewhat precise manner we did in other chapters is not easy. As many critics have observed, a systematic and precise definition of concepts was not a quality which characterized the sociological work of Max Weber. This is particularly true of his thesis on "Protestant Asceticism and the Spirit of Capitalism". As Bryan Turner observes, this theory lends itself to different and conflicting interpretations. One such interpretation places Weber as an idealist who believed that capitalism in Europe was able to develop largely due to people's religious convictions, namely Protestantism.

The Protestant ethic of hard labour taught by Calvin, provides, according to Weber, the primary source for capitalist accumulation. Capital in this theory is accumulated through the "Labour Ethics" of the Calvinist school of faith which asserts that hard work, savings and the reinvestment of these savings in bigger enterprises during one's life are the most important principles of the Protestant "worldly" ethic. Weber, in other words, constructs his theory of "the Spirit of Capitalism" not by examining the internal dynamics of capitalist accumulation itself, seen in reference to Marx as an essential process for understanding capitalist production and accumulation; instead, Weber uses the theory to address the question of *why* capitalism has developed only in the Christian Occident and failed to do so in the non-Christian (Hindu, Buddhist, Muslim,...etc.,) Orient.

In his attempt at probing this question, critics maintain, Weber has indulged himself in a number of assumptions and assertions about people's modes of behaviour, attitudes towards life and spiritual convictions, leading in a number of instances to false, if not racially based statements about the Oriental "Other". This text presents a clear picture of the Us-vs-Them dichotomy referred to in the first chapter. The text can be read as a treatise on the superiority of the Occidental West over the Oriental East. While both were seen as equally developed in terms of both science and technology, the Occident, armed with religious motivation, was able to achieve a higher level of civilization. Since this superiority is established comparatively, embedded in the notion of superiority of the Occident is also the inferiority of the Orient.

The other part of the text is taken from *Society and Economy*. This text is intended to introduce the reader to Weber's methodology on sociological enquiry. The part on "Basic Sociological Terms" provides definitions to various sociological terms. In this text, one reads about the importance of constructing the ideal type as an explanatory tool for social phenomenon. Limitations of space have precluded me from including a chapter which, otherwise, would have been useful; that is, the section on "Value-judgment in Social Science", which familiarises the student with Weber's approach to psychological research. A reference to this part, nevertheless, would not be out of place. Central to Weber's argument here is the ethical or moral question of the involvement of the individual (subject) researcher in the process, design and conclusion of their research.

Weber tries to establish a relationship between objectivity and neutrality in conducting sociological research. He asserts that in order to establish an objective research, the latter must be "value-neutral". The subject/researcher must take a neutral position by not imparting his value system or political stand on the object of enquiry. Such research, according to Weber, is not only possible but rather necessary if the research is to be scientific and objective.

Weber's interpretation of objective and scientific research, one may argue, is qualitatively different than that manifested in the Marxist methodology, which does not refrain from using concepts that may be interpreted as "biased" or "value-laden". Concepts such as exploitation and alienation, which are value-laden concepts, are essential to the Marxist theory and methodology. For Marx any social research within the capitalist context must begin with the fact that society is already plagued with contradictions, exploitations and conflicts on social class lines and, therefore, any research that intends to understand these relations in order to change them will have to determine on which side it will lie.

Because Weber's sociology is interpretive sociology, namely, concerned with defining and interpreting social phenomena without any commitment to changing it, Weber, one may argue, can afford the luxury of stepping outside the complex of social inequality. In the absence of a research methodology concerned with understanding the reasons of conflict in order to change them, Weber's interpretive methodology takes a different meaning.

Sociological research based on the Weberian principles often uses "observation" as a primary means to conduct research. The same methodology discourages other techniques of collecting data such as "participant observation" or "oral history" since they imply a degree of the individual/subject's involvement in the formation of data and the conclusions thereof. The Weberian model of research, one may add, is largely used and strongly encouraged by agencies and state institutions, for the so-called neutral or objective results assumed in this type of research.

THE DEFINITION OF SOCIOLOGY AND OF SOCIAL ACTION

Sociology (in the sense in which this highly ambiguous word is used here) is a science concerning itself with the interpretive understanding of social action and thereby with a causal explanation of its course and consequences. We shall speak of "action" insofar as the acting individual attaches a subjective meaning to his behavior — be it overt or covert, omission or acquiescence. Action is "social" insofar as its subjective meaning takes account of the behavior of others and is thereby oriented in its course.[1]

A. Methodological Foundations[2]

I. "Meaning" may be of two kinds. The term may refer first to the actual existing meaning in the given concrete case of a particular actor, or to the average or approximate meaning attributable to a given plurality of actors; or secondly to the theoretically conceived *pure type*[3] of subjective meaning attributed to the hypothetical actor or actors in a given type of action. In no case does it refer to an objectively "correct" meaning or one which is "true" in some metaphysical sense. It is this which distinguishes the empirical sciences of action, such as sociology and history, from the dogmatic disciplines in that area, such as jurisprudence, logic, ethics, and esthetics, which seek to ascertain the "true" and "valid" meanings associated with the objects of their investigation.

2. The line between meaningful action and merely reactive behavior to which no subjective meaning is attached, cannot be sharply drawn empirically. A very considerable part of all sociologically relevant behavior, especially purely traditional behavior, is marginal between the two. In the case of some psychophysical processes, meaningful, i.e., subjectively understandable, action

is not to be found at all; in others it is discernible only by the psychologist. Many mystical experiences which cannot be adequately communicated in words are, for a person who is not susceptible to such experiences, not fully understandable. At the same time the ability to perform a similar action is not a necessary prerequisite to understanding; "one need not have been Caesar in order to understand Caesar." "Recapturing an experience" is important for accurate understanding, but not an absolute precondition for its interpretation. Understandable and non-understandable components of a process are often intermingled and bound up together.

3. All interpretation of meaning, like all scientific observations, strives for clarity and verifiable accuracy of insight and comprehension (*Evidenz*).[4] The basis for certainty in understanding can be either rational, which can be further subdivided into logical and mathematical, or it can be of an emotionally empathic or artistically appreciative quality. Action is rationally evident chiefly when we attain a completely clear intellectual grasp of the action-elements in their intended context of meaning. Empathic or appreciative accuracy is attained when, through sympathetic participation, we can adequately grasp the emotional context in which the action took place. The highest degree of rational understanding is attained in cases involving the meanings of logically or mathematically related propositions; their meaning may be immediately and unambiguously intelligible. We have a perfectly clear understanding of what it means when somebody employs the proposition $2 \times 2 = 4$ or the Pythagorean theorem in reasoning or argument, or when someone correctly carries out a logical train of reasoning according to our accepted modes of thinking. In the same way we also understand what a person is doing when he tries to achieve certain ends by choosing appropriate means on the basis of the facts of the situation, as experience has accustomed us to interpret them. The interpretation of such rationally purposeful action possesses, for the understanding of the choice of means, the highest degree of verifiable certainty. With a lower degree of certainty, which is, however, adequate for most purposes of explanation, we are able to understand errors, including confusion of problems of the sort that we ourselves are liable to, or the origin of which we can detect by sympathetic self-analysis.

On the other hand, many ultimate ends or values toward which experience shows that human action may be oriented, often cannot be understood completely, though sometimes we are able to grasp them intellectually. The more radically they differ from our own ultimate values, however, the more difficult it is for us to understand them empathically. Depending upon the circumstances of the particular case we must be content either with a purely intellectual understanding of such values or when even that fails, sometimes we must simply accept them as given data. Then we can try to understand the action motivated by them on the basis of whatever opportunities for approximate emotional and intellectual interpretation seem to be available at different points in its course. These difficulties confront, for instance, people not susceptible to unusual acts of religious and charitable zeal, or persons who abhor extreme rationalist fanaticism (such as the fanatic advocacy of the "rights of man").

The more we ourselves are susceptible to such emotional reactions as anxiety, anger, ambition, envy, jealousy, love, enthusiasm, pride, vengefulness, loyalty, devotion, and appetites of all sorts, and to the "irrational" conduct which grows out of them, the more readily can we empathize with them. Even when such emotions are found in a degree of intensity of which the observer himself is completely incapable, he can still have a significant degree of emotional understanding of their meaning and can interpret intellectually their influence on the course of action and the selection of means.

For the purposes of a typological scientific analysis it is convenient to treat all irrational, affectually determined elements of behavior as factors of deviation from a conceptually pure type of rational action. For example a panic on the stock exchange can be most conveniently analysed by attempting to determine first what the course of action would have been if it had not been influenced by irrational affects; it is then possible to introduce the irrational components as accounting for the observed deviations from this hypothetical course. Similarly, in analysing a political or military campaign it is convenient to determine in the first place what would have been a rational course, given the ends of the participants and adequate knowledge of all the circumstances. Only in this way is it possible to assess the causal significance of irrational factors as accounting for the deviations from this type. The construction of a purely rational course of action in such cases serves the sociologist as a type (ideal type) which has the merit of clear understandability and lack of ambiguity. By comparison with this it is possible to understand the ways in which actual action is influenced by irrational factors of all sorts, such as affects and errors, in that they account for the deviation from the line of conduct which would be expected on the hypothesis that the action were purely rational.

Only in this respect and for these reasons of methodological convenience is the method of sociology "rationalistic." It is naturally not legitimate to interpret this procedure as involving a rationalistic bias of sociology, but only as a methodological device. It certainly does not involve a belief in the actual predominance of rational elements in human life, for on the question of how far this predominance does or does not exist, nothing whatever has been said. That there is, however, a danger of rationalistic interpretations where they are out of place cannot be denied. All experience unfortunately confirms the existence of this danger.

4. In all the sciences of human action, account must be taken of processes and phenomena which are devoid of subjective meaning, in the role of stimuli, results, favoring or hindering circumstances. To be devoid of meaning is not identical with being lifeless or non-human; every artifact, such as for example a machine, can be understood only in terms of the meaning which its production and use have had or were intended to have; a meaning which may derive from a relation to exceedingly various purposes. Without reference to this meaning such an object remains wholly unintelligible. That which is intelligible or understandable about it is thus its relation to human action in the role either of means or of end; a relation of which the actor or actors can be said to have been aware and to which their action has been oriented. Only in terms of such categories is it possible to "understand" objects of this kind. On the other hand processes or conditions, whether they are animate or inanimate, human or non-human, are in the present sense devoid of meaning in so far as they cannot be related to an intended purpose. That is to say they are devoid of meaning if they cannot be related to action in the role of means or ends but constitute only the stimulus, the favoring or hindering circumstances. It may be that the flooding of the Dollart [at the mouth of the Ems river near the Dutch-German border] in 1277 had historical significance as a stimulus to the beginning of certain migrations of considerable importance. Human mortality, indeed the organic life cycle from the helplessness of infancy to that of old age, is naturally of the very greatest sociological importance through the various ways in which human action has been oriented to these facts. To still another category of facts devoid of meaning belong certain psychic or psychophysical phenomena such as fatigue, habituation, memory, etc.; also certain typical states of euphoria under some conditions of ascetic mortification; finally, typical variations in the reactions of individuals according to reaction-time, precision, and other modes. But in the last analysis the same principle applies to these as to other phenomena which are devoid of meaning. Both the actor and the sociologist must accept them as data to be taken into account.

It is possible that future research may be able to discover noninterpretable uniformities underlying what has appeared to be specifically meaningful action, though little has been accomplished in this direction thus far. Thus, for example, differences in hereditary biological constitution, as of "races," would have to be treated by sociology as given data in the same way as the physiological facts of the need of nutrition or the effect of senescence on action. This would be the case if, and insofar as, we had statistically conclusive proof of their influence on sociologically relevant behavior. The recognition of the causal significance of such factors would not in the least alter the specific task of sociological analysis or of that of the other sciences of action, which is the interpretation of action in terms of its subjective meaning. The effect would be only to introduce certain non-interpretable data of the same order as others which are already present, into the complex of subjectively understandable motivation at certain points. (Thus it may come to be known that there are typical relations between the frequency of certain types of teleological orientation of action or of the degree of certain kinds of rationality and the cephalic index or skin color or any other biologically inherited characteristic.)

5. Understanding may be of two kinds: the first is the direct observational understanding[5] of the subjective meaning of a given act as such, including verbal utterances. We thus understand by direct observation, in this case, the meaning of the proposition $2 \times 2 = 4$ when we hear or read it. This is a case of the direct rational understanding of ideas. We also understand an outbreak of anger as manifested by facial expression, exclamations or irrational movements. This is direct observational understanding of irrational emotional reactions. We can understand in a similar observational way the action of a woodcutter or of somebody who reaches for the knob to shut a door or who aims a gun at an animal. This is rational observational understanding of actions.

Understanding may, however, be of another sort, namely explanatory understanding. Thus we understand in terms of *motive* the meaning an actor attaches to the proposition twice two equals four, when he states it or writes it down, in that we understand what makes him do this at precisely this moment and in these circumstances. Understanding in this sense is attained if we know that he is engaged in balancing a ledger or in making a scientific demonstration, or is engaged in some other task of which this particular act would be an appropriate part. This is rational understanding or motivation, which consists in placing the act in an intelligible and more inclusive context of meaning.[6] Thus we understand the chopping of wood or aiming of a gun in terms of motive in addition to direct observation if we know that the woodchopper is working for a wage or is chopping a supply of firewood for his own use or possibly is doing it for recreation. But he might also be working off a fit of rage, an irrational case. Similarly we understand the motive of a person aiming a gun if we know that he has been commanded to shoot as a member of a firing squad, that he is fighting against an enemy, or that he is doing it for revenge. The last is affectually determined and thus in a certain sense irrational. Finally we have a motivational understanding of the outburst of anger if we know that it has been provoked by jealousy, injured pride, or an insult. The last examples are all affectually determined and hence derived from irrational motives. In all the above cases the particular act has been placed in an understandable sequence of motivation, the understanding of which can be treated as an explanation of the actual course of behavior. Thus for a science which is concerned with the subjective meaning of action, explanation requires a grasp of the complex of meaning in which an actual course of understandable action thus interpreted belongs. In all such cases, even where the processes are largely affectual, the subjective meaning of the action, including that also of the relevant meaning complexes, will be called the intended meaning.[7] (This involves a departure from ordinary usage, which speaks of intention in this sense only in the case of rationally purposive action.)

6. In all these cases understanding involves the interpretive grasp of the meaning present in one of the following contexts: (a) as in the historical approach, the actually intended meaning for concrete individual action; or (b) as in cases of sociological mass phenomena, the average of, or an approximation to, the actually intended meaning; or (c) the meaning appropriate to a scientifically formulated pure type (an ideal type) of a common phenomenon. The concepts and "laws" of pure economic theory are examples of this kind of ideal type. They state what course a given type of human action would take if it were strictly rational, unaffected by errors or emotional factors and if, furthermore, it were completely and unequivocally directed to a single end, the maximization of economic advantage. In reality, action takes exactly this course only in unusual cases, as sometimes on the stock exchange; and even then there is usually only an approximation to the ideal type. (On the purpose of such constructions, see my essay in *AfS*, 19 [cf. n. 5] and point 11 below.)

Every interpretation attempts to attain clarity and certainty, but no matter how clear an interpretation as such appears to be from the point of view of meaning, it cannot on this account claim to be the causally valid interpretation. On this level it must remain only a peculiarly plausible hypothesis. In the first place the "conscious motives" may well, even to the actor himself, conceal the various "motives" and "repressions" which constitute the real driving force of his action. Thus in such cases even subjectively honest self-analysis has only a relative value. Then it is the task of the sociologist to be aware of this motivational situation and to describe and analyse it, even though it has not actually been concretely part of the conscious intention of the actor; possibly not at all, at least not fully. This is a borderline case of the interpretation of meaning. Secondly, processes of action which seem to an observer to be the same or similar may fit into exceedingly various complexes of motive in the case of the actual actor. Then even though the situations appear superficially to be very similar we must actually understand them or interpret them as very different, perhaps, in terms of meaning, directly opposed. (Simmel, in his *Probleme der Geschichtsphilosophie*, gives a number of examples.) Third, the actors in any given situation are often subject to opposing and conflicting impulses, all of which we are able to understand. In a large number of cases we know from experience it is not possible to arrive at even an approximate estimate of the relative strength of conflicting motives and very often we cannot be certain of our interpretation. Only the actual outcome of the conflict gives a solid basis of judgment.

More generally, verification of subjective interpretation by comparison with the concrete course of events is, as in the case of all hypotheses, indispensable. Unfortunately this type of verification is feasible with relative accuracy only in the few very special cases susceptible of psychological experimentation. In very different degrees of approximation, such verification is also feasible in the limited number of cases of mass phenomena which can be statistically described and unambiguously interpreted. For the rest there remains only the possibility of comparing the largest possible number of historical or contemporary processes which, while otherwise similar, differ in the one decisive point of their relation to the particular motive or factor the role of which is being investigated. This is a fundamental task of comparative sociology. Often, unfortunately, there is available only the uncertain procedure of the "imaginary experiment" which consists in thinking away certain elements of a chain of motivation and working out the course of action which would then probably ensue, thus arriving at a causal judgment.[8]

For example, the generalization called Gresham's Law is a rationally clear interpretation of human action under certain conditions and under the assumption that it will follow a purely rational course. How far any actual course of action corresponds to this can be verified only by the available statistical evidence for the actual disappearance of under-valued monetary units from circulation. In this case our information serves to demonstrate a high degree of accuracy. The facts of experience were known before the generalization, which was formulated afterwards; but without this successful interpretation our need for causal understanding would evidently be left unsatisfied. On the other hand, without the demonstration that what can here be assumed to be a theoretically adequate interpretation also is in some degree relevant to an actual course of action, a "law," no matter how fully demonstrated theoretically, would be worthless for the understanding of action in the real world. In this case the correspondence between the theoretical interpretation of motivation and its empirical verification is entirely satisfactory and the cases are numerous enough so that verification can be considered established. But to take another example, Eduard Meyer has advanced an ingenious theory of the causal significance of the battles of Marathon, Salamis, and Platea for the development of the cultural peculiarities of Greek, and hence, more generally, Western, civilization.[9] This is derived from a meaningful interpretation of certain symptomatic facts having to do with the attitudes of the Greek oracles and prophets towards the Persians. It can only be directly verified by reference to the examples of the conduct of the Persians in cases where they were victorious, as in Jerusalem, Egypt, and Asia Minor, and even this verification must necessarily remain unsatisfactory in certain respects. The striking rational plausibility of the hypothesis must here necessarily be relied on as a support. In very many cases of historical interpretation which seem highly plausible, however, there is not even a possibility of the order of verification which was feasible in this case. Where this is true the interpretation must necessarily remain a hypothesis.

7. A motive is a complex of subjective meaning which seems to the actor himself or to the observer an adequate ground for the conduct in question. The interpretation of a coherent course of conduct is "subjectively adequate" (or "adequate on the level of meaning"), insofar as, according to our habitual modes of thought and feeling, its component parts taken in their mutual relation are recognized to constitute a "typical" complex of meaning.[10] It is more common to say "correct." The interpretation of a sequence of events will on the other hand be called *causally* adequate insofar as, according to established generalizations from experience, there is a probability that it will always actually occur in the same way. An example of adequacy on the level of meaning in this sense is what is, according to our current norms of calculation or thinking, the correct solution of an arithmetical problem. On the other hand, a causally adequate interpretation of the same phenomenon would concern the statistical probability that, according to verified generalizations from experience, there would be a correct or an erroneous solution of the same problem. This also refers to currently accepted norms but includes taking account of typical errors or of typical confusions. Thus causal explanation depends on being able to determine that there is a probability, which in the rare ideal case can be numerically stated, but is always in some sense calculable, that a given observable event (overt or subjective) will be followed or accompanied by another event.

A correct causal interpretation of a concrete course of action is arrived at when the overt action and the motives have both been correctly apprehended and at the same time their relation has become meaningfully comprehensible. A correct causal interpretation of typical action means that the process which is claimed to be typical is shown to be both adequately grasped on the level of meaning and at the same time the interpretation is to some degree causally adequate. If adequacy in respect to meaning is lacking, then no matter how high the degree of uniformity and how precisely its probability can be numerically determined, it is still an incomprehensible statistical probability, whether we deal with overt or subjective processes. On the other hand, even the most perfect adequacy on the level of meaning has causal significance from a sociological point of view only insofar as there is some kind of proof for the existence of a probability[11] that action in fact normally takes the course which has been held to be meaningful. For this there must be some degree of determinable frequency of approximation to an average or a pure type.

Statistical uniformities constitute understandable types of action, and thus constitute sociological generalizations, only when they can be regarded as manifestations of the understandable subjective meaning of a course of social action. Conversely, formulations of a rational course of subjectively understandable action constitute sociological types of empirical process only when they can be empirically observed with a significant degree of approximation. By no means is the actual likelihood of the occurrence of a given course of overt action always directly proportional to the clarity of subjective interpretation. Only actual experience can prove whether this is so in a given case. There are statistics of processes devoid of subjective meaning, such as death rates, phenomena of fatigue, the production rate of machines, the amount of rainfall, in exactly the same sense as there are statistics of meaningful phenomena. But only when the phenomena are meaningful do we speak of sociological statistics. Examples are such cases as crime rates, occupational distributions, price statistics, and statistics of crop acreage. Naturally there are many cases where both components are involved, as in crop statistics.

8. Processes and uniformities which it has here seemed convenient not to designate as sociological phenomena or uniformities because they are not "understandable," are naturally not on that account any the less important. This is true even for sociology in our sense which is restricted to subjectively understandable phenomena — a usage which there is no intention of attempting to impose on anyone else. Such phenomena, however important, are simply treated by a different method from the others; they become conditions, stimuli, furthering or hindering circumstances of action.

9. Action in the sense of subjectively understandable orientation of behavior exists only as the behavior of one or more individual human beings. For other cognitive purposes it may be useful or necessary to consider the individual, for instance, as a collection of cells, as a complex of bio-chemical reactions, or to conceive his psychic life as made up of a variety of different elements, however these may be defined. Undoubtedly such procedures yield valuable knowledge of causal relationships. But the behavior of these elements, as expressed in such uniformities, is not subjectively understandable. This is true even of psychic elements because the more precisely they are formulated from a point of view of natural science, the less they are accessible to subjective understanding. This is never the road to interpretation in terms of subjective meaning. On the contrary, both for sociology in the present sense, and for history, the object of cognition is the subjective meaning-

complex of action. The behavior of physiological entities such as cells, or of any sort of psychic elements, may at least in principle be observed and an attempt made to derive uniformities from such observations. It is further possible to attempt, with their help, to obtain a causal explanation of individual phenomena, that is, to subsume them under uniformities. But the subjective understanding of action takes the same account of this type of fact and uniformity as of any others not capable of subjective interpretation. (This is true, for example, of physical, astronomical, geological, meteorological, geographical, botanical, zoological, and anatomical facts, of those aspects of psycho-pathology which are devoid of subjective meaning, or of the natural conditions of technological processes.)

For still other cognitive purposes — for instance, juristic ones — or for practical ends, it may on the other hand be convenient or even indispensable to treat social collectivities, such as states, associations, business corporations, foundations, as if they were individual persons. Thus they may be treated as the subjects of rights and duties or as the performers of legally significant actions. But for the subjective interpretation of action in sociological work these collectivities must be treated as *solely* the resultants and modes of organization of the particular acts of individual persons, since these alone can be treated as agents in a course of subjectively understandable action. Nevertheless, the sociologist cannot for his purposes afford to ignore these collective concepts derived from other disciplines. For the subjective interpretation of action has at least three important relations to these concepts. In the first place it is often necessary to employ very similar collective concepts, indeed often using the same terms, in order to obtain an intelligible terminology. Thus both in legal terminology and in everyday speech the term "state" is used both for the legal concept of the state and for the phenomena of social action to which its legal rules are relevant. For sociological purposes, however, the phenomenon "the state" does not consist necessarily or even primarily of the elements which are relevant to legal analysis; and for sociological purposes there is no such thing as a collective personality which "acts." When reference is made in a sociological context to a state, a nation, a corporation, a family, or an army corps, or to similar collectivities, what is meant is, on the contrary, *only* a certain kind of development of actual or possible social actions of individual persons. Both because of its precision and because it is established in general usage the juristic concept is taken over, but is used in an entirely different meaning.

Secondly, the subjective interpretation of action must take account of a fundamentally important fact. These concepts of collective entities which are found both in common sense and in juristic and other technical forms of thought, have a meaning in the minds of individual persons, partly as of something actually existing, partly as something with normative authority. This is true not only of judges and officials, but of ordinary private individuals as well. Actors thus in part orient their action to them, and in this role such ideas have a powerful, often a decisive, causal influence on the course of action of real individuals. This is above all true where the ideas involve normative prescription or prohibition. Thus, for instance, one of the important aspects of the existence of a modern state, precisely as a complex of social interaction of individual persons, consists in the fact that the action of various individuals is oriented to the belief that it exists or should exist, thus that its acts and laws are valid in the legal sense. This will be further discussed below. Though extremely pedantic and cumbersome, it would be possible, if purposes of sociological terminology alone were involved, to eliminate such terms entirely, and substitute newly-coined words. This would be possible even though the word "state" is used ordinarily not only to designate the legal concept but also the real process of action. But in the above important connexion, at least, this would naturally be impossible.

Thirdly, it is the method of the so-called "organic" school of sociology — classical example: Schäffle's brilliant work, *Bau und Leben des sozialen Körpers* — to attempt to understand social interaction by using as a point of departure the "whole" within which the individual acts. His action and behavior are then interpreted somewhat in the way that a physiologist would treat the role of an organ of the body in the "economy" of the organism, that is from the point of view of the survival of the latter. (Compare the famous dictum of a well-known physiologist: "Sec. 10. The spleen. Of the spleen, gentlemen, we know nothing. So much for the spleen." Actually, of course, he knew a good deal about the spleen — its position, size, shape, etc.; but he could say nothing about its function, and it was his inability to do this that he called "ignorance." How far in other disciplines this type of functional analysis of the relation of "parts" to a "whole" can be regarded as definitive, cannot be discussed here; but it is well known that the bio-chemical and bio-physical modes of analysis of the organism are on principle opposed to stopping there. For purposes of sociological analysis two things can be said. First this functional frame of reference is convenient for purposes of practical illustration and for provisional orientation. In these respects it is not only useful but indispensable. But at the same time if its cognitive value is overestimated and its concepts illegitimately "reified,"[12] it can be highly dangerous. Secondly, in certain circumstances this is the only available way of determining just what processes of social action it is important to understand in order to explain a given phenomenon. But this is only the beginning of sociological analysis as here understood. In the case of social collectivities, precisely as distinguished from organisms, we are in a position to go beyond merely demonstrating functional relationships and uniformities. We can accomplish something which is never attainable in the natural sciences, namely the subjective understanding of the action of the component individuals. The natural sciences on the other hand cannot do this, being limited to the formulation of causal uniformities in objects and events and the explanation of individual facts by applying them. We do not "understand" the behavior of cells, but can only observe the relevant functional relationships and generalize on the basis of these observations. This additional achievement of explanation by interpretive understanding, as distinguished from external observation is of course attained only at a price — the more hypothetical and fragmentary character of its results. Nevertheless, subjective understanding is the specific characteristic of sociological knowledge.

It would lead too far afield even to attempt to discuss how far the behavior of animals is subjectively understandable to us and vice versa; in both cases the meaning of the term understanding and its extent of application would be highly problematical. But in so far as such understanding existed it would be theoretically possible to formulate a sociology of the relations of men to animals, both domestic and wild. Thus many animals "understand" commands, anger, love, hostility, and react to them in ways which are evidently often by no means purely instinctive and mechanical and in some sense both consciously meaningful and affected by experience. In a way, our ability to share the feelings of primitive men is not very much greater. We either do not have any reliable means of determining the subjective state of mind of an animal or what we have is at best very unsatisfactory. It is well known that the problems of animal psychology, however interesting, are very thorny ones. There are in particular various forms of social organization among animals: monogamous and polygamous "families," herds, flocks, and finally "states," with a functional division of labour. (The extent of functional differentiation found in these animal societies is by no means, however, entirely a matter of the degree of organic or morphological differentiation of the individual members of the species. Thus, the functional differentiation found among the termites, and in consequence that of the products of their social activities, is much more advanced than in the case of the bees and ants.) In this field it goes without saying that a purely functional point of view is often the best that can, at least for the present, be attained, and the investigator must be content with it. Thus it is possible to study the ways in which the species provides for its survival; that is, for nutrition, defence, reproduction, and reconstruction of the social units. As the principal bearers of these functions, differentiated types of individuals can be identified: "kings," "queens," "workers," "soldiers," "drones," "propagators," "queen's substitutes," and so on. Anything more than that was for a long time merely a matter of speculation or of an attempt to determine the extent to which heredity on the one hand and environment on the other would be involved in the development of these "social" proclivities. This was particularly true of the controversies between Götte and Weismann.[13] The latter's conception in *Die Allmacht der Naturzüchtung* was largely based on wholly non-empirical deductions. But all serious authorities are naturally fully agreed that the limitation of analysis to the functional level is only a necessity imposed by our present ignorance, which it is hoped will only be temporary. (For an account of the state of knowledge of the termites, for example, see the study by Karl Escherich, *Die Termiten oder weissen Ameisen*, 1909.)

The researchers would like to understand not only the relatively obvious survival functions of these various differentiated types, but also the bearing of different variants of the theory of heredity or its reverse on the problem of explaining how these differentiations have come about. Moreover, they would like to know first what factors account for the original differentiation of specialized types from the still neutral undifferentiated species-type. Secondly, it would be important to know what leads the differentiated individual in the typical case to behave in a way which actually serves the survival of the organized group. Wherever research has made any progress in the solution of these problems it has been through the experimental demonstration of the probability or possibility of the role of chemical stimuli or physiological processes, such as nutritional states, the effects of parasitic castration, etc., in the case of the individual organism. How far there is even a hope that the existence of "subjective" or "meaningful" orientation could be made experimentally probable, even the specialist today would hardly be in a position to say. A verifiable conception of the state of mind of these social animals accessible to meaningful understanding, would seem to be attainable even as an ideal goal only within narrow limits. However that may be, a contribution to the understanding of human social action is hardly to be expected from this quarter. On the contrary, in the field of animal psychology, human analogies are and must be continually employed. The most that can be hoped for is, then, that these biological analogies may some day be useful in suggesting significant problems. For instance they may throw light on the question of the relative role in the early stages of human social differentiation of mechanical and instinctive factors, as compared with that of the factors which are accessible to subjective interpretation generally, and more particularly to the role of consciously rational action. It is necessary for the sociologist to be thoroughly aware of the fact that in the early stages even of human development, the first set of factors is completely predominant. Even in the later stages he must take account of their continual interaction with the others in a role which is often of decisive importance. This is particularly true of all "traditional" action and of many aspects of charisma, which contain the seeds of certain types of psychic "contagion" and thus give rise to new social developments. These types of action are very closely related to phenomena which are understandable either only in biological terms or can be interpreted in terms of subjective motives only in fragments. But all these facts do not discharge sociology from the obligation, in full awareness of the narrow limits to which it is confined, to accomplish what it alone can do.

The various works of Othmar Spann [1878-1950] are often full of suggestive ideas though at the same time he is guilty of occasional misunderstandings and above all of arguing on the basis of pure value judgments which have no place in an empirical investigation. But he is undoubtedly correct in doing something to which, however, no one seriously objects, namely, emphasizing the sociological significance of the functional point of view for preliminary orientation to problems. This is what he calls the "universalistic method." It is true that we must know what kind of action is functionally necessary for "survival," but even more so for the maintenance of a cultural type and the continuity of the corresponding modes of social action, before it is possible even to inquire how this action has come about and what motives determine it. It is necessary to know what a "king," an "official," an "entrepreneur," a "procurer," or a "magician" does, that is, what kind of typical action, which justifies classifying an individual in one of these categories, is important and relevant for an analysis, before it is possible to undertake the analysis itself. (This is what Rickert means by *Wertbezogenheit.*) But it is only this analysis itself which can achieve the sociological understanding of the actions of typically differentiated human (and only human) individuals, and which hence constitutes the specific function of sociology. It is a tremendous misunderstanding to think that an "individualistic" *method* should involve what is in any conceivable sense an individualistic system of *values.* It is as important to avoid this error as the related one which confuses the unavoidable tendency of sociological concepts to assume a rationalistic character with a belief in the predominance of rational motives, or even a positive valuation of rationalism. Even a socialistic economy would have to be understood sociologically in exactly the same kind of "individualistic" terms; that is, in terms of the action of individuals, the types of officials found in it, as would be the case with a system of free exchange analysed in terms of the theory of marginal utility or a "better," but in this respect similar theory). The real empirical sociological investigation begins with the question: What motives determine and lead the individual members and participants in this socialistic community to behave in such a way that the community came into being in the first place and that it continues to exist? Any form of functional analysis which proceeds from the whole to the parts can accomplish only a preliminary preparation for this investigation — a preparation, the utility and indispensability of which, if properly carried out, is naturally beyond question.

10. It is customary to designate various sociological generalizations, as for example "Gresham's Law," as "laws." These are in fact typical probabilities confirmed by observation to the effect that under certain given conditions an expected course of social action will occur, which is understandable in terms of the typical motives and typical subjective intentions of the actors. These generalizations are both understandable and definite in the highest degree insofar as the typically observed course of action can be understood in terms of the purely rational pursuit of an end, or where for reasons of methodological convenience such a theoretical type can be heuristically employed. In such cases the relations of means and end will be clearly understandable on grounds of experience, particularly where the choice of means was "inevitable." In such cases it is legitimate to assert that insofar as the action was rigorously rational it could not have taken any other course because for technical reasons, given their clearly defined ends, no other means were available to the actors. This very case demonstrates how erroneous it is to regard any kind of psychology as the ultimate foundation of the sociological interpretation of action. The term psychology, to be sure, is today understood in a wide variety of senses. For certain quite specific methodological purposes the type of treatment which attempts to follow the procedures of the natural sciences employs a distinction between "physical" and "psychic" phenomena which is entirely foreign to the disciplines concerned with human action, at least in the present sense. The results of a type of psychological investigation which employs the methods of the natural sciences in any one of various possible ways may naturally, like the results of any other science, have outstanding significance for sociological problems; indeed this has often happened. But this use of the results of psychology is something quite different from the investigation of human behavior in terms of its subjective meaning. Hence sociology has no closer relationship on a general analytical level to this type of psychology than to any other science. The source of error lies in the concept of the "psychic." It is held that everything which is not physical is *ipso facto* psychic. However, the *meaning* of a train of mathematical reasoning which a person carries out is not in the relevant sense "psychic." Similarly the rational deliberation of an actor as to whether the results of a given proposed course of action will or will not promote certain specific interests, and the corresponding decision, do not become one bit more understandable by taking "psychological" considerations into account. But it is precisely on the basis of such rational assumptions that most of the laws of sociology, including those of economics, are built up. On the other hand, in

explaining the irrationalities of action sociologically, that form of psychology which employs the method of subjective understanding undoubtedly can make decisively important contributions. But this does not alter the fundamental methodological situation.

11. We have taken for granted that sociology seeks to formulate type concepts and generalized uniformities of empirical process. This distinguishes it from history, which is oriented to the causal analysis and explanation of individual actions, structures, and personalities possessing cultural significance. The empirical material which underlies the concepts of sociology consists to a very large extent, though by no means exclusively, of the same concrete processes of action which are dealt with by historians. An important consideration in the formulation of sociological concepts and generalizations is the contribution that sociology can make toward the causal explanation of some historically and culturally important phenomenon. As in the case of every generalizing science the abstract character of the concepts of sociology is responsible for the fact that, compared with actual historical reality, they are relatively lacking in fullness of concrete content. To compensate for this disadvantage, sociological analysis can offer a greater precision of concepts. This precision is obtained by striving for the highest possible degree of adequacy on the level of meaning. It has already been repeatedly stressed that this aim can be realized in a particularly high degree in the case of concepts and generalizations which formulate rational processes. But sociological investigation attempts to include in its scope various irrational phenomena, such as prophetic, mystic, and affectual modes of action, formulated in terms of theoretical concepts which are adequate on the level of meaning. In *all* cases, rational or irrational, sociological analysis both abstracts from reality and at the same time helps us to understand it, in that it shows with what degree of approximation a concrete historical phenomenon can be subsumed under one or more of these concepts. For example, the same historical phenomenon may be in one aspect feudal, in another patrimonial, in another bureaucratic, and in still another charismatic. In order to give a precise meaning to these terms, it is necessary for the sociologist to formulate pure ideal types of the corresponding forms of action which in each case involve the highest possible degree of logical integration by virtue of their complete adequacy on the level of meaning. But precisely because this is true, it is probably seldom if ever that a real phenomenon can be found which corresponds exactly to one of these ideally constructed pure types. The case is similar to a physical reaction which has been calculated on the assumption of an absolute vacuum. Theoretical differentiation (*Kasuistik*) is possible in sociology only in terms of ideal or pure types. It goes without saying that in addition it is convenient for the sociologist from time to time to

employ average types of an empirical statistical character, concepts which do not require methodological discussion. But when reference is made to "typical" cases, the term should always be understood, unless otherwise stated, as meaning *ideal* types, which may in turn be rational or irrational as the case may be (thus in economic theory they are always rational), but in any case are always constructed with a view to adequacy on the level of meaning.

It is important to realize that in the sociological field as elsewhere, averages, and hence average types, can be formulated with a relative degree of precision only where they are concerned with differences of degree in respect to action which remains qualitatively the same. Such cases do occur, but in the majority of cases of action important to history or sociology the motives which determine it are qualitatively heterogeneous. Then it is quite impossible to speak of an "average" in the true sense. The ideal types of social action which for instance are used in economic theory are thus unrealistic or abstract in that they always ask what course of action would take place if it were purely rational and oriented to economic ends alone. This construction can be used to aid in the understanding of action not purely economically determined but which involves deviations arising from traditional restraints, affects, errors, and the intrusion of other than economic purposes or considerations. This can take place in two ways. First, in analysing the extent to which in the concrete case, or on the average for a class of cases, the action was in part economically determined along with the other factors. Secondly, by throwing the discrepancy between the actual course of events and the ideal type into relief, the analysis of the non-economic motives actually involved is facilitated. The procedure would be very similar in employing an ideal type of mystical orientation, with its appropriate attitude of indifference to worldly things, as a tool for analysing its consequences for the actor's relation to ordinary life — for instance, to political or economic affairs. The more sharply and precisely the ideal type has been constructed, thus the more abstract and unrealistic in this sense it is, the better it is able to perform its functions in formulating terminology, classifications, and hypotheses. In working out a concrete causal explanation of individual events, the procedure of the historian is essentially the same. Thus in attempting to explain the campaign of 1866, it is indispensable both in the case of Moltke and of Benedek to attempt to construct imaginatively how each, given fully adequate knowledge both of his own situation and of that of his opponent, would have acted. Then it is possible to compare with this the actual course of action and to arrive at a causal explanation of the observed deviations, which will be attributed to such factors as misinformation, strategical errors, logical fallacies, personal temperament, or considerations outside the realm of strategy. Here, too, an ideal-typical construction of rational action is actually employed even though it is not made explicit.

The theoretical concepts of sociology are ideal types not only from the objective point of view, but also in their application to subjective processes. In the great majority of cases actual action goes on in a state of inarticulate half-consciousness or actual unconsciousness of its subjective meaning. The actor is more likely to "be aware" of it in a vague sense than he is to "know" what he is doing or be explicitly self-conscious about it. In most cases his action is governed by impulse or habit. Only occasionally and, in the uniform action of large numbers, often only in the case of a few individuals, is the subjective meaning of the action, whether rational or irrational, brought clearly into consciousness. The ideal type of meaningful action where the meaning is fully conscious and explicit is a marginal case. Every sociological or historical investigation, in applying its analysis to the empirical facts, must take this fact into account. But the difficulty need not prevent the sociologist from systematizing his concepts by the classification of possible types of subjective meaning. That is, he may reason as if action actually proceeded on the basis of clearly self-conscious meaning. The resulting deviation from the concrete facts must continually be kept in mind whenever it is a question of this level of concreteness, and must be carefully studied with reference both to degree and kind. It is often necessary to choose between terms which are either clear or unclear. Those which are clear will, to be sure, have the abstractness of ideal types, but they are none the less preferable for scientific purposes. (On all these questions see "'Objectivity' in Social Science and Social Policy.")

B. Social Action

1. Social action, which includes both failure to act and passive acquiescence, may be oriented to the past, present, or expected future behavior of others. Thus it may be motivated by revenge for a past attack, defence against present, or measures of defence against future aggression. The "others" may be individual persons, and may be known to the actor as such, or may constitute an indefinite plurality and may be entirely unknown as individuals. (Thus, money is a means of exchange which the actor accepts in payment because he orients his action to the expectation that a large but unknown number of individuals he is personally unacquainted with will be ready to accept it in exchange on some future occasion.)

2. Not every kind of action, even of overt action, is "social" in the sense of the present discussion. Overt action is non-social if it is oriented solely to the behavior of inanimate objects. Subjective attitudes constitute social action only so far as they are oriented to the behavior of others. For example,

religious behavior is not social if it is simply a matter of contemplation or of solitary prayer. The economic activity of an individual is social only if it takes account of the behavior of someone else. Thus very generally it becomes social insofar as the actor assumes that others will respect his actual control over economic goods. Concretely it is social, for instance, if in relation to the actor's own consumption the future wants of others are taken into account and this becomes one consideration affecting the actor's own saving. Or, in another connexion, production may be oriented to the future wants of other people.

3. Not every type of contact of human beings has a social character; this is rather confined to cases where the actor's behavior is meaningfully oriented to that of others. For example, a mere collision of two cyclists may be compared to a natural event. On the other hand, their attempt to avoid hitting each other, or whatever insults, blows, or friendly discussion might follow the collision, would constitute "social action."

4. Social action is not identical either with the similar actions of many persons or with every action influenced by other persons. Thus, if at the beginning of a shower a number of people on the street put up their umbrellas at the same time, this would not ordinarily be a case of action mutually oriented to that of each other, but rather of all reacting in the same way to the like need of protection from the rain. It is well known that the actions of the individual are strongly influenced by the mere fact that he is a member of a crowd confined within a limited space. Thus, the subject matter of studies of "crowd psychology," such as those of Le Bon, will be called "action conditioned by crowds." It is also possible for large numbers, though dispersed, to be influenced simultaneously or successively by a source of influence operating similarly on all the individuals, as by means of the press. Here also the behavior of an individual is influenced by his membership in a "mass" and by the fact that he is aware of being a member. Some types of reaction are only made possible by the mere fact that the individual acts as part of a crowd. Others become more difficult under these conditions. Hence it is possible that a particular event or mode of human behavior can give rise to the most diverse kinds of feeling — gaiety, anger, enthusiasm, despair, and passions of all sorts — in a crowd situation which would not occur at all or not nearly so readily if the individual were alone. But for this to happen there need not, at least in many cases, be any meaningful relation between the behavior of the individual and the fact that he is a member of a crowd. It is not proposed in the present sense to call action "social" when it is merely a result of the effect on the individual of the existence of a crowd as such and the action is not oriented to that fact on the level of meaning. At the same time the borderline is naturally highly indefinite. In such cases as that of the influence of the demagogue, there may be a wide variation in the extent to

which his mass clientele is affected by a meaningful reaction to the fact of its large numbers; and whatever this relation may be, it is open to varying interpretations.

But furthermore, mere "imitation" of the action of others, such as that on which Tarde had rightly laid emphasis, will not be considered a case of specifically social action if it is purely reactive so that there is no meaningful orientation to the actor imitated. The borderline is, however, so indefinite that it is often hardly possible to discriminate. The mere fact that a person is found to employ some apparently useful procedure which he learned from someone else does not, however, constitute, in the present sense, social action. Action such as this is not oriented to the action of the other person, but the actor has, through observing the other, become acquainted with certain objective facts; and it is these to which his action is oriented. His action is then *causally* determined by the action of others, but not meaningfully. On the other hand, if the action of others is imitated because it is fashionable or traditional or exemplary, or lends social distinction, or on similar grounds, it is meaningfully oriented either to the behavior of the source of imitation or of third persons or of both. There are of course all manner of transitional cases between the two types of imitation. Both the phenomena discussed above, the behavior of crowds and imitation, stand on the indefinite borderline of social action. The same is true, as will often appear, of traditionalism and charisma. The reason for the indefiniteness of the line in these and other cases lies in the fact that both the orientation to the behavior of others and the meaning which can be imputed by the actor himself, are by no means always capable of clear determination and are often altogether unconscious and seldom fully self-conscious. Mere "influence" and meaningful orientation cannot therefore always be clearly differentiated on the empirical level. But conceptually it is essential to distinguish them, even though merely reactive imitation may well have a degree of sociological importance at least equal to that of the type which can be called social action in the strict sense. Sociology, it goes without saying, is by no means confined to the study of social action; this is only, at least for the kind of sociology being developed here, its central subject matter, that which may be said to be decisive for its status as a science. But this does not imply any judgment on the comparative importance of this and other factors.

Types of Social Action

Social action, like all action, may be oriented in four ways. It may be:

(1) *instrumentally rational* (*zweckrational*), that is, determined by expectations

as to the behavior of objects in the environment and of other human beings; these expectations are used as "conditions" or "means" for the attainment of the actor's own rationally pursued and calculated ends;

(2) *value-rational* (*wertrational*), that is, determined by a conscious belief in the value for its own sake of some ethical, aesthetic, religious, or other form of behavior, independently of its prospects of success;

(3) *affectual* (especially emotional), that is, determined by the actor's specific affects and feeling states;

(4) *traditional*, that is, determined by ingrained habituation.

1. Strictly traditional behavior, like the reactive type of imitation discussed above, lies very close to the borderline of what can justifiably be called meaningfully oriented action, and indeed often on the other side. For it is very often a matter of almost automatic reaction to habitual stimuli which guide behavior in a course which has been repeatedly followed. The great bulk of all everyday action to which people have become habitually accustomed approaches this type. Hence, its place in a systematic classification is not merely that of a limiting case because, as will be shown later, attachment to habitual forms can be upheld with varying degrees of self-consciousness and in a variety of senses. In this case the type may shade over into value rationality (*Wertrationalität*).

2. Purely affectual behavior also stands on the borderline of what can be considered "meaningfully" oriented, and often it, too, goes over the line. It may, for instance, consist in an uncontrolled reaction to some exceptional stimulus. It is a case of sublimation when affectually determined action occurs in the form of conscious release of emotional tension. When this happens it is usually well on the road to rationalization in one or the other or both of the above senses.

3. The orientation of value-rational action is distinguished from the affectual type by its clearly self-conscious formulation of the ultimate values governing the action and the consistently planned orientation of its detailed course to these values. At the same time the two types have a common element, namely that the meaning of the action does not lie in the achievement of a result ulterior to it, but in carrying out the specific type of action for its own sake. Action is affectual if it satisfies a need for revenge, sensual gratification, devotion, contemplative bliss, or for working off emotional tensions (irrespective of the level of sublimation).

Examples of pure value-rational orientation would be the actions of persons who, regardless of possible cost to themselves, act to put into practice their convictions of what seems to them to be required by duty, honor, the pursuit of beauty, a religious call, personal loyalty, or the importance of some "cause" no matter in what it consists. In our terminology, value-rational action always involves "commands" or "demands" which, in the actor's opinion, are binding on him. It is only in cases where human action is motivated by the fulfillment of such unconditional demands that it will be called value-rational. This is the case in widely varying degrees, but for the most part only to a relatively slight extent. Nevertheless, it will be shown that the occurrence of this mode of action is important enough to justify its formulation as a distinct type; though it may be remarked that there is no intention here of attempting to formulate in any sense an exhaustive classification of types of action.

4. Action is instrumentally rational (*zweckrational*) when the end, the means, and the secondary results are all rationally taken into account and weighed. This involves rational consideration of alternative means to the end, of the relations of the end to the secondary consequences, and finally of the relative importance of different possible ends. Determination of action either in affectual or traditional terms is thus incompatible with this type. Choice between alternative and conflicting ends and results may well be determined in a value-rational manner. In that case, action is instrumentally rational only in respect to the choice of means. On the other hand, the actor may, instead of deciding between alternative and conflicting ends in terms of a rational orientation to a system of values, simply take them as given subjective wants and arrange them in a scale of consciously assessed relative urgency. He may then orient his action to this scale in such a way that they are satisfied as far as possible in order of urgency, as formulated in the principle of "marginal utility." Value-rational action may thus have various different relations to the instrumentally rational action. From the latter point of view, however, value-rationality is always irrational. Indeed, the more the value to which action is oriented is elevated to the status of an absolute value, the more "irrational" in this sense the corresponding action is. For, the more unconditionally the actor devotes himself to this value for its own sake, to pure sentiment or beauty, to absolute goodness or devotion to duty, the less is he influenced by considerations of the consequences of his action. The orientation of action wholly to the rational achievement of ends without relation to fundamental values is, to be sure, essentially only a limiting case.

5. It would be very unusual to find concrete cases of action, especially of social action, which were oriented *only* in one or another of these ways. Furthermore, this classification of the modes of orientation of action is in no sense meant to exhaust the possibilities of the field, but only to formulate in conceptually pure form certain sociologically important types to which actual action is more or less closely approximated or, in much the more common case, which constitute its elements. The usefulness of the classification for the purposes of this investigation can only be judged in terms of its results.

3. The Concept of Social Relationship

The term "social relationship" will be used to denote the behavior of a plurality of actors insofar as, in its meaningful content, the action of each takes account of that of the others and is oriented in these terms. The social relationship thus consists entirely and exclusively in the existence of a probability that there will be a meaningful course of social action — irrespective, for the time being, of the basis for this probability.

1. Thus, as a defining criterion, it is essential that there should be at least a minimum of mutual orientation of the action of each to that of the others. Its content may be of the most varied nature: conflict, hostility, sexual attraction, friendship, loyalty, or economic exchange. It may involve the fulfillment, the evasion, or the violation of the terms of an agreement; economic, erotic, or some other form of "competition"; common membership in status, national or class groups (provided it leads to social action). Hence, the definition does not specify whether the relation of the actors is co-operative or the opposite.

2. The "meaning" relevant in this context is always a case of the meaning imputed to the parties in a given concrete case, on the average, or in a theoretically formulated pure type — it is never a normatively "correct" or a metaphysically "true" meaning. Even in cases of such forms of social organization as a state, church, association, or marriage, the social relationship consists exclusively in the fact that there has existed, exists, or will exist a probability of action in some definite way appropriate to this meaning. It is vital to be continually clear about this in order to avoid the "reification" of those concepts. A "state," for example, ceases to exist in a sociologically relevant sense whenever there is no longer a probability that certain kinds of meaningfully oriented social action

178 / Sociological Thought

will take place. This probability may be very high or it may be negligibly low. But in any case it is only in the sense and degree in which it does exist that the corresponding social relationship exists. It is impossible to find any other clear meaning for the statement that, for instance, a given "state" exists or has ceased to exist.

3. The subjective meaning need not necessarily be the same for all the parties who are mutually oriented in a given social relationship; there need not in this sense be "reciprocity." "Friendship," "love," "loyalty," "fidelity to contracts," "patriotism," on one side, may well be faced with an entirely different attitude on the other. In such cases the parties associate different meanings with their actions, and the social relationship is insofar objectively "asymmetrical" from the points of view of the two parties. It may nevertheless be a case of mutual orientation insofar as, even though partly or wholly erroneously, one party presumes a particular attitude toward him on the part of the other and orients his action to this expectation. This can, and usually will, have consequences for the course of action and the form of the relationship. A relationship is objectively symmetrical only as, according to the typical expectations of the parties, the meaning for one party is the same as that for the other. Thus the actual attitude of a child to its father may be a least approximately that which the father, in the individual case, on the average or typically, has come to expect. A social relationship in which the attitudes are completely and fully corresponding is in reality a limiting case. But the absence of reciprocity will, for terminological purposes, be held to exclude the existence of a social relationship only if it actually results in the absence of a mutual orientation of the action of the parties. Here as elsewhere all sorts of transitional cases are the rule rather than the exception.

4. A social relationship can be of a very fleeting character or of varying degrees of permanence. In the latter case there is a probability of the repeated recurrence of the behavior which corresponds to its subjective meaning and hence is expected. In order to avoid fallacious impressions, let it be repeated that it is *only* the existence of the probability that, corresponding to a given subjective meaning, a certain type of action will take place which constitutes the "existence" of the social relationship. Thus that a "friendship" or a "state" exists or has existed means this and only this: that we, the observers, judge that there is or has been a probability that on the basis of certain kinds of known subjective attitude of certain individuals there will result in the average sense a certain specific type of action. For the purposes of legal reasoning it is essential to be able to decide

whether a rule of law does or does not carry legal authority, hence whether a legal relationship does or does not "exist." This type of question is not, however, relevant to sociological problems.

5. The subjective meaning of a social relationship may change, thus a political relationship once based on solidarity may develop into a conflict of interests. In that case it is only a matter of terminological convenience and of the degree of continuity of the change whether we say that a new relationship has come into existence or that the old one continues but has acquired a new meaning. It is also possible for the meaning to be partly constant, partly changing.

6. The meaningful content which remains relatively constant in a social relationship is capable of formulation in terms of maxims which the parties concerned expect to be adhered to by their partners on the average and approximately. The more rational in relation to values or to given ends the action is, the more is this likely to be the case. There is far less possibility of a rational formulation of subjective meaning in the case of a relation of erotic attraction or of personal loyalty or any other affectual type than, for example, in the case of a business contract.

7. The meaning of a social relationship may be agreed upon by mutual consent. This implies that the parties make promises covering their future behavior, whether toward each other or toward third persons. In such cases each party then normally counts, so far as he acts rationally, in some degree on the fact that the other will orient his action to the meaning of the agreement as he (the first actor) understands it. In part he orients his action rationally (*zweckrational*) to these expectations as given facts with, to be sure, varying degrees of subjectively "loyal" intention of doing his part. But in part also he is motivated value-rationally by a sense of duty, which makes him adhere to the agreement as he understands it. This much may be anticipated.

PROTESTANT ASCETICISM AND THE SPIRIT OF CAPITALISM

In order to grasp the connexions between the fundamental religious ideas of ascetic Protestantism and its maxims of everyday economic life, it is necessary above all to refer to those theological writings which can be seen to have had their origins in pastoral practice. For, in a time when the next world was everything, when the social position of the Christian depended on his admission to communion, and when the influence exercised by the clergy in the cure of souls, in church discipline and in preaching, was of a kind which (as the merest glance at the collections of *'consilia'*, *'casus conscientiae'*, etc. will show) we modern men simply cannot any longer begin to imagine, the religious forces at work in pastoral practice are the decisive influences in forming 'national character'.

For the purposes of our discussion in this section, as opposed to later discussions, we may treat ascetic Protestantism as a single undifferentiated whole. But since that kind of English Puritanism which had its roots in Calvinism affords the most consistent attempt to work out the basis of the idea of the 'calling', we may, in accordance with our principle, take one of its representatives as the focus of our discussion. Richard Baxter is distinguished above many other literary representatives of the Puritan ethic by his eminently practical and conciliatory attitude, and also by the universal recognition of his constantly republished and translated works. A Presbyterian and an apologist for the Westminster Synod, he nevertheless gradually, like so many of the best minds of his time, moved away in his doctrinal views from the extreme Calvinist position. He was at heart an opponent of Cromwell's usurpation, as of every revolution, with a distaste for sectarianism, above all for the fanatical zeal of the 'Saints', but a very liberal attitude towards peculiarities of external practice, combined with an objective approach to his opponents. He sought his field of work essentially in the direction of the practical advancement of the moral life of the Church, and in this work he was willing to serve, as one of the most successful pastors known to history,[1] indifferently under the Parliamentary regime, Cromwell or the Restoration. He finally retired under the Restoration — before St Bartholomew's day. His 'Christian Directory' is the most comprehensive compendium of Puritan moral theology, relating its theology at every point to his own practical experience as a pastor. For comparison, we have taken Spener's *'Theologische Bedenken'* to represent German Pietism and Barclay's 'Apology' to represent Quakerism, together with other representatives of the ascetic ethic;[2] to save space, these comparisons will be made as far as possible in the footnotes.[3]

To pick up Baxter's 'Saints Everlasting Rest' or his 'Christian Directory', or some similar works by other writers,[4] is immediately to be struck by the emphasis placed, in the judgments on riches[5] and their acquisition, precisely on the Ebionitic elements in New Testament teaching.[6] Riches as such are a grave danger, their temptations unremitting, the effort[7] to acquire them not only senseless when compared with the surpassing importance of the Kingdom of God, but also morally hazardous. Asceticism seems in these passages to be directed against all striving to acquire temporal goods, to a much greater extent than in Calvin, who found in riches no hindrance to the clergy's activity, but on the contrary a totally desirable means of increasing their authority, and who allowed them to invest their wealth at a profit as long as they avoided scandal. Examples of this kind of condemnation of the pursuit of money and possessions can readily and abundantly be found in Puritan writings, and contrasted with late medieval ethical literature, which was much more free and easy in this respect. Moreover, the intentions behind these reflections were absolutely serious: though it is only on a somewhat closer examination that their decisive ethical meaning and implications become clear. The real object of moral condemnation is, in particular, relaxation in the possession of property[8] and enjoyment of riches, resulting in sloth and the lusts of the flesh, and above all in distraction from the pursuit of a 'holy' life. And it is only because possessions bring with them the risk of this kind of relaxation that they are hazardous. For the 'Saints' everlasting rest' lies in the next world: on earth, however, man too must, if he is to be sure of being in a state of grace, 'work the works of Him that sent him, while it is day'. Not sloth and enjoyment, but only activity, according to the unambiguously revealed will of God, serves to increase His glory.[9]

To waste time is thus the first and, in principle, the worst of all sins. The span of life is infinitely short and precious if one is to 'make sure of' one's election. To lose time through sociability, 'idle talk',[10] extravagance,[11] even through more sleep than is necessary for health[12] (six to at most eight hours), is considered worthy of total moral condemnation.[13] Franklin's remark that 'Time is money' is not yet found, but the proposition is true, so to speak, in a spiritual sense: it is infinitely valuable, since every hour lost is taken away from work in the service of God's glory.[14] Hence, passive contemplation is also valueless, indeed in some cases actually objectionable, at least when indulged in at the expense of work in one's calling.[15] For to God it is less pleasing than the active fulfilment of His will in one's calling.[16] Besides, Sunday exists for that purpose, and it is, according to Baxter, always those who are lazy in their calling who have no time for God even at the hour appointed for that purpose.[17]

Accordingly, Baxter's principal work has as one of its central themes a constantly repeated, at times almost passionate, advocacy of hard, unremitting, physical or intellectual work.[18] Two motifs are combined here.[19] First, work is a well-tried ascetic method, and in the Western Church, in sharp contrast not only with the Eastern, but also with almost all forms of monasticism anywhere in the world,[20] it has been approved as such from earliest times.[21] It is especially the specific prophylactic against all those temptations which Puritanism subsumes under the concept of 'unclean life'; and their role is by no means negligible. Indeed, sexual asceticism differs only in degree, not in underlying principle, from monasticism and precisely because its conception of marriage is more far-reaching. For even in marriage, sexual intercourse is permissible only as the means willed by God to increase His glory, in accordance with the commandment 'Be fruitful and multiply'.[22] The prescription against all sexual temptations, as against religious doubt and the torments of excessive self-examination, is (apart from moderation in diet, vegetarianism and cold baths) 'Labour hard in your calling'.[23]

But over and above that, and most important of all, labour is a divinely commanded ultimate end of life as a whole.[24] St. Paul's assertion, 'If any would not work, neither should he eat', holds unconditionally and for everyone.[25] Disinclination for work is a symptom of a fall from the state of grace.[26]

The difference from the medieval attitude is clearly to be seen here. Thomas Aquinas had also offered an interpretation of the saying just quoted. But according to him[27] work is necessary only in a naturalistic sense for the preservation of the life of the individual and the community. Where this purpose no longer applies, the commandment is no longer valid. It applies only to the species as a whole, not to every individual member. Anyone who can live off his property without work is not included in the commandment, and equally, contemplation, as a spiritual activity in the Kingdom of God, is naturally outside the scope of the commandment in its literal interpretation. For popular theology, finally, the highest form of monastic 'productivity' lay in its contribution to the 'treasury of the Church' through prayer and choral singing. Not only does Baxter, however, naturally not permit such exceptions to the ethical obligation to work: he also preaches with the greatest possible emphasis that even wealth does not excuse anyone from that unconditional commandment.[28] Even the man of property may not eat without working, for, even if he is not compelled to work in order to supply his needs, there is still God's commandment, which he must obey as much as the poor man.[29] For divine providence has prepared for everyone without distinction a particular *calling*, which he must recognise and in which he must work, and this calling is not, as in Lutheranism,[30] a fate to which one must submit and with which one must be content, but a commandment of God to the individual to work to His glory. This apparently slight shade of difference had far-reaching psychological consequences, and went together with the further evolution of that providential interpretation of the economic order which was already current in Scholasticism.

The phenomenon of the division of labour and the distribution of occupations in society had already been interpreted by, amongst others, Thomas Aquinas (to whom we can again most conveniently refer) as flowing directly from the divine plan for the world. But the classification of men within this cosmic order results from natural causes and is, in the Scholastic terminology, 'contingent'. For Luther, as we saw, the classification of men into given estates and occupations resulting from an objective historical order was taken to flow directly from the divine will, and it therefore became for him a religious duty for the individual to persevere in the position and within the limits assigned to him by God.[31] This was all the more true, in that the relationship of Lutheran piety to the 'world' in general was initially, and continued to be, uncertain. It was impossible to extract from Luther's system of ideas, which never entirely shed its Pauline indifference to the world, any ethical principles for the organisation of the world: the world had to be taken as it was, and this alone constituted one's religious duty.

In the Puritan view, on the other hand, there is a different nuance to the providential character of the interplay of private economic interest. True to the Puritan scheme of pragmatic interpretation, the providential purpose of the classification of occupations is to be recognised by their fruits. On these Baxter expresses himself in ways which, at more than one point, are directly reminiscent of Adam Smith's well-known apotheosis of the division of labour.[32] The specialisation of occupations, because it gives scope for the *skill* of the worker, leads to a quantitative and qualitative increase in the performance of work and so serves the common good, or 'common best', which is identified with the good of the greatest possible number. If the motivation is so far purely utilitarian and closely related to a number of views which had already become commonplace in the secular literature of the time,[33] the characteristically Puritan overtones become obvious as soon as Baxter begins his discussion with the theme, 'Outside of a well-marked calling the accomplishments of a man are only casual and irregular, and he spends more time in idleness than at work', and when he concludes by saying, 'and he [the worker with a calling] will carry out his work in order while another remains in constant confusion, and his business knows neither time nor place[34]... therefore is a certain calling the best for everyone.' The irregular work in which the ordinary day-labourer is compelled to engage is an often unavoidable, but always regrettable compromise. The life of those without a calling lacks the systematic and methodical character required, as we saw, by inner-worldly asceticism.

In the Quaker ethic, too, the working life of man is to be a consistent ascetic exercise in virtue, a proof of one's state of grace in the conscientiousness which is apparent in the careful and methodical way in which one follows one's calling.[35] Not work as such, but rational work in a calling, is what God requires. In the Puritan idea of the 'calling' the emphasis is always on this methodical asceticism in the practice of one's calling, not, as in Luther, on contentment with the lot once and for all assigned to one by God.[36] Hence, not only will the question whether anyone can combine several callings be answered with an unconditional 'Yes', provided it is beneficial either for the general good or for one's own[37] and not injurious to anyone else, and provided that it does not lead to unconscientiousness or 'unfaithfulness' in one of the callings so combined. But also it will not be regarded as in any way in itself objectionable to change one's calling, provided it is not done frivolously but in order to take up a calling which will be more pleasing to God,[38] that is, in accordance with the general principle, a more useful one. Above all, how useful a calling is, and so how pleasing it is to God, depends in the first instance on its moral benefits, secondly on the degree of importance for the community of the goods to be produced in it, and thirdly (and this is naturally the most important from the practical point of view) on its 'profitability' for the individual.[39] For, if the God Whom the Puritan sees at work in all the coincidences of life reveals a chance of profit to one of His own, He has a purpose in so doing. Consequently, the faithful Christian must follow this call, by turning it to good account.[40] 'If God show you a way in which you may lawfully get more than in another way (without wrong to your soul or to any other), if you refuse this, and choose the less gainful way, you cross one of the ends of your calling, and you refuse to be God's steward, and to accept His gifts and use them for Him when He requireth it: you may labour to be rich for God, though not for the flesh and sin'.[41] Riches are only dangerous as a temptation to idle repose and sinful enjoyment of life, and the endeavour to acquire them is only suspect when its purpose is to enable one later to live a life of frivolity and gaiety. When it is engaged in as part of the duties of the calling, however, it is not only morally permissible but positively commanded.[42] The parable of the servant who was rejected because he had not profited from the talent which was entrusted to him seemed to express that idea in explicit terms.[43] To wish to be poor was, as was frequently argued, the same as to wish to be ill:[44] as a form of justification by works, it would be objectionable and detrimental to the glory of God. Finally, begging by anyone fit to work is not only sinful in that it is an instance of sloth, but also, in the Apostle's words, contrary to the love of one's neighbour.[45]

As the teaching of the ascetic significance of a regular calling sheds an ethical aura around the modern specialised expert, so the providential interpretation of the chances of profit does for the businessman.[46] The aristocratic self-indulgence of the seigneur and the parvenu ostentation of the snob are equally hateful to asceticism. On the other and, the full radiance of ethical approval falls on the sober bourgeois self-made man:[47] 'God blesseth his trade' is a standard way of referring to those Saints[48] who have successfully followed up the divine dispensation. The whole weight of the Old Testament God, Who rewards His own for their piety precisely in *this* life,[49] was bound to influence in the same direction the Puritan, who, following Baxter's advice, checked his own state of grace by comparing it with the spiritual condition of the Biblical heroes,[50] and in so doing interpreted the statements of the Bible 'as if they were paragraphs in a code of law'.

In themselves, indeed, the statements of the Old Testament were not entirely unambiguous. We saw that, linguistically speaking, Luther was the first to use the term 'calling' in the worldly sense in his translation of a passage in Jesus Sirach. The book of Jesus Sirach, however, in spite of the Hellenistic influences at work in it, belongs in its whole atmosphere to the traditionalist sections of the (expanded) Old Testament. It is characteristic that, right up to the present day, this book seems to enjoy a special popularity among the Lutheran peasantry of Germany,[51] just as the fundamentally Lutheran character of the main tendencies in German Pietism used to find expression in the popularity of Jesus Sirach.[52] The Puritans rejected the Apocrypha on the grounds that it was not inspired, in conformity with their strict 'either-or' attitude to the distinction between the divine and the creaturely.[53] This meant that, among the canonical books, the Book of Job had all the greater impact, with its combination of, on the one hand, a sublime glorification of God's absolutely sovereign and totally superhuman majesty — so congenial as it was to Calvinist views — with the sense of certainty which overflows again in the conclusion (as trivial for Calvin as it was important for Puritanism) that God will bless His own also and precisely — and, in the Book of Job, only! — in this life and in material terms.[54] The Oriental quietism which pervades several of the most moving verses of the Psalms and the Book of Proverbs was explained away in the same way as Baxter explained away the traditionalist overtones of the passage in the First Epistle to the Corinthians which was definitive for the concept of the calling. For this reason all the more emphasis was laid on those passages in the Old Testament which extol formal righteousness as the criterion of conduct which is pleasing to God. The theory that the Mosaic Law had only lost its validity under the new convenant to the extent that it contained ceremonial or historically limited prescriptions for the Jewish people, but that otherwise it was an expression of Natural Law and so had always had and still retained its validity,[55] made it possible, on the one hand, to eliminate prescriptions which were simply inappropriate to modern life, while giving free rein to the considerable reinforcement of that spirit of self-righteous and sober legalism so characteristic of the inner-worldly asceticism of this kind of Protestantism, by the many related features of Old Testament morality.[56]

Thus, if several contemporaries, like a number of more recent writers, dubbed the basic ethical temper of English Puritanism in particular 'English Hebraism',[57] this was, rightly understood, a perfectly apt description. It is not, however, the Palestinian Judaism of the time when the Old Testament writings were emerging which should come to mind, but the Judaism which gradually evolved under the influence of many centuries of formalistic education in the Law and the Talmud, and even then one must be extremely cautious about drawing parallels. The temper of ancient Judaism, which was on the whole inclined to the tolerant appreciation of life as such, was very different from the specific character of Puritanism. Equally different — and this should not be overlooked — were the economic ethics of medieval and modern Judaism in those respects which were decisive for the place which both hold in the development of the capitalist ethos. Judaism was on the side of the politically or speculatively orientated 'adventurist capitalism': its ethos was, in a word, that the pariah capitalism. Puritanism, on the other hand, was the vehicle for the ethos of the rational bourgeois enterprise and the rational organisation of labour. It took from the Jewish ethos only what fitted into this framework.

It would be impossible, within the limits of this sketch, to analyse the characterological consequences of this permeation of life by Old Testament standards, though this would be an exciting task, which has not, however, as yet been undertaken even for Judaism itself.[58] Apart from the connexions already pointed out, one feature of the general mental attitude of the Puritan which above all deserves consideration is that in him there was a spectacular rebirth of the belief that one belonged to God's chosen people.[59] Even the gentle Baxter thanks God for the fact that He has allowed him to be born in England and in the true Church and not anywhere else: and in the same way this gratitude for the freedom from sin achieved for the individual by God's grace permeated the attitude to life[60] of the Puritan bourgeoisie and gave rise to that formalistically correct hardness of character typical of the representatives of that heroic epoch of capitalism.

We shall now seek to elucidate the special points at which the Puritan conception of the calling and the requirement of asceticism in one's conduct of life were bound to have a direct influence on the development of the capitalist mode of life. As we saw, asceticism turns with full force against one thing above all — the relaxed enjoyment of life and the pleasures which it has to offer. This feature is well expressed in its most characteristic form in the controversy over the 'Book of Sports',[61] which James I and Charles I sought to enforce by law with the avowed aim of attacking Puritanism, and which Charles I commanded to be read aloud from all pulpits. When the Puritans fought like madmen against the King's decree legally permitting certain traditional popular amusements on Sundays outside the times of church services, it was not only the disturbance of the Sabbath peace which enraged them, but the whole deliberate deviation from the ordered way of life of the Saints. And when the King threatened to impose severe penalties on every attack on the legality of those sports, his purpose was precisely to break that asceticism, which was dangerous to the state because it was anti-authoritarian. The monarchic and feudal society protected those who wanted to amuse themselves against the emergent bourgeois morality and the ascetic conventicle, with its hostile attitude to authority, just as today capitalist society protects those who want to work against the class morality of the workers and the trade union, with its hostile attitude to authority. The Puritans defended against this their most important characteristic, the principle of the ascetic conduct of life. For, apart from this, the antipathy of the Puritans, even of the Quakers, for sport was not a pure matter of principle. They required only that sport should serve a rational purpose, the recreation necessary to enable one to be physically capable of work. As a means of pure relaxed enjoyment for unruly instincts, on the other hand, it was suspect to the Puritan; and to the extent that it became a straightforward means of pleasure or aroused competitive jealousy, raw instinct or the irrational desire to gamble, it was obviously utterly objectionable. Instinctive enjoyment of life, which attracts one away from work at one's calling as much as from religious devotion, was equally the enemy of rational asceticism, whether it took the form of 'aristocratic' sport or of the ordinary man's visits to dance halls or taverns.[62]

The attitude to those cultural goods which do not have a directly religious value is correspondingly distrustful, and often hostile. It is not as if a dismal, philistine contempt for culture was any part of the Puritan ideal. Exactly the opposite is true, at least in the case of science — with the exception of the abhorred Scholasticism. The greatest figures of the Puritan movement, moreover, are steeped in the culture of the Renaissance: the sermons of the Presbyterian wing of the movement drip with classicisms,[63] and even those of the Radicals do not disdain that kind of learning in theological polemics, despite the fact that they certainly found it cause for scandal. Never, perhaps has any country so abounded in 'graduates' as did New England in the first generation of its existence. The satires of their opponents, such as Butler's 'Hudibras', were directed precisely against the book-learning and sophisticated dialectical skills of the Puritans; and this fits in partly with their religious evaluation of knowledge, which follows from their attitude to the Catholic conception of 'implicit faith'.

Quite a different situation confronts one as soon as one enters the realm of non-scientific literature[64] and even more when one considers the visual arts. Here, it must be admitted, asceticism lay like a frost on the life of Merry England. And it was not only the secular festivals which were affected by it. The passionate hatred of the Puritan for everything which smelt of 'superstition', for everything reminiscent of magical or ritual means of grace, pursued the Christian festival of Christmas as much as it did the Maypole[65] or the easy-going religious use of art. The fact that there was still room in Holland for the development of a great tradition of often robustly realistic art[66] shows merely how little could be achieved in this direction by the attempt in that country at an authoritarian regulation of morals on its own against the influence of the Court and the Regents (a class of *rentiers*). It also shows, however, the joy in life of the newly rich petty bourgeois, after the brief domination of the Calvinist theocracy had settled down into a more prosaic state church and Calvinism had thus perceptibly lost its power of propaganda in the cause of asceticism.[67]

The theatre was abhorrent to the Puritans,[68] and with the rigorous exclusion of eroticism and nudity from the domain of what was possible, the more radical approach, in literature as in art, could not continue to exist. The concepts of 'idle talk', 'superfluities',[69] 'vain ostentation', all of which referred to forms of behaviour which were irrational and purposeless, and so not ascetic, and serving the glory of man rather than God, were ready to hand to give decisive support to sober purposiveness against every kind of use of artistic motifs. Finally, this applied also to all forms of direct adornment of the person, as, for example, in styles of clothing.[70] The powerful tendency towards uniformity in styles of life which is nowadays supported by the capitalist interest in the 'standardisation' of production[71] had its intellectual origin in the rejection of the 'idolatry of the creature'.[72] Certainly, it should not be forgotten in all this that Puritanism contained within itself a world of contradictions, that the instinctive feeling for what is timelessly great in art was certainly stronger among its leaders than in the milieu of the Cavaliers,[73] and that a unique genius like Rembrandt, however far his mode of life may have fallen short of finding complete favour in the eyes of the Puritan God, was certainly greatly influenced in the direction which his creative activity took by his sectarian environment.[74] But that alters nothing in the general picture, to the extent that the powerfully intensified sense of personality, which accompanied and which was, indeed, partly a result of the further development of the Puritan atmosphere, had its most beneficial effects in literature, and even there not until later generations.

Without being able to enter into a more detailed discussion here of the influence of Puritanism in all these directions, we should remember only that there was always at least one characteristic limit to the toleration of delight in the kind of cultural goods which are valued only for the sake of aesthetic or sporting pleasure: that was that they should not cost anything. Man is but the steward of the goods allotted to him by God's grace, and, like the servant in the Bible, he has to give an account of every penny entrusted to him:[75] it is at the very least questionable, therefore, to spend any of his money for a purpose which serves, not God's grace, but his own pleasure.[76] Who is there who keeps his eyes open who has not encountered people who think in this way even in the present day?[77] The thought that man has obligations towards the possessions entrusted to him, to which he subordinated himself either as obedient steward or actually as a 'machine for acquisition', lays its chilly hand on life. The greater the possessions become, the sterner becomes — provided the ascetic attitude to life can stand the test — the sense of responsibility for them, the feeling that one must preserve them undiminished for God's glory and increase them by unceasing labour. The genesis of this way of life, too, like so many elements of the modern capitalist spirit, reaches back in its individual parts to the Middle Ages,[78] but its first coherent ethical foundations are to be found in the ethic of ascetic Protestantism. Its importance for the development of capitalism is clear to see.[79]

We might summarise what has been said so far by saying that inner-worldly Protestant asceticism used all its power against the relaxed enjoyment of possessions: it sets limits to consumption, especially luxury consumption. On the other hand, it had the psychological effect of liberating the acquisition of goods from the restrictions of the traditionalist ethic: it burst the shackles confining the profit-motive, in that not only did it make it lawful, it even (in the sense described) looked upon it directly as the will of God. The struggle against fleshly lust and the fondness for external goods was, as not only the Puritans but also the great apologist for Quakerism, Barclay, expressly state, not a struggle against rational acquisition, but against the irrational use of possessions. This was, however, above all a matter of the value placed on the luxurious forms of outward display so dear to feudal sensibility, which were to be condemned as 'idolatry of the creature',[80] as opposed to the divinely willed rational and utilitarian use of possessions to serve the ends of life for the individual and the community. It was not mortification of the flesh[81] which Puritanism wished to impose on the rich man, but the use of his possessions for necessary and practically useful purposes. The concept of 'comfort' characteristically encompasses the range of ethically permissible purposes for which possessions might be used, and it is of course no accident that the development of the style of life associated with that concept is to be observed at its earliest and clearest precisely among the most consistent representatives of this whole view of life, the Quakers. Against the tinsel and show of Cavalier pomp, which, resting as it does on an unsound economic basis, prefers shabby elegance to sober simplicity, they set as their ideal the neat and solid comfort of the bourgeois 'home'.[82]

On the side of the production of private economic wealth, asceticism attacked with equal force both dishonesty and purely impulsive greed: for it was the latter that the Puritans rejected under the name of 'covetousness', 'Mammonism' and so forth — the pursuit of riches for no purpose beyond that of being rich. For possessions were in themselves a source of temptation. In this regard, however, asceticism was a force which 'always wills the good and always creates evil' — by which I mean 'evil' in its own sense, of possessions and the temptations they offer. For not only did it, like the Old Testament and in perfect parallel with its ethical evaluation of 'good works', regard the pursuit of riches as an end in itself as supremely reprehensible, but the achievement of wealth as the fruit of work in a calling as an expression of God's blessing. But also, and still more important, the religious valuation of unceasing, constant, systematic, worldly labour in a calling as simply the highest form of asceticism and at the same time the surest and most visible proof of regeneration and genuineness of faith must certainly have been the most powerful lever imaginable for the expansion of that conception of life which we have here referred to as the 'spirit' of capitalism.[83] And if we put together the limitation of consumption referred to earlier and this breaking of the shackles on acquisitiveness, then the outward result is obvious: capital accumulation resulting from an ascetic compulsion to save.[84] The restrictions imposed on the consumption of what was acquired were bound to have a beneficial effect on its productive use as investment capital.

The exact extent of this effect naturally cannot be mathematically determined. In New England, the connexion was so palpable that it had already not escaped the notice of such an excellent historian as Doyle.[85] But in Holland, too, which was only really dominated by strict Calvinism for seven years, the greater simplicity of life which prevailed in the religiously more earnest circles led, when combined with enormous wealth, to an immoderate passion for capital accumulation.[86] It is further obvious that the tendency which has always existed, and is still operative amongst us today, to 'ennoble' bourgeois wealth must have been considerably restricted by the antipathy of Puritanism towards feudal forms of life. English mercantilist writers of the seventeenth century attributed the greater power of capital in Holland as compared with England to the fact that, in that country, newly acquired wealth did not, as in England, seek ennoblement in the normal course of events through investment in land and (for it was this, and not just the purchase of land in itself, which was at issue) through a change to feudal habits of life, in which it would be withdrawn from capitalist use.[87] Further, the esteem in which the Puritans held agriculture, as a specially important type of industry which was also especially conducive to piety, did not apply (in Baxter for instance) to the big landowner, but to the yeoman and the farmer; and in the eighteenth century, it applied not to the country squire but to the 'rational' farmer.[88] A constant theme in English society ever since the seventeenth century has been the quarrel between the 'squirearchy', who stand for the traditions of 'Merry England', and the Puritan circles, which vary considerably in their social strengths.[89] Both traits, that of an uninhibited naive joy in life and that of a severely controlled and reserved self-restraint and subjection to conventional ethical standards, are even today juxtaposed in the portrait of the English 'national character'.[90] An equally persistent theme in the earliest history of North American colonisation is the sharp contrast between the 'adventurers', who ran plantations with the labour of indentured servants and aspired to the life of a seigneur, and the specifically bourgeois attitudes of the Puritans.[91]

Wherever the power of the Puritan conception of life reached, it in all circumstances — and this is, of course, far more important than the mere promotion of capital accumulation — favoured the tendency towards a bourgeois, economically rational, way of life: it gave to that way of life its most essential and, above all, its only consistent support. It stood by the cradle of modern 'economic man'. To be sure, these Puritan ideals gave way under the extreme stresses presented by those 'temptations' of wealth which were so familiar to the Puritans themselves. We usually find the most sincere upholders of the Puritan spirit amongst those strata of petty bourgeois and farmers[92] who are in the early stages of their social ascent, while the 'beati possidentes', even among the Quakers, are all to often ready to abandon the old ideals.[93]

It was, indeed, the same fate to which the predecessor of inner-worldly asceticism, the monastic asceticism of the Middle Ages, succumbed again and again: when the rational conduct of the economy, in a place where life was strictly regulated and consumption restricted, had achieved its full effect, the wealth so acquired either fell directly, as in pre-Reformation times, into the hands of the nobility or else threatened to disrupt monastic discipline and required the institution of one of the numerous 'reformations'. Thus, the whole history of monastic life is in a sense a constantly renewed struggle with the problem of the secularising influence of property.

The same is true, on a larger scale, of Puritan inner-worldly asceticism. The powerful Methodist 'revival' which preceded the full flowering of British industry towards the end of the eighteenth century may be compared in many respects with such a reformation of the monasteries. A passage from John Wesley himself[94] might well be quoted at this point: it would be a very suitable motto to inscribe over all that has been said so far. For it shows that the leaders of the ascetic movements themselves were clear about the apparently so paradoxical connexions discussed here, and that their understanding of them was throughout along precisely the lines suggested here.[95] Wesley wrote, 'I fear, wherever riches have increased, the essence of religion has decreased in the same proportion. Therefore I do not see how it is possible, in the nature of things, for any revival of true religion to continue long. For religion must necessarily produce both industry and frugality, and these cannot but produce riches. But as riches increase, so will pride, anger and love of the world in all its branches. How then is it possible that Methodism, that is, a religion of the heart, though it flourishes now as a green bay tree, should continue in this state? For the Methodists in every place grow diligent and frugal; consequently they increase in goods. Hence they proportionately increase in pride, in anger, in the desire of the flesh, the desire of the eyes, and the pride of life. So, although the form of religion remains, the spirit is swiftly vanishing away. Is there no way to prevent this — the continual decay of pure religion? We ought not to prevent people from being diligent and frugal; *we must exhort all Christians to gain all they can, and to save all they can; that is, in effect, to grow rich.*' (Then follows the admonition that those who 'gain all they can and save all they can' should also 'give all they can', in order in this way to grow in grace and to lay up treasure in Heaven.) Clearly, the connexions analysed here are present in every detail.[96]

Just as Wesley says here, these powerful religious movements, whose importance in economic development lay initially in their ascetic educational influence, usually did not achieve their full economic effect until after the peak of purely religious enthusiasm had already passed, when the convulsive quest for the Kingdom of God was beginning gradually to settle down into sober virtue in one's calling and when the religious roots were slowly withering, to give way to a utilitarian concern with this world. This was the time when, as Dowden puts it, the place occupied in the popular imagination by Bunyan's 'Pilgrim', hastening through 'Vanity Fair' in a solitary inward quest of the Kingdom of Heaven, was taken by 'Robinson Crusoe', the isolated economic man who happens also to carry on missionary work.[97] When, as a further step, the principle of 'making the best of both worlds' began to prevail, then, as again Dowden has already put it, a good conscience was liable to become simply one of the means of comfortable bourgeois life, as is neatly expressed too in the German proverb about the 'soft pillow'. The bequest of that religiously lively period of the seventeenth century to its utilitarian heirs, however, was above all an exceedingly good — let us be bold and say, a pharisaically good — conscience about the acquisition of money, as long as it was acquired only by legal means. All relics of the doctrine *'Deo placere vix potest'* had vanished.[98] A specifically bourgeois work ethic had developed. With the consciousness that he stood in God's full grace and was visibly blessed by Him, the bourgeois entrepreneur could and should pursue his acquisitive interests, provided that he kept within the bounds of formal correctness, that his moral conduct was irreproachable and that the use which he made of his riches was not an improper one. The power of religious asceticism, moreover, placed at his disposal workers who were sober, conscientious, extremely industrious and loyal to their job as their divinely appointed purpose in life.[99] It also gave him the soothing assurance that the unequal distribution of worldly goods was the special work of God's providence, God in these distinctions as in His purely particular grace following His own secret and, to us, unknown ends.[100] Calvin had already uttered the often quoted remark that only when the 'people', in other words, the mass of workers and artisans, was kept poor did it remain obedient to God.[101] The Netherlanders, Pieter de la Court and others, had then 'secularised' this idea, arguing that most men work only when necessity drives them to it, and this formulation of a recurrent theme in capitalist economics then went to swell the flood of theories about the 'productivity' of low wages. In this case too, the utilitarian interpretation was imperceptibly imposed on the idea as its religious roots withered, fully in accordance with the pattern of development which we have observed over and over again. Medieval ethics had not only tolerated begging, but had actually gloried in the mendicant orders. Even nonreligious beggars, since they gave the wealthy the opportunity to do good works by giving alms, were sometimes actually singled out and treated as an 'estate'. The Anglican social ethic of the Stuart period was still in essence very close to this attitude. It was left to Puritan asceticism to elaborate the harsh English Poor Laws, which in this respect led to a change in principle. This was possible because begging was in fact unknown among the Protestant sects and the generality of strict Puritan communities in their midst.[102]

Considering matters from the other side, from the workers' point of view, Zinzendorf's variety of Pietism, for instance, glorified the worker who was true to his calling and was not acquisitive as following the model of the Apostles and so as gifted with the charisma of discipleship.[103] Still more radical were similar views which spread first among the Baptists. Of course, the whole corpus of ascetic literature of almost all denominations is steeped in the view that the faithful work, even at low wages, by those who have otherwise had no chances in life, is something highly pleasing to God. In that respect there is nothing new in Protestant asceticism. But not only did it powerfully add a whole new depth to the view, it also created for that ideal something which was absolutely essential if it was to be effective, namely a psychological stimulus in the form of the conception of such work as a calling, as the most excellent, indeed often in the end the only, means of becoming sure of one's state of grace.[104] And on the other hand, it made it lawful to exploit this specific willingness to work, in that it also interpreted the acquisition of money by the entrepreneur as his 'calling'.[105] It is obvious how greatly the 'productivity' of labour in the capitalist sense must have been advanced by such exclusive pursuit of the Kingdom of God through fulfilment of the duty to work in a calling and the strict asceticism which church discipline naturally imposed precisely on the non-property-owning classes.

The interpretation of work as a 'calling' became as characteristic of the modern worker as the corresponding conception of acquisition became for the entrepreneur. It was in response to this, at that time new, situation that such an acute Anglican observer as Sir William Petty attributed the economic strength of the Dutch in the seventeenth century to the fact that the 'Dissenters' (Calvinists and Baptists) who were specially numerous among them were people who looked on 'Labour and Industry as their duty towards God'. The 'organic' social order in the fiscal-monopolistic form which it took in Anglican thinking under the Stuarts, especially in Laud — that is, the alliance of state and Church with the 'monopolists' on the basis of a Christian social structure — was contrasted by Puritan thought, whose representatives were all among the passionate opponents of this kind of capitalism based on state privileges, putting out and colonisation, with the individualistic incentives of rational legal acquisition in virtue of one's own ability and initiative. While the monopoly industries of England, with their state privileges, soon vanished again without trace, the Puritans said, rational legal acquisition played a decisive part in the creation of industries which were built up without the support of the governmental authorities, and partly in spite of and contrary to them.[106] The Puritans, such as Prynne and Parker, refused to have anything to do with the 'courtiers and project-makers' of the large-scale capitalist type, whom they looked on as an ethically suspect class; they were proud of their own superior bourgeois business morality, which was the real reason for the persecutions to which they were subjected by those circles. Defoe proposed to win the struggle against Dissent by boycotting bank credit and calling in deposits. The contrast between the two kinds of capitalist activity ran to a large extent in parallel with the contrasts in religion. The opponents of the Nonconformists, even in the eighteenth century, continually scoffed at them as embodiments of the 'spirit of shopkeepers' and persecuted them for undermining traditional English ideals. Here also lay the roots of the contrast between the Puritan and the Jewish economic ethos: contemporaries such as Prynne already knew that it was the former rather than the latter which represented the true bourgeois economic ethic.[107]

One of the constituents of the modern capitalist spirit, and not only of this, but of modern civilisation generally, the rational conduct of life on the basis of the idea of the calling, thus has its origins, as the present discussion should have shown, in the spirit of Christian asceticism. One has only to re-read again now Franklin's treatise cited at the beginning of this essay to see that the essential elements of the frame of mind there referred to as the 'spirit of capitalism' are precisely those to which we have pointed in the foregoing discussion as forming the content of the Puritan asceticism of the calling,[108] only without the religious foundation which had already crumbled even in Franklin's time. The idea that modern work in a calling is ascetic in character is not, indeed, a new one. In his most profound insights, in *Wilhelm Meister's Journeyman Years* and the ending which he gave to his *Faust*, Goethe too[109] sought to teach us that it is in the present-day world a condition of doing anything of value that one should confine oneself to specialised work, with all the renunciation of man's Faustian omnicompetence which that implies; that therefore 'doing' and 'renunciation' are today inextricably linked — which is the ascetic basis of the bourgeois style of life, if indeed it is to be a style of life and not a lack of style. For Goethe, this knowledge meant a renunciatory parting from a time of complete and beautiful humanity, which will no more be repeated in the course of our cultural development than will the period of the flowering of ancient Athens.

The Puritan wanted to be a man with a calling; we are compelled to be. For when asceticism was transferred from the monastic cell to the life of the calling and moral concern with this world began to predominate, this helped to create that powerful modern economic world, bound to the technical and economic conditions of mechanical production, which today shapes the way of life of all who are born into it (not only those who are directly employed in the economy) with overwhelming pressure, and will perhaps continue to do so until the last hundredweight of fossil fuel has been burned to ashes. In Baxter's view, concern for external goods should lie on the shoulders of the Saints only like 'a light cloak, which can be thrown aside at any moment'.[110] But fate has allowed that cloak to become a casing as hard as steel. Because asceticism undertook to rebuild the world and to express itself in the world, the external goods of this world have acquired an increasing and ultimately inescapable power over men, such as they have never had before in history. Today, its spirit (whether finally or not, who knows?) has escaped from these confines. Capitalism in its triumph did not need this support any longer, since it rests on mechanical foundations. Even the rosy disposition of its smiling heir, the Enlightenment, seems finally to be fading, and the idea of 'duty in one's calling' haunts our present life like the ghost of our former religious beliefs. Where 'fulfilment of one's calling' cannot be directly related to the highest spiritual values of culture, or where it is not necessarily felt subjectively as simple economic pressure, the individual today generally ceases to reflect on it. In the United States, where it has been given most freedom, acquisitiveness, stripped of its religious and ethical meaning, tends today to be associated with purely competitive passions, which often give it the character of a sporting contest.[111] No one knows as yet who will live within these confines in future, and whether, at the end of this vast development, totally new prophets will emerge or there will be a powerful revival of old ideas and ideals, or, if neither of these, whether there will be a state of mechanised petrification, embellished by a kind of frenzied self-importance. In that case it might indeed become true to say of the 'last men' of this cultural development: 'specialists without soul, hedonists without heart: this cipher flatters itself that it has reached a stage of humanity never before attained'.

At this point, indeed, we enter the domain of value-judgments and confessions of faith, which should not burden such a purely historical discussion as this. The task would rather be to demonstrate the significance of ascetic rationalism, only touched upon in the foregoing sketch, for social and political ethics, and so for the mode of organisation and the functions of social groups from the conventicle to the state. Then there must be an analysis of its relations with humanistic rationalism[112] and its ideals and cultural influences, and further to the development of philosophical and scientific empiricism, to technological development and the spiritual values of our culture. Finally, there should be an historical study of its historical development from its medieval origins through inner-worldly asceticism to the stage where it becomes pure utilitarianism, covering all the different areas in which ascetic forms of religion have played a part. Only in this way could the extent of the cultural significance of ascetic Protestantism in relation to other formative elements of modern culture be established. In the present essay an attempt has been made to refer to their causes the fact and the nature of its influence in one, admittedly important, respect. The way in which the development and the special characteristics of Protestant asceticism have in their turn been influenced by the totality of socio-cultural conditions, especially economic conditions, must then be made clear.[113] For although modern man is on the whole usually incapable, even with the best will in the world, of conceiving the importance which religious ideas and sentiments have had for the conduct of life, for culture and for national character as being as great as it in fact has been, it nevertheless cannot be the intention to substitute for a one-sidedly 'spiritualist' interpretation. Both are equally possible,[114] but both are of equally little service to the interests of historical truth if they claim to be, not preliminaries to enquiry, but its conclusion.[115]

(*Gesammelte Aufsätze zur Religionssoziologie*,
2nd edn, Tübingen, 1922, I, pp. 163-206.
First published in this form in 1920;
original publication 1905.)

ENDNOTES

The Definition of Sociology and of Social Action

Unless otherwise noted, all notes in this chapter are by Talcott Parsons. For Parson's exposition and critique of Weber's methodology, see his introduction to *The Theory of Social and Economic Organization* and his *Structure of Social Action*.

1   In this series of definitions Weber employs several important terms which need discussion. In addition to *Verstehen*, which has already been commented upon, there are four important ones: *Deuten*, *Sinn*, *Handeln*, and *Verhalten*. *Deuten* has generally been translated as "interpret." As used by Weber in this context it refers to the interpretation of subjective states of mind and the meanings which can be imputed as intended by an actor. Any other meaning of the word "interpretation" is irrelevant to Weber's discussion. The term *Sinn* has generally been translated as "meaning"; and its variations, particularly the corresponding adjectives, *sinnhaft*, *sinnvoll*, *sinnfremd*, have been dealt with by appropriately modifying the term *meaning*. The reference here again is always to features of the content of subjective states of mind or symbolic systems which are ultimately referable to such states of mind.

The terms *Handeln* and *Verhalten* are directly related. *Verhalten* is the broader term referring to any mode of behavior of human individuals, regardless of the frame of reference in terms of which it is analysed. "Behavior" has seemed to be the most appropriate English equivalent. *Handeln*, on the other hand, refers to the concrete phenomenon of human behavior only insofar as it is capable of "understanding," in Weber"s technical sense, in terms of subjective categories. The most appropriate English equivalent has seemed to be "action." This corresponds to [Parson's] usage in *The Structure of Social Action* and would seem to be fairly well established. "Conduct" is also similar and has sometimes been used. *Deuten*, *Verstehen*, and *Sinn* are thus applicable to human behavior only insofar as it constitutes action or conduct in this specific case.

2   Weber's text in Part One is organized in a manner frequently found in the German academic literature of his day, in that he first lays down certain fundamental definitions and then proceeds to comment on them. These comments, which apparently were not intended to be "read" in the ordinary sense, but rather serve as reference material for the clarification and systematization of the theoretical concepts and their implications, are in the German edition printed in a smaller type, a convention which we have followed for the rest of Part One. However, while in most cases the comments are relatively brief, under the definitions of "sociology" and "social action" Weber wrote what are essentially methodological essays (sec. I:A-B), which because of their length have been printed in ordinary type.

Protestant Asceticism and the Spirit of Capitalism

1   See the fine character sketch in Dowden's *Puritan and Anglican*. There is a reasonably good guide to Baxter's theology, after he had gradually modified his strict belief in the 'double decree', in the Introduction (by Jenkyn) to the selection of his works printed in the *Works of the Puritan Divines*. His attempt to combine 'universal redemption' and 'personal election' satisfied nobody. For us, the crucial point is only that even at that time he remained firm on personal election, or in other words on the ethically decisive feature of the doctrine of predestination. It is important, on the other hand, that he weakened the forensic interpretation of the doctrine of justification, since that represented a move in the direction of the Baptists.

2   Treatises and sermons by Thomas Adams, John Howe, Matthew Henry, J. Janeway, Stuart Charnock, Baxter and Bunyan have been collected in the ten volumes of the *Works of the Puritan Divines* (London, 1845-48), though the selection is often somewhat arbitrary. The work of Bailey referred to is *Praxis Pietatis* (Leipzig, 1724); that of Sedgwick is *Bussund Gnadenlehre*, in the German translation of 1689; and that of Hoornbeek is *Theologia Practica* (Utrecht, 1663).

3   Voët or other continental representatives of inner-worldly asceticism might equally well have been referred to. Brentano's view that this development was 'merely Anglo-Saxon' is totally mistaken. The choice depends on a wish to give expression, not exclusively but as far as possible, to the ascetic movement of the second half of the seventeenth century, immediately before it turned into utilitarianism. In the framework of this sketch we have unfortunately had to deny ourselves the chance to pursue the fascinating problem of additionally illuminating the style of life of ascetic Protestantism from the biographical literature: the Quaker literature in particular, since it is relatively unknown in Germany, would be worth citing.

4   One might equally well refer to the writings of Gisbert Voët, the proceedings of the Huguenot synods or the Dutch Baptist literature. It is most unfortunate that Sombart and Brentano have singled out precisely those 'Ebionitic' elements in Baxter which I have myself emphasised so strongly, in order to confront me with the undoubted backwardness (from the capitalist point of view) of his teachings. But first of all, one must have a really thorough acquaintance with this literature as a whole in order to make proper use of it; and secondly, it should not be overlooked that I have actually tried to show how, in spite of this 'anti-Mammonistic' teaching, the spirit of this ascetic form of religion, just as in the monastic economics, gave birth to economic rationalism, because it rewarded the ascetically determined rational pursuits which played the decisive role in this process. This alone is the nub of the matter and precisely this is the point of the present argument.

5   It is the same in Calvin, who was certainly no admirer of bourgeois wealth (see the vehement attacks on Venice and Antwerp in *Jes. Opp.*, III 140a, 308a).

6   *Saints' Everlasting Rest*, Chapters X and XII. Compare Bailey, *Praxis Pietatis*,

p. 182, or Matthew Henry, 'The Worth of the Soul', *Works of the Puritan Divines*, p. 319: 'Those that are eager in pursuit of worldly wealth despise their soul, not only because the soul is neglected and the body preferred before it, but because it is employed in these pursuits: Psalm 127, 2.' (On the same page, however, can be found the remark to be quoted later about the sinfulness of all forms of wasting time, especially in 'recreations'.) The same is true of the whole religious literature of English and Dutch Puritanism. See, for example, Hoornbeek's Philippics (*Theolgia Practica*, x, Ch. 18, 18) against '*avaritia*' (avarice). In the case of the latter writer there are also sentimental influences of a pietistic kind at work: see his praise of a 'tranquillity of spirit' which is pleasing to God, as against the 'cares' of this world. Bailey too (*Praxis Pietatis*, p. 182), alluding to a familiar passage in the Bible, expresses the opinion that 'A rich man is not easily saved'. The Methodist catechisms also warn against 'laying up for oneself treasure on earth'. In Pietism this is absolutely self-evident. And the case is no different with the Quakers. Compare Barclay (*The Apology for the True Christian Divinity*, p. 517), '...and therefore beware of such temptation as to use their callings and engine to be richer'.

7   Not just riches, but the instinctive pursuit of gain (or what was considered as such) were condemned with equal sharpness. In the Netherlands, the Synod of South Holland in 1574 explained, in answer to an enquiry, that money-lenders, even though their business was carried on legally, should not be admitted to communion; the Provincial Synod of Deventer in 1598 (Article 24) extended this to those employed by money-lenders; the Synod at Gorichem in 1606 laid down harsh and humiliating conditions for the admission of the wives of 'usurers'; and it was still a matter for discussion in 1644 and 1657 whether money-lenders should be admitted to communion. (This is evidence especially against Brentano, who cites his Catholic forebears — although there have been merchants and bankers of foreign birth throughout the European and Asiatic world for millenia.) Finally, Gisbert Voët (*Disp. Theol.*, IV, 1667, *de usuris*, p. 665) could still exclude the 'Trapezites' (that is, the Lombard or Piedmontese money-lenders) from communion. The situation was no different in the Huguenot synods. It was certainly not the capitalist strata of this kind who embodied the frame of mind and the mode of life which are at issue here. What is more, they were nothing new, as compared with the ancient world and the Middle Ages.

8   A theme which is exhaustively developed in Chapter Ten of the *Saints' Everlasting Rest*. Anyone who would seek lasting rest in possessions, which God gives as merely a 'lodging', is stricken by God even in this life. To rest content on the riches which one has already gained nearly always presages moral failure. Could we have all that we were able to have in this world, would this yet be all that we could hope for? Satisfaction is not to be attained in this world, since God has willed that it should not be.

9   *Christian Directory*, I, pp. 375-76, 'It is for action that God maintaineth us and our activities: work is the moral as well as the natural end of power... It is action that God is most served and honoured by...The public welfare or the good of many is to be valued above our own.' Here we see the starting point for the

development from the will of God to the purely utilitarian point of view of later liberal theory. On the religious sources of utilitarianism, see further below and above.

10 Beginning with the Biblical threat of punishment for every idle word, the command to be silent has been, especially since the Cluniac monks, a tried and tested ascetic method for cultivating self-control. Baxter too goes exhaustively into the sinfulness of vain speech. The characterological significance of this has already been assessed by Sanford (*Studies and Reflections of the Great Rebellion*, pp. 90f). The 'melancholy' and 'moroseness' of the Puritans, which made such a deep impression on their contemporaries, were a consequence of the disintegration of the spontaneity of the 'natural state' and the prohibition of thoughtless speech was meant to serve this end.

When Washington Irving (*Bracebridge Hall*, Ch. xxx) seeks the reason which leads to a sense of personal responsibility, partly in the 'calculating spirit' of capitalism and partly in the effects of political freedom, it should be pointed out that the same effect was not produced amongst the Latin nations and that in England the situation was that, first, Puritanism enabled its adherents to create free institutions and so to become a world power, and secondly, that it changed the spirit of 'calculation' (as Sombart calls it), which is indeed constitutive of capitalism, from an economic instrument into the principle of a whole mode of life.

11 *Op. cit.*, I, p. III.

12 *Christian Directory*, I, pp. 383f.

13 There is a similar point about the preciousness of time in Barclay, *The Apology for the True Christian Divinity*, p. 14.

14 Baxter, *op. cit.*, p. 79, 'Keep up a high esteem of time and be every day more careful that you lose none of your time, than you are that you lose none of your gold and silver. And if vain recreation, dressings, feastings, idle talk, unprofitable company, or sleep, be any of them temptations to rob you of any of your time, accordingly heighten your watchfulness.' 'Those that are prodigal of their time despise their own souls' is the view of Matthew Henry ('Worth of the Soul', *Works of the Puritan Divines*, p. 315). Here again Protestant asceticism is following well-trodden paths. We usually look on it as specific to modern man in his professional life that the 'has no time', and even, for instance, — as Goethe was already doing in his *Wanderjahren* — measure the extent of capitalist development by the fact that the clocks strike the quarter-hours (as Sombart also says in his *Kapitalismus*). But we should not forget that the first man to take account of the divisions of time in his life (in the Middle Ages) was the monk, and that the church bell had first to provide for his need to divide time.

15 Compare Baxter's discussion of the calling, *op. cit.*, I, pp. 108f, where the following passage is found: 'Question: But may I not cast off the world that I may only think of my salvation? — Answer: You may cast off all such excess of worldly cares or business as unnecessarily hinder you in spiritual things. But

you may not cast off all bodily employment and mental labour in which *you may serve the common good*. Everyone as a member of Church or Commonwealth must employ their parts to the utmost for the good of the Church and the Commonwealth. To neglect this and say: I will pray and meditate, is as if your servant should refuse your greatest work and tye himself to some lesser easier part. And *God hath commanded you some way or other to labour for your daily bread and not to live as drones of the sweat of others only.*' God's commandment to Adam, 'In the sweat of thy face shalt thou eat bread', and St Paul's admonition, 'If any would not work, neither should he eat' were cited in this connexion. It has long been known of the Quakers that, even amongst the most wealthy, their sons were put to learn a trade — for ethical, not, as Alberti suggests, for utilitarian reasons.

16   Here there are some respects in which Pietism, because of its emphasis on feeling, follows a different path. For Spener (see his '*Theologische Bedenken*', III, p. 445), despite his completely Lutheran emphasis on the idea that work in a calling is the service of God, it is settled (and this too is Lutheran) that the agitation of activity in a calling draws one away from God — an extremely characteristic antithesis to Puritanism.

17   *Op. cit.*, p. 242: 'It's they that are lazy in their callings that can find no time for holy duties'. This is the origin of the view that the towns, the home of the bourgeoisie engaged in rational acquisition, were also pre-eminently the homes of the ascetic virtues. Baxter says of his hand-loom weavers in Kidderminster: 'And their constant converse and traffic with London doth much to promote civility and piety among tradesmen' (in his *Autobiography* — excerpt in the *Works of the Puritan Divines*, p. xxxviii). The idea that the proximity of the capital should have the effect of strengthening virtue would astonish the clergy today, at least in Germany. But there are also similar views to be found in Pietism. Spener, for instance, writes in passing to a young colleague: 'At least it will be seen that, among the great numbers in the towns, though most are utterly wicked, still a few good souls are on the other hand to be found, with whom to achieve something good; but I fear that sometimes in villages there is scarcely anything entirely good to be found in a whole community' ('*Theologische Bedenken*', I, 66, p. 303). The peasant is little fitted for the ascetic rational conduct of life. His ethical glorification is very modern. We will not here go into the significance of these and similar statements for the question of how far asceticism is determined by class.

18   Consider for example the following passages (*op. cit.*, pp. 336f): 'Be wholly taken up in diligent business for your lawful callings when you are not exercised in the more immediate service of God'. 'Labour hard in your callings'. 'See that you have a calling which will find you employment for all the time which God's immediate service spareth'.

19   That the specific ethical valuation of work and its 'dignity' was not in origin an idea unique to, or even characteristic of, Christianity has again been strongly emphasised recently by Harnack (*Mitt. des Ev.-Soz. Kongr.*, 14, Folge, 1905, Nos. 3/4, p. 48).

20   The basis of this important contrast, which has been obvious since the Benedictine rule, can only be clarified by a much more thorough discussion.

21   So also in Pietism (Spener, '*Theologische Bedenken*', III, pp. 429-30). The characteristic Pietist turn given to the idea is that loyalty to one's calling, which is imposed on us as a punishment because of the Fall, helps to mortify the individual will. Work in a calling, as a form of service expressing love for one's neighbour, is a duty of gratitude for God's grace (a Lutheran conception), and so it is not pleasing to God when it is done unwillingly and with ill humour (III, p. 272). The Christian will therefore 'show himself as diligent in his work as a worldly man' (III, p. 278). That obviously falls short of the Puritan way of thinking.

22   'A sober procreation of children' is its purpose according to Baxter. Similarly in Spener, though he makes concessions to the coarse Lutheran view according to which a secondary purpose is to avoid immorality, which cannot be restrained in any other way. Concupiscence, as a feeling which accompanies copulation, is sinful even within marriage and, according to Spener's interpretation, for example, is a consequence of the Fall, which in this way turned a natural and divinely willed process into something unavoidably associated with sinful feelings, and so into something shameful. According to the conception of some pietistic movements, moreover, the highest form of Christian marriage is that in which virginity is preserved, the next highest, that in which sexual relations serve exclusively for procreation, and so on down to those which are entered into for purely sexual motives or simply for the sake of outward appearances and are, ethically regarded, no better than concubinage. Further, among the lower forms of marriage, that which is entered into simply for the sake of outward appearances is preferred to marriage for purely sexual motives, on the grounds that it does still involve rational considerations. The Herrnhut theory and practice need not concern us here. Rationalist philosophy, in the person of Christian Wolff, took over the ascetic theory in the sense that what was ordained as a means to an end (concupiscence and its appeasement) should not be made into an end in itself.

The shift to the purely hygienic concerns of utilitarianism was already complete by the time of Franklin, who adopts the ethical standpoint of the modern doctor, taking 'chastity' to mean the limitation of sexual intercourse to what is desirable on grounds of health, and, as is well known, also expressing views on how that aim should be achieved. This development has begun everywhere as soon as these questions have become a subject for purely rational consideration. The Puritan and the hygienic sexual rationalist follow very different paths, but at this point they 'understand each other'. In a lecture (the theme was brothels and arrangements for regulating them) an enthusiastic advocate of 'hygenic' prostitution supported his claim that 'extra-marital intercourse', because of its hygienic utility, was morally admissible by referring to its poetic glorification in the characters of Faust and Gretchen. Both these notions — that Gretchen should be considered as a prostitute, and that the powerful sway of human passions should be identified with hygienic sex — would be entirely acceptable to Puritan ways of thinking. The same is true, for instance, of the typical specialist's attitude embodied in the view occasionally advocated by very distinguished doctors that a question such as that of the meaning of sexual abstinence, which bears on the subtlest problems of personality and culture, belongs 'exclusively' within the province of the medical man, who is the 'specialist' in this field. For the Puritans, the specialist was the moral theorist, here it is the hygienic expert: but the principle of 'competence' to settle the question, which to us can so easily seem philistine, is the same, though of course it operates in the reverse direction. However, the powerful idealism of the Puritan viewpoint, with all it pruderies, can also point to positive successes, from the point of view of racial conservation and in purely 'hygienic' terms; whereas modern sexual hygiene, because of its inevitable appeal to 'open-mindedness', runs the risk of allowing the very source of its own strength to drain away.

Naturally, it is impossible to discuss here the way in which, in the setting of the rational interpretation of sexual relations to be found in those nations which were influenced by Puritanism, marital relationships ultimately achieved a degree of refinement and permeation by spiritual and ethical ideals, and marital chivalry flourished, in contrast with the patriarchal miasma which still lingers in Germany, often in considerable pockets, through all ranks right up to the intellectual aristocracy. (Baptist influences have also played their part in the emancipation of women; the defence of women's freedom of conscience and the extension to women of the idea of 'the priesthood of all believers' were also among the first breaches in patriarchalism.)

23   A constantly recurring theme in Baxter. The Scriptural basis is either the passage quoted by Franklin which we already know (Proverbs 22. 29) or the eulogy of work in Proverbs 31. 16. Cf. *Christian Directory*, I, p. 382, p. 377, etc.

24   Even Zinzendorf says on one occasion: 'One does not work only that one may live, but one lives in order to work, and if one has no more work to do, then one either suffers or dies' (Plitt, I, p. 428).

25   A Mormon symbol also ends (after quotations) with the words: 'But a lazy or indolent man cannot be a Christian and be saved. He is destined to be struck down and cast from the hive'. However, here it was principally the impressive discipline, following the middle path between monastery and factory, which confronted the individual with the choice between working and perishing and — together, of course, with religious enthusiasm and only made possible by it — produced the astounding economic achievements of that sect.

26   Hence its symptoms are carefully analysed, Baxter, *Christian Directory*, I, p. 380. 'Sloth' and 'idleness' are such particularly grave sins, just because they have a *dispositional* character. They are regarded by Baxter actually as 'destroyers of grace' (I, pp. 279-80). They are indeed the antitheses of the methodical life.

27   See Thomas Aquinas, *Quaest. quodlibetal.*, VII, Article 17c.

28   Baxter, *Christian Directory*, I, pp. 108ff. The following passages are especially striking: 'Question: But will not wealth excuse us? — Answer: It may excuse you from some sordid sort of work, by making you more serviceable to another,

but you are no more excused from service of work...than the poorest man', and further, on p. 376: 'Though they [the rich] have no outward want to urge them, they have as great a necessity to obey God...God hath strictly commanded it [work] to all.'

[29] Similarly in Spener ('*Theologische Bedenken*', III, pp. 338, 425), who for this reason is particularly opposed to the tendency to premature retirement, considering it to be morally hazardous; also, in rejecting criticism of the legitimacy of charging interest on the grounds that living on interest leads to idleness, stresses that someone who could live on his interest would still be obliged by God's commandment to work.

[30] Including Pietism. Whenever the question of change of occupation arises, Spener always takes the view that once one has entered upon a certain calling, it is a duty of obedience to God's providence that one should continue in it and reconcile oneself to it.

[31] The tremendous emotional power, dominating the whole conduct of life, with which the Indian doctrine of salvation associates occupational traditionalism with the chances of rebirth, has been discussed at length in my essays on 'The Economic Ethics of the World Religions'. This is a particularly good point at which to learn to recognise the difference between merely theoretical ethical concepts and the creation of psychological incentives of a particular kind by religion. The pious Hindu could only secure favourable chances of rebirth by a strictly traditional fulfilment of the obligations of his native caste, and that is the strongest imaginable religious foundation for traditionalism. Indian ethics is in fact in this respect the most consistent antithesis of Puritan ethics, just as in another regard (the traditionalism of its status group structure) it is the most consistent antithesis of Judaism.

[32] Baxter, *Christian Directory*, I, p. 377.

[33] But not for that reason historically derivable from it. A much more important influence in it is the genuinely Calvinist idea that the ordered system of the 'world' serves the glory of God, His Self-glorification. The utilitarian development of this idea, that the economic cosmos ought to serve the purpose of prolonging the life of everyone ('good of the many', 'common good', etc.), resulted from the notion that any other interpretation would lead to a typically aristocratic 'idolatry of the creature', or would serve, not to glorify God, but the purposes of creaturely 'culture'. God's will, however, as expressed in the purposeful ordering of the economic cosmos, may take the form, as far as worldly ends in general come into consideration, only of the well-being of the 'commonwealth', or in other words of an impersonal 'utility'. Utilitarianism is thus, as was said earlier, a consequence of the impersonal construction of the 'love of one's neighbour' and the repudiation of all forms of glorification of the world resulting from the exclusivity of the Puritan conception of '*ad majorem Dei gloriam*'. The degree of intensity to which the whole ascetic Protestantism was dominated by the idea that all glorification of the creature was detrimental to the glory of God and so utterly objectionable is clearly to be seen in the scruples and mental anguish

which it cost even Spener, who certainly could never be suspected of 'democratic' sympathies, to uphold the use of titles as 'indifferent' in the face of numerous enquiries. He reassures himself finally with the reflection that, even in the Bible, the praetor Festus was addressed with the title 'Most Noble' by the Apostle. The political aspect of the matter is not relevant in this connexion.

34   'The inconstant man is a stranger in his own house', says also Thomas Adams (*Works of the Puritan Divines*, p. 77).

35   See especially on this point George Fox's statements in W. and T. Evans, eds., *The Friends' Library* (Philadelphia, 1837), I, p. 130.

36   It would of course be altogether wrong to look on this turning-point in religious ethics as a mere reflection of the actual economic relationships. The specialisation of occupations had of course gone much further in medieval Italy than in the England of the period under consideration.

37   For God, as is very often emphasised in the Puritan literature, never commanded man to love his neighbour *more* than himself, but *as* himself. Thus, there is also an obligation to love oneself. For example, if someone knows that he himself uses his possessions more purposefully and so to the greater glory of God than his neighbour could, he is not obliged by his love of his neighbour to give him any of them.

38   Spener also comes close to this view. But he is still extremely cautious and inclined to be opposed to it even when it is a case of moving from the calling of a merchant, which is morally particularly dangerous, to theology ('*Theologische Bedenkin*', III, pp. 435-443: I, p. 524). The frequent recurrence of answers to precisely this question (about the permissibility of a change of calling) in Spener's naturally well-considered judgment shows, by the way, how distinctly practical in terms of everyday life the various types of interpretation of I Corinthians 7 were.

39   Nothing of this kind is to be found in the writings at least of the leading continental Pietists. Spener's attitude to 'profit' vacillates between the Lutheran view, that it has to do with sustenance, and Mercantilist arguments about the utility of commercial prosperity and the like ('*Theologische Bedenken*', III, pp. 330, 332; cf. I, p. 418: the cultivation of tobacco brings money into the country and hence is useful, so not sinful! Cf. also III, pp. 426, 427, 429, 434). He does not fail to point out, however, that, as the example of the Quakers and the Mennonites shows, it is possible to make a profit and remain pious: indeed that specially high profits may — a point we shall return to later — be a direct product of piety and honesty (p. 435).

40   Such views in Baxter are not a mere reflection of the economic environment in which he lived. On the contrary, his autobiography makes it clear that a decisive element in the success of his home mission was that those tradesmen who lived in Kidderminster were not rich, but only earned enough for 'food and raiment', and that the guild masters had to live no better than their workers, indeed 'from hand to mouth'. 'It is the poor that receive the glad tidings of the Gospel'.

Thomas Adams comments on the pursuit of profit, 'He (the knowing man) knows...that money may make a man richer, not better, and thereupon chooseth rather to sleep with a good conscience than a full purse...therefore desires no more wealth than an honest man may bear away' — *but he does want that much* (Thomas Adams, *Works of the Puritan Divines*, LI), and that means that all formally honest means of earning a living are also legitimate.

⁴¹ Thus Baxter, *Christian Directory*, I, Ch. x, Tit. I Dir. 9 (Section 24), p. 378, col. 2. Proverbs 23-4, 'Labour not to be rich' means only 'Riches for our fleshly ends must not ultimately be intended'. Wealth used in the feudal or seigneurial way is what is hateful (cf. the remark in I, p. 380 about 'the debauched part of the gentry'), not wealth as such.

Milton in his first '*Defensio pro populo Anglicano*' puts forward the well-known theory that only the 'middle class' can embody virtue — meaning by 'middle class' the 'bourgeoisie' as opposed to the 'aristocracy', as is shown by the argument that 'luxury' as well as 'distress' may be an obstacle to the exercise of virtue.

⁴² This is the decisive point. Once again, the general comment may be made that we are here, of course, concerned, not so much with the intellectual development of theological ethical theories, as with the morality which had force in the practical life of the believers: in other words, with the practical effect of the religious orientation of the work ethic. Occasionally, at least, it is possible to find discussions in Catholic casuistical literature, especially in Jesuit sources, which for instance on the question of the permissibility of interest, which does not concern us here, have a similar ring to those of many Protestant casuists, which indeed seem to go further than them on the question of what is 'permissible' or 'approvable' (the Puritans have in later times often enough faced the objection that the Jesuit ethics are in principle essentially the same as their own). As the Calvinists often cited Catholic moral theologians — not only Thomas Aquinas, Bernard of Clairvaux, and Bonaventure, but also their own contemporaries — so Catholic casuists frequently took account of heretical ethics (though we shall not go further into this point here). But, quite apart from the decisive fact that the ascetic life was recommended for the laity, the all-important difference even in theory is that these latitudinarian views were in Catholicism the results, not sanctioned by the authority of the Church, of specifically lax ethical theories, repudiated by precisely the most earnest and strictest adherents of the Church, whereas conversely, the Protestant idea of the calling had the effect of leading precisely the most earnest followers of the ascetic life to pursue the life of capitalist acquisition. What in the one case was permissible under certain conditions seemed in the other to be a positive moral good. The fundamental differences between the two ethics, so important in practice, have been finally defined for the modern world, since the time of the Jansenist controversy and the Bull '*Unigenitus*'.

⁴³ 'You may labour in that manner as tendeth most to your success and lawful gain. You are bound to improve all your talents...' Then follows the passage quoted above in the text. A direct parallel is drawn between the pursuit of riches in the

Kingdom of God and the pursuit of success in an earthly calling, e.g. in Janeway, 'Heaven upon Earth' (in *Works of the Puritan Divines*, p. 275).

44 Already in Duke Christoph von Württemberg's Lutheran Confession, which was submitted to the Council of Trent, it was urged against the vow of poverty that, while anyone who is poor in his estate should accept his lot, if he vows to remain so, this is the same as if he vowed to be chronically ill or to have a bad name.

45 This is to be found in Baxter and e.g. in Duke Christoph's Confession. Cf. further such passages as the following: '...the vagrant rogues whose lives are nothing but an exorbitant course: the main begging...', etc. (Thomas Adams, *Works of the Puritan Divines*, p. 259). Calvin had already strictly prohibited begging and the Dutch synods inveigh against licences and certificates to beg. Whereas the Stuarts, especially Laud's regime under Charles I, had developed the principle of governmental poor relief and provision of work for the unemployed, the Puritan war-cry was 'Giving alms is no charity' (later to be the title of Defoe's well-known work), and towards the end of the seventeenth century there began the system of deterrence, in the form of 'Workhouses' for the unemployed (cf. Leonard, *Early History of English Poor Relief*, Cambridge, 1900, and H. Levy, *Die Grundlagen des ökonomischen Liberalismus in der Geschichte der englischen Volkswirtschaft*, Jena, 1912, pp. 69ff).

46 The president of the Baptist Union of Great Britain and Ireland, G. White, said emphatically in his inaugural address for the assembly in London in 1903 ('Baptist Handbook', 1904, p. 104): 'The best men on the roll of our Puritan churches were men of affairs, who believed that religion should permeate the whole of life.'

47 This is the characteristic point of contrast with all feudal conceptions. In the feudal view, only the descendants of the political or social parvenu can enjoy the benefits of his success and the line which he founded. (This is characteristically expressed in the Spanish word *hidalgo*, i.e. *hijo d'algo or filius de aliquo*, where the *aliquid* (or 'something') is one of the ancestors from whom wealth has been inherited.) However much these differences may be fading today in the rapid transformation and Europeanisation of the American national character, still one occasionally finds there even today the precisely opposite, specifically bourgeois, view which glorifies success in business and acquisition as symptoms of spiritual achievement and which has on the contrary no respect at all for purely inherited wealth. On the other hand, in Europe (as James Bryce has already pointed out in one place) virtually any social position is in effect to be bought for money, provided the man of property has not himself stood behind the counter and carries out the necessary transformation of his property (foundation of trusts, etc.). See the criticism of the honour of lineage, e.g. in Thomas Adams, *Works of the Puritan Divines*, p. 216.

48 This was so, e.g. already in the case of the founder of the Familist sect, Hendrik Niklaes, who was a merchant. (Barclay, *Inner Life of the Religious Communities of the Commonwealth*, p. 34.)

208 / Sociological Thought

49   This is absolutely settled, e.g. for Hoornbeek, since Matthew 5.5 and I Timothy 4.8 also made purely earthly promises to the Saints (*Theologia Practica*, I, p. 193). Everything results from God's providence, but He has a special care for His own: p. 192, '*Super alios autem summa cura et modis singularissimis versatur Dei providential circa fideles*'. ('Above others, God's providence deals with the faithful with supreme care and in the most singular ways'.) Then follows a discussion about the means of knowing whether a stroke of luck results, not from the '*communis providentia*' (general providence), but from that special provision. Bailey too (*Praxis Pietatis*, p. 191) refers success in one's calling to God's providence. That prosperity is 'often' the reward for godly living is a constantly recurring theme in the writings of the Quakers (see, e.g. a statement of this kind from as late as 1848 in *Selection from the Christian Advices issued by the General Meeting of the Society of Friends in London*, 6th edn. London, 1851, p. 209). We shall return again to the connexion with the Quaker ethic.

50   As an example of this concern with the patriarchs — which is at the same time characteristic of the Puritan view of life — Thomas Adams' analysis of the quarrel between Jacob and Esau may serve (*Works of the Puritan Divines*, p. 235): 'His (Esau's) folly may be argued from the base estimation of the birthright' (this passage is also important for the development of the idea of the birthright, of which more later), 'that he would so lightly pass from it and on so easy condition as a pottage.' But he was then perfidious in not wanting to recognise the sale as valid on the grounds that he had been cheated. He is indeed a 'cunning hunter, a man of the fields', an irrational barbarian, whereas Jacob 'a plain man, dwelling in tents', represents the 'man of grace'. The feeling of an inner affinity with Judaism, still expressed in Roosevelt's well-known writings, was found by Köhler (*Die Niederl. Ref. Kirche*) to be widespread also among Dutch peasants. On the other hand, however, Puritanism was fully conscious of its opposition to Jewish ethics in its practical dogmatics, as Prynne's pamphlet against the Jews (on the occasion of Cromwell's plan for toleration) clearly shows. See below, Note 58.

51   *Zur bäuerlichen Glaubens- und Sittenlehre.* By a Thuringian parson (2nd edn; Gotha, 1890), p. 16. The peasants here depicted are characteristic products of Lutheran churchmanship. I have again and again written the word 'Lutheran' in the margin, where the esteemed author has imagined he is discussing a general 'peasant' form of religion.

52   Cf. e.g. the reference in Ritschl, *Pietismus*, II, p. 158. Spener likewise bases his objections to change of occupation and the pursuit of profit in part on remarks of Jesus Sirach, '*Theologische Bedenken*', III, p. 426.

53   Admittedly, Bailey, for instance, recommends reading them nevertheless, and there are quotations from the Apocrypha to be found here and there, but naturally not often. I do not remember (though this may be just accidental) any such from Jesus Sirach.

54   Where outward success is the lot of those who are clearly damned, the Calvinist,

such as Hoornbeek, consoles himself, in accordance with the 'theory of hardening of the heart', with the certainty that God allows them to prosper in order to harden their hearts and so condemn them to all the more certain perdition.

55 We shall not discuss this point in any greater detail in this connexion. The point of interest here is only the formalistic character of 'righteousness'. On the significance of the Old Testament ethic for Natural Law, there is much in Troeltsch's *Soziallehren*.

56 The ethical standards of the Scriptures are binding, according to Baxter (*Christian Directory*, III, pp. 173f), to the extent that (i) they are merely a 'transcript' of the 'Law of Nature' or (ii) they bear the 'express character of universality and perpetuity'.

57 For example, Dowden (with reference to Bunyan), *Puritan and Anglican*, p. 39.

58 There is a more detailed discussion of this in my essays on the 'Economic Ethics of the World Religions'. It is impossible here to analyse the enormous influence exerted on the characterological development of Judaism, on its rationalistic opposition to all cultivation of the senses, by, for instance, the second commandment in particular ('Thou shalt not make unto thee any graven image'). Nevertheless, it is perhaps worth mentioning as characteristic a remark made to me by one of the leaders of the 'Educational Alliance' in the United States. This is an organisation which with astonishing success and enormous resources attempts the Americanisation of Jewish immigrants, and he told me that the primary aim of the process of assimilation, to achieve which all kinds of artistic and social instruction are used, is 'emancipation from the second commandment'.

In Puritanism there corresponds to the Israelite prohibition of all anthropomorphisation of God the prohibition of all idolatry of the creature, which is somewhat different, but related in its effects. As for Talmudic Judaism, the principal features of Puritan morality are certainly very similar to it. When, for instance, in the Talmud (in Wünsche, *Babyl. Talmud*, II, p. 34) the injunction is found that it is better and more richly rewarded by God when one does something good from a sense of duty than when one does a good deed which one is not obliged to do by the Law — in other words, the loveless fulfilment of duty is ethically higher than emotional philanthropy — the Puritan ethic would accept that in all essentials, just as Kant was later to come close to it, influenced by his Scottish ancestry and his strictly pietistic upbringing. (Several of his formulations are directly derived from the ideas of ascetic Protestantism, though this is a point we cannot discuss here.) Nevertheless, the Talmudic ethic is steeped in Oriental traditionalism: 'Rabbi Tanchum ben Chanilai said, "Let man never alter a custom" (*Gemara to Mishna*, VII, I Fol. 86b, No. 93 in Wünsche: the topic is the diet of day-labourers), and this obligation fails to apply only in relation to strangers.

However, the Puritan conception of 'lawfulness' as a validation, as opposed to the Jewish view of it as the mere fulfilment of commandments, obviously gave a much stronger incentive to positive activity. The idea that success is a sign of God's blessing is of course not unknown in Judaism. But the radically different religious and ethical meaning which it took on in consequence of the double ethical standard, internal and external, in Judaism, ruled out any similarity in outcome precisely in this decisive respect. In relation to 'strangers', actions were permitted which were forbidden in relation to 'brothers'. For this reason alone, it was impossible for success in the area of what was in this way not 'commanded' but only 'permitted' to be a criterion of religious validation and an incentive to a methodical ordering of one's life in the sense it was for the Puritan. On this whole problem, whose treatment by Sombart in his book *Die Juden und das Wirtschaft* is in many ways unsatisfactory, see the essays cited above. Detailed discussion would be out of place here. The Jewish ethic, strange as it may appear at first sight, remained markedly traditionalist. Equally, we cannot here go into the enormous shift in inner attitudes to the world which resulted from the Christian interpretation of the concepts of 'grace' and 'salvation', which always in a unique way concealed within itself the seeds of new possibilities of development. On Old Testament 'legalism', cf. also, e.g. Ritschl, *Rechtfertigung und Vershönung*, II, p. 265.

To the English Puritans, the Jews of their own time represented the type of capitalism which they themselves found abhorrent — orientated as it was towards war, state contracts, state monopolies, speculative enterprises and princely projects of building and finance. In fact, the contrast can be formulated in general terms, with the always unavoidable reservations, in this way: Jewish capitalism was speculative pariah capitalism; Puritan capitalism was the bourgeois organisation of labour.

[59] The truth of Holy Scripture follows for Baxter ultimately from the 'wonderful difference of the godly and ungodly', the absolute difference between the 'renewed man' and others, and God's obviously special provision for the spiritual welfare of His own (which may, of course, be manifested in the form of 'trials') — *Christian Directory*, I, p. 165, Col. 2, margin.

[60] To get some sense of this, one has only to read the tortuous attempts made by Bunyan (who after all comes close at times to the mood of Luther's *Freedom of a Christian* — as in 'Of the Law and a Christian', *Works of the Puritan Divines*, p. 254) to come to terms with the parable of the Pharisee and the Publican (see his sermon 'The Pharisee and the Publican', pp. 100f). Why is the Pharisee rejected? He does not truly keep God's commandments: he is obviously a sectarian, concerned only with external trivialities and ceremonies (p. 107); above all, however, he ascribes merit to himself and yet, 'as the Quakers do', thanks God for his virtue, misusing the name of God; he sinfully relies on the merits of his own virtue (p. 126) and in so doing implicitly denies God's election to grace (pp. 139f). His prayer is thus idolatry of the creature and that is what is sinful in it. On the other hand, the Publican, as the sincerity of his confession shows, is inwardly born again, for, as it is expressed, in a characteristic Puritan weakening of the Lutheran idea of conviction of sin, 'to a right and sincere conviction of sin there must be a conviction of the probability of mercy' (p. 209).

61 Reprinted in Gardiner's *Constitutional Documents*. This struggle against anti-authoritarian asceticism may be compared with Louis XIV's persecution of Port-Royal and the Jansenists.

62 Calvin's attitude was in this regard essentially more lenient, at least as far as the more refined aristocratic forms of enjoyment were concerned. The Bible alone determines the limits; anyone who keeps to it and preserves a good conscience is not required anxiously to suspect every impulse in himself to enjoy life. The relevant statements on this point in Chapter X of the *Institution of the Christian Religion* (e.g. *nec fugere ea quoque possumus quae videntur oblectationi magis quam necessitati inservire*) ('and we cannot avoid those things which seem to serve pleasure rather than necessity') could in themselves have opened the door to very lax practices. Along with the increasing anxiety about the certainty of salvation among later generations, another important fact in this respect (which we shall evaluate in another place) is that in the area of the 'church militant' it was the petty bourgeoisie who were responsible for the ethical development of Calvinism.

63 Thomas Adams (*Works of the Puritan Divines*, p. 3), for example, begins a sermon on 'the three divine sisters' ('But the greatest of these is charity') with the allusion that even Paris gave the apple to Aphrodite!

64 Novels and the like are 'wastetimes' and should therefore not be read (Baxter, *Christian Directory*, I, p. 51, Col. 2). The aridity of lyric poetry and folk song, not only of drama, after the Elizabethan period in England is well known. In the visual arts, Puritanism perhaps did not find all that much to suppress. There is, however, a striking decline of musical talent, which seems to have been very good (the part played by England in the history of music was not insignificant) until it reached that nadir which we observe among the Anglo-Saxon nations later, and still today, in that regard. Apart from the Negro churches, and except for the professional singers now engaged by the churches as 'attractions' (Trinity Church, Boston, engaged such a singer in 1904 at a fee of $8,000 a year), all that is usually to be heard in America is a kind of caterwauling, unbearable to German ears, which goes by the name of 'community singing'. (To some extent, a similar development has taken place also in Holland.)

65 It was just the same in Holland, as is clear from the proceedings of the synods. (See the resolution on the Maypole in the Reitsma Collection, VI, 78.139 and *passim*).

66 It is plausible to suppose that the 'Renaissance of the Old Testament' and the pietistic preoccupation with certain Christian feelings of hostility to beauty, ultimately derived from Deutero-Isiah and Psalm 22, must have contributed in the arts to the greater possibility of using ugliness as the subject-matter of art, and that the Puritan rejection of all idolatry of the creature must also have played some part in this. But it is still not possible to be certain about all the details. In the Roman Church, quite different, demagogic, motives produced outwardly similar phenomena — but with totally different artistic results. Anyone who stands before Rembrandt's 'Saul and David' in the Mauritshuis believes himself

to be directly experiencing the powerful impact of Puritan feeling. The brilliant analysis of Dutch cultural influences in Carl Neumann's *Rembrandt* probably indicates the extent of what we can know at present about how far positively beneficial artistic effects can be attributed to ascetic Protestantism.

[67] The relatively less extensive penetration of the Calvinist ethic into practical life in Holland, the weakening of the ascetic spirit there, which began as early as the beginning of the seventeenth century (the English Congregationalists who fled to Holland in 1608 found the inadequate observance of the Sabbath in Holland shocking) but was complete by the time of the Stadtholder Friedrich Heinrich, and the smaller power of expansion of Dutch Puritanism generally were caused by a variety of factors which it would be impossible to go into here. They lay in part in the political system, which was a federation of particularistic towns and districts, and in the much less warlike attitude: the War of Independence was fought in the main with the money of Amsterdam and with mercenaries; English preachers used to illustrate the story of the Tower of Babel by referring to the Dutch army. In this way the seriousness of the religious struggle to a large extent affected others, but at the same time their chance of participating in political power was thrown away. By contrast, Cromwell's army, though in part impressed, felt itself to be a citizen army. Admittedly, it was all the more characteristic that it was just this army which included in its programme the abolition of the duty of bearing arms, on the grounds that it was permissible to fight to the greater glory of God in a cause which could in conscience be known to be right, but not for the whims of princes. The constitution of the English army, which to traditional German ways of thinking is 'immoral', resulted, in its historical origins, from very 'moral' motives and was demanded by soldiers who had never been defeated: only after the Restoration was it used to further the interests of the Crown. The Dutch *schutterijen*, who were the embodiments of Calvinism in the period of the great war, can be seen in Hals' pictures, just half a generation after the Synod of Dordrecht, behaving in a far from 'ascetic' way. The protests from the synods about their manner of life become more and more frequent. The Dutch concept of *Deftigkeit* ('soundness') is a mixture of rational bourgeois 'respectability' and patrician consciousness of status. The gradation of church pews by classes in Dutch churches shows the aristocratic character of this kind of church life even today. The continuation of the town economy retarded industry. It was only through refugees that it received a fresh impetus, and even then it only lasted for a short time in each case. In Holland too, however, the inner-worldly asceticism of Calvinism and Pietism had its effect, and in precisely the same direction as elsewhere. This was true also in the sense of that 'ascetic compulsion to save' which is likewise to be discussed shortly, as Groen van Prinsterer testifies in the passage cited in Note 86 below. The almost complete lack of good literature in Calvinist Holland is naturally no accident. (See on Holland, e.g. Busken-Huët, *Het land van Rembrandt*, which has also been published in German translation by von der Ropp.) The significance of Dutch religion as 'the ascetic compulsion to save' is clearly evident even in the eighteenth century, for example in Albertus Haller's sketches. For the special characteristics of Dutch artistic judgment and its motives compare, for example,

Constantine Huyghens' autobiographical sketches (written in 1629-31) in *Oud Holland*, 1891. (Groen van Prinsterer's work already cited, *La Hollande et l'influence de Calvin* (1864) has nothing decisive to say about our problems.) The colony of New Holland in America was socially a half-feudal domination by 'patrons', that is, merchants who advanced capital, and in contrast with New England it was difficult to induce the 'little man' to emigrate there.

68 It may be recalled that the Puritan town council closed the theatre in Stratford-on-Avon even in Shakespeare's lifetime, indeed while he was spending the last years of his life there. (Shakespeare's hatred and contempt for the Puritans come out at every opportunity.) As late as 1777, the town of Birmingham refused to allow a theatre because it encouraged 'idleness' and so was detrimental to trade. (See Ashley, *Birmingham Industry and Commerce*, 1913, pp. 7-8.)

69 The decisive point here too is that for the Puritans it was simply a matter of 'either-or' — either the will of God or the vanity of His creatures. For this reason there could be nothing 'indifferent' for them. As already pointed out, Calvin's own attitude was different in this regard: what one eats, what clothes one wears and so forth are matters of indifference, as long as they do not have the consequences of enslaving the soul to the power of desire. Freedom from the 'world' should be expressed, as with the Jesuits, in indifference, that is, in Calvin's view, in undiscriminating, dispassionate use of those goods which the earth offers (pp. 409ff of the original edition of the *Institution of the Christian Religion*). This is an attitude which obviously comes closer in effect to the Lutheran than the stricter views of his later followers.

70 Quaker practice in this respect is well known. But already at the beginning of the seventeenth century the exiled congregations in Amsterdam were shaken for a whole decade by the most severe storms over the fashionable hats and dresses of a pastor's wife. (There is an amusing account of this in Dexter's *Congregationalism of the Last Three Hundred Years*.) Sanford (*Studies and Reflections of the Great Rebellion*) has already pointed out that present-day male hair-styles are those of the much-derided 'Roundheads' and that the equally derided style of male clothing of the Puritans is essentially the same, at any rate in underlying principle, as that of the present day.

71 On this point see again Veblen's book (already cited), *The Theory of Business Enterprise*.

72 This is an attitude to which we are constantly coming back. It explains statements like the following: 'Every penny, which is paid upon yourselves and children and friends must be done as by God's own appointment and to serve and please Him. Watch narrowly, or else that thievish carnal self will leave God nothing' (Baxter, *op. cit.*, I, p. 108, bottom right). That is the decisive point: anything used for personal purposes is taken away from the service of God's glory.

73 It is right that we should often be reminded, as we are by Dowden (*Puritan and Anglican*), that, for instance, Cromwell saved Raphael's cartoons and Mantegna's 'Triumph of Caesar' from destruction, while Charles II tried to sell them. As is well known, Restoration society was extremely cool towards English national

literature, or even actually rejected it. In courts everywhere the influence of Versailles was indeed all-powerful.

To analyse in detail the influence exercised on the minds of the highest type of Puritans and those who passed through their schools by this turning away from the unreflecting enjoyment of everyday life would be a task impossible to complete, at any rate within the limits of the present essay. Washington Irving (*Bracebridge Hall*) formulates in the customary English terminology the effect which it had: 'It [political freedom, in his opinion: we should rather say, Puritanism] evinces less play of the fancy, but more power of imagination'. It is only necessary to think of the position of the Scots in science, literature, technical invention, even in business life in England, to feel that this comment, though somewhat narrow in its formulations, is on the right lines.

We shall not speak here of its significance for the development of technology and the empirical sciences. The relationship is evident in all aspects of everyday life. For the Quakers, for instance, the following 'recreations' are permissible (according to Barclay): visiting friends, reading works of history, mathematical and physical experiments, gardening, conversation about business matters and other events in the world and so on. The reason is the one explained earlier.

[74]   Brilliantly analysed in Carl Neumann's *Rembrandt*, which should in general be read in conjunction with the above remarks.

[75]   Thus Baxter in the passage cited earlier, I, p. 108 bottom.

[76]   Compare for example the well-known picture of Colonel Hutchinson in his widow's biography (often quoted, e.g. by Sanford, *Studies and Reflections of the Great Rebellion*, p. 57). After an account of all his chivalrous virtues and his natural tendency towards an unruffled enjoyment of life, it continues: 'He was wonderfully neat, cleanly and genteel in his habit, and had a very good fancy in it; but he left off very early the wearing of anything that was costly...' The ideal Puritan woman depicted in Baxter's funeral oration over Mary Hammer (*Works of the Puritan Divines*, p. 533) is very similar: generous and cultivated, but economical with two things, time and expenditure on 'pomp' and pleasure.

[77]   Among many examples, I remember in particular one industrialist, unusually successful in his business life and in his later years very well-to-do who, when his doctor recommended him to take a few oysters every day for the treatment of a persistent digestive weakness, could only be persuaded to do so with the greatest difficulty. The considerable endowments which he made, during his lifetime, for charitable purposes and his general open-handedness showed, on the other hand, that this was merely a matter of residual 'ascetic' feelings, according to which personal enjoyment of wealth is morally dangerous, and had nothing in common with any form of 'meanness'.

[78]   The separation of workplace, office and 'business' in general from private residence, of firm from name and of business capital from private wealth, together with the tendency to make the 'business' into a 'mystical entity' initially, at least, the corporate wealth), all lay in this direction. On this point, see my *Zur Geschichte der Handelsgesellschaften im Mittelalter*.

79   In some passages in the first edition of his *Kapitalismus*, Sombart has already
      rightly alluded to this characteristic phenomenon. However, it should be noted
      that capital accumulation may stem from two very different psychological
      sources. One can be found at work far back into the mists of antiquity and is
      expressed in the form of bequests, family estates, trusts and so on as well as, or
      rather much more purely and clearly than, in the urge to die sometime encumbered
      with a great weight of material possessions and above all to secure the continued
      existence of the 'business', albeit by damaging the personal interests of the
      majority of one's heirs. In these cases, there is not only a wish to prolong one's
      life (in imagination at least) beyond the grave in one's own creations, but also a
      desire to uphold the splendour of the family, that is, a form of vanity which, so to
      speak, applies to the extended personality of the donor: at all events, it is a
      question of basically egocentric goals. It is quite different in the case of the
      'bourgeois' motive with which we have to do here: there, the principle of
      asceticism, 'Thou shalt deny thyself', is given a positive, capitalist turn, 'Thou
      shalt acquire', and confronts us, plain and unvarnished in its irrationality, as a
      kind of categorical imperative. God's glory and the individual's duty, not human
      vanity, are here, for the Puritans, the only motive; and today, the only motive is
      duty to one's 'calling'. Anyone who enjoys illustrating ideas by their extreme
      consequences should remember the theory of certain American millionaires,
      that the millions one has acquired should not be left to one's children, so that
      they should not be deprived of the moral benefits of having to work and get rich
      themselves: today that is admittedly a purely 'theoretical' fancy.

80   It must be stressed again and again that this is the ultimately decisive religious
      motive, together with the purely ascetic idea of mortifying the flesh: this is
      particularly obvious in the case of the Quakers.

81   Baxter (*Saints' Everlasting Rest*, 12) rejects this, on much the same grounds as
      were commonly given by the Jesuits: the body should be provided with its
      needs, or else one will become its slave.

82   This ideal clearly existed in Quakerism in particular, even in the earliest period
      of its development, as has been shown in important respects by Weingarten in
      his '*Englische Revolutionskirchen*'. Barclay's detailed discussions (*The Apology
      for the True Christian Divinity*, pp. 519ff and 533) also illustrate this very
      clearly. What is to be avoided is, first, creaturely vanity, and so all forms of
      ostentation, finery and use of things which have no practical purpose or are
      valued only for their rarity (that is, out of vanity); secondly, unconscientious use
      of wealth, as in expenditure on less necessary requirements which is
      disproportionate in relation to the necessary requirements of life and provision
      for the future: one might say that the Quaker was thus a walking 'law of
      marginal utility'. 'Moderate use of the creature' is perfectly legitimate, but, in
      particular, attention might be paid to the quality and solidity of materials and so
      forth, insofar as this did not lead to 'vanity'. On all this, cf. *Morgenblatt für
      gebildete Leser*, 1846, No. 216ff. (For comfort and solidity of materials among
      the Quakers in particular, cf. Schneckenburger, *Vorlesungen*, pp. 96f.)

83   It has already been stated above that we shall not consider here the question of the class determinants of religious movements (on this, see my essays on the 'Economic Ethics of the World Religions'). But in order to see that, for instance, Baxter, whom we have used as our principal example, did not see the world through the spectacles of the 'bourgeoisie' of his time, it is sufficient to bear in mind that, even for him, the learned callings were followed in the order of pleasingness to God first by the husbandman, then by mariners, clothiers, booksellers, tailors, etc. in a colourful throng. Moreover, the 'mariners' who are thus characteristically mentioned are perhaps thought of at least as much as fishermen as sailors. In this respect, several of the statements in the Talmud express a different attitude. Cf., e.g. in Wünsche, '*Babyl. Talmud*', II[1], pp. 20, 21, the admittedly not unchallenged statements of Rabbi Eleasar, all to the effect that commerce is better than agriculture. (An intermediate view in II[2], p. 68 on the prudent investment of capital: 1/3 in land, 1/3 in goods, 1/3 as ready money.)

For the sake of those whose conscience cannot be appeased without finding economic ('materialist', as they are unfortunately still called) explanations, it may be remarked here that I consider the influence of economic development on the destiny of systems of religious ideas to be very important, and that I shall later attempt to examine the way in which, in this case, the processes of mutual adaptation and the general relationships between the two came to be what they were. But the content of those religious ideas can by no means be deduced from the 'economic' influences: they are themselves — let us be quite firm about this — the most powerful formative elements of 'national character', they follow their own laws and have compelling power purely in their own right. And furthermore, the most important differences, those between Lutheranism and Calvinism, are primarily the result of *political* causes, to the extent that any extra-religious factors have any part to play.

84   This is what Eduard Bernstein is thinking of when he says in his essay in volume I of the *History of Socialism* (p. 681 and p. 625): 'Asceticism is a bourgeois virtue'. His discussion in this work was the first to point out these important connexions in general. The connexion is, however, much more far-reaching than he supposes. For what was central was not the mere accumulation of capital, but the ascetic rationalisation of the whole of working life.

For the American colonies, Doyle has already clearly emphasised the contrast between the Puritan North, where, as a result of the 'ascetic compulsion to save', there was always capital available for investment, and the situation of the South.

85   Doyle, *The English in America*, II, Ch. I. The existence of iron-working companies (1643), cloth-weaving for the market (1659), and also the flourishing condition of handicrafts in New England in the first generation after the founding of the colony are, from a purely economic point of view, anachronisms. They contrast strikingly, not only with the situation in the South, but also with the non-Calvinist system in Rhode Island, where complete freedom of conscience was enjoyed, and where, despite the excellent harbour, the report of the Governor and Council could still say in 1686, 'The great obstruction concerning trade is

the want of merchants and men of considerable Estates amongst us' (Arnold, *History of the State of Rhode Island*, I, p. 490). It can hardly be doubted in fact that some part was played in this by the pressure towards constant re-investment of saved capital exerted by the Puritan limitation of consumption. Some part was also played by church discipline, though we shall not go further into that here.

[86] That these circles in the Netherlands admittedly rapidly declined is shown by Busken-Huët's discussion (*Het land van Rembrandt*, II, Ch. III and IV). For all that, Groen van Prinsterer (*Handb. d. Gesch. v. h. V.*, 3rd edn, Section 303, Note to p. 254) says: '*De Nederlanders verkoopen veel en verbruiken wenig*', even in the period after the Peace of Westphalia.

[87] For England, it was recommended by, for example, a petition submitted by an aristocratic Royalist after Charles II's entry into London (quoted by Ranke, '*Englische Geschichte*', IV, p. 197) that it should be forbidden by law to acquire landed estates with bourgeois capital, so that such capital would be forced to be applied only to trade.

The 'Regents' in Holland distinguished themselves as an 'Estate' from the bourgeois patriciate of the towns by buying up the old knightly estates. (See on this point the complaint from the year 1652, cited in Fruin, *Tien jaren uit den tachtigjaren oorlog*, that the Regents were now *rentiers* and no longer merchants.) Admittedly, these circles were never inwardly or seriously Calvinist in their attitudes. And the notorious pursuit of nobility and titles which was widespread among the Dutch bourgeoisie in the second half of the seventeenth century shows in itself that one must be cautious, at least in relation to this period, about accepting that contrast between the English and the Dutch situations. The superior strength of inherited wealth here broke through the ascetic spirit.

[88] The extensive purchase of English landed estates by bourgeois capital was followed by the great age of English agriculture.

[89] Even as late as the present century, Anglican landlords have often refused to accept Nonconformists as tenants. (At present, both church parties are approximately equal in numbers, but in the past the Nonconformists were always the minority.)

[90] H. Levy, in his recent paper in *Archiv für Sozialwissenschaft*, XLVI, pp. 605f, has rightly drawn attention to the fact that the English national character, as it can be inferred from a number of its features, made the English less receptive to an ascetic ethos and bourgeois virtues than other nations: an essential feature of their character was, and still is, a certain robust, if crude, vitality. The power of Puritan asceticism in the period of its dominance can be seen precisely in the astonishing degree to which it was able to moderate this character-trait in its adherents.

[91] A constantly recurring theme also in Doyle's discussion. The decisive influence in determining the Puritans' attitudes was always the religious motive (though of course it was not always the sole determinant). In Massachusetts, the colony, under Winthrop's leadership, tended to permit the immigration of gentlemen, even an upper house with an hereditary nobility, provided the gentlemen joined

the church. Settlement was restricted for the sake of church discipline. The colonisation of New Hampshire and Maine was carried out by great Anglican merchants, who established large cattle plantations. Here there was very much less social cohesion.) There were complaints as early as 1632 about the New Englanders' inordinate desire for profit (see, e.g. Weeden's *Economic and Social History of New England*, I, p. 125).

92   This has already been emphasised by Petty in his *Political Arithmetick*; all the contemporary sources without exception speak especially about the members of the Puritan sects (Baptists, Quakers, Mennonites) as belonging to a stratum of society which was partly without resources and partly consisted of small capitalists, contrasting them both with the aristocracy of great merchants and with the financial adventurers. It was precisely this stratum of small capitalists, however, not the great financiers, the monopolists, state contractors, state money-lenders, colonial entrepreneurs, promoters and so forth, which was responsible for the characteristic feature of Western capitalism — the bourgeois, private enterprise organisation of industrial labour. (See, e.g. Unwin, *Industrial Organisation in the 16th and 17th Centuries*, London, 1914, pp. 196ff.) This contrast was familiar to contemporaries themselves: cf. Parker's *Discourse concerning Puritans of 1641*, where likewise the contrast with project-makers and courtiers is emphasised.

93   For the way in which this was expressed in the politics of Pennsylvania in the eighteenth century, especially also in the War of Independence, see Sharpless, *A Quaker Experiment in Government* (Philadelphia, 1902).

94   See Southey's *Life of Wesley*, Ch. 29. The reference, which I did not know, was communicated to me in a letter from Professor Ashley (1913). Ernst Troeltsch, to whom I communicated it for this purpose, has already cited it on occasion.

95   This passage is recommended reading for all those today who think themselves more informed and cleverer on these matters than the leaders and contemporaries of those movements themselves: as can be seen, they knew very well what they were doing and also what risks they were taking. It really will not do to dispute facts which are absolutely indisputable and have never so far been disputed by anyone, and which I have merely tried to relate a little more closely to their underlying causes, and to dispute them so casually as have, unfortunately, some of my critics. No one in the seventeenth century had any doubts about these connexions (cf. Manley, *Usury of 6% Examined*, 1669, p. 137). Quite apart from the modern writers already cited, poets like Heine and Keats, as well as scholars such as Macaulay, Cunningham, and Rogers or writers like Matthew Arnold have taken them for granted. Among the most recent literature, see Ashley, *Birmingham Industry and Commerce* (1913). Ashley has also subsequently expressed his full agreement with me in correspondence. On the whole problem, see Note 4, p. 194 of H. Levy's article cited above.

96   Perhaps there could be no clearer proof of the fact that exactly the same connexions were evident already to the Puritans of the classical period than the argument which Bunyan actually puts into the mouth of Mr. Money-Love: one may become religious in order to become rich, for instance to increase one's

custom. For it does not matter *why* one became religious (p. 114 of Tauchnitz edition).

97   Defoe was a keen Nonconformist.

98   Spener too (*'Theologische Bedenken'*, pp. 426f, 429, 432ff) holds the calling of the merchant to be full of temptations and snares, but he explains in answer to an enquiry, 'It pleases me to see that my dear friend has no scruples as regards trade, but recognises it as a form of life, as it is, in which much that is useful to the human race can be accomplished and so love can be exercised in accordance with God's will'. In various other places there is a more detailed case for this, based on mercantilist arguments. If Spener occasionally, in typically Lutheran fashion, treats the desire to be rich as the principal snare, in accordance with I Timothy 6. 8 and 9 and with an appeal to Jesus Sirach (*v. sup.*), and recommends that it should be unconditionally put aside, and if he adopts the view that wealth is only to be pursued as far as is necessary to meet physical needs (*'Theologische Bedenken'*, III, p. 435 top), he weakens this position on the other hand by referring to those sectaries who prosper and yet live godly lives (see Note 39). Even he does not regard riches as objectionable if they are the result of diligent work in one's calling. Because of the Lutheran elements in his position, it is less consistent than Baxter's.

99   Baxter (*Christian Directory*, II, p. 16) warns against taking on 'heavy, flegmatic, sluggish, fleshly, slothful persons' as 'servants' and recommends that preference be given to 'godly' servants: not only because 'ungodly' servants would be mere 'eye-servants', but above all because 'a truly godly servant will do all your service in obedience to God, as if *God Himself had bid him do it'*. Others, in contrast, would be inclined 'to make no great matter of conscience of it'. Conversely, among workers it is not the outward confession of religion, but the 'conscience to do their duty' which is the mark of the Saint. As can be seen, the interests of God and the employer here merge suspiciously with each other: Spener too (*'Theologische Bedenken'*, II, p. 272), for all his insistent exhortations in other places to set aside time for thinking of God, takes for granted the assumption that workers must be content with the bare minimum of free time (even on Sundays). English writers have rightly called the Protestant immigrants the 'pioneers of skilled labour'. See also the evidence in H. Levy, *'Die Grundlagen des ökonomischen Liberalismus'*, p. 53.

100   The analogy between the predestination of only a few — so 'unjust' by human standards — and the distribution of wealth, equally unjust, but equally the will of God, was brought home continually, e.g. in Hoornbeek, *Theologia Practica*, I, p. 153. Besides, as Baxter says, *op. cit.*, I, p. 380, poverty is very often a symptom of sinful idleness.

101   In Thomas Adams' opinion too (*Works of the Puritan Divines*, p. 158), God in particular probably allows so many to remain poor because He knows they are not mature enough to cope with the temptations which riches bring with them. For riches all too often drive religion from men's minds.

102   See above, Note 45, and the work by H. Levy cited there. Exactly the same point

is emphasised by all the accounts (for instance, by Manley for the Huguenots).

[103] Similar phenomena were also found in England. To that category belong, for instance, the kind of Pietism which was associated with Law's *Serious Call* (1728) and which preached poverty, chastity and — initially — separation from the world.

[104] Baxter's work in Kidderminster, in a parish which had been going to rack and ruin before his arrival, was not only almost unparalleled in the history of the ministry in its degree of success, but also a typical example of the way in which asceticism prepared the masses for labour (or, in Marxist terms, for 'the production of surplus value'), and so in general first made it possible to use them in conditions of capitalist labour (domestic industry, weaving, etc.). The causal relationship generally takes this form. Seen from Baxter's side, he used this process of fitting his charges into the machinery of capitalism to further his own religious and ethical interests. From the point of view of the development of capitalism, these interests of Baxter's helped to further the development of the capitalist 'spirit'.

[105] One further point: it is open to doubt how much power, as a psychological force, there was in the 'joy' of the medieval craftsman in 'what he had created', of which so much play is made. Nevertheless, there is undoubtedly something in it. At all events, asceticism stripped work of all charms in this world (nowadays capitalism has once and for all destroyed them), and directed it to the other world. Work in a calling as such is the will of God. The impersonality of present-day labour, its joylessness and pointlessness for the individual, is here hallowed by religion. Capitalism in the period of its emergence needed workers who would be available for economic use on grounds of conscience. Today it is in the saddle and can compel their labour without rewards in the next world.

[106] See, on these conflicts and developments, H. Levy in the book cited earlier. The historical origins of the typically English and very powerful opposition of public opinion to monopolies lay in an association between the political struggle for power against the Crown (the Long Parliament excluded the monopolists from Parliament) and the ethical motives of Puritanism and the economic interests of bourgeois small and middle capitalism against the financial magnates in the seventeenth century. The Declaration of the Army of 2 August 1652 and also the Petition of the Levellers of 28 January 1653 demand, along with the abolition of excises, tolls, and indirect taxes and the introduction of a single tax on estates, above all 'free trade': that is, abolition of all monopolistic limitations on internal and external trade on the grounds that they violate human rights. There had already been something similar in the 'Grand Remonstrance'.

[107] Cf. on this point H. Levy, *Die Grundlagen des ökonomischen Liberalismus*, pp. 51f.

[108] It perhaps would be more appropriate to a somewhat different context to point out that even here those elements which have not yet been traced back to their religious roots, especially the dictum that 'honesty is the best policy' (in Franklin's discussion of credit), are of Puritan origin. (See my essay on 'The Protestant

Sects and the Spirit of Capitalism'.) Here I shall simply reproduce the following remarks by J.A. Rowntree (*Quakerism Past and Present*, pp. 95-6), to which Eduard Bernstein has drawn my attention: 'Is it merely a coincidence, or is it a consequence, that the lofty profession of spirituality made by the Friends has gone hand in hand with shrewdness and tact in the transaction of mundane affairs? Real piety favours the success of a trader by insuring his integrity, and fostering habits of prudence and forethought: — important items in obtaining that standing and credit in the commercial world, which are requisite for the steady accumulation of wealth'. (See the essay on 'The Protestant Sects'.) 'Honest as a Huguenot' was as proverbial in the seventeenth century as the integrity of the Dutch which Sir William Temple so admired, and as, a century later, was that of the English, compared with the Continentals who had not passed through this ethical school.

109   Well analysed in Bielschowsky's *Goethe*, II, Ch. 18. For the development of the scientific 'cosmos', cf. the similar view expressed, e.g. by Windelband at the conclusion of his '*Blütezeit der deutschen Philosophie*' (the second volume of his *Geschichte der neueren Philosophie*).

110   *Saints' Everlasting Rest*, Ch. XII.

111   'Couldn't the old man rest content with his $75,000 a year? No! The front of the store must be widened to 400 feet. Why? That beats everything, he thinks. Evenings, when his wife and daughter read together, he just longs to go to bed; Sundays, he's looking at the clock every five minutes to see when the day will end: what a misguided life!' This was the verdict of the son-in-law (a German immigrant) of the leading dry-goods man of a town in Ohio on his father-in-law — a verdict which no doubt seemed to the 'old man' for his part totally incomprehensible and a symptom of German lack of energy.

112   This remark (which I have here allowed to stand unaltered) ought to have shown Brentano (*Die Anfänge des modernen Kapitalismus*) in itself that I have never doubted its independent significance. That humanism too was not pure 'rationalism' has recently been strongly emphasised again by Borinski in *Abhandl. der Münchener Ak. der Wiss.* (1919).

113   Not this problem, but that of the Reformation in general, especially Luther, is the concern of von Below's Academic Address, *Die Ursachen der Reformation* (Freiburg, 1916). For the topic treated here, especially the controversies relating to this study, reference may be made to Hermelink's *Reformation und Gegenreformation*, although that is primarily concerned with other problems.

114   For the foregoing sketch has deliberately concerned itself only with those relationships in which there is no doubt about the influence of religious consciousness on 'material' civilisation. It would have been easy to go on from that to a neat 'construction', in which all that is most 'characteristic' of modern culture would have been logically deduced from Protestant rationalism. But that kind of thing is best left to the type of dilettante who believes in the 'uniformity' of the 'collective psyche' and the possibility of reducing it to a single formula.

It should, however, be remarked that, of course, the period of capitalist development which preceded that considered in our study was everywhere influenced in part by Christianity, which both retarded and advanced it. The nature of these influences belongs in a later chapter. Furthermore, whether any of the wider problems outlined above can be discussed within the framework of the *Archiv für Sozialwissenschaft und Sozialpolitik* is not certain, in view of the type of problems with which the journal deals. But the idea of writing thick tomes which would have to rely as heavily as they would in this case on the works of foreign theologians and historians is not one which fills me with much enthusiasm. (I have allowed these sentences to stand here unaltered.) For the tension between ideals and reality in the 'early capitalist' period before the Reformation see Strieder, *Studien zur Geschichte der kapitalistischen Organisationsformen* (1914), Book II (also against the work by Keller referred to earlier and used by Sombart).

[115] It seems to me that this sentence and the immediately preceding remarks and notes should be more than enough to obviate all misunderstanding of what this study has tried to achieve and I can see no reason to amend it in any way. I have abandoned my original intention of proceeding directly along the lines of the further programme suggested above, and have now decided, partly for accidental reasons, especially because of the appearance of Troeltsch's *Soziallehren der christlichen Kirchen* (which has settled several of the problems which I should have had to consider in a way which I, as a non-theologian, could not have done), but partly also in order to take these studies out of their isolation and place them in the context of general cultural development, that I shall first set down the results of comparative studies on the connexions between religion and society in world history. These follow here. They are preceded merely by a short essay written for the occasion intended to clarify the concept of a 'sect' used above and also to examine the significance of the Puritan conception of the church for the modern capitalist spirit.

5️⃣ Karl Marx

The chapter on Marx begins with excerpts from Feuerbach intended to familiarize the student with Marxist methodology of historical and dialectical materialism. Taken from *The German Ideology*, this text shows, through the critique of the Hegelian and neo-Hegelian schools, the primacy of the material conditions of production and reproduction. In this text Marx asserts that the material conditions of production form the bases upon which certain forms of ideologies are developed and reflected. But the relationship is not one-sided. These ideologies, in turn, impact on the material conditions and, along with the latter, contribute to changes in the social structure. The relationship between the material base, the economic conditions, known also as the structure, on the one hand, and ideology or the superstructure on the other, is perceived by Marx as one of dialectical character, whereby both the structure and the superstructure reflect and impact on each other.

The relationship between structure and superstructure is demonstrated through a number of examples, such as the relationship of state and law to property. As we shall see later in this introduction, Marx in Part VIII of *Capital* Vol. 1 paid special attention to the role of the British state, which, through the use of legal and extra-legal means, was able to speed up the process of capitalist production.

Capital Vol. 1, from which one of the following texts is taken, is about the history of the development of capital in Western Europe. Capital, Marx reminds us, is not a thing, it is not a sum of articles, commodities or money; rather it is an expression of social relations of production. Capitalism as a system or mode of production, Marx asserts, is a historical phenomenon. It developed under specific historical, social and economic conditions with the help of certain political and ideological forces.

Marx traces the development of capitalism through its simplest form, "simple commodity production". Simple commodity production refers to a historic period where direct producers produced commodities primarily for consumption. Goods or commodities at this stage were not for sale nor were they oriented for the market. Self-sufficiency and a low level of productive forces or means of production were characteristic of this stage of production.

Increasing population and demand, combined with the introduction of the steam engine and the development in general of the forces of production, have pushed production to a higher level, shifting its orientation from one based on local sufficiency to one oriented towards the national or even the international market.

Essential to the understanding of the capitalist mode of production, Marx maintains, is recognizing the shift or change in the use, meaning and value of labour. While in pre-capitalist modes of production, labour power was invested in producing use-value or goods for immediate consumption; in capitalism, labour power is hired to produce exchange-value or commodities for the market. The significance of this change lies in the ability of capitalism to mask the actual relations of production and distort the origin of capital. To explain the process which mystifies production relations, Marx develops the labour theory of value. According to this theory, the value of a commodity represents the labour power and consequently the labour-time necessary in the production of the item/commodity. In the same way one should measure the value of labour power or the labourer which under capitalism is turned into a commodity. The value of the labourer, thus, is the total sum necessary for his or her reproduction.

Yet, the value of the labourer identified above is only partial, since it covers only the bare necessities of the labourer's daily survival. As Marx observes, the capitalist does not live from day to day, he must have long-term plans. For that reason, the capitalist must ensure a new generation of workers that is also equipped with the skills necessary at that historical moment. Put together, the value of the labourer — expressed in the wage, salary he or she receives — would have to cover both daily maintenance as well as generational and historical reproduction. It is clear that workers do not receive the value of their labour power under capitalism.

Marx identifies two forms of labour; live labour, which refers to the capacity to work or the time and energy invested by the worker in creating new values; and dead labour, which refers to already produced commodities. These include the very items, tools and machines, the labourer uses during the production process. This theory, known as the labour theory of value, figures prominently in all of Marx's works and particularly *Capital*.

Through the labour theory of value, Marx intended to demonstrate one simple fact. Namely, that capital is not a trans-historical phenomenon. It is not a thing that can be found, like in fairy-tales of treasures in distant lands, nor is it generated by the capitalists as we come to assume. Instead, capital is the product, the labour of the labourers, it is the product of the labour-time invested by the workers in the production or creation process. Capital, in other words, is labour, both the dead and live portions of labour. The main question here is: If capital is the product of the labourer, how is it then that the capitalist and not the labourer owns capital? It is at this juncture that Marx elaborates on the concept of "surplus" as the means to express the relationship of contradictions between the two major classes: the proletariat and the bourgeoisie.

The proletariat refers to the social class which does not own the means of production and is forced to sell its labour power to survive. The bourgeoisie, on the other hand, refers to the class which owns the means of production, yet does not labour. To simplify the relationship, Marx envisaged a meeting between the two (a capitalist and a labourer). The capitalist offers the workplace, tools, machines and raw materials and the labourer invests his labour-time converting raw materials into commodities. At the end of the working day, the labourer receives a certain sum of money and the capitalist, after selling the product, receives value, which exceeds that which he invested at the beginning of the labour day. To this additional value Marx refers as "surplus value". This value represents the extra, additional or surplus labour-time which the labourer invests and is not paid for. In other words, "surplus value" represents "free" labour-time by the worker.

Because of the unequal relationship to the means of production within which the two classes begin the production process, a class of dispossessed and a class of owners, the relationship between the two necessarily becomes one of exploitation. This necessary relationship keeps the two apart and in constant contradictions. This contradiction is reinforced during the production process, as the workers are required to produce surplus value to which they have no access. During the production process the relations of contradictions become relations of exploitation.

Marx identifies another force that develops in the process of capitalist development and contributes further to the alienation and estrangement of the two classes, particularly the proletariat. This is the concept of the division of labour. The division of labour, which refers to the division between town/ country, agriculture/industry, mental/physical labour...etc., is a force that contributes to widening the gap between society's social classes. Unlike the meaning attributed to the division of labour by Emile Durkheim, Marx has no doubts that the division of labour characteristic of capitalism is but a source of further friction, contradiction and socio-economic alienation.

To eliminate contradictions one needs to eliminate exploitation or the generation of surplus, and to do that the whole system of the relations of production has to transform into a new one based on different relations of production. In other words, an alternative system to capitalist production must develop.

In *Capital* Marx is not only concerned with the scientific economic laws that govern the movement of capital and the dynamics of capitalist production. As we see in the text he is also concerned with the historic conditions that give rise to the emergence of these classes. Marx's discussion of the historical context for the emergence of capitalism appears in Part VIII (the last chapter of *Capital*). In this chapter, Marx analyzes the socio-political and historic conditions and forces that lead to the destruction of the indigenous natural economy, the feudal mode of production in Europe and its replacement with the capitalist mode of production. In effect, one can make the argument that on grounds of both logical and historical reasons, Part VIII of *Capital* was supposed to be the first part in the book, for it provides the grounds and genesis for the development of capitalism.

Marx challenges the theories that assume that the transition to capitalism is a peaceful process. By criticising the so-called primitive accumulation, he demonstrates, through the case study of British history, the harsh and rather brutal conditions under which the agricultural direct producers were forced out of their land, expropriated from the land, freed from their natural possession of and direct access to the means of production and forced to become sellers of their labour power. Forced expropriation was not done by the capitalists alone. They were reinforced throughout the process by the state, itself described by Marx as largely the protector of the interests of the capitalist class.

Force, violence, legal and extra-legal force, Marx asserts, have accompanied the whole process of capitalist development. The intervention of the British state, whether in the expropriation of the land, expropriation of the peasants or through the regulation of the relations of exploitation is analyzed throughout these pages.

FEUERBACH
OPPOSITION OF THE MATERIALIST AND IDEALIST OUTLOOK

A. Idealism and Materialism

The Illusions of German Ideology

As we hear from German ideologists, Germany has in the last few years gone through an unparalleled revolution. The decomposition of the Hegelian philosophy, which began with Strauss, has developed into a universal ferment into which all the powers of the past are swept. In the general chaos mighty empires have arisen only to meet with immediate doom, heroes have emerged momentarily only to be hurled back into obscurity by bolder and stronger rivals. It was a revolution beside which the French Revolution was child's play, a world struggle beside which the struggles of the Diadochi [successors of Alexander the Great] appear insignificant. Principles ousted one another, heroes of the mind overthrew each other with unheard-of rapidity, and in the three years 1842-45 more of the past was swept away in Germany than at other times in three centuries.

All this is supposed to have taken place in the realm of pure thought.

Certainly it is an interesting event we are dealing with: the putrescence of the absolute spirit. When the last spark of its life had failed, the various components of this *caput mortuum* began to decompose, entered into new combinations and formed new substances. The industrialists of philosophy, who till then had lived on the exploitation of the absolute spirit, now seized upon the new combinations. Each with all possible zeal set about retailing his apportioned share. This naturally gave rise to competition, which, to start with, was carried on in moderately staid bourgeois fashion. Later when the German market was glutted, and the commodity in spite of all efforts found no response in the world market, the business was spoiled in the usual German manner by fabricated and fictitious production, deterioration in quality, adulteration of the raw materials, falsification of labels, fictitious purchases, bill-jobbing and a credit system devoid of any real basis. The competition turned into a bitter struggle, which is now being extolled and interpreted to us as a revolution of world significance, the begetter of the most prodigious results and achievements.

If we wish to rate at its true value this philosophic charlatanry, which awakens even in the breast of the honest German citizen a glow of national pride, if we wish to bring out clearly the pettiness, the parochial narrowness of this whole Young-Hegelian movement and in particular the tragicomic contrast between the illusions of these heroes about their achievements and the actual achievements themselves, we must look at the whole spectacle from a standpoint beyond the frontiers of Germany.

German criticism has, right up to its latest efforts, never quitted the realm of philosophy. Far from examining its general philosophic premises, the whole body of its inquiries has actually sprung from the soil of a definite philosophical system, that of Hegel. Not only in their answers but in their very questions there was a mystification. This dependence on Hegel is the reason why not one of these modern critics has even attempted a comprehensive criticism of the Hegelian system, however much each professes to have advanced beyond Hegel. Their polemics against Hegel and against one another are confined to this — each extracts one side of the Hegelian system and turns this against the whole system as well as against the sides extracted by the others. To begin with they extracted pure unfalsified Hegelian categories such as substance and "self-consciousness", later they desecrated these categories with more secular names such as "species", "the Unique", "Man", etc.

The entire body of German philosophical criticism from Strauss to Stirner is confined to criticism of *religious* conceptions. The critics started from real religion and actual theology. What religious consciousness and a religious conception really meant was determined variously as they went along. Their advance consisted in subsuming the allegedly dominant metaphysical, political, juridical, moral and other conceptions under the class of religious or theological conceptions; and similarly in pronouncing political, juridical, moral consciousness as religious or theological, and the political, juridical, moral man — "*man*" in the last resort — as religious. The dominance of religion was taken for granted. Gradually every dominant relationship was pronounced a religious relationship and transformed into a cult, a cult of law, a cult of the State, etc. On all sides it was only a question of dogmas and belief in dogmas. The world sanctified to an ever-increasing extent till at last our venerable Saint Max was able to canonise it *en bloc* and thus dispose of it once for all.

The Old Hegelians had *comprehended* everything as soon as it was reduced to an Hegelian logical category. The Young Hegelians *criticised* everything by attributing to it religious conceptions or by pronouncing it a theological matter. The Young Hegelians are in agreement with the Old Hegelians in their belief in the rule of religion, of concepts, of a universal principle in the existing world. Only, the one party attacks this dominion as usurpation, while the other extols it as legitimate.

Since the Young Hegelians consider conceptions, thoughts, ideas, in fact all the products of consciousness, to which they attribute an independent existence, as the real chains of men (just as the Old Hegelians declared them the true bonds of human society) it is evident that the Young Hegelians have to fight only against these illusions of consciousness. Since, according to their fantasy, the relationships of men, all their doings, their chains and their limitations are products of their consciousness, the Young Hegelians logically put to men the moral postulate of exchanging their present consciousness for human, critical or egoistic consciousness, and thus of removing their limitations. This demand to change consciousness amounts to a demand to interpret reality in another way, i.e. to recognise it by means of another interpretation. The Young-Hegelian ideologists, in spite of their allegedly "world-shattering" statements, are the staunchest conservatives. The most recent of them have found the correct expression for their activity when they declare they are only fighting against *"phrases"*. They forget, however, that to these phrases they themselves are only opposing other phrases, and that they are in no way combating the real existing world when they are merely combating the phrases of this world. The only results which this philosophic criticism could achieve were a few (and at that thoroughly one-sided) elucidations of Christianity from the point of view of religious history; all the rest of their assertions are only further embellishments of their claim to have furnished, in these unimportant elucidations, discoveries of universal importance.

It has not occurred to any one of these philosophers to inquire into the connection of German philosophy with German reality, the relation of their criticism to their own material surroundings.

First Premises of Materialist Method

The premises from which we begin are not arbitrary ones, not dogmas, but real premises from which abstraction can only be made in the imagination. They are the real individuals, their activity and the material conditions under which they live, both those which they find already existing and those produced by their activity. These premises can thus be verified in a purely empirical way.

The first premise of all human history is, of course, the existence of living human individuals. Thus the first fact to be established is the physical organisation of these individuals and their consequent relation to the rest of nature. Of course, we cannot here go either into the actual physical nature of man, or into the natural conditions in which man finds himself — geological, oreohydrographical, climatic and so on. The writing of history must always set out from these natural bases and their modification in the course of history through the action of men.

Men can be distinguished from animals by consciousness, by religion or anything else you like. They themselves begin to distinguish themselves from animals as soon as they begin to *produce* their means of subsistence, a step which is conditioned by their physical organisation. By producing their means of subsistence men are indirectly producing their actual material life.

The way in which men produce their means of subsistence depends first of all on the nature of the actual means of subsistence they find in existence and have to reproduce. This mode of production must not be considered simply as being the production of the physical existence of the individuals. Rather it is a definite form of activity of these individuals, a definite form of expressing their life, a definite *mode of life* on their part. As individuals express their life, so they are. What they are, therefore, coincides with their production, both with what they produce and with *how* they produce. The nature of individuals thus depends on the material conditions determining their production.

This production only makes its appearance with the *increase of population*. In its turn this presupposes the *intercourse [Verkehr]*[1] of individuals with one another. The form of this intercourse is again determined by production.

The relations of different nations among themselves depend upon the extent to which each has developed its productive forces, the division of labour and internal intercourse. This statement is generally recognised. But not only the relation of one nation to others, but also the whole internal structure of the nation itself depends on the stage of development reached by its production and its internal and external intercourse. How far the productive forces of a nation are developed is shown most manifestly by the degree to which the division of labour has been carried. Each new productive force, insofar as it is not merely a quantitative extension of productive forces already known (for instance the bringing into cultivation of fresh land), causes a further development of the division of labour.

The division of labour inside a nation leads at first to the separation of industrial and commercial from agricultural labour, and hence to the separation of *town* and *country* and to the conflict of their interests. Its further development leads to the separation of commercial from industrial labour. At the same time through the division of labour inside these various branches there develop various divisions among the individuals co-operating in definite kinds of labour. The relative position of these individual groups is determined by the methods employed in agriculture, industry and commerce (patriarchalism, slavery, estates, classes). These same conditions are to be seen (given a more developed intercourse) in the relations of different nations to one another.

The various stages of development in the division of labour are just so many different forms of ownership, i.e. the existing stage in the division of labour determines also the relations of individuals to one another with reference to the material, instrument, and product of labour.

The first form of ownership is tribal [*Stammeigentum*][2] ownership. It corresponds to the undeveloped stage of production, at which a people lives by hunting and fishing, by the rearing of beasts or, in the highest stage, agriculture. In the latter case it presupposes a great mass of uncultivated stretches of land. The division of labour is at this stage still very elementary and is confined to a further extension of the natural division of labour existing in the family. The social structure is, therefore, limited to an extension of the family; patriarchal family chieftains, below them the members of the tribe, finally slaves. The slavery latent in the family only develops gradually with the increase of population, the growth of wants, and with the extension of external relations, both of war and of barter.

The second form is the ancient communal and State ownership which proceeds especially from the union of several tribes into a *city* by agreement or by conquest, and which is still accompanied by slavery. Beside communal ownership we already find movable, and later also immovable, private property developing, but as an abnormal form subordinate to communal ownership. The citizens hold power over their labouring slaves only in their community, and on this account alone, therefore, they are bound to the form of communal ownership. It is the communal private property which compels the active citizens to remain in this spontaneously derived form of association over against their slaves. For this reason the whole structure of society based on this communal ownership, and with it the power of the people, decays in the same measure as, in particular, immovable private property evolves. The division of labour is already more developed. We already find the antagonism of town and country; later the antagonism between those states which represent town interests and those which represent country interests, and inside the towns themselves the antagonism between industry and maritime commerce. The class relation between citizens and slaves is now completely developed.

With the development of private property, we find here for the first time the same conditions which we shall find again, only on a more extensive scale, with modern private property. On the one hand, the concentration of private property, which began very early in Rome (as the Licinian agrarian law proves[3]) and proceeded very rapidly from the time of the civil wars and especially under the Emperors; on the other hand, coupled with this, the transformation of the plebeian small peasantry into a proletariat, which, however, owing to its intermediate position between propertied citizens and slaves, never achieved an independent development.

The third form of ownership is feudal or estate property. If antiquity started out from the *town* and its little territory, the Middle Ages started out from the *country*. This different starting-point was determined by the sparseness of the population at that time, which was scattered over a large area and which received no large increase from the conquerors. In contrast to Greece and Rome, feudal development at the outset, therefore, extends over a much wider territory, prepared by the Roman conquests and the spread of agriculture at first associated with it. The last centuries of the declining Roman Empire and its conquest by the barbarians destroyed a number of productive forces; agriculture had declined, industry had decayed for want of a market, trade had died out or been violently suspended, the rural and urban population had decreased. From these conditions and the mode of organisation of the conquest determined by them, feudal property developed under the influence of the Germanic military constitution. Like tribal and communal ownership, it is based again on a community; but the directly producing class standing over against it is not, as in the case of the ancient community, the slaves, but the enserfed small peasantry. As soon as feudalism is fully developed, there also arises antagonism to the towns. The hierarchical structure of landownership, and the armed bodies of retainers associated with it, gave the nobility power over the serfs. This feudal organisation was, just as much as the ancient communal ownership, an association against a subjected producing class; but the form of association and the relation to the direct producers were different because of the different conditions of production.

This feudal system of landownership had its counterpart in the *towns* in the shape of corporative property, the feudal organisation of trades. Here property consisted chiefly in the labour of each individual person. The necessity for association against the organised robber-nobility, the need for communal covered markets in an age when the industrialist was at the same time a merchant, the growing competition of the escaped serfs swarming into the rising towns, the feudal structure of the whole country: these combined to bring about the *guilds*. The gradually accumulated small capital of individual craftsmen and their stable numbers, as against the growing population, evolved the relation of journeyman and apprentice, which brought into being in the towns a hierarchy similar to that in the country.

Thus the chief form of property during the feudal epoch consisted on the one hand of landed property with serf labour chained to it, and on the other of the labour of the individual with small capital commanding the labour of journeymen. The organisation of both was determined by the restricted conditions of production — the small-scale and primitive cultivation of the land, and the craft type of industry. There was little division of labour in the heyday of feudalism. Each country bore in itself the antithesis of town and country; the division into estates was certainly strongly marked; but apart from the differentiation of princes, nobility, clergy and peasants in the country, and masters, journeymen, apprentices and soon also the rabble of casual labourers in the towns, no division of importance took place. In agriculture it was rendered difficult by the strip-system, beside which the cottage industry of the peasants themselves emerged. In industry there was no division of labour at all in the individual trades themselves, and very little between them. The separation of industry and commerce was found already in existence in older towns; in the newer it only developed later, when the towns entered into mutual relations.

The grouping of larger territories into feudal kingdoms was a necessity for the landed nobility as for the towns. The organisation of the ruling class, the nobility, had, therefore, everywhere a monarch at its head.

The fact is, therefore, that definite individuals who are productively active in a definite way enter into these definite social and political relations. Empirical observation must in each separate instance bring out empirically, and without any mystification and speculation, the connection of the social and political structure with production. The social structure and the State are continually evolving out of the life-process of definite individuals, but of individuals, not as they may appear in their own or other people's imagination, but as they *really* are; i.e. as they operate, produce materially, and hence as they work under definite material limits, presuppositions and conditions independent of their will.

The production of ideas, of conceptions, of consciousness, is at first directly interwoven with the material activity and the material intercourse of men, the language of real life. Conceiving, thinking, the mental intercourse of men, appear at this stage as the direct efflux of their material behaviour. The same applies to mental production as expressed in the language of politics, laws, morality, religion, metaphysics, etc. of a people. Men are the producers of their conceptions, ideas, etc. — real, active men, as they are conditioned by a definite development of their productive forces and of the intercourse corresponding to these, up to its furthest forms. Consciousness can never be anything else than conscious existence, and the existence of men is their actual life-process. If in all ideology men and their circumstances appear upside-down as in a *camera obscura*, this phenomenon arises just as much from their historical life-process as the inversion of objects on the retina does from their physical life-process.

In direct contrast to German philosophy which descends from heaven to earth, here we ascend from earth to heaven. That is to say, we do not set out from what men say, imagine, conceive, nor from men as narrated, thought of, imagined, conceived, in order to arrive at men in the flesh. We set out from real, active men, and on the basis of their real life-process we demonstrate the development of the ideological reflexes and echoes of this life-process. The phantoms formed in the human brain are also, necessarily, sublimates of their material life-process, which is empirically verifiable and bound to material premises. Morality, religion, metaphysics, all the rest of ideology and their corresponding forms of consciousness, thus no longer retain the semblance of independence. They have no history, no development; but men, developing their material production and their material intercourse, alter, along with this their real existence, their thinking and the products of their thinking. Life is not determined by consciousness, but consciousness by life. In the first method of approach the starting-point is consciousness taken as the living individual; in the second method, which conforms to real life, it is the real living individuals themselves, and consciousness is considered solely as *their* consciousness.

This method of approach is not devoid of premises. It starts out from the real premises and does not abandon them for a moment. Its premises are men, not in any fantastic isolation and rigidity, but in their actual, empirically perceptible process of development under definite conditions. As soon as this active life-process is described, history ceases to be a collection of dead facts as it is with the empiricists (themselves still abstract), or an imagined activity of imagined subjects, as with the idealists.

Where speculation ends — in real life — there real, positive science begins: the representation of the practical activity, of the practical process of development of men. Empty talk about consciousness ceases, and real knowledge has to take its place. When reality is depicted, philosophy as an independent branch of knowledge loses its medium of existence. At the best its place can only be taken by a summing-up of the most general results, abstractions which arise from the observation of the historical development of men. Viewed apart from real history, these abstractions have in themselves no value whatsoever. They can only serve to facilitate the arrangement of historical material, to indicate the sequence of its separate strata. But they by no means afford a recipe of schema, as does philosophy, for neatly trimming the epochs of history. On the contrary, our difficulties begin only when we set about the observation and the arrangement — the real depiction — of our historical material, whether of a past epoch or of the present. The removal of these difficulties is governed by premises which it is quite impossible to state here, but which only the study of the actual life-process and the activity of the individuals of each epoch will make evident. We shall select here some of these abstractions, which we use in contradistinction to the ideologists, and shall illustrate them by historical examples.

History: Fundamental Conditions

Since we are dealing with the Germans, who are devoid of premises, we must begin by stating the first premise of all human existence and, therefore, of all history, the premise, namely, that men must be in a position to live in order to be able to "make history". But life involves before everything else eating and drinking, a habitation, clothing and many other things. The first historical act is thus the production of the means to satisfy these needs, the production of material life itself. And indeed this is an historical act, a fundamental condition of all history, which today, as thousands of years ago, must daily and hourly be fulfilled merely in order to sustain human life. Even when the sensuous world is reduced to a minimum, to a stick as with Saint Bruno [Bauer], it presupposes the action of producing the stick. Therefore in any interpretation of history one has first of all to observe this fundamental fact in all its significance and all its implications and to accord it its due importance. It is well known that the Germans have never done this, and they have never, therefore, had an *earthly* basis for history and consequently never an historian. The French and the English, even if they have conceived the relation of this fact with so-called history only in an extremely one-sided fashion, particularly as long as they remained in the toils of political ideology, have nevertheless made the first attempts to give the writing of history a materialistic basis by being the first to write histories of civil society, of commerce and industry.

The second point is that the satisfaction of the first need (the action of satisfying, and the instrument of satisfaction which has been acquired) leads to new needs; and this production of new needs is the first historical act. Here we recognise immediately the spiritual ancestry of the great historical wisdom of the Germans who, when they run out of positive material and when they can serve up neither theological nor political nor literary rubbish, assert that this is not history at all, but the "prehistoric era". They do not, however, enlighten us as to how we proceed from this nonsensical "prehistory" to history proper; although, on the other hand, in their historical speculation they seize upon this "prehistory" with especial eagerness because they imagine themselves safe there from interference on the part of "crude facts", and, at the same time, because there they can give full rein to their speculative impulse and set up and knock down hypotheses by the thousand.

The third circumstance which, from the very outset, enters into historical development, is that men, who daily remake their own life, begin to make other men, to propagate their kind: the relation between man and woman, parents and children, the *family*. The family, which to begin with is the only social relationship, becomes later, when increased needs create a new social relations and the increased population new needs, a subordinate one (except in Germany), and must then be treated and analysed according to the existing empirical data, not according to the concept of the family, as is the custom in Germany.[4] These three aspects of social activity are not of course to be taken as three different stages, but just as three aspects or, to make it clear to the Germans, "three moments", which have existed simultaneously since the dawn of history and the first men, and which still assert themselves in history today.

The production of life, both of one's own in labour and of fresh life in procreation, now appears as a double relationship: on the one hand as a natural, on the other as a social relationship. By social we understand the co-operation of several individuals, no matter under what conditions, in what manner and to what end. It follows from this that a certain mode of production, or industrial stage, is always combined with a certain mode of co-operation, or social stage, and this mode of co-operation is itself a "productive force". Further, that the multitude of productive forces accessible to men determines the nature of society, hence, that the history of humanity must always be studied and treated in relation to the history of industry and exchange, But it is also clear how in Germany it is impossible to write this sort of history, because the Germans lack not only the necessary power of comprehension and the material but also the "evidence of their senses", for across the Rhine you cannot have any experience of these things since history has stopped happening. Thus it is quite obvious from the start that there exists a materialistic connection of men with one another, which is determined by their needs and their mode of production, and which is as old as men themselves. This connection is ever taking on new forms, and thus presents a "history" independently of the existence of any political or religious nonsense which in addition may hold men together.

Only now, after having considered four moments, four aspects of the primary historical relationships, do we find that man also possesses "consciousness", but, even so, not inherent, not "pure" consciousness. From the start the "spirit" is afflicted with the curse of being "burdened" with matter, which here makes its appearance in the form of agitated layers of air, sounds, in short, of language. Language is as old as consciousness, language *is* practical consciousness that exists also for other men, and for that reason alone it really exists for me personally as well; language, like consciousness, only arises from the need, the necessity, of intercourse with other men. Where there exists a relationship, it exists for me: the animal does not enter into "*relations*" with anything, it does not enter into any relation at all. For the animal, its relation to others does not exist as a relation. Consciousness is, therefore, from the very beginning a social product, and remains so as long as men exist at all. Consciousness is at first, of course, merely consciousness concerning the *immediate* sensuous environment and consciousness of the limited connection with other persons and things outside the individual who is growing self-conscious. At the same time it is consciousness of nature, which first appears to men as a completely alien, all-powerful and unassailable force, with which men's relations are purely animal and by which they are overawed like beasts; it is thus a purely animal consciousness of nature (natural religion) just because nature is as yet hardly modified historically. (We see here immediately: this natural religion or this particular relation of men to nature is determined by the form of society and vice versa. Here, as everywhere, the identity of nature and man appears in such a way that the restricted relation of men to nature determines their restricted relation to one another, and their restricted relation to one another determines men's restricted relation to nature.) On the other hand, man's consciousness of the necessity of associating with the individuals around him is the beginning of the consciousness that he is living in society at all. This beginning is as animal as social life itself at this stage. It is mere herd-consciousness, and at this point man is only distinguished from sheep by the fact that with him consciousness takes the place of instinct or that his instinct is a conscious one. This sheep-like or tribal consciousness receives its further development and extension through increased productivity, the increase of needs, and, what is fundamental to both of these, the increase of population. With these there develops the division of labour, which was originally nothing but the division of labour in the sexual act, then that division of labour which develops spontaneously or "naturally" by virtue of natural predisposition (e.g. physical strength), needs, accidents, etc. etc. Division of labour only becomes truly such from the moment when a division of material and mental labour appears. (The first form of ideologists, *priests*, is concurrent.) From this moment onwards consciousness *can* really flatter itself that it is something other than consciousness of existing practice, that it *really* represents something without representing something real; from now on consciousness is in a position to emancipate itself from the world and to proceed to the formation of pure theory, theology, philosophy, ethics, etc. But even if this theory, theology, philosophy, ethics, etc. comes into contradiction with the existing relations, this can only occur because existing social relations have come into contradiction with existing forces of production; this, moreover, can also occur in a particular national sphere of relations through the appearance of the contradiction, not within the national orbit, but between this national consciousness and the practice of other nations, i.e. between the national and the general consciousness of a nation (as we see it now in Germany).

Moreover, it is quite immaterial what consciousness starts to do on its own: out of all such muck we get only the one inference that these three moments, the forces of production, the state of society, and consciousness, can and must come into contradiction with one another, because the *division of labour* implies the possibility, nay the fact that intellectual and material activity — enjoyment and labour, production and consumption — devolve on different individuals, and that the only possibility of their not coming into contradiction lies in the negation in its turn of the division of labour. It is self-evident, moreover, that "spectres", "bonds", "the higher being", "concept", "scruple", are merely the idealistic, spiritual expression, the conception apparently of the isolated individual, the image of very empirical fetters and limitations, within which the mode of production of life and the form of intercourse coupled with it move.

Private Property and Communism

With the division of labour, in which all these contradictions are implicit, and which in its turn is based on the natural division of labour in the family and the separation of society into individual families opposed to one another, is given simultaneously the *distribution*, and indeed the *unequal* distribution, both quantitative and qualitative, of labour and its products, hence property: the nucleus, the first form, of which lies in the family, where wife and children are the slaves of the husband. This latent slavery in the family, though still very crude, is the first property, but even at this early stage it corresponds perfectly to the definition of modern economists who call it the power of disposing of the labour-power of others. Division of labour and private property are, moreover, identical expressions: in the one the same thing is affirmed with reference to activity as is affirmed in the other with reference to the product of the activity.

Further, the division of labour implies the contradiction between the interest of the separate individual or the individual family and the communal interest of all individuals who have intercourse with one another. And indeed, this communal interest does not exist merely in the imagination, as the "general interest", but first of all in reality, as the mutual interdependence of the individuals among whom the labour is divided. And finally, the division of labour offers us the first example of how, as long as man remains in natural society, that is, as long as a cleavage exists between the particular and the common interest, as long, therefore, as activity is not voluntarily, but naturally, divided, man's own deed becomes an alien power opposed to him, which enslaves him instead of being controlled by him. For as soon as the distribution of labour comes into being, each man has a particular, exclusive sphere of activity, which is forced upon him and from which he cannot escape. He is a hunter, a fisherman, a shepherd, or a critical critic, and must remain so if he does not want to lose his means of livelihood; while in communist society, where nobody has one exclusive sphere of activity but each can become accomplished in any branch he wishes, society regulates the general production and thus makes it possible for me to do one thing today and another tomorrow, to hunt in the morning, fish in the afternoon, rear cattle in the evening, criticise after dinner, just as I have a mind, without ever becoming hunter, fisherman, shepherd or critic. This fixation of social activity, this consolidation of what we ourselves produce into an objective power above us, growing out of our control, thwarting our expectations, bringing to naught our calculations, is one of the chief factors in historical development up till now.

[5](And out of this very contradiction between the interest of the individual and that of the community the latter takes an independent form as the *State*,

divorced from the real interests of individual and community, and at the same time as an illusory communal life, always based, however, on the real ties existing in every family and tribal conglomeration — such as flesh and blood, language, division of labour on a larger scale, and other interests — and especially, as we shall enlarge upon later, on the classes, already determined by the division of labour, which in every such mass of men separate out, and of which one dominates all the others. It follows from this that all struggles within the State, the struggle between democracy, aristocracy, and monarchy, the struggle for the franchise, etc. etc. are merely the illusory forms in which the real struggles of the different classes are fought out among one another. Of this the German theoreticians have not the faintest inkling, although they have received a sufficient introduction to the subject in the *Deutsch-Französische Jahrbücher* and *Die heilige Familie*. Further, it follows that every class which is struggling for mastery, even when its domination, as is the case with the proletariat, postulates the abolition of the old form of society in its entirety and of domination itself, must first conquer for itself political power in order to represent its interest in turn as the general interest, which immediately it is forced to do. Just because individuals seek *only* their particular interest, which for them does not coincide with their communal interest, the latter will be imposed on them as an interest "alien" to them, and "independent" of them, as in its turn a particular, peculiar "general" interest; or they themselves must remain within this discord, as in democracy. On the other hand, too, the *practical* struggle of these particular interests, which constantly *really* run counter to the communal and illusory communal interests, makes *practical* intervention and control necessary through the illusory "general" interest in the form of the State.)

The social power, i.e. the multiplied productive force, which arises through the co-operation of different individuals as it is determined by the division of labour, appears to these individuals, since their co-operation is not voluntary but has come about naturally, not as their own united power, but as an alien force existing outside them, of the origin and goal of which they are ignorant, which they thus cannot control, which on the contrary passes through a peculiar series of phases and stages independent of the will and the action of man, nay even being the prime governor of these.

How otherwise could for instance property have had a history at all, have taken on different forms, and landed property, for example, according to the different premises given, have proceeded in France from parcellation to centralisation in the hands of a few, in England from centralisation in the hands of a few to parcellation, as is actually the case today? Or how does it happen that trade, which after all is nothing more than the exchange of products of various individuals and countries, rules the whole world through the relation of supply and demand — a relation which, as an English economist says, hovers over the earth like the fate of the ancients, and with invisible hand allots fortune and misfortune to men, sets up empires and overthrows empires, causes nations to rise and to disappear — while with the abolition of the basis of private property, with the communistic regulation of production (and, implicit in this, the destruction of the alien relation between men and what they themselves produce), the power of the relation of supply and demand is dissolved into nothing, and men get exchange, production, the mode of their mutual relation, under their own control again?

In history up to the present it is certainly an empirical fact that separate individuals have, with the broadening of their activity into world-historical activity, become more and more enslaved under a power alien to them (a pressure which they have conceived of as a dirty trick on the part of the so-called universal spirit, etc.), a power which has become more and more enormous and, in the last instance, turns out to be the *world market*. But it is just as empirically established that, by the overthrow of the existing state of society by the communist revolution (of which more below) and the abolition of private property which is identical with it, this power, which so baffles the German theoreticians, will be dissolved; and that then the liberation of each single individual will be accomplished in the measure in which history becomes transformed into world history. From the above it is clear that the real intellectual wealth of the individual depends entirely on the wealth of his real connections. Only then will the separate individuals be liberated from the various national and local barriers, be brought into practical connection with the material and intellectual production of the whole world and be put in a position to acquire the capacity to enjoy this all-sided production of the whole earth (the creations of man). *All-round* dependence, this natural form of the *world-historical* co-operation of individuals, will be transformed by this communist revolution into the control and conscious mastery of these powers, which, born of the action of men on one another, have till now overawed and governed men as powers completely alien to them. Now this view can be expressed again in speculative-idealistic, i.e. fantastic, terms as "self-generation of the species" ("society as the subject"), and thereby the consecutive series of interrelated individuals connected with each other can be conceived as a single individual, which accomplishes the mystery of generating itself. It is clear here that individuals certainly make *one another*, physically and mentally, but do not make themselves.

This "alienation" (to use a term which will be comprehensible to the philosophers) can, of course, only be abolished given two *practical* premises. For it to become an "intolerable" power, i.e. a power against which men make a revolution, it must necessarily have rendered the great mass of humanity "propertyless", and produced, at the same time, the contradiction of an existing world of wealth and culture, both of which conditions presuppose a great increase in productive power, a high degree of its development. And, on the other hand, this development of productive forces (which itself implies the actual empirical existence of men in their *world-historical*, instead of local, being) is an absolutely necessary practical premise because without it *want* is merely made general, and with *destitution* the struggle for necessities and all the old filthy business would necessarily be reproduced; and furthermore, because only with this universal development of productive forces is a *universal* intercourse between men established, which produces in all nations simultaneously the phenomenon of the "propertyless" mass (universal competition), makes each nation dependent on the revolutions of the others, and finally has put *world-historical*, empirically universal individuals in place of local ones. Without this (I) communism could only exist as a local event; (2) the *forces* of intercourse themselves could not have developed as *universal*, hence intolerable powers: they would have remained home-bred conditions surrounded by superstition; and (3) each extension of intercourse would abolish local communism. Empirically, communism is only possible as the act of the dominant peoples "all at once" and simultaneously, which presupposes the universal development of productive forces and the world intercourse bound up with communism. Moreover, the mass of *propertyless* workers — the utterly precarious position of labour-power on a mass scale cut off from capital or from even a limited satisfaction and, therefore, no longer merely temporarily deprived of work itself as a secure source of life — presupposes the *world market* through competition. The proletariat can thus only exist *world-historically*, just as communism, its activity, can only have a "world-historical" existence. World-historical existence of individuals means, existence of individuals which is directly linked up with world history.

Communism is for us not a *state of affairs* which is to be established, an *ideal* to which reality [will] have to adjust itself. We call communism the real movement which abolishes the present state of things. The conditions of this movement result from the premises now in existence.

Ruling Class and Ruling Ideas

The ideas of the ruling class are in every epoch the ruling ideas, i.e. the class which is the ruling *material* force of society, is at the same time its ruling *intellectual* force. The class which has the means of material production at its disposal, has control at the same time over the means of mental production,

242 / Sociological Thought

so that thereby, generally speaking, the ideas of those who lack the means of mental production are subject to it. The ruling ideas are nothing more than the ideal expression of the dominant material relationships, the dominant material relationships grasped as ideas; hence of the relationships which make the one class the ruling one, therefore, the ideas of its dominance. The individuals composing the ruling class possess among other things consciousness, and therefore think. Insofar, therefore, as they rule as a class and determine the extent and compass of an epoch, it is self-evident that they do this in its whole range, hence among other things rule also as thinkers, as producers of ideas, and regulate the production and distribution of the ideas of their age: thus their ideas are the ruling ideas of the epoch. For instance, in an age and in a country where royal power, aristocracy, and bourgeoisie are contending for mastery and where, therefore, mastery is shared, the doctrine of the separation of powers proves to be the dominant idea and is expressed as an "eternal law".

The division of labour, which we already saw above as one of the chief forces of history up till now, manifests itself also in the ruling class as the division of mental and material labour, so that inside this class one part appears as the thinkers of the class (its active, conceptive ideologists, who make the perfecting of the illusion of the class about itself their chief source of livelihood), while the others' attitude to these ideas and illusions is more passive and receptive, because they are in reality the active members of this class and have less time to make up illusions and ideas about themselves. Within this class this cleavage can even develop into a certain opposition and hostility between the two parts, which, however, in the case of a practical collision, in which the class itself is endangered, automatically comes to nothing, in which case there also vanishes the semblance that the ruling ideas were not the ideas of the ruling class and had a power distinct from the power of this class. The existence of revolutionary ideas in a particular period presupposes the existence of a revolutionary class; about the premises for the latter sufficient has already been said above.

If now in considering the course of history we detach the ideas of the ruling class from the ruling class itself and attribute to them an independent existence, if we confine ourselves to saying that these or those ideas were dominant at a given time, without bothering ourselves about the conditions of production and the producers of these ideas, if we thus ignore the individuals and world conditions which are the source of the ideas, we can say, for instance, that during the time that the aristocracy was dominant, the concepts honour, loyalty, etc. were dominant, during the dominance of the bourgeoisie the concepts freedom, equality, etc. The ruling class itself on the whole imagines this to be so. This conception of history, which is common to all historians, particularly since the eighteenth century, will necessarily come up against the phenomenon that increasingly abstract ideas hold sway, i.e. ideas which increasingly take on the form of universality. For each new class which puts itself in the place of one ruling before it, is compelled, merely in order to carry through its aim, to represent its interest as the common interest of all the members of society, that is, expressed in ideal form: it has to give its ideas the form of universality, and represent them as the only rational, universally valid ones. The class making a revolution appears from the very start, if only because it is opposed to a *class*, not as a class but as the representative of the whole of society; it appears as the whole mass of society confronting the one ruling class.[9] It can do this because, to start with, its interest really is more connected with the common interest of all other non-ruling classes, because under the pressure of hitherto existing conditions its interest has not yet been able to develop as the particular interest of a particular class. Its victory, therefore, benefits also many individuals of the other classes which are not winning a dominant position, but only insofar as it now puts these individuals in a position to raise themselves into the ruling class. When the French bourgeoisie overthrew the power of the aristocracy, it thereby made it possible for many proletarians to raise themselves above the proletariat, but only insofar as they become bourgeois. Every new class, therefore, achieves its hegemony only on a broader basis than that of the class ruling previously, whereas the opposition of the non-ruling class against the new ruling class later develops all the more sharply and profoundly. Both these things determine the fact that the struggle to be waged against this new ruling class, in its turn, aims at a more decided and radical negation of the previous conditions of society than could all previous classes which sought to rule.

This whole semblance, that of the rule of a certain class is only the rule of certain ideas, comes to a natural end, of course, as soon as class rule in general ceases to be the form in which society is organised, that is to say, as soon as it is no longer necessary to represent a particular interest as general or the "general interest" as ruling.

Once the ruling ideas have been separated from the ruling individuals and, above all, from the relationships which result from a given stage of the mode of production, and in this way the conclusion has been reached that history is always under the sway of ideas, it is very easy to abstract from these various ideas "*the* idea", the notion, etc. as the dominant force in history, and thus to understand all these separate ideas and concepts as "forms of self-determination" on the part of *the* concept developing in history. It follows then naturally, too, that all the relationships of men can be derived from the concept of man, man as conceived, the essence of man,

Man. This has been done by the speculative philosophers. Hegel himself confesses at the end of the *Geschichtsphilosophie* that he "has considered the progress of the *concept* only" and has represented in history the "true *theodicy*". (pp. 446.) Now one can go back again to the producers of the "concept", to the theorists, ideologists and philosophers, and one comes then to the conclusion that the philosophers, the thinkers as such, have at all times been dominant in history: a conclusion, as we see, already expressed by Hegel. The whole trick of proving the hegemony of the spirit in history (hierarchy Stirner calls it) is thus confined to the following three efforts.

No. I. One must separate the ideas of those ruling for empirical reasons, under empirical conditions and as empirical individuals, from these actual rulers, and thus recognise the rule of ideas or illusions in history.

No. 2. One must bring an order into this rule of ideas, prove a mystical connection among the successive ruling ideas, which is managed by understanding them as "acts of self-determination on the part of the concept" (this is possible because by virtue of their empirical basis these ideas are really connected with one another and because, conceived as *mere* ideas, they become self-distinctions, distinctions made by thought).

No. 3. To remove the mystical appearance of this "self-determining concept" it is changed into a person — "Self-Consciousness" — or, to appear thoroughly materialistic, into a series of persons, who represent the "concept" in history, into the "thinkers", the "philosophers", the ideologists, who again are understood as the manufacturers of history, as the "council of guardians", as the rulers. Thus the whole body of materialistic elements has been removed from history and now full rein can be given to the speculative steed.

Whilst in ordinary life every shopkeeper is very well able to distinguish between what somebody professes to be and what he really is, our historians have not yet won even this trivial insight. They take every epoch at its word and believe that everything it says and imagines about itself is true.

This historical method which reigned in Germany, and especially the reason why, must be understood from its connection with the illusion of ideologists in general, e.g. the illusions of the jurist, politicians (of the practical statesmen among them, too), from the dogmatic dreamings and distortions of these fellows; this is explained perfectly easily from their practical position in life, their job, and the division of labour.

C. The Real Basis of Ideology

Division of Labour: Town and Country

[...][10] From the first there follows the premise of a highly developed division of labour and an extensive commerce; from the second, the locality. In the first case the individuals must be brought together; in the second they find themselves alongside the given instrument of production as instruments of production themselves. Here, therefore, arises the difference between natural instruments of production and those created by civilisation. The field (water, etc.) can be regarded as a natural instrument of production. In the first case, that of the natural instrument of production, individuals are subservient to nature; in the second, to a product of labour. In the first case, therefore, property (landed property) appears as direct natural domination, in the second, as domination of labour particularly of accumulated labour, capital. The first case presupposes that the individuals are united by some bond: family, tribe, the land itself, etc.; the second, that they are independent of one another and are only held together by exchange. In the first case, what is involved is chiefly an exchange between men and nature in which the labour of the former is exchanged for the products of the latter; in the second, it is predominantly an exchange of men among themselves. In the first case, average, human common sense is adequate — physical activity is as yet not separated from mental activity; in the second, the division between physical and mental labour must already be practically completed. In the first case, the domination of the proprietor over the propertyless may be based on a personal relationship, on a kind of community; in the second, it must have taken on a material shape in a third party — money. In the first case, small industry exists, but determined by the utilisation of the natural instrument of production and therefore without the distribution of labour among various individuals; in the second, industry exists only in and through the division of labour.

The greatest division of material and mental labour is the separation of town and country. The antagonism between town and country begins with the transition from barbarism to civilisation, from tribe to State, from locality to nation, and runs through the whole history of civilisation to the present day (the Anti-Corn Law League).

The existence of the town implies, at the same time, the necessity of administration, police, taxes, etc.; in short, of the municipality, and thus of politics in general. Here first became manifest the division of the population into two great classes, which is directly based on the division of labour and on the instruments of production. The town already is in actual fact the concentration of the population, of the instruments of production, of capital, of pleasures, of needs, while the country demonstrates just the opposite fact, isolation and separation. The antagonism between town and country can only exist within the framework of private property. It is the most crass expression of the subjection of the individual under the division of labour, under a definite activity forced upon him — a subjection which makes one man into a restricted town-animal, the other into a restricted country-animal, and daily creates anew the conflict between their interests. Labour is here again the chief thing, power *over* individuals, and as long as the latter exists, private property must exist. The abolition of the antagonism between town and country is one of the first conditions of communal life, a condition which again depends on a mass of material premises and which cannot be fulfilled by the mere will, as anyone can see at the first glance. (These conditions have still to be enumerated.) The separation of town and country can also be understood as the separation of capital and landed property, as the beginning of the existence and development of capital independent of landed property — the beginning of property having its basis only in labour and exchange.

In the towns which, in the Middle Ages, did not derive ready-made from an earlier period but were formed anew by the serfs who had become free, each man's own particular labour was his only property apart from the small capital he brought with him, consisting almost solely of the most necessary tools of his craft. The competition of serfs constantly escaping into the town, the constant war of the country against the towns and thus the necessity of an organised municipal military force, the bond of common ownership in a particular kind of labour, the necessity of common buildings for the sale of their wares at a time when craftsmen were also traders, and the consequent exclusion of the unauthorised from these buildings, the conflict among the interests of the various crafts, the necessity of protecting their laboriously acquired skill, and the feudal organisation of the whole of the country: these were the causes of the union of the workers of each craft in guilds. We have not at this point to go further into the manifold modifications of the guild-system, which arise through later historical developments. The flight of the serfs into the towns went on without interruption right through the Middle Ages. These serfs, persecuted by their lords in the country, came separately into the towns, where they found an organised community, against which they were powerless and in which they had to subject themselves to the station assigned to them by the demand for their labour and the interest of their organised urban competitors. These workers, entering separately, were never able to attain to any power, since, if their labour was of the guild type which had to be learned, the guild-masters bent them to their will and organised them according to their interest; or if their labour was not such as had to be learned, and therefore not of the guild type, they became day-labourers and never managed to organise, remaining an unorganised rabble. The need for day-labourers in the towns created the rabble.

These towns were true "associations", called forth by the direct need, the care of providing for the protection of property, and of multiplying the means of production and defence of the separate members. The rabble of these towns was devoid of any power, composed as it was of individuals strange to one another who had entered separately, and who stood unorganised over against an organised power, armed for war, and jealously watching over them. The journeymen and apprentices were organised in each craft as it best suited the interest of the masters. The patriarchal relationship existing between them and their masters gave the latter a double power — on the one hand because of their influence on the whole life of the journeymen, and on the other because, for the journeymen who worked with the same master, it was a real bond which held them together against the journeymen of other masters and separated them from these. And finally, the journeymen were bound to the existing order by their simple interest in becoming masters themselves. While, therefore, the rabble at least carried out revolts against the whole municipal order, revolts which remained completely ineffective because of their powerlessness, the journeymen never got further than small acts of insubordination within separate guilds, such as belong to the very nature of the guild-system. The great risings of the Middle Ages all radiated from the country, but equally remained totally ineffective because of the isolation and consequent crudity of the peasants.

In the towns, the division of labour between the individual guilds was as yet [quite naturally derived] and, in the guilds themselves, not at all developed between the individual workers. Every workman had to be versed in a whole round of tasks, had to be able to make everything that was to be made with his tools. The limited commerce and the scanty communication between the individual towns, the lack of population and the narrow needs did not allow of a higher division of labour, and therefore every man who wished to become a master had to be proficient in the whole of his craft. Thus there is found with medieval craftsmen an interest in their special work and in proficiency in it, which was capable of rising to a narrow artistic sense. For this very reason, however, every medieval craftsman was completely absorbed in his work, to which he had a contented, slavish relationship, and to which he was subjected to a far greater extent than the modern worker, whose work is a matter of indifference to him.

Capital in these towns was a naturally derived capital, consisting of a house, the tools of the craft, and the natural, hereditary customers; and not being realisable, on account of the backwardness of commerce and the lack of circulation, it descended from father to son. Unlike modern capital, which can be assessed in money and which may be indifferently invested in this thing or that, this capital was directly connected with the particular work of the owner, inseparable from it and to this extent *estate* capital.

The next extension of the division of labour was the separation of production and commerce, the formation of a special class of merchants; a separation which, in the towns bequeathed by a former period, had been handed down (among other things with the Jews) and which very soon appeared in the newly formed ones. With this there was given the possibility of commercial communications transcending the immediate neighbourhood, a possibility, the realisation of which depended on the existing means of communication, the state of public safety in the countryside, which was determined by political conditions (during the whole of the Middle Ages, as is well known, the merchants travelled in armed caravans), and on the cruder or more advanced needs (determined by the stage of culture attained) of the region accessible to intercourse.

With commerce the prerogative of a particular class, with the extension of trade through the merchants beyond the immediate surroundings of the town, there immediately appears a reciprocal action between production and commerce. The towns enter into relations *with one another*, new tools are brought from one town into the other, and the separation between production and commerce soon calls forth a new division of production between the individual towns, each of which is soon exploiting a predominant branch of industry. The local restrictions of earlier times begin gradually to be broken down.

It depends purely on the extension of commerce whether the productive forces achieved in a locality, especially inventions, are lost for later development or not. As long as there exists no commerce transcending the immediate neighbourhood, every invention must be made separately in each locality, and mere chances such as irruptions of barbaric peoples, even ordinary wars, are sufficient to cause a country with advanced productive forces and needs to have to start right over again from the beginning. In primitive history every invention had to be made daily anew and in each locality independently. How little highly developed productive forces are safe from complete destruction, given even a relatively very extensive commerce, is proved by the Phoenicians, whose inventions were for the most part lost for a long time to come through the ousting of this nation from commerce, its conquest by Alexander and its consequent decline. Likewise, for instance, glass-painting in the Middle Ages. Only when commerce has become the world commerce and has as its basis large-scale industry, when all nations are drawn into the competitive struggle, is the permanence of the acquired productive forces assured.

The Rise of Manufacturing

The immediate consequence of the division of labour between the various towns was the rise of manufactures, branches of production which had outgrown the guild-system. Manufactures first flourished, in Italy and later in Flanders, under the historical premise of commerce with foreign nations. In other countries, England and France for example, manufactures were at first confined to the home market. Besides the premises already mentioned manufactures depend on an already advanced concentration of population, particularly in the countryside, and of capital, which began to accumulate in the hands of individuals, partly in the guilds in spite of the guild regulations, partly among the merchants.

That labour which from the first presupposed a machine, even of the crudest sort, soon showed itself the most capable of development. Weaving, earlier carried on in the country by the peasants as a secondary occupation to procure their clothing, was the first labour to receive an impetus and a further development through the extension of commerce. Weaving was the first and remained the principal manufacture. The rising demand for clothing materials, consequent on the growth of population, the growing accumulation and mobilisation of natural capital through accelerated circulation, the demand for luxuries called forth by the latter and favoured generally by the gradual extension of commerce, gave weaving a quantitative and qualitative stimulus, which wrenched it out of the form of production hitherto existing. Alongside the peasants weaving for their own use, who continued, and still continue, with this sort of work, there emerged a new class of weavers in the towns, whose fabrics were destined for the whole home market and usually for foreign markets too.

Weaving, an occupation demanding in most cases little skill and soon splitting up into countless branches, by its whole nature resisted the trammels of the guild. Weaving was, therefore, carried on mostly in villages and market-centres without guild organisation, which gradually became towns, and indeed the most flourishing towns in each land.

With guild-free manufacture, property relations also quickly changed. The first advance beyond naturally derived estate capital was provided by the rise of merchants whose capital was from the beginning movable, capital in the modern sense as far as one can speak of it, given the circumstances of those times. The second advance came with manufacture, which again made mobile a mass of natural capital, and altogether increased the mass of movable capital as against that of natural capital.

At the same time, manufacture became a refuge of the peasants from the guilds which excluded them or paid them badly, just as earlier the guild-towns had [served] as a refuge for the peasants from [the oppressive landed nobility].

Simultaneously with the beginning of manufactures there was a period of vagabondage caused by the abolition of the feudal bodies of retainers, the disbanding of the swollen armies which had flocked to serve the kings against their vassals, the improvement of agriculture, and the transformation of great strips of tillage into pasture land. From this alone it is clear how this vagabondage is strictly connected with the disintegration of the feudal system. As early as the thirteenth century we find isolated epochs of this kind, but only at the end of the fifteenth and the beginning of the sixteenth does this vagabondage make a general and permanent appearance. These vagabonds, who were so numerous that, for instance, Henry VIII of England had 72,000 of them hanged, were only prevailed upon to work with the greatest difficulty and through the most extreme necessity, and then only after long resistance. The rapid rise of manufactures, particularly in England, absorbed them gradually.

With the advent of manufactures, the various nations entered into a competitive relationship, the struggle for trade, which was fought out in wars, protective duties and prohibitions, whereas earlier the nations, insofar as they were connected at all, had carried on an inoffensive exchange with each other. Trade had from now on a political significance.

With the advent of manufacture the relationship between worker and employer changed. In the guilds the patriarchal relationship between journeyman and master continued to exist; in manufacture its place was taken by the monetary relation between worker and capitalist — a relationship which in the countryside and in small towns retained a patriarchal tinge, but in the larger, the real manufacturing towns, quite early lost almost all patriarchal complexion.

Manufacture and the movement of production in general received an enormous impetus through the extension of commerce which came with the discovery of America and the sea-route to the East Indies. The new products imported thence, particularly the masses of gold and silver which came into circulation and totally changed the position of the classes towards one another, dealing a hard blow to feudal landed property and to the workers; the expeditions of adventurers, colonisation; and above all the extension of markets into a world market, which had now become possible and was daily becoming more and more a fact, called forth a new phase of historical development, into which in general we cannot here enter further. Through the colonisation of the newly discovered countries the commercial struggle of the nations amongst one another was given new fuel and accordingly greater extension and animosity.

The expansion of trade and manufacture accelerated the accumulation of movable capital, while in the guilds, which were not stimulated to extend their production, natural capital remained stationary or even declined. Trade and manufacture created the big bourgeoisie; in the guilds was concentrated the petty bourgeoisie, which no longer was dominant in the towns as formerly, but had to bow to the might of the great merchants and manufacturers. Hence the decline of the guilds, as soon as they came into contact with manufacture.

The intercourse of nations took on, in the epoch of which we have been speaking, two different forms. At first the small quantity of gold and silver in circulation involved the ban on the export of these metals; and industry, for the most part imported from abroad and made necessary by the need for employing the growing urban population, could not do without those privileges which could be granted not only, of course, against home competition, but chiefly against foreign. The local guild privilege was in these original prohibitions extended over the whole nation. Customs duties originated from the tributes which the feudal lords exacted as protective levies against robbery from merchants passing through their territories, tributes later imposed likewise by the towns, and which, with the rise of the modern states, were the Treasury's most obvious means of raising money.

The appearance of American gold and silver on the European markets, the gradual development of industry, the rapid expansion of trade and the consequent rise of the non-guild bourgeoisie and of money, gave these measures another significance. The State, which was daily less and less able to do without money, now retained the ban on the export of gold and silver out of fiscal considerations; the bourgeois, for whom these masses of money which were hurled on to the market became the chief object of speculative buying, were thoroughly content with this; privileges established earlier became a source of income for the government and were sold for money; in the customs legislation there appeared the export duty, which, since it only [placed] a hindrance in the way of industry, had a purely fiscal aim.

The second period began in the middle of the seventeenth century and lasted almost to the end of the eighteenth. Commerce and navigation had expanded more rapidly than manufacture, which played a secondary role; the colonies were becoming considerable consumers; and after long struggles the separate nations shared out the opening world market among themselves. This period begins with the Navigation Laws[11] and colonial monopolies. The competition of the nations among themselves was excluded as far as possible by tariffs, prohibitions and treaties; and in the last resort the competitive struggle was carried on and decided by wars (especially naval wars). The mightiest maritime nation, the English, retained preponderance in trade and manufacture. Here, already, we find concentration in one country.

Manufacture was all the time sheltered by protective duties in the home market, by monopolies in the colonial market, and abroad as much as possible by differential duties. The working-up of home-produced material was encouraged (wool and linen in England, silk in France), the export of home-produced raw material forbidden (wool in England), and the [working-up] of imported material neglected or suppressed (cotton in England). The nation dominant in sea trade and colonial power naturally secured for itself also the greatest quantitative and qualitative expansion of manufacture. Manufacture could not be carried on without protection, since, if the slightest change takes place in other countries, it can lose its market and be ruined; under reasonably favourable conditions it may easily be introduced into a country, but for this very reason can easily be destroyed. At the same time through the mode in which it is carried on, particularly in the eighteenth century, in the countryside, it is to such an extent interwoven with the vital relationships of a great mass of individuals, that no country dare jeopardise its existence by permitting free competition. Insofar as it manages to export, it therefore depends entirely on the extension or restriction of commerce, and exercises a relatively very small reaction [on the latter]. Hence its secondary [importance] and the influence of [the merchants] in the eighteenth century. It was the merchants and especially the shippers who more than anybody else pressed for State protection and monopolies; the manufacturers also demanded and indeed received protection, but all the time were inferior in political importance to the merchants. The commercial towns, particularly the maritime towns, became to some extent civilised and acquired the outlook of the big bourgeoisie, but in the factory towns an extreme petty-bourgeois outlook persisted. Cf. Aikin,[12] etc. The eighteenth century was the century of trade. Pinto says this expressly: "*Le commerce fait la marotte du siècle*";[13] and: "*Depuis quelque temps il n'est plus question que de commerce, de navigation et de marine.*"[14]

This period is also characterised by the cessation of the bans on the export of gold and silver and the beginning of the trade in money; by banks, national debts, paper money; by speculation in stocks and shares and stockjobbing in all articles; by the development of finance in general. Again capital lost a great part of the natural character which had still clung to it.

The concentration of trade and manufacture in one country, England, developing irresistibly in the seventeenth century, gradually created for this country a relative world market, and thus a demand for the manufactured products of this country, which could no longer be met by the industrial productive forces hitherto existing. This demand, outgrowing the productive forces, was the motive power which, by producing big industry — the application of elemental forces to industrial ends, machinery and the most complex division of labour — called into existence the third period of private ownership since the Middle Ages. There already existed in England the other pre-conditions of this new phase: freedom of competition inside the nation, the development of theoretical mechanics, etc. (Indeed, the science of mechanics perfected by Newton was altogether the most popular science in France and England in the eighteenth century.) (Free competition inside the nation itself had everywhere to be conquered by a revolution — 1640 and 1688 in England, 1789 in France.) Competition soon compelled every country that wished to retain its historical role to protect its manufactures by renewed customs regulations (the old duties were no longer any good against big industry) and soon after to introduce big industry under protective duties. Big industry universalised competition in spite of these protective measures (it is practical free trade; the protective duty is only a palliative, a measure of defence *within* free trade), established means of communication and the modern world market, subordinated trade to itself, transformed all capital into industrial capital, and thus produced the rapid circulation (development of the financial system) and the centralisation of capital. By universal competition it forced all individuals to strain their energy to the utmost. It destroyed as far as possible ideology, religion, morality, etc. and where it could not do this, make them into a palpable lie. It produced world history for the first time, insofar as it made all civilised nations and every individual member of them dependent for the satisfaction of their wants on the whole world, thus destroying the former natural exclusiveness of separate nations. It made natural science subservient to capital and took from the division of labour the last semblance of its natural character. It destroyed natural growth in general, as far as this is possible while labour exists, and resolved all natural relationships into money relationships. In the place of naturally grown towns it created the modern, large industrial cities which have sprung up overnight. Wherever it penetrated, it destroyed the crafts and all earlier stages of industry. It completed the victory of the commercial town over the countryside. [Its first premise] was the automatic system. [Its development] produced a mass of productive forces, for which private [property] became just as much a fetter as the guild had been for manufacture and the small, rural workshop for the developing craft. These productive forces received under the system of private property a one-sided development only, and became for the majority destructive forces; moreover, a great multitude of such forces could find no application at all within the system. Generally speaking, big industry created everywhere the same relations between the classes of society, and thus destroyed the peculiar individuality of the various nationalities. And finally, while the bourgeoisie of each nation still retained separate national interests, big industry created a class, which in all nations has the same interest and with which nationality is already dead; a class which is really rid of all the old world and at the same time stands pitted against it. Big industry makes for the worker not only the relation to the capitalist, but labour itself, unbearable.

It is evident that big industry does not reach the same level of development in all districts of a country. This does not, however, retard the class movement of the proletariat, because the proletarians created by big industry assume leadership of this movement and carry the whole mass along with them, and because the workers excluded from big industry are placed by it in a still worse situation than the workers in big industry itself. The countries in which big industry is developed act in a similar manner upon the more or less non-industrial countries, insofar as the latter are swept by universal commerce into the universal competitive struggle.[15]

These different forms are just so many forms of the organisation of labour, and hence of property. In each period a unification of the existing productive forces takes place, insofar as this has been rendered necessary by needs.

The Relation of State and Law to Property

The first form of property, in the ancient world as in the Middle Ages, is tribal property, determined with the Romans chiefly by war, with the Germans by the rearing of cattle. In the case of the ancient peoples, since several tribes live together in one town, the tribal property appears as State property, and the right of the individual to it as mere "possession" which, however, like tribal property as a whole, is confined to landed property only. Real private property began with the ancients, as with modern nations, with movable property. — (Slavery and community) (*dominium ex jure Quiritum* [16]). In the case of the nations which grew out of the Middle Ages, tribal property evolved through various stages — feudal landed property, corporative movable property, capital invested in manufacture — to modern capital, determined by big industry and universal competition, i.e. pure private property, which has cast off all semblance of a communal institution and has shut out the State from any influence on the development of property. To this modern private property corresponds the modern State, which, purchased gradually by the owners of property by means of taxation, has fallen entirely into their hands through the national debt, and its existence has become wholly dependent on the commercial credit which the owners of property, the bourgeois, extend to it, as reflected in the rise and fall of State funds on the stock exchange. By the mere fact that it is a *class* and no longer an *estate*, the bourgeoisie is forced to organize itself no longer locally, but nationally, and to give a general form to its mean average interest. Through the emancipation of private property from the community, the State has become separate entity, beside and outside civil society; but it is nothing more than the form of organisation which the bourgeoisie necessarily adopt both for internal and external purposes, for the mutual guarantee of their property and interests.

The independence of the State is only found nowadays in those countries where the estates, done away with in more advanced countries, still have a part to play, and where there exists a mixture; countries, that is to say, in which no one section of the population can achieve dominance over the others. This is the case particularly in Germany. The most perfect example of the modern State is North America. The modern French, English and American writers all express the opinion that the State exists only for the sake of private property, so that this fact has penetrated into the consciousness of the normal man.

Since the State is the form in which the individuals of a ruling class assert their common interests, and in which the whole civil society of an epoch is epitomised, it follows that the State mediates in the formation of all common institutions and that the institutions receive a political form. Hence the illusion that law is based on the will, and indeed on the will divorced from its real basis — on *free* will. Similarly, justice is in its turn reduced to the actual laws.

Civil law develops simultaneously with private property out of the disintegration of the natural community. With the Romans the development of private property and civil law had no further industrial and commercial consequences, because their whole mode of production did not alter. (Usury!)

With modern peoples, where the feudal community was disintegrated by industry and trade, there began with the rise of private property and civil law a new phase, which was capable of further development. The very first town which carried on an extensive maritime trade in the Middle Ages, Amalfi, also developed maritime law. As soon as industry and trade developed private property further, first in Italy and later in other countries, the highly developed Roman civil law was immediately adopted again and raised to authority. When later the bourgeoisie had acquired so much power that the princes took up its interests in order to overthrow the feudal nobility by means of the bourgeoisie, there began in all countries — in France in the sixteenth century — the real development of law, which in all countries except England proceeded on the basis of the Roman Codex. In England, too, Roman legal principles had to be introduced to further the development of civil law (especially in the case of movable property). (It must not be forgotten that law has just as little an independent history as religion.)

In civil law the existing property relationships are declared to be the result of the general will. The *jus utendi et abutendi*[17] itself asserts on the one hand the fact that private property has become entirely independent of the community, and on the other the illusion that private property itself is based solely on the private will, the arbitrary disposal of the thing. In practice, the *abuti*[17] has very definite economic limitations for the owner of private property, if he does not wish to see his property and hence his *jus abutendi* pass into other hands, since actually the thing, considered merely with reference to his will, is not a thing at all, but only becomes a thing, true property in intercourse, and independently of the law (a *relationship*, which the philosophers call an idea). This juridical illusion, which reduces law to the mere will, necessarily leads, in the further development of property relationships, to the position that a man may have a legal title to a thing without really having the thing. If, for instance, the income from a piece of land is lost owing to the competition, then the proprietor has certainly his legal title to it along with the *jus utendi et abutendi*. But he can do nothing with it: he owns nothing as a landed proprietor if in addition he has not enough capital to cultivate his ground. This illusion of the jurists also explains the fact that for them, as for every code, it is altogether fortuitous that individuals enter into relationships among themselves (e.g. contracts); it explains why they consider that these relationships [can] be entered into or not at will, and that their content rests purely on the individual [free] will of the contracting parties.

Whenever, through the development of industry and commerce, new forms of intercourse have been evolved (e.g. assurance companies, etc.), the law has always been compelled to admit them among the modes of acquiring property.

THE FETISHISM OF COMMODITIES AND THE SECRET THEREOF

A commodity appears, at first sight, a very trivial thing, and easily understood. Its analysis shows that it is, in reality, a very queer thing, abounding in metaphysical subtleties and theological niceties. So far as it is a value in use, there is nothing mysterious about it, whether we consider it from the point of view that by its properties it is capable of satisfying human wants, or from the point that those properties are the product of human labour. It is as clear as noon-day, that man, by his industry, changes the forms of the materials furnished by Nature, in such a way as to make them useful to him. The form of wood, for instance, is altered, by making a table out of it. Yet, for all that, the table continues to be that common, every-day thing, wood. But, so soon as it steps forth as a commodity, it is changed into something transcendent. It not only stands with its feet on the ground, but, in relation to all other commodities, it stands on its head, and evolves out of its wooden brain grotesque ideas, far more wonderful than "table-turning" ever was.

The mystical character of commodities does not originate, therefore, in their use-value. Just as little does it proceed from the nature of the determining factors of value. For, in the first place, however varied the useful kinds of labour, or productive activities, may be, it is a physiological fact, that they are functions of the human organism, and that each such function, whatever may be its nature or form, is essentially the expenditure of human brain, nerves, muscles, &c. Secondly, with regard to that which forms the ground-work for the quantitative determination of value, namely, the duration of that expenditure, or the quantity of labour, it is quite clear that there is a palpable difference between its quantity and quality. In all states of society, the labour-time that it costs to produce the means of subsistence, must necessarily be an object of interest to mankind, though not of equal interest in different stages of development.[1] And lastly, from the moment that men in any way work for one another, their labour assumes a social form.

Whence, then, arises the enigmatical character of the product of labour, so soon as it assumes the form of commodities? Clearly from this form itself. The equality of all sorts of human labour is expressed objectively by their products all being equally values; the measure of the expenditure of labour-power by the duration of that expenditure, takes the form of the quantity of value of the products of labour; and finally, the mutual relations of the producers, within which the social character of their labour affirms itself, take the form of a social relation between the products.

A commodity is therefore a mysterious thing, simply because in it the social character of men's labour appears to them as an objective character stamped upon the product of that labour; because the relation of the producers to the sum total of their own labour is presented to them as a social relation, existing not between themselves, but between the products of their labour. This is the reason why the products of labour become commodities, social things whose qualities are at the same time perceptible and imperceptible by the senses. In the same way the light from an object is perceived by us not as the subjective excitation of our optic nerve, but as the objective form of something outside the eye itself. But, in the act of seeing, there is at all events, an actual passage of light from one thing to another, from the external object to the eye. There is a physical relation between physical things. But it is different with commodities. There, the existence of the things quâ commodities, and the value-relation between the products of labour which stamps them as commodities, have absolutely no connexion with their physical properties and with the material relations arising therefrom. There it is a definite social relation between men, that assumes, in their eyes, the fantastic form of a relation between things. In order, therefore, to find an analogy, we must have recourse to the mist-enveloped regions of the religious world. In that world the productions of the human brain appear as independent beings endowed with life, and entering into relation both with one another and the human race. So it is in the world commodities with the products of men's hands. This I call the Fetishism which attaches itself to the products of labour, so soon as they are produced as commodities, and which is therefore inseparable from the production of commodities.

This Fetishism of commodities has its origin, as the foregoing analysis has already shown, in the peculiar social character of the labour that produces them.

As a general rule, articles of utility become commodities, only because they are products of the labour of private individuals or groups of individuals who carry on their work independently of each other. The sum total of the labour of all these private individuals forms the aggregate labour of society. Since the producers do not come into social contact with each other until they exchange their products, the specific social character of each producer's labour does not show itself except in the act of exchange. In other words, the labour of the individual asserts itself as a part of the labour of society, only by means of the relations which the act of exchange establishes directly between the products, and indirectly, through them, between the producers. To the latter, therefore, the relations connecting the labour of one individual with that of the rest appear, not as direct social relations between individuals at work, but as what they really are, material relations between persons and social relations between things. It is only by being exchanged that the products of labour acquire, as values, one uniform social status, distinct from their varied forms of existence as objects of utility. This division of a product into a useful thing and a value becomes practically important, only when exchange has acquired such an extension that useful articles are produced for the purpose of being exchanged, and their character as values has therefore to be taken into account, beforehand, during production. From this moment the labour of the individual producer acquires socially a two-fold character. On the one hand, it must, as a definite useful kind of labour, satisfy a definite social want, and thus hold its place as part and parcel of the collective labour of all, as a branch of a social division of labour that has sprung up spontaneously. On the other hand, it can satisfy the manifold wants of the individual producer himself, only in so far as the mutual exchangeability of all kinds of useful private labour is an established social fact, and therefore the private useful labour of each producer ranks on an equality with that of all others. The equalisation of the most different kinds of labour can be the result only of an abstraction from their inequalities, of reducing them to their common denominator, viz., expenditure of human labour-power or human labour in the abstract. The two-fold social character of the labour of the individual appears to him, when reflected in his brain, only under those forms which are impressed upon that labour in every-day practice by the exchange of products. In this way, the character that his own labour possesses of being socially useful takes the form of the condition, that the product must be not only useful, but useful for others, and the social character that his particular labour has of being the equal of all other particular kinds of labour, takes the form that all the physically different articles that are the products of labour, have one common quality, viz., that of having value.

Hence, when we bring the products of our labour into relation with each other as values, it is not because we see in these articles the material receptacles of homogeneous human labour. Quite the contrary: whenever, by an exchange, we equate as values our different products, by that very act, we also equate, as human labour, the different kinds of labour expended upon them. We are not aware of this, nevertheless we do it.[2] Value, therefore, does not stalk about with a label describing what it is. It is value, rather, that converts every product into a social hieroglyphic. Later on, we try to decipher the hieroglyphic, to get behind the secret of our own social products; for to stamp an object of utility as a value, is just as much a social product as language. The recent scientific discovery, that the products of labour, so far as they are values, are but material expressions of the human labour spent in their production, marks, indeed, an epoch in the history of the development of the human race, but, by no means, dissipates the mist through which the social character of labour appears to us to be an objective character of the products themselves. The fact, that in the particular form of production with which we are dealing, viz., the production of commodities, the specific social character of private labour carried on independently, consists in the equality of every kind of that labour, by virtue of its being human labour, which character, therefore, assumes in the product the form of value — this fact appears to the producers, notwithstanding the discovery above referred to, to be just as real and final, as the fact, that, after the discovery by science of the component gases of air, the atmosphere itself remained unaltered.

What, first of all, practically concerns producers when they make an exchange, is the question, how much of some other product they get for their own? in what proportions the products are exchangeable? When these proportions have, by custom, attained a certain stability, they appear to result from the nature of the products, so that, for instance, one ton of iron and two ounces of gold appear as naturally to be of equal value as a pound of gold and a pound of iron in spite of their different physical and chemical qualities appear to be of equal weight. The character of having value, when once impressed upon products, obtains fixity only by reason of their acting and re-acting upon each other as quantities of value. These quantities vary continually, independently of the will, foresight and action of the producers. To them, their own social action takes the form of the action of objects, which rule the producers instead of being ruled by them. It requires a fully developed production of commodities before, from accumulated experience alone, the scientific conviction springs up, that all the different kinds of private labour, which are carried on independently of each other, and yet as spontaneously developed branches of the social division of labour, are continually being reduced to the quantitative proportions in which society requires them. And why? Because, in the midst of all the accidental and ever fluctuating exchange-relations between the products, in labour-time socially necessary for their production forcibly asserts itself like an over-riding law of Nature. The law of gravity thus asserts itself when a house falls about our ears.[3] The determination of the magnitude of value by labour-time is therefore a secret, hidden under the apparent fluctuation in the relative values of commodities. Its discovery, while removing all appearance of mere accidentality from the determination of the magnitude of the values of products, yet in no way alters the mode in which that determination takes place.

Man's reflections on the forms of social life, and consequently, also, his scientific analysis of those forms, take a course directly opposite to that of their actual historical development. He begins, post festum, with the results of the process of development ready to hand before him. The characters that stamp products as commodities, and whose establishment is a necessary preliminary to the circulation of commodities, have already acquired the stability of natural, self-understood forms of social life, before man seeks to decipher, not their historical character, for in his eyes they are immutable, but their meaning. Consequently it was the analysis of the prices of commodities that alone led to the determination of the magnitude of value, and it was the common expression of all commodities in money that alone led to the establishment of their characters as values. It is, however, just this ultimate money-form of the world of commodities that actually conceals, instead of disclosing, the social character of private labour, and the social relations between the individual producers. When I state that coats or boots stand in a relation to linen, because it is the universal incarnation of abstract human labour, the absurdity of the statement is self-evident. Nevertheless, when the producers of coats and boots compare those articles with linen, or, what is the same thing, with gold or silver, as the universal equivalent, they express the relation between their own private labour and the collective labour of society in the same absurd form.

The categories of bourgeois economy consist of such like forms. They are forms of thought expressing with social validity the conditions and relations of a definite, historically determined mode of production, viz., the production of commodities. The whole mystery of commodities, all the magic and necromancy that surrounds the products of labour as long as they take the form of commodities, vanishes therefore, so soon as we come to other forms of production.

Since Robinson Crusoe's experiences are a favourite theme with political economists,[4] let us take a look at him on his island. Moderate though he may be, yet some few wants he has to satisfy, and must therefore do a little useful work of various sorts, such as making tools and furniture, taming goats, fishing and hunting. Of his prayers and the like we take no account, since they are a source of pleasure to him, and he looks upon them as so much recreation. In spite of the variety of his work, he knows that his labour, whatever its form, is but the activity of one and the same Robinson, and consequently, that it consists of nothing but different modes of human labour. Necessity itself compels him to apportion his time accurately between his different kinds of work. Whether one kind occupies a greater space in his general activity than another, depends on the difficulties, greater or less as the case may be, to be overcome in attaining the useful effect aimed at. This our friend Robinson soon learns by experience, and having rescued a watch, ledger, and pen and ink from the wreck, commences, like a true-born Briton, to keep a set of books. His stock-book contains a list of the objects of utility that belong to him, of the operations necessary for their production; and lastly, of the labour-time that definite quantities of those objects have, on an average, cost him. All the relations between Robinson and the objects that form this wealth of his own creation, are here so simple and clear as to be intelligible without exertion, even to Mr. Sedley Taylor. And yet those relations contain all that is essential to the determination of value.

Let us now transport ourselves from Robinson's island bathed in light to the European middle ages shrouded in darkness. Here, instead of the independent man, we find everyone dependent, serfs and lords, vassals and suzerains, laymen and clergy Personal dependence here characterises the social relations of production just as much as it does the other spheres of life organised on the basis of that production. But for the very reason that personal dependence forms the ground-work of society, there is no necessity for labour and its products to assume a fantastic form different from their reality. They take the shape, in the transactions of society, of services in kind and payments in kind. Here the particular and natural form of labour, and not, as in a society based on production of commodities, its general abstract form is the immediate social form of labour. Compulsory labour is just as properly measured by time, as commodity-producing labour; but every serf knows that what he expends in the service of his lord, is a definite quantity of his own personal labour-power. The tithe to be rendered to the priest is more matter of fact than his blessing. No matter, then, what we may think of the parts played by the different classes of people themselves in this society, the social relations between individuals in the performance of their labour, appear at all events as their own mutual personal relations, and are not disguised under the shape of social relations between the products of labour.

For an example of labour in common or directly associated labour, we have no occasion to go back to that spontaneously developed form which we find on the threshold of the history of all civilised races.[5] We have one close at hand in the patriarchal industries of a peasant family, that produces corn, cattle, yarn, linen, and clothing for home use. These different articles are, as regards the family, so many products of its labour, but as between themselves, they are not commodities. The different kinds of labour, such as tillage, cattle tending, spinning, weaving and making clothes, which result in the various products, are in themselves, and such as they are, direct social functions, because functions of the family, which, just as much as a society based on the production of commodities, possess a spontaneously developed system of division of labour. The distribution of the work within the family, and the regulation of the labour-time of the several members, depend as well upon differences of age and sex as upon natural conditions varying with the seasons. The labour-owner of each individual, by its very nature, operates in this case merely as a definite portion of the whole labour-power of the family, and therefore, the measure of the expenditure of individual labour-power by its duration, appears here by its very nature as a social character of their labour.

Let us now picture to ourselves, by way of change, a community of free individuals, carrying on their work with the means of production in common, in which the labour-power of all the different individuals is consciously applied as the combined labour-power of the community. All the characteristics of Robinson's labour are here repeated, but with this difference, that they are social, instead of individual. Everything produced by him was exclusively the result of his own personal labour, and therefore simply an object of use for himself. The total product of our community is a social product. One portion serves as fresh means of production and remains social. But another portion is consumed by the members as means of subsistence. A distribution of this portion amongst them is consequently necessary. The mode of this distribution will vary with the productive organisation of the community, and the degree of historical development attained by the producers. We will assume, but merely for the sake of a parallel with the production of commodities, that the share of each individual producer in the means of subsistence is determined by his labour-time. Labour-time would, in that case, play a double part. Its apportionment in accordance with a definite social plan maintains the proper proportion between the different kinds of work to be done and the various wants of the community. On the other hand, it also serves as a measure of the portion of the common labour borne by each individual, and of his share in the part of the total product destined for individual consumption. The social relations of the individual producers, with regard both to their labour and to its products, are in this case perfectly simple and intelligible, and that with regard not only to production but also to distribution.

The religious world is but the reflex of the real world. And for a society based upon the production of commodities, in which the producers in general enter into social relations with one another by treating their products as commodities and values, whereby they reduce their individual private labour to the standard of homogeneous human labour — for such a society, Christianity with its *cultus* of abstract man, more especially in its bourgeois developments, Protestantism, Deism, &c., is the most fitting form of religion. In the ancient Asiatic and other ancient modes of production, we find that the conversion of products into commodities, and therefore the conversion of men into producers of commodities, holds a subordinate place, which, however, increases in importance as the primitive communities approach nearer and nearer to their dissolution. Trading nations, properly so called, exist in the ancient world only in its interstices, like the gods of Epicurus in the Intermundia, or like Jews in the pores of Polish society. Those ancient social organisms of production are, as compared with bourgeois society, extremely simple and transparent. But they are founded either on the immature development of man individually, who has not yet severed the umbilical cord that unites him with his fellowmen in a primitive tribal community, or upon direct relations of subjection. They can arise and exist only when the development of the productive power of labour has not risen beyond a low stage, and when, therefore, the social relations within the sphere of material life, between man and man, and between man and Nature, are correspondingly narrow. This narrowness is reflected in the ancient worship of Nature, and in the other elements of the popular religions. The religious reflex of the real world can, in any case, only then finally vanish, when the practical relations of every-day life offer to man none but perfectly intelligible and reasonable relations with regard to his fellowmen and to Nature.

The life-process of society, which is based on the process of material production, does not strip off its mystical veil until it is treated as production by freely associated men, and is consciously regulated by them in accordance with a settled plan. This, however, demands for society a certain material ground-work or set of conditions of existence which in their turn are the spontaneous product of a long and painful process of development.

Political Economy has indeed analysed, however incompletely,[6] value and its magnitude, and has discovered what lies beneath these forms. But it has never once asked the question why labour is represented by the value of its product and labour-time by the magnitude of that value.[7] These formulae, which bear it stamped upon them in unmistakable letters that they belong to a state of society, in which the process of production has the mastery over man, instead of being controlled by him, such formulae appear to the bourgeois intellect to be as much a self-evident necessity imposed by Nature as productive labour itself. Hence forms of social production that preceded the bourgeois form, are treated by the bourgeoisie in much the same way as the Fathers of the Church treated pre-Christian religions.[8]

To what extent some economists are misled by the Fetishism inherent in commodities, or by the objective appearance of the social characteristics of labour, is shown, amongst other ways, by the dull and tedious quarrel over the part played by Nature in the formation of exchange-value. Since exchange-value is a definite social manner of expressing the amount of labour bestowed upon an object, Nature has no more to do with it, than it has in fixing the course of exchange.

The mode of production in which the product takes the form of a commodity, or is produced directly for exchange, is the most general and most embryonic form of bourgeois production. It therefore makes its appearance at an early date in history, though not in the same predominating and characteristic manner as now-a-days. Hence its Fetish character is comparatively easy to be seen through. But when we come to more concrete forms, even this appearance of simplicity vanishes. Whence arose the illusions of the monetary system? To it gold and silver, when serving as money, did not represent a social relation between producers, but were natural objects with strange social properties. And modern economy, which looks down with such disdain on the monetary system, does not its superstition come out as clear as noon-day, whenever it treats of capital? How long is it since economy discarded the physiocratic illusion, that rents grow out of the soil and not out of society?

But not to anticipate, we will content ourselves with yet another example relating to the commodity-form. Could commodities themselves speak, they would say: Our use-value may be a thing that interests men. It is no part of us as objects. What, however, does belong to us as objects, is our value. Our natural intercourse as commodities proves it. In the eyes of each other we are nothing but exchange-values. Now given how those commodities speak through the mouth of the economist. "Value" — (*i.e.*, exchange-value) "is a property of things, riches" — *i.e.*, use-value) "of man. Value, in this sense, necessarily implies exchanges, riches do not."[9] "Riches" (use-value) "are the attribute of men, value is the attribute of commodities. A man or a community is rich, a pearl or a diamond is valuable... A pearl or a diamond is valuable" as a pearl or a diamond.[10] So far no chemist has ever discovered exchange-value either in a pearl or a diamond. The economic discoverers of this chemical element, who by-the-way lay special claim to critical acumen, and however that the use-value of objects belongs to them independently of their material properties, while their value, on the other hand, forms a part of them as objects. What confirms them in this view, is the peculiar circumstance that the use-value of objects is realised without exchange, by means of a direct relation between the objects and man, while, on the other hand, their value is realised only by exchange, that by means of a social process, Who fails here to call to mind our good friend Dogberry, who informs neighbour Seacoal, that, "To be a well-favoured man is the gift of fortune; but reading and writing comes by Nature."[11]

THE SECRET OF PRIMITIVE ACCUMULATION

We have seen how money is changed into capital; how through capital surplus-value is made, and from surplus-value more capital. But the accumulation of capital pre-supposes surplus-value; surplus-value pre-supposes capitalistic production; capitalistic production pre-supposes the pre-existence of considerable masses of capital and of labour-power in the hands of producers of commodities. The whole movement, therefore, seems to turn in a vicious cycle, out of which we can only get by supposing a primitive accumulation (previous accumulation of Adam Smith) preceding a capitalistic accumulation; an accumulation not the result of the capitalist mode of production, but its starting-point.

This primitive accumulation plays in Political Economy about the same part as original sin in theology. Adam bit the apple, and thereupon sin fell on the human race. Its origin is supposed to be explained when it is told as an anecdote of the past. In times long gone by there were two sorts of people; one, the diligent, intelligent, and, above all, frugal elite; the other, lazy rascals, spending their substance, and more, in riotous living. The legend of theological original sin tells us certainly how man came to be condemned to eat his bread in the sweat of his brow; but the history of economic original sin reveals to us that there are people to whom this is by no means essential. Never mind! Thus it came to pass that the former sort accumulated wealth, and the latter sort had at last nothing to sell except their own skins. And from this original sin dates the poverty of the great majority that, despite all its labour, has up to now nothing to sell but itself, and the wealth of the few that increases constantly although they have long ceased to work. Such insipid childishness is every day preached to us in the defence of property. M. Thiers, *e.g.*, had the assurance to repeat it with all the solemnity of a statesman, to the French people, once so *spirituel*. But as soon as the question of property crops up, it becomes a sacred duty to proclaim the intellectual food of the infant as the one thing fit for all ages and for all stages of development. In actual history it is notorious that conquest, enslavement, robbery, murder, briefly force, play the great part. In the tender annals of Political Economy, the idyllic reigns from time immemorial. Right and "labour" were from all time the sole means of enrichment, the present year of course always excepted. As a matter of fact, the methods of primitive accumulation are anything but idyllic.

In themselves money and commodities are no more capital than are the means of production and of subsistence. They want transforming into capital. But this transformation itself can only take place under certain circumstances that centre in this, viz., that two very different kinds of commodity-possessors must come face to face and into contact; on the one hand, the owners of money, means of production, means of subsistence, who are eager to increase the sum of values they possess, by buying other people's labour-power; on the other hand, free labourers, the sellers of their own labour-power, and therefore the sellers of labour. Free labourers, in the double sense that neither they themselves form part and parcel of the means of production, as in the case of slaves, bondsmen, &c., nor do the means of production belong to them, as in the case of peasant-proprietors; they are, therefore, free from, unencumbered by, any means of production of their own. With this polarisation of the market for commodities, the fundamental conditions of capitalist production are given. The capitalist system pre-supposes the complete separation of the labourers from all property in the means by which they can realise their labour. As soon as capitalist production is once on its own legs, it not only maintains this separation, but reproduces it on a continually extending scale. The process, therefore, that clears the way for the capitalist system, can be none other than the process which takes away from the labourer the possession of his means of production; a process that transforms, on the one hand, the social means of subsistence and of production into capital, on the other, the immediate producers into wage-labourers. The so-called primitive accumulation, therefore, is nothing else than the historical process of divorcing the producer from the means of production. It appears as primitive, because it forms the pre-historic stage of capital and of the mode of production corresponding with it.

The economic structure of capitalistic society has grown out of the economic structure of feudal society. The dissolution of the latter set free the elements of the former.

The immediate producer, the labourer, could only dispose of his own person after he had ceased to be attached to the soil and ceased to be the slave, serf, or bondman of another. To become a free seller of labour-power, who carries his commodity wherever he finds a market, he must further have escaped from the regime of the guilds, their rules for apprentices and journeymen, and the impediments of their labour regulations. Hence, the historical movement which changes the producers into wage-workers, appears, on the one hand, as their emancipation from serfdom and from the fetters of the guilds, and this side alone exists for our bourgeois historians. But, on the other hand, these new freedmen became sellers of themselves only after they had been robbed of all their own means of production, and of all the guarantees of existence afforded by the old feudal arrangements. And the history of this, their expropriation, is written in the annals of mankind in letters of blood and fire.

The industrial capitalists, these new potentates, had on their part not only to displace the guild masters of handicrafts, but also the feudal lords, the possessors of the sources of wealth. In this respect their conquest of social power appears as the fruit of a victorious struggle both against feudal lordship and its revolting prerogatives, and against the guilds and the fetters they laid on the free development of production and the free exploitation of man by man. The chevaliers d'industrie, however, only succeeded in supplanting the chevaliers of the sword by making use of events of which they themselves were wholly innocent. They have risen by means as vile as those by which the Roman freedman once on a time made himself the master of his *patronus*.

The starting-point of the development that gave rise to the wage-labourer as well as to the capitalist, was the servitude of the labourer. The advance consisted in a change of form of this servitude, in the transformation of feudal exploitation into capitalist exploitation. To understand its march, we need not go back very far. Although we come across the first beginnings of capitalist production as early as the 14th or 15th century, sporadically, in certain towns of the Mediterranean, the capitalistic era dates from the 16th century. Wherever it appears, the abolition of serfdom has been long effected, and the highest development of the middle ages, the existence of sovereign towns, has been long on the wane.

In the history of primitive accumulation, all revolutions are epoch-making that act as levers for the capitalist class in course of formation; but, above all, those moments when great masses of men are suddenly and forcibly torn from their means of subsistence, and hurled as free and "unattached" proletarians on the labour-market. The expropriation of the agricultural producer, of the peasant, from the soil, is the basis of the whole process. The history of this expropriation, in different countries, assumes different aspects, and runs through its various phases in different orders of succession, and at different periods. In England alone, which we take as our example, has it the classic form.[1]

EXPROPRIATION OF THE AGRICULTURAL POPULATION FROM THE LAND

In England, serfdom had practically disappeared in the last part of the 14th century. The immense majority of the population[1] consisted then, and to a still larger extent, in the 15th century, of free peasant proprietors, whatever was the feudal title under which their right of property was hidden. In the large seignorial domains, the old bailiff, himself a serf, was displaced by the free farmer. The wage-labourers of agriculture consisted partly of peasants, who utilised their leisure time by working on the large estates, partly of an independent special class of wage-labourers, relatively and absolutely few in numbers. The latter also were practically at the same time peasant farmers, since, besides their wages, they had allotted to them arable land to the extent of 4 or more acres, together with their cottages. Besides they, with the rest of the peasants, enjoyed the usufruct of the common land, which gave pasture to their cattle, furnished them with timber, fire-wood, turf, &c.[2] In all countries of Europe, feudal production is characterised by division of the soil amongst the greatest possible number of sub-feudatories. The might of the feudal lord, like that of the sovereign, depended not on the length of his rent-roll, but on the number of his subjects, and the latter depended on the number of peasant proprietors.[3] Although, therefore, the English land, after the Norman conquest, was distributed in gigantic baronies, one of which often included some 900 of the old Anglo-Saxon lordships, it was bestrewn with small peasant properties, only here and there interspersed with great seignorial domains. Such conditions, together with the prosperity of the towns so characteristic of the 15th century, allowed of that wealth of the people which Chancellor Fortescue so eloquently paints in his "Laudes legum Angliae"; but it excluded the possibility of capitalistic wealth.

The prelude of the revolution that laid the foundation of the capitalist mode of production, was played in the last third of the 15th, and the first decade of the 16th century. A mass of free proletarians was hurled on the labour-market by the breaking-up of the bands of feudal retainers, who, as Sir James Steuart well says, "everywhere uselessly filled house and castle."

Although the royal power, itself a product of bourgeois development, in its strife after absolute sovereignty forcibly hastened on the dissolution of these bands of retainers, it was by no means the sole cause of it. In insolent conflict with king and parliament, the great feudal lords created an incomparably larger proletariat by the forcible driving of the peasantry from the land, to which the latter had the same feudal right as the lord himself, and by the usurpation of the common lands. The rapid rise of the Flemish wool manufactures, and the corresponding rise in the price of wool in England, gave the direct impulse to these evictions. The old nobility had been devoured by the great feudal wars. The new nobility was the child of its time, for which money was the power of all powers. Transformation of arable land into sheepwalks was, therefore, its cry. Harrison, in his "Description of England, prefixed to Holinshed's Chronicles," describes how the expropriation of small peasants is ruining the country. "What care our great encroachers?" The dwellings of the peasants and the cottages of the labourers were razed to the ground or doomed to decay. "If," says Harrison, "the old records of euerie manour be sought... it will soon appear that in some manour seventeene, eighteene, or twentie houses are shrunk... that England was neuer less furnished with people than at the present.... Of cities and townes either utterly decaied or more than a quarter or half diminished, though some one be a little increased here or there; of townes pulled downe for sheepe-walks, and no more but the lordships now standing in them.... I could saie somwhat." The complaints of these old chroniclers are always exaggerated, but they reflect faithfully the impression made on contemporaries by the revolution in the conditions of production. A comparison of the writings of Chancellor Fortescue and Thomas More reveals the gulf between the 15th and 16th century. As Thornton rightly has it, the English working-class was precipitated without any transition from its golden into its iron age.

Legislation was terrified at this revolution. It did not yet stand on that height of civilisation where the "wealth of the nation" (*i.e.*, the formation of capital, and the reckless exploitation and impoverishing of the mass of the people) figure as the *ultima Thule* of all state-craft. In his history of Henry VII., Bacon says: "Inclosures at that time (1489) began to be more frequent, whereby arable land (which could not be manured without people and families) was turned into pasture, which was easily rid by a few herdsmen; and tenancies for years, lives, and at will (whereupon much of the yeomanry lived) were turned into demesnes. This bred a decay of people, and (by consequence) a decay of towns, churches, tithes, and the like... In remedying of this inconvenience the king's wisdom was admirable, and the parliament's at that time...they took a course to take away depopulating inclosures, and depopulating pasturage." An Act of Henry VII., 1489, cap. 19, forbad the destruction of all "houses of husbandry" to which at least 20 acres of land belonged. By an Act, 25 Henry VIII., the same law was renewed. It recites, among other things, that many farms and large flocks of cattle, especially of sheep, are concentrated in the hands of a few men, whereby the rent of land has much risen and tillage has fallen off, churches and houses have been pulled down, and marvellous numbers of people have been deprived of the means wherewith to maintain themselves and their families. The Act, therefore, ordains the rebuilding of the decayed farm-steads, and fixes a proportion between corn land and pasture land, &c. An Act of 1533 recites that some owners possess 24,000 sheep, and limits the number to be owned to 2,000.[4] The cry of the people and the legislation directed, for 150 years after Henry VII., against the expropriation of the small farmers and peasants, were alike fruitless. The secret of their inefficiency Bacon, without knowing it, reveals to us, "The device of King Henry VII., " says Bacon, in his "Essays, Civil and Moral." Essay 29, "was profound and admirable, in making farms and houses of husbandry of a standard; that is, maintained with such a proportion of land unto them as may breed a subject to live in convenient plenty, and no servile condition, and to keep the plough in the hands of the owners and not mere hirelings."[5] What the capitalist system demanded was, on the other hand, a degraded and almost servile condition of the mass of the people, the transformation of them into mercenaries, and of their means of labour into capital. During this transformation period, legislation also strove to retain the 4 acres of land by the cottage of the agricultural wage-labourer, and forbad him to take lodgers into his cottage. In the reign of James I., 1627, Roger Crocker of Front Mill, was condemned for having built a cottage on the manor of Front Mill without 4 acres of land attached to the same in perpetuity. As late as Charles I.'s reign, 1638, a royal commission was appointed to enforce the carrying out of the old laws, especially that referring to the 4 acres of land. Even in Cromwell's time, the building of a house within 4 miles of London was forbidden unless it was endowed with 4 acres of land. As late as the first half of the 18th century complaint is made if the cottage of the agricultural labourer has not an adjunct of one or two acres of land. Nowadays, he is lucky if it is furnished with a little garden, or if he may rent, far away from his cottage, a few roods. "Landlords and farmers," says Dr. Hunter, "work here hand in hand. A few acres to the cottage would make the labourers too independent."[6]

The process of forcible expropriation of the people received in the 16th century a new and frightful impulse from the Reformation, and from the consequent colossal spoliation of the church property. The Catholic church was, at the time of the Reformation, feudal proprietor of a great part of the English land. The suppression of the monasteries, &c., hurled their inmates into the proletariat. The estates of the church were to a large extent given away to rapacious royal favourites, or sold at a nominal price to speculating farmers and citizens, who drove out, *en masse*, the hereditary sub-tenants and threw their holdings into one. The legally guaranteed property of the poorer folk in a part of the church's tithes was tacitly confiscated.[7] "Pauper ubique jacet," cried Queen Elizabeth, after a journey through England. In the 43rd year of her reign the nation was obliged to recognise pauperism officially by the introduction of a poor-rate. "The authors of this law seem to have been ashamed to state the grounds of it, for [contrary to traditional usage] it has no preamble whatever."[8] By the 16th of Charles I., ch. 4, it was declared perpetual, and in fact only in 1834 did it take a new and harsher form.[9] These immediate results of the Reformation were not its most lasting ones. The property of the church formed the religious bulwark of the traditional conditions of landed property. With its fall these were no longer tenable.[10]

Even in the last decade of the 17th century, the yeomanry, the class of independent peasants, were more numerous than the class of farmers. They had formed the backbone of Cromwell's strength, and, even according to the confession of Macaulay, stood in favourable contrast to the drunken squires and to their servants, the country clergy, who had to marry their masters' cast-off mistresses. About 1750, the yeomanry had disappeared,[11] and so had, in the last decade of the 18th century, the last trace of the common land of the agricultural labourer. We leave on one side here the purely economic causes of the agricultural revolution. We deal only with the forcible means employed.

After the restoration of the Stuarts, the landed proprietors carried, by legal means, an act of usurpation, effected everywhere on the Continent without any legal formality. They abolished the feudal tenure of land, *i.e.*, they got rid of all its obligations to the State, "indemnified" the State by taxes on the peasantry and the rest of the mass of the people, vindicated for themselves the rights of modern private property in estates to which they had only a feudal title, and, finally, passed those laws of settlement, which, *mutatis mutandis*, had the same effect on the English agricultural labourer, as the edict of the Tartar Boris Godunof on the Russian peasantry.

The "glorious Revolution" brought into power, along with William of Orange, the landlord and capitalist appropriators of surplus-value.[12] They inaugurated the new era by practising on a colossal scale thefts of state lands, thefts that had been hitherto managed more modestly. These estates were given away, sold at a ridiculous figure, or even annexed to private estates by direct seizure.[13] All this happened without the slightest observation of legal etiquette. The Crown lands thus fraudulently appropriated, together with the robbery of the Church estates, as far as these had not been lost again during the republican revolution, form the basis of the to-day princely domains of the English oligarchy.[14] The bourgeois capitalists favoured the operation with the view, among others, to promoting free trade in land, to extending the domain of modern agriculture on the large farm-system, and to increasing their supply of the free agricultural proletarians ready to hand. Besides, the new landed aristocracy was the natural ally of the new bankocracy, of the newly-hatched *haute finance*, and of the large manufacturers, then depending on protective duties. The English bourgeoisie acted for its own interest quite as wisely as did the Swedish bourgeoisie who, reversing the process, hand in hand with their economic allies, the peasantry, helped the kings in the forcible resumption of the Crown lands from the oligarchy. This happened since 1604 under Charles X. and Charles XI.

Communal property — always distinct from the State property just dealt with — was an old Teutonic institution which lived on under cover of feudalism. We have seen how the forcible usurpation of this, generally accompanied by the turning of arable into pasture land, begins at the end of the 15th and extends into the 16th century. But, at that time, the process was carried on by means of individual acts of violence against which legislation, for a hundred and fifty years, fought in vain. The advance made by the 18th century shows itself in this, that the law itself becomes now the instrument of the theft of the people's land, although the large farmers make use of their little independent methods as well.[15] The parliamentary form of the robbery is that of Acts for enclosures of Commons, in other words, decrees by which the landlords grant themselves the people's land as private property, decrees of expropriation of the people. Sir F. M. Eden refutes his own crafty special pleading, in which he tries to represent communal property as the private property of the great landlords who have taken the place of the feudal lords, when he, himself, demands a "general Act of Parliament for the enclosure of Commons" (admitting thereby that a parliamentary *coup d'etat* is necessary for its transformation into private property), and moreover calls on the legislature for the indemnification for the expropriated poor.[16]

Whilst the place of the independent yeoman was taken by tenants at will, small farmers on yearly leases, a servile rabble dependent on the pleasure of the landlords, the systematic robbery of the Communal lands helped especially, next to the theft of the State domains, to see all those large farms, that were called in the 18th century capital farms[17] or merchant farms,[18] and to "set free" the agricultural population as proletarians for manufacturing industry.

The 18th century, however, did not yet recognise as fully as the 19th the identity between national wealth and the poverty of the people. Hence the most vigorous polemic, in the economic literature of that time, on the "enclosure of commons." From the mass of materials that lie before me, I give a few extracts that will throw a strong light on the circumstances of the time. "In several parishes of Hertfordshire," writes one indignant person, "24 farms, numbering on the average 50-150 acres, have been melted up into three farms."[19] "In Northamptonshire and Leicestershire the enclosure of common lands has taken place on a very large scale, and most of the new lordships, resulting from the enclosure, have been turned into pasturage, in consequence of which many lordships have not now 50 acres ploughed yearly, in which 1,500 were ploughed formerly. The ruins of former dwelling-houses, barns, stables, &c.," are the sole traces of the former inhabitants. "An hundred houses and families have in some open-field villages... dwindled to eight or ten... The landholders in most parishes that have been enclosed only 15 or 20 years, are very few in comparison of the numbers who occupied them in the open-field state. It is no uncommon thing for 4 or 5 wealthy graziers to engross a large enclosed lordship which was before in the hands of 20 or 30 farmers, and as many smaller tenants and proprietors. All these are hereby thrown out of their livings with their families and many other families who were chiefly employed and supported by them."[20] It was not only the land that lay waste, but often land cultivated either in common or held under a definite rent paid to the community, that was annexed by the neighbouring landlords under pretext of enclosure. "I have here in view enclosures of open fields and lands already improved. It is acknowledged by even the writers in defence of enclosures that these diminished villages increase the monopolies of farms, raise the prices of provisions, and produce depopulation... and even the enclosure of waste lands (as now carried on) bears hard on the poor, by depriving them of a part of their subsistence, and only goes towards increasing farms already too large."[21] "When," says Dr. Price, "this land gets into the hands of a few great farmers, the consequence must be that the little farmers" (earlier designated by him "a multitude of little proprietors and tenants, who maintain themselves and families by the produce of the ground they occupy by sheep kept on a common, by poultry, hogs, &c., and who therefore have little occasion to purchase any of the means of subsistence") "will be converted into a body of men who earn their subsistence by working for others, and who will be under a necessity of going to market for all they want.... There will, perhaps, be more labour, because there will be more compulsion to it.... Towns and manufactures will increase, because more will be driven to them in quest of places and employment. This is the way in which the engrossing of farms naturally operates. And this is the way in which, for many years, it has been actually operating in this kingdom."[22] He sums up the effect of the enclosures thus: "Upon the whole, the circumstances of the lower ranks of men are altered in almost every respect for the worse. From little occupiers of land, they are reduced to the state of day-labourers and hirelings; and, at the same time, their subsistence in that state has become more difficult."[23] In fact, usurpation of the common lands and the revolution in agriculture accompanying this, told so acutely on the agricultural labourers that, even according to Eden, between 1765 and 1780, their wages began to fall below the minimum, and to be supplemented by official poor-law relief. Their wages, he says, "were not more than enough for the absolute necessaries of life."

Let us hear for a moment a defender of enclosures and an opponent of Dr. Price. "Not is it a consequence that there must be depopulation, because men are not seen wasting their labour in the open field.... If, by converting the little farmers into a body of men who must work for others, more labour is produced, it is an advantage which the nation" (to which, of course, the "converted" ones do not belong) "should wish for... the produce being greater when their joint labours are employed on one farm, there will be a surplus of manufactures, and by this means manufactures, one of the mines of the nation, will increase, in proportion to the quantity of corn produced."[24]

The stoical peace of mind with which the political economist regards the most shameless violation of the "sacred rights of property" and the grossest acts of violence to persons, as soon as they are necessary to lay the foundations of the capitalistic mode of production, is shown by Sir F. M. Eden, philanthropist and tory to boot. The whole series of thefts, outrages, and popular misery, that accompanied the forcible expropriation of the people, from the last third of the 15th to the end of the 18th century, lead him merely to the comfortable conclusion: "The due proportion between arable land and pasture had to be established. During the whole of the 14th and the greater part of the 15th century, there was one acre of pasture to 2, 3, and even 4 of arable land. About the middle of the 16th century the proportion was changed of 2 acres of pasture to 2, later on, of 2 acres of pasture to one of arable, until at last the proportion of 3 acres of pasture to one of arable land was attained."

In the 19th century, the very memory of the connexion between the agricultural labourer and the communal property had, of course, vanished. To say nothing of more recent times, have the agricultural population received a farthing of compensation for the 3,511,770 acres of common land which between 1801 and 1831 were stolen from them by parliamentary devices presented to the landlords by the landlords?

The last process of wholesale expropriation of the agricultural population from the soil is, finally, the so-called clearing of estates, *i.e.*, the sweeping men off them. All the English methods hitherto considered culminated in "clearing." As we saw in the picture of modern conditions given in a former chapter, where there are no more independent peasants to get rid of, the "clearing" of cottages begins; so that the agricultural labourers do not find on the soil cultivated by them even the spot necessary for their own housing.

But what "clearing of estates" really and properly signifies, we learn only in the promised land of modern romance, the Highlands of Scotland. There the process is distinguished by its systematic character, by the magnitude of the scale on which it is carried out at one blow (in Ireland landlords have gone to the length of sweeping away several villages at once; in Scotland areas as large as German principalities are dealt with), finally by the peculiar form of property, under which the embezzled lands were held.

The Highland Celts were organised in clans, each of which was the owner of the land on which it was settled. The representative of the clan, its chief or "great man," was only the titular owner of this property, just as the Queen of England is the titular owner of all the national soil. When the English government succeeded in suppressing the intestine wars of these "great men," and their constant incursions into the Lowland plains, the chiefs of the clans by no means gave up their time-honoured trade as robbers; they only changed its form. On their own authority they transformed their nominal right into a right of private property, and as this brought them into collision with their clansmen, resolved to drive them out by open force. "A king of England might as well claim to drive his subjects into the sea," says Professor Newman.[25] This revolution, which began in Scotland after the last rising of the followers of the Pretender, can be followed through its first phases in the writings of Sir James Steuart[26] and James Anderson.[27] In the 18th century the hunted-out Gaels were forbidden to emigrate from the country, with a view to driving them by force to Glasgow and other manufacturing towns.[28] As an example of the method[29] obtaining in the 19th century, the "clearing" made by the Duchess of Sutherland will suffice here. This person, well instructed in economy, resolved, on entering upon her government, to effect a radical cure, and to turn the whole country, whose population had already been, by earlier processes of the like kind, reduced to 15,000, into a sheep-walk. From 1814 to 1820 these 15,000 inhabitants, about 3,000 families, were systematically hunted and rooted out. All their villages were destroyed and burnt, all their fields turned into pasturage. British soldiers enforced this eviction, and came to blows with the inhabitants. One old woman was burnt to death in the flames of the hut, which she refused to leave. Thus this fine lady appropriated 794,000 acres of land that had from time immemorial belonged to the clan. She assigned to the expelled inhabitants about 6,000 acres on the sea-shore — 2 acres per family. The 6,000 acres had until this time lain waste, and brought in no income to their owners. The Duchess, in the nobility of her heart, actually went so far as to let these at an average rent of 2s. 6d. per acre to the clansmen, who for centuries had shed their blood for her family. The whole of the stolen clanland she divided into 29 great sheep farms, each inhabited by a single family, for the most part imported English farm-servants. In the year 1835 the 15,000 Gaels were already replaced by

131,000 sheep. The remnant of the aborigines flung on the sea-shore, tried to live by catching fish. They became amphibious and lived, as an English author says, half on land and half on water, and withal only half on both.[30]

But the brave Gaels must expiate yet more bitterly their idolatry, romantic and of the mountains, for the "great men" of the clan. The smell of their fish rose to the noses of the great men. They scented some profit in it, and let the sea-shore to the great fishmongers of London. For the second time the Gaels were hunted out.[31]

But, finally, part of the sheep-walks are turned into deer preserves. Every one knows that there are no real forests in England. The deer in the parks of the great are demurely domestic cattle, fat as London aldermen. Scotland is therefore the last refuge of the "noble passion." "In the Highlands," says Somers in 1848, "new forests are springing up like mushrooms. Here, on one side of Gaick, you have the new forest of Glenfeshie; and there on the other you have the new forest of Ardverikie. In the same line you have the Black Mount, an immense waste also recently erected. From east to west — from the neighbourhood of Aberdeen to the crags of Oban — you have now a continuous line of forests; while in other parts of the Highlands there are the new forests of Loch Archaig, Glengarry, Glenmoriston, &c. Sheep were introduced into glens which had been the seats of communities of small farmers; and the latter were driven to seek subsistence on coarser and more sterile tracks of soil. Now deer are supplanting sheep; and these are once more dispossessing the small tenants, who will necessarily be driven down upon still coarser land and to more grinding penury. Deer-forests[32] and the people cannot co-exist. One or other of the two must yield. Let the forests be increased in number and extent during the next quarter of a century, as they have been in the last, and the Gaels will perish from their native soil.... This movement among the Highland proprietors is with some a matter of ambition...with some love of sport...while others, of a more practical cast, follow the trade in deer with an eye solely to profit. For it is a fact, that a mountain range laid out in forest is, in many cases, more profitable to the proprietor than when let as a sheep-walk....The huntsman who wants a deer-forest limits his offers by no other calculation than the extent of his purse....Sufferings have been inflicted in the Highlands scarcely less severe than those occasioned by the policy of the Norman kings. Deer have received extended ranges, while men have been hunted within a narrower and still narrower circle....One after one the liberties of the people have been cloven down....And the oppressions are daily on the increase....The clearance and dispersion of the people is pursued by the proprietors as a settled principle, as an agricultural necessity, just as trees and brushwood are cleared from the wastes of America or Australia; and the operation goes on in a quiet, business-like way, &c."[33]

The spoliation of the church's property, the fraudulent alienation of the State domains, the robbery of the common lands, the usurpation of feudal and clan property, and its transformation into modern private property under circumstances of reckless terrorism, were just so many idyllic methods of primitive accumulation. They conquered the field for capitalistic agriculture, made the soil part and parcel of capital, and created for the town industries the necessary supply of a "free" and outlawed proletariat.

BLOODY LEGISLATION AGAINST THE EXPROPRIATED, FROM THE END OF THE 15TH CENTURY. FORCING DOWN OF WAGES BY ACTS OF PARLIAMENT

The proletariat created by the breaking up of the bands of feudal retainers and by the forcible expropriation of the people from the soil, this "free" proletariat could not possibly be absorbed by the nascent manufactures as fast as it was thrown upon the world. On the other hand, these men, suddenly dragged from their wonted mode of life, could not as suddenly adapt themselves to the discipline of their new condition. They were turned *en masse* into beggars, robbers, vagabonds, partly from inclination, in most cases from stress of circumstances. Hence at the end of the 15th and during the whole of the 16th century, throughout Western Europe a bloody legislation against vagabondage. The fathers of the present working-class were chastised for their enforced transformation into vagabonds and paupers. Legislation treated them as "voluntary" criminals, and assumed that it depended on their own good will to go on working under the old conditions that no longer existed.

In England this legislation began under Henry VII.

Henry VIII. 1530: Beggars old and unable to work receive a beggar's licence. On the other hand, whipping and imprisonment for sturdy vagabonds. They are to be tied to the cart-tail and whipped until the blood streams from their bodies, then to swear an oath to go back to their birthplace or to where they have lived the last three years and to "put themselves to labour." What grim irony! In 27 Henry VIII. the former statute is repeated, but strengthened with new clauses. For the second arrest for vagabondage the whipping is to be repeated and half the ear sliced off; but for the third relapse the offender is to be executed as a hardened criminal and enemy of the common weal.

Edward VI.: A statute of the first year of his reign, 1547, ordains that if anyone refuses to work, he shall be condemned as a slave to the person who has denounced him as an idler. The master shall feed his slave on bread and water, weak broth and such refuse meat as he thinks fit. He has the right to force him to do any work, no matter how disgusting, with whip and chains. If the slave is absent a fortnight, he is condemned to slavery for life and is to be branded on forehead or back with the letter S; if he runs away thrice, he is to be executed as a felon. The master can sell him, bequeath him, let him out on hire as a slave, just as any other personal chattel or cattle. If the slaves attempt anything against the masters, they are also to be executed. Justices of the peace, on information, are to hunt the rascals down. If it happens that a vagabond has been idling about for three days, he is to be taken to his birthplace, branded with a redhot iron with the letter V on the breast and be set to work, in chains, in the streets or at some other labour. If the vagabond gives a false birthplace, he is then to become the slave for life of this place, of its inhabitants, or its corporation, and to be branded with an S. All persons have the right to take away the children of the vagabonds and to keep them as apprentices, the young men until the 24th year, the girls until the 20th. If they run away, they are to become up to this age the slaves of their masters, who can put them in irons, whip them, &c., if they like. Every master may put an iron ring round the neck, arms or legs of his slave, by which to know him more easily and to be more certain of him.[1] The last part of this statute provides that certain poor people may be employed by a place or by persons, who are willing to give them food and drink and to find them work. This kind of parish-slaves was kept up in England until far into the 19th century under the name of "roundsmen."

Elizabeth, 1572: Unlicensed beggars above 14 years of age are to be severely flogged and branded on the left ear unless some one will take them into service for two years; in case of a repetition of the offence, if they are over 18, they are to be executed, unless some one will take them into service for two years; but for the third offence they are to be executed without mercy as felons. Similar statutes: 18 Elizabeth, c. 13, and another of 1597.[2]

James I: Any one wandering about and begging is declared a rogue and a vagabond. Justices of the peace in petty sessions are authorised to have them publicly whipped and for the first offence to imprison them for 6 months, for the second for 2 years. Whilst in prison they are to be whipped as much and as often as the justices of the peace think fit.... Incorrigible and dangerous rogues are to be branded with an R on the left shoulder and set to hard labour, and if they are caught begging again, to be executed without mercy. These statutes, legally binding until the beginning of the 18th century, were only repealed by 12 Anne, c. 23.

Similar laws in France, where by the middle of the 17th century a kingdom of vagabonds (truands) was established in Paris. Even at the beginning of Louis XVI.'s reign (Ordinance of July 13th, 1777) every man in good health from 16 to 60 years of age, if without means of subsistence and not practising a trade, is to be sent to the galleys. Of the same nature are the statute of Charles V. for the Netherlands (October, 1537), the first edict of the States and Towns of Holland (March 10, 1614), the "Plakaat" of the United Provinces (June 26, 1649), &c.

Thus were the agricultural people, first forcibly expropriated from the soil, driven from their homes, turned into vagabonds, and then whipped, branded, tortured by laws grotesquely terrible, into the discipline necessary for the wage system.

It is not enough that the conditions of labour are concentrated in a mass, in the shape of capital, at the one pole of society, while at the other are grouped masses of men, who have nothing to sell but their labour-power. Neither is it enough that they are compelled to sell it voluntarily. The advance of capitalist production develops a working-class, which by education, tradition, habit, looks upon the conditions of that mode of production as self-evident laws of Nature. The organisation of the capitalist process of production, once fully developed, breaks down all resistance. The constant generation of a relative surplus-population keeps the law of supply and demand of labour, and therefore keeps wages, in a rut that corresponds with the wants of capital. The dull compulsion of economic relations completes the subjection of the labourer to the capitalist. Direct force, outside economic conditions, is of course still used, but only exceptionally. In the ordinary run of things, the labourer can be left to the "natural laws of production," *i.e.*, to his dependence on capital, a dependence springing from, and guaranteed in perpetuity by, the conditions of production themselves. It is otherwise during the historic genesis of capitalist production. The bourgeoisie, at its rise, wants and uses the power of the state to "regulate" wages, *i.e.*, to force them within the limits suitable for surplus-value making, to lengthen the working-day and to keep the labourer himself in the normal degree of dependence. This is an essential element of the so-called primitive accumulation.

The class of wage-labourers, which arose in the latter half of the 14th century, formed then and in the following century only a very small part of the population, well protected in its position by the independent peasant proprietary in the country and the guild-organisation in the town. In country and town master and workmen stood close together socially. The subordination of labour to capital was only formal — *i.e.*, the mode of production itself had as yet no specific capitalistic character. Variable capital preponderated greatly over constant. The demand for wage-labour grew, therefore, rapidly with every accumulation of capital, whilst the supply of wage-labour followed but slowly. A large part of the national product, changed later into a fund of capitalist accumulation, then still entered into the consumption-fund of the labourer.

Legislation on wage-labour (from the first, aimed at the exploitation of the labourer and, as it advanced, always equally hostile to him),[3] is started in England by the Statute of Labourers, of Edward III., 1349. The ordinance of 1350 in France, issued in the name of King John, corresponds with it. English and French legislation run parallel and are identical in purport. So far as the labour-statutes aim at compulsory extension of the working-day, I do not return to them, as this point was treated earlier (Chap. X., Section 5).

The Statute of Labourers was passed at the urgent instance of the House of Commons. A Tory says naively: "Formerly the poor demanded such *high* wages as to threaten industry and wealth. Next, their wages are so low as to threaten industry and wealth equally and perhaps more, but in another way."[4] A tariff of wages was fixed by law for town and country, for piece-work and day-work. The agricultural labourers were to hire themselves out by the year, the town ones "in open market." It was forbidden, under pain of imprisonment, to pay higher wages than those fixed by the statute, but the taking of higher wages was more severely punished than the giving them. [So also in Sections 18 and 19 of the Statute of Apprentices of Elizabeth, ten days' imprisonment is decreed for him that pays the higher wages, but twenty-one days for him that receives them.] A statute of 1360 increased the penalties and authorised the masters to extort labour at the legal rate of wages by corporal punishment. All combinations, contracts, oaths, &c., by which masons and carpenters reciprocally bound themselves, were declared null and void. Coalition of the labourers is treated as a heinous crime from the 14th century to 1825, the year of the repeal of the laws against Trades' Unions. The spirit of the Statute of Labourers of 1349 and of its offshoots, comes out clearly in the fact, that indeed a maximum of wages is dictated by the State, but on no account a minimum.

In the 16th century, the condition of the labourers had, as we know, become much worse. The money wage rose, but not in proportion to the depreciation of money and the corresponding rise in the prices of commodities. Wages, therefore, in reality fell. Nevertheless, the laws for keeping them down remained in force, together with the ear-clipping and branding of those "whom no one was willing to take into service." By the Statute of Apprentices 5 Elizabeth, c. 3, the justices of the peace were empowered to fix certain wages and to modify them according to the time of the year and the price of commodities. James I. extended these regulations of labour also to weavers, spinners, and all possible categories of workers.[5] George II. extended the laws against coalitions of labourers to manufacturers. In the manufacturing period *par excellence*, the capitalist mode of production had become sufficiently strong to render legal regulation of wages as impracticable as it was unnecessary; but the ruling classes were unwilling in case of necessity to be without the weapons of the old arsenal. Still, 8 George II. forbade a higher day's wage than 2s. 7 1/2 d. for journeymen tailors in and around London, except in cases of general mourning; still, 13 George III., c. 68, gave the regulation of the wages of silk-weavers to the justices of the peace; still, in 1706, it required two judgments of the higher courts to decide, whether the mandates of justices of the peace as to wages held good also for non-agricultural labourers; still, in 1799, an act of Parliament ordered that the wages of the Scotch miners should continue to be regulated by a statute of Elizabeth and two Scotch acts of 1661 and 1671. How completely in the meantime circumstances had changed, is proved by an occurrence unheard-of before in the English Lower House. In that place, where for more than 400 years laws had been made for the maximum, beyond which wages absolutely must not rise, Whitbread in 1796 proposed a legal minimum wage for agricultural labourers. Pitt opposed this, but confessed that the "condition of the poor was cruel." Finally, in 1813, the laws for the regulation of wages were repealed. They were an absurd anomaly, since the capitalist regulated his factory by his private legislation, and could by the poor-rates make up the wage of the agricultural labourer to the indispensable minimum. The provisions of the labour statutes as to contracts between master and workman, as to giving notice and the like, which only allow of a civil action against the contract-breaking master, but on the contrary permit a criminal action against the contract-breaking workman, are to this hour (1873) in full force. The barbarous laws against Trades' Unions fell in 1825 before the threatening bearing of the proletariat. Despite this, they fell only in part. Certain beautiful fragments of the old statute vanished only in 1859. Finally, the act of Parliament of June 29, 1871, made a pretence of removing the last traces of this class of legislation by legal recognition of Trades' Unions. But an act of Parliament of the same date (an act to amend the criminal law relating to violence, threats, and molestation), re-established, in point of fact, the former state of things in a new shape. By this Parliamentary escamotage the means which the labourers could use in a strike or lock-out were withdrawn from the laws common to all citizens, and placed under exceptional penal legislation, the interpretation of which fell to the masters themselves in their capacity as justices of the peace. Two years earlier, the same House of Commons and the same Mr. Gladstone in the well-known straightforward fashion brought in a bill for the abolition of all exceptional penal legislation against the working-class. But this was never allowed to go beyond the second reading, and the matter was thus protracted until at last the "great Liberal party," by an alliance with the Tories, found courage to turn against the very proletariat that had carried it into power. Not content with this treachery, the "great

Liberal party" allowed the English judges, ever complaisant in the service of the ruling classes, to dig up again the earlier laws against "conspiracy," and to apply them to coalitions of labourers. We see that only against its will and under the pressure of the masses did the English Parliament give up the laws against Strikes and Trades' Unions, after it had itself, for 500 years, held, with shameless egoism, the position of a permanent Trades' Union of the capitalists against the labourers.

During the very first storms of the revolution, the French bourgeoisie dared to take away from the workers the right of association but just acquired. By a decree of June 14, 1791, they declared all coalition of the workers as "an attempt against liberty and the declaration of the rights of man," punishable by a fine of 500 livres, together with deprivation of the rights of an active citizen for one year.[6] This law which, by means of State compulsion, confined the struggle between capital and labour within limits comfortable for capital, has outlived revolutions and changes of dynasties. Even the Reign of Terror left it untouched. It was but quite recently struck out of the Penal Code. Nothing is more characteristic than the pretext for this bourgeois *coup d'etat*. "Granting," says Chapelier, the reporter of the Select Committee on this law, "that wages ought to be a little higher than they are,... that they ought to be high enough for him that receives them, to be free from that state of absolute dependence due to the want of the necessaries of life, and which is almost that of slavery," yet the workers must not be allowed to come to any understanding about their own interests, nor to act in common and thereby lessen their "absolute dependence, which is almost that of slavery;" because, forsooth, in doing this they injure "the freedom of their cidevant masters, the present entrepreneurs," and because a coalition against the despotism of the quondam masters of the corporations is — guess what! — is a restoration of the corporations abolished by the French constitution.[7]

GENESIS OF THE CAPITALIST FARMER

Now that we have considered the forcible creation of a class of outlawed proletarians, the bloody discipline that turned them into wage-labourers, the disgraceful action of the State which employed the police to accelerate the accumulation of capital by increasing the degree of exploitation of labour, the question remains: whence came the capitalists originally? For the expropriation of the agricultural population creates, directly, none but great landed proprietors. As far, however, as concerns the genesis of the farmer, we can, so to say, put our hand on it, because it is a slow process evolving through many centuries. The serfs, as well as the free small proprietors, held land under very different tenures, and were therefore emancipated under very different economic conditions. In England the first form of the farmer is the bailiff, himself a serf. His position is similar to that of the old Roman *villicus*, only in a more limited sphere of action. During the second half of the 14th century he is replaced by a farmer, whom the landlord provides with seed, cattle and implements. His condition is not very different from that of the peasant. Only he exploits more wage-labour. Soon he becomes a métayer, a half-farmer. He advances one part of the agricultural stock, the landlord the other. The two divide the total product in proportions determined by contract. This form quickly disappears in England, to give place to the farmer proper, who makes his own capital breed by employing wage-labourers, and pays a part of the surplus-product, in money or in kind, to the landlord as rent. So long, during the 15th century, as the independent peasant and the farm-labourer working for himself as well as for wages, enriched themselves by their own labour, the circumstances of the farmer, and his field of production, were equally mediocre. The agricultural revolution which commenced in the last third of the 15th century, and continued during almost the whole of the 16th (excepting, however, its last decade), enriched him just as speedily as it impoverished the mass of the agricultural people.[1]

The usurpation of the common lands allowed him to augment greatly his stock of cattle, almost without cost, whilst they yielded him a richer supply of manure for the tillage of the soil. To this, was added in the 16th century, a very important element. At that time the contracts for farms ran for a long time, often for 99 years. The progressive fall in the value of the precious metals, and therefore of money, brought the farmers golden fruit. Apart from all the other circumstances discussed above, it lowered wages. A portion of the latter was now added to the profits on the farm. The continuous rise in the price of corn, wool, meat, in a word of all agricultural produce, swelled the money capital of the farmer without any action on his part, whilst the rent he paid (being calculated on the old value of money) diminished in reality.[2] Thus they grew rich at the expense both of their labourers and their landlords. No wonder therefore, that England, at the end of the 16th century, had a class of capitalist farmers, rich, considering the circumstances of the time.[3]

REACTION OF THE AGRICULTURAL REVOLUTION ON INDUSTRY. CREATION OF THE HOME-MARKET FOR INDUSTRIAL CAPITAL

The expropriation and expulsion of the agricultural population, intermittent but renewed again and again, supplied, as we say, the town industries with a mass of proletarians entirely unconnected with the corporate guilds and unfettered by them; a fortunate circumstance that make old A. Anderson (not

284 / Sociological Thought

to be confounded with James Anderson) in his "History of Commerce," believe in the direct intervention of Providence. We must still pause a moment on this element of primitive accumulation. The thinning-out of the independent, self-supporting peasants not only brought about the crowding together of the industrial proletariat, in the way that Geoffroy Saint Hilaire explained the condensation of cosmical matter at one place, by its rarefaction at another.[1] In spite of the smaller number of its cultivators, the soil brought forth as much or more produce, after as before, because the revolution in the conditions of landed property was accompanied by improved methods of culture, greater co-operation, concentration of the means of production, &c., and because not only were the agricultural wage-labourers put on the strain more intensely,[2] but the field of production on which they worked for themselves, became more and more contracted. With the setting free of a part of the agricultural population, therefore, their former means of nourishment were also set free. They were now transformed into material elements of variable capital. The peasant, expropriated and cast adrift, must buy their value in the form of wages, from his new master, the industrial capitalist. That which holds good of the means of subsistence holds with the raw materials of industry dependent upon home agriculture. They were transformed into an element of constant capital. Suppose, *e.g.*, a part of the Westphalian peasants, who, at the time of Frederick II., all span flax, forcibly expropriated and hunted from the soil; and the other part that remained, turned into day-labourers of large farmers. At the same time arise large establishments for flax-spinning and weaving, in which the men "set free" now work for wages. The flax looks exactly as before. Not a fibre of it is changed, but a new social soul has popped into its body. It forms now a part of the constant capital of the master manufacturer. Formerly divided among a number of small producers, who cultivated it themselves and with their families spun it in retail fashion, it is now concentrated in the hand of one capitalist, who sets others to spin and weave it for him. The extra labour expended in flax-spinning realises itself formerly in extra income to numerous peasant families, or maybe, in Frederick II.'s time, in taxes pour le roi de Prusse. It realises itself now in profit for a few capitalists. The spindles and looms, formerly scattered over the face of the country, are now crowded together in a few great labour-barracks, together with the labourers and the raw material. And spindles, looms, raw material, are now transformed, from means of independent existence for the spinners and weavers, into means for commanding them and sucking out of them unpaid labour.[3] One does not perceive, when looking at the large manufactories and the large farms, that they have originated from the throwing into one of many small centres of production, and have been built up by the expropriation of many small independent producers. Nevertheless, the popular intuition was not at fault.

In the time of Mirabeau, the lion of the Revolution, the great manufactories were still called manufactures réunies, workshops thrown into one, as we speak of fields thrown into one. Says Mirabeau: "We are only paying attention to the grand manufactories, in which hundreds of men work under a director and which are commonly called *manufactures réunies*. Those where a very large number of labourers work, each separately and on his own account, are hardly considered; they are placed at an infinite distance from the others. This is a great error, as the latter alone make a really important object of national prosperity.... The large workshop (manufacture réunie) will enrich prodigiously one or two entrepreneurs, but the labourers will only be journeymen, paid more or less, and will not have any share in the success of the undertaking. In the discrete workshop (manufacture séparée), on the contrary, no one will become rich, but many labourers will be comfortable; the saving and the industrious will be able to amass a little capital, to put by a little for the birth of a child, for an illness, for themselves or their belongings. The number of saving and industrious labourers will increase, because they will see in good conduct, in activity, a means of essentially bettering their condition, and not of obtaining a small rise of wages that can never be of any importance of the future, and whose sole result is to place men in the position to live a little better, but only from day to day.... The large workshops, undertakings of certain private persons who pay labourers from day to day to work for their gain, may be able to put these private individuals at their ease, but they will never be an object worth the attention of governments. Discrete workshops, for the most part combined with cultivation of small holdings, are the only free ones."[4] The expropriation and eviction of a part of the agricultural population not only set free for industrial capital, the labourers, their means of subsistence, and material for labour; it also created the home-market.

In fact, the events that transformed the small peasants into wage-labourers, and their means of subsistence and of labour into material elements of capital, created, at the same time, a home-market for the latter. Formerly, the peasant family produced the means of subsistence and the raw materials, which they themselves, for the most part, consumed. These raw materials and means of subsistence have now become commodities; the large farmer sells them, he finds his market in manufactures. Yarn, linen, coarse woollen stuffs — things whose raw materials had been within the reach of every peasant family, had been spun and woven by it for its own use — were now transformed into articles of manufacture, to which the country districts at once served for markets. The many scattered customers, whom stray artisans until now had found in the numerous small producers working on their own account, concentrate themselves now into one great market provided for by industrial capital.[5] Thus, hand in hand with the expropriation of the self-supporting peasants, with their separation from their means of production, goes the destruction of rural domestic industry, the process of separation between manufacture and agriculture. And only the destruction of rural domestic industry can give the internal market of a country that extension and consistence which the capitalist mode of production requires. Still the manufacturing period, properly so called, does not succeed in carrying out this transformation radically and completely. It will be remembered that manufacture, properly so called, conquers but partially the domain of national production, and always rests on the handicrafts of the town and the domestic industry of the rural districts as its ultimate basis. If it destroys these in one form, in particular branches, at certain points, it calls them up again elsewhere, because it needs them for the preparation of raw material up to a certain point. It produces, therefore, a new class of small villagers who, while following the cultivation of the soil as an accessory calling, find their chief occupation in industrial labour, the products of which they sell to the manufacturers directly, or through the medium of merchants. This is one, though not the chief, cause of a phenomenon which, at first, puzzles the student of English history. From the last third of the 15th century he finds continually complaints, only interrupted at certain intervals, about the encroachment of capitalist farming in the country districts, and the progressive destruction of the peasantry. On the other hand, he always finds this peasantry turning up again, although in diminished number, and always under worse conditions.[6] The chief reason is: England is at one time chiefly a cultivator of corn, at another chiefly a breeder of cattle, in alternate periods, and with these the extent of peasant cultivation fluctuates. Modern Industry alone, and finally, supplies, in machinery, the lasting basis of capitalistic agriculture, expropriates radically the enormous majority of the agricultural population, and completes the separation between agriculture and rural domestic industry, whose roots — spinning and weaving — it tears up.[7] It therefore also, for the first time, conquers for industrial capital the entire home-market.[8]

ENDNOTES

Feuerbach: Opposition of the Materialist and Idealist Outlook

[1]   In *The German Ideology* the word *"Verkehr"* is used in a very wide sense, encompassing the material and spiritual intercourse of separate individuals, social groups and entire countries. Marx and Engels show that material intercourse, and above all the intercourse of men with each other in the production process, is the basis of every other form of intercourse.

The terms *"Verkehrstorm"* (form of intercourse), *"Verkehrsweise"* (mode of intercourse) and *"Verkehrsverhaltnisse"* (relations, or conditions, of intercourse) which we encounter in *The German Ideology* are used by Marx and Engels to express the concept "relations of production" which during that period was taking shape in their mind.

The ordinary dictionary meanings of *"Verkehr"* are traffic, intercourse, commerce. In this translation the word *"Verkehr"* has been mostly rendered as "intercourse" and occasionally as "association" or "commerce". — Ed.

2   The term *"Stamm"* — rendered in the present volume by the word "tribe" — played a considerably greater part in historical works written during the forties of the last century than it does at present. It was used to denote a community of people descended from a common ancestor, and comprised the modern concepts of "gens" and "tribe". The first to define and differentiate these concepts was Lewis Henry Morgan in his work *Ancient Society; or, Researches in the Lines of Human Progress from Savagery Through Barbarism to Civilisation*, London, 1877. This outstanding American ethnographer and historian showed for the first time the significance of the gens as the nucleus of the primitive communal system and thereby laid the scientific foundations for the history of primitive society as a whole. Engels drew the general conclusions from Morgan's discoveries and made a comprehensive analysis of the meaning of the concepts "gens" and "tribe" in his work *The Origin of the Family, Private Property and the State* (1884). — Ed.

3   The *Licinian agrarian law* — the agrarian law of Licinius and Sextius, Roman tribunes of the people, passed in 367 B.C. as a result of the struggle which the plebeians waged against the patricians. According to this law a Roman citizen could not hold more than 500 Yugera (approximately 309 acres) of common land (*ager publicus*). — Ed.

4   The building of houses. With savages each family has as a matter of course its own cave or hut like the separate family tent of the nomads. This separate domestic economy is made only the more necessary by the further development of private property. With the agricultural peoples a communal domestic economy is just as impossible as a communal cultivation of the soil. A great advance was the building of towns. In all previous periods, however, the abolition of individual economy, which is inseparable from the abolition of private property, was impossible for the simple reason that the material conditions governing it were not present. The setting-up of a communal domestic economy presupposes the development of machinery, of the use of natural forces and of many other productive forces — e.g. of water-supplies, of gas-lighting, steam-heating, etc., the removal [of the antagonism] of town and country. Without these conditions a communal economy would not in itself form a new productive force; lacking any material basis and resting on a purely theoretical foundation, it would be a mere freak and would end in nothing more than a monastic economy — What was possible can be seen in the towns brought about by condensation and the erection of communal buildings for various definite purposes (prisons, barracks, etc.). That the abolition of individual economy is inseparable from the abolition of the family is self-evident.

⁵ In the manuscript this paragraph occurs as a marginal note beside the previous paragraph. — Ed.

⁹ [Marginal note by Marx:] Universality corresponds to (I) the class versus the estate, (2) the competition, world-wide intercourse, etc., (3) the great numerical strength of the ruling class, (4) the illusion of the *common* interests (in the beginning this illusion is true), (5) the delusion of the ideologies and the division of labour.

¹⁰ Four pages of the manuscript are missing here. — Ed.

¹¹ *Navigation Laws* — a series of Acts passed in England from 1381 onwards to protect English shipping against foreign competition. The best known was that of 1651, directed mainly against the Dutch, who controlled most of the carrying trade. It prohibited the importation of any goods not carried in English ships or the ships of the country where the goods were produced, and laid down that British coasting trade and commerce with the colonies was to be carried on only by English boats. The Navigation Laws were modified in the early nineteenth century and repealed in 1849 except for a reservation regarding coasting trade, which was revoked in 1854. — Ed.

¹² The movement of capital, although considerably accelerated, still remained, however, relatively slow. The splitting-up of the world market into separate parts, each of which was exploited by a particular nation, the exclusion of competition among themselves on the part of the nations, the clumsiness of production itself and the fact that finance was only evolving from its early stages, greatly impeded circulation. The consequence of this was a haggling, mean and niggardly spirit which still clung to all merchants and to the whole mode of carrying on trade. Compared with the manufacturers, and above all with the craftsmen, they were certainly big bourgeois; compared with the merchants and industrialists of the next period they remain petty bourgeois. Cf. Adam Smith.

¹³ "Commerce is the rage of the century." — Ed.

¹⁴ "For some time now people have been talking only about commerce, navigation and the navy." — Ed.

¹⁵ Competition separates individuals from one another, not only the bourgeois but still more the workers, in spite of the fact that it brings them together. Hence it is a long time before these individuals can unite, apart from the fact that for the purposes of this union — if it is not to be merely local — the necessary means, the great industrial cities and cheap and quick communications, have first to be produced by big industry. Hence every organised power standing over against these isolated individuals, who live in relationships, daily reproducing this isolation, can only be overcome after long struggles. To demand the opposite would be tantamount to demanding that competition should not exist in this definite epoch of history, or that the individuals should banish from their minds relationships over which in their isolation they have no control.

¹⁶ Ownership in accordance with the law applying to full Roman citizens. — Ed.

¹⁷ The right of using and consuming (also: abusing), i.e. of disposing of a thing at will. — Ed.

The Fetishism of Commodities and the Secret Thereof

1   Among the ancient Germans the unit for measuring land was what could be harvested in a day, and was called Tagwerk, Tagwanne (jurnale, or terra jurnalis, or diornalis), Mannsmaad, &c. (See G. L. von Maurer, "Einleitung zur Geschichte der Mark —, &c. Verfassung," München, 1854, p. 129 sq.)

2   When, therefore, Galiani says: Value is a relation between persons — "La Ricchezza è una ragione tra due persone," — he ought to have added: a relation between persons expressed as a relation between things. (Galiani: Della Moneta, p. 221, V. III. of Custodi's collection of "Scrittori Classici Italiani di Economia Politica." Parte Moderna, Milano, 1803.)

3   "What are we to think of a law that asserts itself only by periodical revolutions? It is just nothing but a law of Nature, founded on the want of knowledge of those whose action is the subject of it." (Friedrich Engels: "Umrisse zu einer Kritik der National-ökonomi," in the "Deutsch-Französische Jahrbücher," edited by Arnold Ruge and Karl Marx. Paris, 1844.)

4   Even Ricardo has his stories a la Robinson. "He makes the primitive hunter and the primitive fisher straightaway, as owners of commodities, exchange fish and game in the proportion in which labour-time is incorporated in these exchange-values. On this occasion he commits the anachronism of making these men apply to the calculation, so far as their implements have to be taken into account, the annuity tables in current use on the London Exchange in the year 1817. 'The parallelograms of Mr. Owen' appear to be the only form of society, besides the bourgeois form, with which he was acquainted." (Karl Marx: "Zur Kritik, &c." pp. 38, 39)

5   "A ridiculous presumption has latterly got abroad that common property in its primitive form is specifically a Slavonian, or even exclusively Russian form. It is the primitive form that we can prove to have existed amongst Romans, Teutons, and Celts, and even to this day we find numerous examples, ruins though they be, in India. A more exhaustive study of Asiatic, and especially of Indian forms of common property, would show how from the different forms of primitive common property, different forms of its dissolution have been developed. Thus, for instance, the various original types of Roman and Teutonic private property are deducible from different forms of Indian common property." (Karl Marx, "Zur Kritik, &c.," p. 10.)

6   The insufficiency of Ricardo's analysis of the magnitude of value, and his analysis is by far the best, will appear from the 3rd and 4th books of this work. As regards value in general, it is the weak point of the classical school of Political Economy that it nowhere, expressly and with full consciousness, distinguishes between labour, as it appears in the value of a product and the same labour, as it appears in the use-value of that product. Of course the distinction is practically made, since this school treats labour, at one time under its quantitative aspect, at another under its qualitative aspect. But it has not the least idea, that when the difference between various kinds of labour is treated as purely quantitative, their qualitative unity or equality, and therefore their reduction

to abstract human labour, is implied. For instance, Ricardo declares that he agrees with Destutt de Tracy in this proposition: "As it is certain that our physical and moral faculties are alone our original riches, the employment of those faculties, labour of some kind, is our only original treasure, and it is always from this employment that all those things are created, which we call riches.... It is certain, too, that all those things only represent the labour which has created them, and if they have a value, or even two distinct values, they can only derive them from that (the value) of the labour from which they emanate." (Ricardo, "The Principles of Pol. Econ.," 3 Ed. Lond. 1821, p. 334.) We would here only point out, that Ricardo puts his own more profound interpretation upon the words of Destutt. What the latter really says is, that on the one hand all things which constitute wealth represent the labour that creates them, but that on the other hand, they acquire their "two different values" (use-value and exchange-value) from "the value of labour." He thus falls into the commonplace error of the vulgar economists, who assume the value of one commodity (in this case labour) in order to determine the values of the rest. But Ricardo reads him as if he had said, that labour (not the value of labour) is embodied both in use-value and exchange-value. Nevertheless, Ricardo himself pays so little attention to the two-fold character of the labour which has a two-fold embodiment, that he devotes the whole of his chapter on "Values and Riches, Their Distinctive Properties," to a laborious examination of the trivialities of a J. B. Say. And at the finish he is quite astonished to find that Destutt on the one hand agrees with him as to labour being the source of value, and on the other hand with J. B. Say as to the notion of value.

7   It is one of the chief failings of classical economy that it has never succeeded, by means of its analysis of commodities, and, in particular, of their value, in discovering that form under which value becomes exchange-value. Even Adam Smith and Ricardo, the best representatives of the school, treat the form of value as a thing of no importance, as having no connexion with the inherent nature of commodities. The reason for this is not solely because their attention is entirely absorbed in the analysis of the magnitude of value. It lies deeper. The value-form of the product of labour is not only the most abstract, but is also the most universal form, taken by the product in bourgeois production, and stamps that production as a particular species of social production, and thereby gives it its special historical character. If then we treat this mode of production as one eternally fixed by Nature for every state of society, we necessarily overlook that which is the differentia specifica of the value-form, and consequently of the commodity-form, and of its further developments, money-form, capital-form, &c. We consequently find that economists, who are thoroughly agreed as to labour-time being the measure of the magnitude of value, have the most strange and contradictory ideas of money, the perfected form of the general equivalent. This is seen in a striking manner when they treat of banking, where the commonplace definitions of money will no longer hold water. This led to the rise of a restored mercantile system (Ganilh, &c.), which sees in value nothing but a social form, or rather the unsubstantial ghost of that form. Once for all I may here state, that by classical Political Economy, I understand that economy

which, since the time of W. Petty, has investigated the real relations of production in bourgeois society, in contradistinction to vulgar economy, which deals with appearances only, ruminates without ceasing on the materials long since provided by scientific economy, and there seeks plausible explanations of the most obtrusive phenomena, for bourgeois daily use, but for the rest, confines itself to systematising in a pedantic way, and proclaiming for everlasting truths, the trite ideas held by the self-complacent bourgeoisie with regard to their own world, to them the best of all possible worlds.

8   "Les économistes ont une singulière manière de procéder. Il n'y a pour eux que deux sortes d'institutions, celles de l'art et celles de la nature. Les institutions de la féodalité sont des institutions artificielles, celles de la bourgeoisie sont des institutions naturelles. Ils ressemblent en ceci aux théologiens, qui eux aussi établissent deux sortes de religions. Toute religion qui n'est pas la leur, est une invention des hommes, tandis que leur propre religion est une émanation de Dieu — Ainsi il y a eu de l'histoire, mais il n'y en a plus." (Karl Marx. Misère de la Philosophie. Réponse à la Philosophie de la Misère par M. Proudhon, 1847, p. 113.) Truly comical is M. Bastiat, who imagines that the ancient Greeks and Romans lived by plunder alone. But when people plunder for centuries, there must always be something at hand for them to seize; the objects of plunder must be continually reproduced. It would thus appear that even Greeks and Romans had some process of production, consequently, an economy, which just as much constituted the material basis of their world, as bourgeois economy constitutes that of our modern world. Or perhaps Bastiat means, that a mode of production based on slavery is based on a system of plunder. In that case he treads on dangerous ground. If a giant thinker like Aristotle erred in his appreciation of slave labour, why should a dwarf economist like Bastiat be right in his appreciation of wage-labour? — I seize this opportunity of shortly answering an objection taken by a German paper in America, to my work, "Zur Kritik der Pol. Oekonomie, 1859." In the estimation of that paper, my view that each special mode of production and the social relations corresponding to it, in short, that the economic structure of society, is the real basis on which the juridical and political superstructure is raised, and to which definite social forms of thought correspond; that the mode of production determines the character of the social, political, and intellectual life generally, all this is very true for our own times, in which material interests preponderate, but not for the middle ages, in which Catholicism, not for Athens and Rome, where politics reigned supreme. In the first place it strikes one as an odd thing for any one to suppose that these well-worn phrases about the middle ages and the ancient world are unknown to anyone else. This much, however, is clear, that the middle ages could not live on Catholicism, nor the ancient world on politics. On the contrary, it is the mode in which they earned a livelihood that explains why here politics, and there Catholicism, played the chief part. For the rest, it requires but a light acquaintance with the history of the Roman republic, for example, to be aware that its secret history is the history of its landed property. On the other hand, Don Quixote long ago paid the penalty for wrongly imagining that knight errantry was compatible with all economic forms of society.

9   "Observations on certain verbal disputes in Pol. Econ., particularly relating to value and to demand and supply." Lond. 1821, p. 16.

10   S. Bailey, l. c., p. 165.

11   The author of "observations" and S. Bailey accuse Ricardo of converting exchange-value from something relative into something examined absolute. The opposite is the fact. He has maintained the apparent relation between objects, such as diamonds and pearls, in which relation they appear as exchange-values, and disclosed the true relation hidden behind the appearances, namely, their relation to each other as mere expressions of human labour. If the followers of Ricardo answer Bailey somewhat rudely, and by no means convincingly, the reason is to be sought in this, that they were unable to find in Ricardo's own works any key to the hidden relations existing between value and its form, exchange-value.

The Secret of Primitive Accumulation

1   In Italy, where capitalistic production developed earliest, the dissolution of serfdom also took place earlier than elsewhere. The serf was emancipated in that country before he had acquired any prescriptive right to the soil. His emancipation at once transformed him into a free proletarian, who, moreover, found his master ready waiting for him in the towns, for the most part handed down as legacies from the Roman time. When the revolution of the world-market, about the end of the 15th century, annihilated Northern Italy's commercial supremacy, a movement in the reverse direction set in. The labourers of the towns were driven *en masse* into the country, and gave an impulse, never before seen, to the *petite culture*, carried on in the form of gardening.

Expropriation of the Agricultural Population from the Land

1   "The petty proprietors who cultivated their own fields with their own hands, and enjoyed a modest competence... then formed a much more important part of the nation than at present. If we may trust the best statistical writers of that age, not less than 160,000 proprietors who, with their families, must have made up more than a seventh of the whole population, derived their subsistence from little freehold estates. The average income of these small landlords... was estimated at between £60 and £70 a year. It was computed that the number of persons who tilled their own land was greater than the number of those who farmed the land of others." Macaulay: "History of England," 10th ed., 1854, I. pp. 333, 334. Even in the last third of the 17th century, 4/5 of the English people were agricultural. (l.c., p. 413). I quote Macaulay, because as systematic falsifier of history he minimises as much as possible facts of this kind.

2   We must never forget that even the serf was not only the owner, if but a tribute-paying owner, of the piece of land attached to his house, but also a co-possessor of the common land. "Le paysan (in Silesia, under Frederick II.) est serf." Nevertheless, these serfs possess common lands. "On n'a pas pu encore engager les Silésiens au partage des communes, tandis que dans la Nouvelle Marche, il

n'y a guère de village où ce partage ne soit exécuté avec le plus grand succès." (Mirabeau: "De la Monarchie Prussienne." Londres, 1788, t. ii, pp. 125, 126.)

3   Japan, with its purely feudal organisation of landed property and its developed *petite culture*, gives a much truer picture of the European middle ages than all our history books, dictated as these are, for the most part, by bourgeois prejudices. It is very convenient to be "liberal" at the expense of the middle ages.

4   In his "Utopia," Thomas More says, that in England "your shepe that were wont to be so meke and tame, and so smal eaters, now, as I heare saye, become so great devourers and so wylde that they eate up, and swallow downe, the very men themselfes." "Utopia," trasnl. by Robinson, ed., Arber, Lond., 1869, p. 41.

5   Bacon shows the connexion between a free, well-to-do peasantry and good infantry. "This did wonderfully concern the might and mannerhood of the kingdom to have farms as it were of a standard sufficient to maintain an able body out of penury, and did in effect amortise a great part of the lands of the kingdom unto the hold and occupation of the yeomanry or middle people, of a condition between gentlemen, and cottageres and peasants.... For it hath been held by the general opinion of men of best judgment in the wars... that the principal strength of an army consisteth in the infantry or foot. And to make good infantry it requireth men bred, not in a servile or indigent fashion, but in some free and plentiful manner. Therefore, if a state run most to noblemen and gentlemen, and that the husbandmen and ploughmen be but as their workfolk and labourers, or else mere cottagers (which are but hous'd beggars), you may have a good cavalry, but never good stable bands of foot....And this is to be seen in France, and Italy, and some other parts abroad, where in effect all is noblesse or peasantry... insomuch that they are informed to employ mercenary bands of Switzers and the like, for their battalions of foot; whereby also it comes to pass that those nations have much people and few soldiers." ("The Reign of Henry VII." Verbatim reprint from Kennet's England. Ed. 1719. Lond., 1870, p. 308.)

6   Dr. Hunter, l. c., p. 134. "The quantity of land assigned (in the old laws) would now be judged too great for labourers, and rather as likely to convert them into small farmers." (George Roberts: "The Social History of the People of the Southern Counties of England in Past Centuries." Lond., 1856, pp. 184-185.

7   "The right of the poor to share in the tithe, is established by the tenour of ancient statutes." (Tuckett, l. c., Vol. II., pp. 804-805.)

8   William Cobbett: "A History of the Protestant Reformation," 471.

9   The "spirit" of Protestantism may be seen from the following, among other things. In the south of England certain landed proprietors and well-to-do farmers put their heads together and propounded ten questions as to the right interpretation of the poor-law of Elizabeth. These they laid before a celebrated jurist of that time, Sergeant Snigge (later a judge under James I.) for his opinion. "Question 9 — Some of the more wealthy farmers in the parish have devised a skilful mode by which all the trouble of executing this Act (the 43rd of Elizabeth) might be avoided. They have proposed that we shall erect a prison in the parish, and then give notice to the neighbourhood, that if any persons are disposed to farm the

poor of this parish, they do give in sealed proposals, on a certain day, of the lowest price at which they will take them off our hands; and that they will be authorised to refuse to any one unless he be shut up in the aforesaid prison. The proposers of this plan conceive that there will be found in the adjoining counties, persons, who, being unwilling to labour and not possessing substance or credit to take a farm or ship, so as to live without labour, may be induced to make a very advantageous offer to the parish. If any of the poor perish under the contractor's care, the sin will lie at his door, as the parish will have done its duty by them. We are, however, apprehensive that the present Act (43 rd of Elizabeth) will not warrant a prudential measure of this kind; but you are to learn that the rest of the freeholders of the county, and of the adjoining county of B, will very readily join in instructing their members to propose an Act to enable the parish to contract with a person to lock up and work the poor; and to declare that if any person shall refuse to be so locked up and worked, he shall be entitled to no relief. This, it is hoped, will prevent persons in distress from wanting relief, and be the means of keeping down parishes." (R. Blakey, "The History of Political Literature from the Earliest Times." Lond., 1855, Vol. II., pp. 84-85.) In Scotland, the abolition of serfdom took place some centuries later than in England. Even in 1698, Fletcher of Saltoun, declared in the Scotch parliament, "The number of beggars in Scotland is reckoned at not less than 200,000. The only remedy that I, a republican on principle, can suggest, is to restore the old state of serfdom, to make slaves of all those who are unable to provide for their own subsistence." Eden, l.c., Book 1., ch. 1, pp. 60-61, says, "The decrease of villenage seems necessarily to have been the era of the origin of the poor. Manufactures and commerce are the two parents of our national poor." Eden, like our Scotch republican on principle, errs only in this: not the abolition of villenage, but the abolition of the property of the agricultural labourer in the soil made him a proletarian, and eventually a pauper. In France, where the expropriation was effected in another way, the ordonnance of Moulins, 1566, and the Edict of 1656, correspond to the English poor-laws.

[10]   Professor Rogers, although formerly Professor of Political Economy in the University of Oxford, the hotbed of Protestant orthodoxy, in his preface to the "History of Agriculture" lays stress on the fact of the pauperisation of the mass of the people by the Reformation.

[11]   "A Letter to Sir. F. C. Bunbury, Bart., on the High Price of Provisions. By a Suffolk Gentleman." Ipswich, 1795, p. 4. Even the fanatical advocate of the system of large farms, the author of the "Inquiry into the Connexion between the Present Price of Provisions," London, 1773, p. 139, says: "I most lament the loss of our yeomanry, that set of men who really kept up the independence of this nation; and sorry I am to see their lands now in the hands of monopolising lords, tenanted out to small farmers, who hold their leases on such conditions as to be little better than vassals ready to attend a summons on every mischievous occasion."

[12]   On the private moral character of this bourgeois hero, among other things: "The large grant of lands in Ireland to Lady Orkney, in 1695, is a public instance of the king's affection, and the lady's influence....Lady Orkney's endearing offices

are supposed to have been — foeda labiorum ministeria." (In the Sloane manuscript Collection, at the British Museum, No. 4224. The Manuscript is entitled: "The character and behaviour of King William, Sunderland, etc., as represented in Original Letters to the Duke of Shrewsbury from Somers Halifax, Oxford, Secretary Vernon, etc." It is full of curiosa.

13   "The illegal alienation of the Crown Estates, partly by sale and partly by gift, is a scandalous chapter in English history... a gigantic fraud on the nation." (F. W. Newman, "Lectures on Political Economy." London, 1851, pp. 129, 130.) [For details as to how the present large landed proprietors of England came into their possessions see "Our Old Nobility. By Noblesse Oblige." London, 1879. — F. E.]

14   Read, *e.g.*, E. Burke's Pamphlet on the ducal house of Bedford, whose offshoot was Lord John Russell, the "tomtit of Liberalism."

15   "The farmers forbid cottagers to keep any living creatures besides themselves and children, under the pretence that if they keep any beasts or poultry, they will steal from the farmer's barns for their support; they also say, keep the cottagers poor and you will keep them industrious, &c., but the real fact I believe, is that the farmers may have the whole right of common to themselves." ("A Political Inquiry into the Consequences of Enclosing Waste Lands." London, 1785, p. 75.)

16   Eden, l. c., preface.

17   "Capital Farms." Two letters on the Flour Trade and the Dearness of Corn. By a person in business. London, 1767, pp. 19, 20.

18   "Merchant Farms." "An Enquiry into the Causes of the Present High Price of Provisions." London, 1767, p. 11. Note. — This excellent work, that was published anonymously, is by the Rev. Nathaniel Forster.

19   Thomas Wright: "A Short Address to the Public on the Monopoly of Large Farms," 1779, pp. 2, 3.

20   Rev. Addington: "Inquiry into the Reasons for or against Enclosing Open Fields," London, 1772, pp. 37, 43 passim.

21   Dr. R. Price, l. c. v. ii., p. 155, Forster, Addington, Kent, Price, and James Anderson, should be read and compared with the miserable prattle of Sycophant MacCulloch in his catalogue: "The Literature of Political Economy," London, 1845.

22   Price, l. c., p. 147.

23   Price, l. c., p. 159. We are reminded of ancient Rome. "The rich had got possession of the greater part of the undivided land. They trusted in the conditions of the time, that these possessions would not be again taken from them, and bought, therefore, some of the pieces of land lying near theirs, and belonging to the poor, with the acquiescence of their owners, and took some by force, so that they now were cultivating widely extended domains, instead of isolated fields. Then they employed slaves in agriculture and cattle-breeding, because freemen would have been taken from labour for military service. The possession of slaves brought them great gain, inasmuch as these, on account of their immunity from military service, could freely multiply and have a multitude of children.

Thus the powerful men drew all wealth to themselves, and all the land swarmed with slaves. The Italians, on the other hand, were always decreasing in number, destroyed as they were by poverty, taxes, and military service. Even when times of peace came, they were doomed to complete inactivity, because the rich were in possession of the soil, and used slaves instead of freemen in the tilling of it." (Appian: "Civil Wars," I.7.) This passage refers to the time before the Licinian rogations. Military service, which hastened to so great an extent the ruin of the Roman plebeians, was also the chief means by which, as in a forcing-house, Charlemagne brought about the transformation of free German peasants into serfs and bondsmen.

[24] "An Inquiry into the Connexion between the Present Price of Provisions, &c., " pp. 124, 129. To the like effect, but with an opposite tendency: "Working-men are driven from their cottages and forced into the towns to seek for employment; but then a larger surplus is obtained, and thus capital is augmented." ("The Perils of the Nation," 2nd ed. London, 1843, p. 14.)

[25] l. c., p. 132.

[26] Steuart says: "If you compare the rent of these lands" (he erroneously includes in this economic category the tribute of the taskmen to the clanchief) "with the extent, it appears very small. If you compare it with the numbers fed upon the farm, you will find that an estate in the Highlands maintains, perhaps, ten times as many people as another of the same value in good and fertile province." (l. c., vol. i., ch. xvi., p. 104).

[27] James Anderson: "Observations on the Means of Exciting a Spirit of National Industry, &c.," Edinburgh, 1777.

[28] In 1860 the people expropriated by force were exported to Canada under false pretences. Some fled to the mountains and neighbouring islands. They were followed by the police, came to blows with them and escaped.

[29] "In the Highlands of Scotland," says Buchanan, the commentator on Adam Smith, 1814, "the ancient state of property is daily subverted.... The landlord, without regard to the hereditary tenant (a category used in error here), now offers his land to the highest bidder, who, if he is an importer, instantly adopts a new system of cultivation. The land, formerly overspread with small tenants or labourers, was peopled in proportion to its produce, but under the new system of improved cultivation and increased rents, the largest possible produce is obtained at the least possible expense: and the useless hands being, with this view, removed, the population is reduced, not to what the land will maintain, but to what it will employ. The dispossessed tenants either seek a subsistence in the neighbouring towns," &c. (David Buchanan: "Observations on, &c., A. Smith's Wealth of Nations." Edinburgh, 1814, vol. iv., p. 144.) "The Scotch grandees dispossessed families as they would grub up coppice-wood, and they treated villages and their people as Indians harassed with wild beasts do, in their vengeance, a jungle with tigers.... Man is bartered for a fleece of a carcase of mutton, nay, held cheaper.... Why, how much worse is it than the intention of the Moguls, who, when they had broken into the northern provinces of China, proposed in council to exterminate the inhabitants, and convert the land into

pasture. This proposal many Highland proprietors have effected in their own country against their own countrymen." (George Ensor: "An Inquiry Concerning the Population of Nations." Lond., 1818, pp. 215, 216.)

30 When the present Duchess of Sutherland entertained Mrs. Beecher Stowe, authoress of "Uncle Tom's Cabin," with great magnificence in London to show her sympathy for the negro slaves of the American republic — a sympathy that she prudently forgot, with her fellow-aristocrats, during the civil war, in which every "noble" English heart beat for the slave-owner — I gave in the *New York Tribune* the facts about the Sutherland slaves. (Epitomised in part by Carey in "The Slave Trade." Philadelphia, 1853, pp. 203, 204.) My article was reprinted in a Scotch newspaper, and led to a pretty polemic between the latter and the sycophants of the Sutherlands.

31 Interesting details on this fish trade will be found in Mr. David Urquhart's Portfolio, new series. — Nassau W. Senior, in this posthumous work, already quoted, terms "the proceedings in Sutherlandshire one of the most beneficent clearings since the memory of man." (l. c.)

32 The deer-forests of Scotland contain not a single tree. The sheep are driven from, and then the deer driven to, the naked hills, and then it is called a deer-forest. Not even timber-planting and real forest culture.

33 Robert Somers: "Letters from the Highlands: or the Famine of 1847." London, 1848, pp. 12-28 passim. These letters originally appeared in *The Times*. The English economists of course explained the famine of the Gaels in 1847, by their over-population. At all events, they "were pressing on their food-supply." The "clearing of estates," or as it is called in Germany, "Bauernlegen," occurred in Germany especially after the 30 years' war, and led to peasant-revolts as late as 1790 in Kursachesen. It obtained especially in East Germany. In most of the Prussian provinces, Frederick II. for the first time secured right of property for the peasants. After the conquest of Silesia he forced the landlords to rebuild the huts, barns, etc., and to provide the peasants with cattle and implements. He wanted soldiers for his army and tax-payers for his treasury. For the rest, the pleasant life that the peasant led under Frederick's system of finance and hodge-podge rule of despotism, bureaucracy and feudalism, may be seen from the following quotation from his admirer, Mirabeau: "Le lin fait donc une des grandes richesses du cultivateur dans le Nord de l'Allemagne. Malheureusement pour l'espèce humaine, ce n'est qu'une ressource contre la misère et non un moyen de bien-être. Les impôts directs, les corvées, les servitudes de tout genre, écrasent le cultivateur allemand, qui paie encore des impôts indirects dans tout ce qu'il achète... et pour comble de ruine, il n'ose pas vendre ses productions où et comme il le veut; il n'ose pas acheter ce dont il a besoin aux marchands qui pourraient le lui livrer au meilleur prix. Toutes ces causes le ruinent insensiblement, et il se trouverait hors d'état de payer les impôts directs à l'échéance sans la filerie; elle lui offre une ressource, en occupant utilement sa femme, ses enfants, ses servants, ses valets, et lui-même; mais quelle pénible vie, même aidée de ce secours. En été, il travaille comme un forçat au labourage et à la récolte; il se couche à 9 heures et se lève à deux, pour suffire aux travaux; en hiver il devrait réparer ses forces par un plus grand repos; mais il manquera

de grains pour le pain et les semailles, s'il se défait des denrées qu'il faudrait vendre pour payer les impôts. Il faut donc filer pour suppléer à ce vide.... il faut y apporter la plus grande assiduité. Aussi le paysan se couche-t-il en hiver à minuit, une heure, et se lève à cinq ou six; ou bien il se couche à neuf, et se lève à deux, et cela tous les jours de la vie si ce n'est le dimanche. Ces excès de veille et de travail usent la nature humaine, et de la vien qu'hommes et femmes vieillissent beaucoup plutôt dans les campagnes que dan les villes." (Mirabeau, l. c., t. III. pp. 212 sqq.)

Note to the second edition. In April 1866, 18 years after the publication of the work of Robert Somers quoted above, Professor Leone Levi gave a lecture before the Society of Arts on the transformation of sheep-walks into deer-forest, in which he depicts the advance in the devastation of the Scottish Highlands. He says, with other things: "Depopulation and transformation into sheep-walks were the most convenient means for getting an income without expenditure.... A deer-forest in place of a sheep-walk was a common change in the Highlands. The landowners turned out the sheep as they once turned out the men from their estates, and welcomed the new tenants — the wild beasts and the feathered birds.... One can walk from the Earl of Dalhousie's estates in Forfarshire to John o'Groats, without ever leaving forest land.... In many of these woods the fox, the wild cat, the marten, the polecat, the weasel and the Apline hare are common; whilst the rabbit, the squirrel and the rat have lately made their way into the country. Immense tracts of land, much of which is described in the statistical account of Scotland as having a pasturage in richness and extent of very superior description, are thus shut out from all cultivation and improvement, and are solely devoted to the sport of a few persons for a very brief period of the year." The London *Economist* of June 2, 1866, says, "Amongst the items of news in a Scotch paper of last week, we read....'One of the finest sheep farms in Sutherlandshire, for which a rent of £1,200 a year was recently offered, on the expiry of the existing lease this year, is to be converted into a deer-forest.' Here we see the modern instincts of feudalism... operating pretty much as they did when the Norman Conqueror... destroyed 36 villages to create the New Forest.... Two millions of acres... totally laid waste, embracing within their area some of the most fertile lands of Scotland. The natural grass of Glen Tilt was among the most nutritive in the country of Perth. The deer-forest of Ben Aulder was by far the best grazing ground in the wide district of Badenoch; a part of the Black Mount forest was the best pasture for black-faced sheep in Scotland. Some idea of the ground laid waste for purely sporting purposes in Scotland may be formed from the fact that it embraced an area larger than the whole country of Perth. The resources of the forest of Ben Aulder might give some idea of the loss sustained from the forced desolations. The ground would pasture 15,000 sheep, and as it was not more than one-thirtieth part of the old forest ground in Scotland... it might, &c....All that forest land is as totally unproductive.... It might thus as well have been submerged under the waters of the German Ocean.... Such extemporised wildernesses or deserts ought to be put down by the decided interference of the Legislature."

Bloody Legislation against the Expropriated

1   The author of the "Essay on Trade, etc.," 1770, says, "In the reign of Edward VI. indeed the English seem to have set, in good earnest, about encouraging manufactures and employing the poor. This we learn from a remarkable statute which runs thus: 'That all vagrants shall be branded, &c.,'" l. c., p. 5.

2   Thomas More says in his "Utopia": "Therfore that on covetous and unsatiable cormaraunte and very plage of his native contrey maye compasse aboute and inclose many thousand akers of grounde together within one pale or hedge, the husbandmen be thrust owte of their owne, or els either by coneyne and fraude, or by violent oppression they be put besydes it, or by wrongs and iniuries thei be so weried that they be compelled to sell all: by one meanes, therfore, or by other, either by hooke or crooke they muste needes departe awaye, poore, selye, wretched soules, men, women, husbands, wiues, fatherlesse children, widowes, wofull mothers with their yonge babes, and their whole householde smal in substance, and muche in numbre, as husbandrye requireth many handes. Awaye thei trudge, I say, owte of their knowen accustomed houses, fyndynge no place to reste in. All their housholde stuffe, which is very little woorthe, thoughe it might well abide the sale: yet beeynge sodainely thruste owte, they be constrayned to sell it for a thing of nought. And when they haue wandered abrode tyll that be spent, what cant they then els doe but steale, and then justly pardy be hanged, or els go about beggyng. And yet then also they be caste in prison as vagaboundes, because they go aboute and worke not: whom no man wyl set a worke though thei neuer so willyngly profre themselues therto." Of these poor fugitives of whom Thomas More says that they were forced to thieve, "7,200 great and petty thieves were put to death," in the reign of Henry VIII. (Holinshed, "Description of England," Vol. 1, p. 186.) In Elizabeth's time, "rogues were trussed up apace, and that there was not one year commonly wherein three or four hundred were not devoured and eaten up by the gallowes." (Strype's "Annals of the Reformation and Establishment of Religion and other Various Occurrences in the Church of England during Queen Elizabeth's Happy Reign." Second ed., 1725, Vol. 2) According to this same Strype, in Somersetshire, in one year, 40 persons were executed, 35 robbers burnt in the hand, 37 whipped, and 183 discharged as "incorrigible vagabonds." Nevertheless, he is of opinion that this large number of prisoners does not comprise even a fifth of the actual criminals, thanks to the negligence of the justices and the foolish compassion of the people; and the other countries of England were not better off in this respect than Somersetshire, while some were even worse.

3   "Whenever the legislature attempts to regulate the differences between masters and their workmen, its counsellors are always the masters," says A. Smith. "L'esprit des lois, c'est la propriété." says Linguet.

4   "Sophisms of Free Trade." By a Barrister. Lond., 1850, p. 206. He adds maliciously: "We were ready enough to interfere for the employer, can nothing now be done for the employed?"

5   From a clause of Statute 2 James I., c. 6, we see that certain clothmakers took upon themselves to dictate, in their capacity of justices of the peace, the official tariff of wages in their own shops. In Germany, especially after the Thirty Years'

War, statutes for keeping down wages were general. "The want of servants and labourers was very troublesome to the landed proprietors in the depopulated districts. All villagers were forbidden to let rooms to single men and women; all the latter were to be reported to the authorities and cast into prison if they were unwilling to become servants, even if they were employed at any other work, such as sowing seeds for the peasants at a daily wage, or even buying and selling corn. (Imperial privileges and sanctions for Silesia, I., 25.) For a whole century in the decrees of the small German potentates a bitter cry goes up again and again about the wicked and impertinent rabble that will not reconcile itself to its hard lot, will not be content with the legal wage; the individual landed proprietors are forbidden to pay more than the State had fixed by a tariff. And yet the conditions of service were at times better after the war than 100 years later; the farm servants of Silensia had, in 1652, meat twice a week, whilst even in our century, districts are known where they have it only three times a year. Further, wages after the war were higher than in the following century." (G. Freytag.)

[6] Article I. of this law runs: "L'anéantissement de toute espèce de corporations du même état et profession étant l'une des bases fondamentales de la constitution francaise, il est défendu de les rétablir de fait sous quelque prétexte et sous quelque forme que ce soit." Article IV. declares, that if "des citoyens attachés aux mêmes professions, arts et métiers prenaient des délibérations, faisaient entre eux des conventions tendantes à refuser de concert ou à n'accorder qu'à un prix déterminé le secours de leur industrie ou de leurs travaux, les dites délibérations et conventions... seront délcarées inconstitutionnelles, attentatoires à la liberté et à la declaration des droits de l'homme, &c."; felony, therefore, as in the old labour-statutes. ("Révolutions de Paris," Paris, 1791, t. III, p. 523.)

[7] Buchez et Roux: "Histoire Parlementaire," t. x., p. 195.

Genesis of the Capitalist Farmer

[1] Harrison in his "Description of England," says "although peradventure foure pounds of old rent be improved to fortie, toward the end of his term, if he have not six of seven yeares rent lieng by him, fiftie or a hundred pounds, yet will the farmer thinke his gaines verie small."

[2] On the influence of the depreciation of money in the 16th century, on the different classes of society, see "A Compendious or Briefe Examination of Certayne Ordinary Complaints of Divers of our Countrymen in these our Days." By W. S., Gentleman. (London 1581.) The dialogue form of this work led people for a long time to ascribe it to Shakespeare, and even in 1751, it was published under his name. Its author is William Stafford. In one place the knight reasons as follows:

"Knight: You, my neighbour, the husbandman, you Maister Mercer, and you Goodman Cooper, with other artificers, may save yourselves metely well. For as much as all things are dearer than they were, so much do you arise in the pryce of your wares and occupations that ye sell agayne. But we have nothing to sell whereby we might advance ye price there of, to countervaile those things that we must buy agayne." In another place the knight asks the doctor: "I pray you, what be those sorts that ye meane. And first, of those that ye thinke should have no loose thereby? — Doctor: I mean all those that live by buying and selling, for as they buy deare, they sell thereafter. Knight: What is the next sort that ye say would win by it? Doctor: Marry, all such as have takings of fearmes in their owne manurance [cultivation] at the old rent, for where they pay after the olde rate they sell after the newe — that is, they paye for theire lande good cheape, and sell all things growing thereof deare. Knight: What sorte is that which, ye sayde should have greater losse hereby, than these men had profit? Doctor: It is all noblemen, gentlemen, and all other that live either by a stinted rent or stypend, or do not manure [cultivation] the ground, or doe occupy no buying and selling."

3   In France, the regisseur, steward, collector of dues for the feudal lords during the earlier part of the middle ages, soon became an homme d'affaires, who by extortion, cheating, &c., swindled himself into a capitalist. These regisseurs themselves were sometimes noblemen. *E.g.*, "C'est li compte que messire Jacques de Thoraine, chevalier chastelain sor Besancon rent ès-seigneur tenant les comptes à Dijon pour monseigneur le duc et comte de Bourgoigne, des rentes appartenant à la dite chastellenie, depuis xxve jour de décembre MCCCLIX jusqu'au xxviiie jour de décembre MCCCLX." (Alexis Monteil: "Traité de Matériaux Manuscrits etc.," pp. 234, 235.) Already it is evident here how in all spheres of social life the lion's share falls to the middleman. In the economic domain, *e.g.*, financiers, stock-exchange speculators, merchants, shoopkeepers skim the cream; in civil matters, the lawyer fleeces his clients; in politics the representative is of more importance than the voters, the minister than the sovereign, in religion God is pushed into the background by the "Mediator," and the latter again is shoved back by the priests, the inevitable middlemen between the good shepherd and his sheep. In France, as in England, the great feudal territories were divided into innumerable small homesteads, but under conditions incomparably more unfavourable for the people. During the 14th century arose the farms of *terriers*. Their number grew constantly, far beyond 100,000. They paid rents varying from 1/12 to 1/5 of the product in money or in kind. These farms were fiefs, sub-fiefs, &c., according the value and extent of the domains, many of them only containing a few acres. But these farmers had rights of jurisdiction in some degree over the dwellers on the soil; there were four grades. The oppression of the agricultural population under all these petty tyrants will be understood. Monteil says that there were once in France 160,000 judges, where to-day, 4,000 tribunals, including justices of the peace, suffice.

Reaction of the Agricultural Revolution on Industry

1   In his "Notions de Philosophie Naturelle," Paris, 1838.

2   A point that Sir James Steuart emphasises.

3   "Je permettrai," says the capitalist, "que vous ayez l'honneur de me servir, à condition que vous me donnez le peu qui vous reste pour la peine que je prends de vous commander." (J. J. Rousseau: "Discours sur l'Economie Politique.")

4   Mirabeau, l. c., t. III., pp. 20-109 passim. That Mirabeau considers the separate workshops more economical and productive than the "combined," and sees in

the latter merely artificial exotics under government cultivation, is explained by the position at that time of a great part of the continental manufactures.

5   "Twenty pounds of wool converted unobtrusively into the yearly clothing of a labourer's family by its own industry in the intervals of other work — this makes no show; but bring it to market, send it to the factory, thence to the broker, thence to the dealer, and you will have great commercial operations, and nominal capital engaged to the amount of twenty times its value.... The working-class is thus emersed to support a wretched factory population, a parasitical shop-keeping class, and a fictitious commercial, monetary, and financial system. (David Urguhart, l. c., p. 120.)

6   Cromwell's time forms an exception. So long as the Republic lasted, the mass of the English people of all grades rose from the degradation into which they had sunk under the Tudors.

7   Tuckett is aware that the modern woollen industry has sprung, with the introduction of machinery, from manufacture proper and from the destruction of rural and domestic industries. "The plough, the yoke, were 'the invention of gods, and the occupation of heroes;' are the loom, the spindle, the distaff, of less noble parentage. You sever the distaff and the plough, the spindle and the yoke, and you get factories and poor-houses, credit and panics, two hostile nations, agricultural and commercial. (David Urquhart, l. c., p. 122.) But now comes Carey, and cries out upon England, surely not with unreason, that it is trying to turn every other country into a mere agricultural nation, whose manufacturer is to be England. He pretends that in this way Turkey has been ruined, because the owners and occupants of land have never been permitted by England to strengthen themselves by the formation of that natural alliance between the plough and the loom, the hammer and the harrow. ("The Slave Trade", p. 125.) According to him, Urquhart himself is one of the chief agents in the ruin of Turkey, where he had made Free-trade propaganda in the English interest. The best of it is that Carey, a great Russophile by the way, wants to prevent the process of separation by the very system of protection which accelerates it.

8   Philanthropic English economists, like Mill, Rogers, Goldwin Smith, Fawcett, &c., and liberal manufacturers like John Bright, & Co., ask the English landed proprietors, as God asked Cain after Abel, Where are our thousands of freeholders gone? But where do *you* come from, then? From the destruction of those freeholders. Why don't you ask further, where are the independent weavers, spinners, and artisans gone?

Rosa Luxemburg

Born in 1870 in Russian Poland, Rosa Luxemburg's life and tragic death symbolize the conditions of oppression, struggle and resistance characteristic of Europe (particularly Germany) in the late 19th and early 20th century. Luxemburg's thirst for social justice placed her at an early age in the revolutionary camp, theorizing and working for the cause of the working classes. Her academic and revolutionary work landed her in prison more than once and ended her life in a brutal way as her body was recovered from a canal days after she was beaten by German soldiers.

The following text, which is taken from her *The Accumulation of Capital*, first published in 1913, is considered as her finest achievement. This book represents a Marxist critique of Marx's theory of the capitalist relations of production as presented in his three volumes of *Capital*. Similar to the structure of *Capital* Vol. 1, as we have already seen, Luxemburg's book deals with capitalist production and relations at two levels. The first is by examining or rather re-examining the internal dynamics of capitalist production and re-evaluating Marx's notion of simple reproduction and reproduction on an expanded scale.

Using an elaborate and complex Marxist economics, Luxemburg tries to show the problems in Marx's analysis of the relationship between capital and labour. One of her major critiques in this respect is that Marx's analysis of the dynamics of capitalism, i.e., its production, reproduction, consumption and accumulation on an expanded scale, has been confined to the two major classes of the proletariat and the bourgeoisie within metropolitan Europe. Thus ignoring the international or global role of capital and its expansion to the Third World.

The second level of analysis concerns Luxemburg's discussion of the expansion or enlarged accumulation of capital. While this discussion is presented from different levels: only one level will be presented here, namely, the social, historical and, one may add, the human cost of the expansion of capital at an extended scale. Luxemburg's analysis here in some ways complements Marx's discussion of the historical genesis of capitalism. Both Marx and Luxemburg are concerned with the impact of capitalist development on the peasantry (the indigenous agricultural direct producers), the destruction of peasant or agrarian forms of production and the expropriation of the peasants as a result of the development of capitalism. Her main thesis is that capital is in constant struggle to obtain fresh and new sources of production.

In Luxemburg's theory the so-called primitive accumulation, discussed by Marx as the historic genesis of capitalism does not stop in Europe. Capital constantly pursues new and untapped natural economies. In detail, she writes:

> [C]apital in its struggle against societies with a natural economy pursues the following ends: 1) To gain immediate possession of important sources of productive forces such as land, game in primeval forests, minerals, precious stones and ores, products of exotic flora such as rubber, etc. 2) To 'liberate' labour power and to coerce it into service. 3). To introduce a commodity economy. And, 4) To separate trade and agriculture. (Luxemburg, 1913:368)

Luxemburg's analysis is, in some respects, also similar to Lenin's theory of imperialism. One of the main differences between her theory and that of Lenin is that she focused her analysis on forms of imperialism prior to the First World War, hence discussing "earlier" forms of capitalist expansion to the Third World. Lenin, on the other hand, has considered the First World War as the European capitalist's ultimate means for the expansion of capitalism. For Lenin, imperialism was seen as the highest stage of capitalism.

In his chapter "The So-Called Primitive Accumulation", Marx lays a special emphasis on the role of the state in facilitating the expropriation of the peasants and further entrenching capitalist production. Luxemburg takes this analysis a step further and demonstrates the crucial role force plays in the accumulation of capital beyond European borders. Her thesis is that at every stage in the accumulation of capital from the colonies the process is accomplished by the use of force, violence and extra-legal measures.

Capitalism, Luxemburg argues, "needs non-capitalist social strata as a market for its surplus value, as a source of supply for its means of production and as a reservoir of labour power for its wage system. For all these purposes, forms of production based upon a natural economy are of no use to capital..."(Luxemburg, 1913:367). To be able to penetrate into these non-capitalist social formations, social formations with natural economies, European capitalists ensure the destruction of the existing production relations via a number of mechanisms. These include gaining immediate possession of important sources of production or productive forces such as land. Citing the cases of British imperialism in India and French imperialism in Algeria, Luxemburg documents the privatization and consequent robbing of indigenous land by foreign capitalists.

As a consequence of land privatization and robbery, capitalists aim at "liberating" labour power and coercing it into its services. Luxemburg criticises the bourgeois notion of peaceful trade or market commodity exchange when she affirms that commodity economy is introduced by force, violence and wars. The Opium War in China is cited as a case in point. The final stage of imperialism or capitalist enlarged accumulation from the colonies involves the separation of trade or industry from agriculture. This process, she insists, is also accompanied with force and violence against the indigenous peoples and their traditional occupations.

Finally, it is possible to view Rosa Luxemburg's work presented in this chapter as the missing link in Western classical theorization. Her emphasis on the social and historical on the one hand and capital's constant search for new natural or peasant economies on the other, provides the linkage between the development of Western civilization (capitalism) and the underdevelopment of the Eastern and Third World civilization. It demonstrates the necessity of the destruction of the latter for the enlarged or expanded reproduction of the former.

THE STRUGGLE AGAINST NATURAL ECONOMY

Capitalism arises and develops historically amidst a non-capitalist society. In Western Europe it is found at first in a feudal environment from which it in fact sprang — the system of bondage in rural areas and the guild system in the towns — and later, after having swallowed up the feudal system, it exists mainly in an environment of peasants and artisans, that is to say in a system of simple commodity production both in agriculture and trade. European capitalism is further surrounded by vast territories of non-European civilisation ranging over all levels of development, from the primitive communist hordes of nomad herdsmen, hunters and gatherers to commodity production by peasants and artisans. This is the setting for the accumulation of capital.

We must distinguish three phases: the struggle of capital against natural economy, the struggle against commodity economy, and the competitive struggle of capital on the international stage for the remaining conditions of accumulation.

The existence and development of capitalism requires an environment of non-capitalist forms of production, but not every one of these forms will serve its ends. Capitalism needs non-capitalist social strata as a market for its surplus value, as a source of supply for its means of production and as a reservoir of labour power for its wage system. For all these purposes, forms of production based upon a natural economy are of no use to capital. In all social organisations where natural economy prevails, where there are primitive peasant communities with common ownership of the land, a feudal system of bondage or anything of this nature, economic organisation is essentially in response to the internal demand; and therefore there is no demand, or very little, for foreign goods, and also, as a rule, no surplus production, or at least no urgent need to dispose of surplus products. What is most important, however, is that, in any natural economy, production only goes on because both means of production and labour power are bound in one form or another. The communist peasant community no less than the feudal *corvée* farm and similar institutions maintain their economic organisation by subjecting the labour power, and the most important means of production, the land, to the rule of law and custom. A natural economy thus confronts the requirements of capitalism at every turn with rigid barriers. Capitalism must therefore always and everywhere fight a battle of annihilation against every historical form of natural economy that it encounters, whether this is slave economy, feudalism, primitive communism, or patriarchal peasant economy. The principal methods in this struggle are political force (revolution, war), oppressive taxation by the state, and cheap goods; they are partly applied simultaneously, and partly they succeed and complement one another. In Europe, force assumed revolutionary forms in the fight against feudalism (this is the ultimate explanation of the bourgeois revolutions in the seventeenth, eighteenth and nineteenth centuries); in the non-European countries, where it fights more primitive social organisations, it assumes the forms of colonial policy. These methods, together with the systems of taxation applied in such cases, and commercial relations also, particularly with primitive communities, form an alliance in which political power and economic factors go hand in hand.

In detail, capital in its struggle against societies with a natural economy pursues the following ends:

(1) To gain immediate possession of important sources of productive forces such as land, game in primeval forests, minerals, precious stones and ores, products of exotic flora such as rubber, etc.

(2) To 'liberate' labour power and to coerce it into service.

(3) To introduce a commodity economy.

(4) To separate trade and agriculture.

At the time of primitive accumulation, i.e. at the end of the Middle Ages, when the history of capitalism in Europe began, and right into the nineteenth century, dispossessing the peasants in England and on the Continent was the most striking weapon in the large-scale transformation of means of production and labour power into capital. Yet capital in power performs the same task even to-day, and on an even more important scale — by modern colonial policy. It is an illusion to hope that capitalism will ever be content with the means of production which it can acquire by way of commodity exchange. In this respect already, capital is faced with difficulties because vast tracts of the globe's surface are in the possession of social organisations that have no desire for commodity exchange or cannot, because of the entire social structure and the forms of ownership, offer for sale the productive forces in which capital is primarily interested. The most important of these productive forces is of course the land, its hidden mineral treasure, and its meadows, woods and water, and further the flocks of the primitive shepherd tribes. If capital were here to rely on the process of slow internal disintegration, it might take centuries. To wait patiently until the most important means of production could be alienated by trading in consequence of this process were tantamount to renouncing the productive forces of those territories altogether. Hence derives the vital necessity for capitalism in its relations with colonial countries to appropriate the most important means of production. Since the primitive associations of the natives are the strongest protection for their social organisations and for their material bases of existence, capital must begin by planning for the systematic destruction and annihilation of all the non-capitalist social units which obstruct its development. With that we have passed beyond the stage of primitive accumulation; this process is still going on. Each new colonial expansion is accompanied, as a matter of course, by a relentless battle of capital against the social and economic ties of the natives, who are also forcibly robbed of their means of production and labour power. Any hope to restrict the accumulation of capital exclusively to 'peaceful competition', i.e. to regular commodity exchange such as takes place between capitalist producer-countries, rests on the pious belief that capital can accumulate without mediation of the productive forces and without the demand of more primitive organisations, and that it can rely upon the slow internal process of a disintegrating natural economy. Accumulation, with its spasmodic expansion, can no more wait for, and be content with, a natural internal disintegration of non-capitalist formations and their transition to commodity economy, than it can wait for, and be content with, the natural increase of the working population. Force is the only solution open to capital; the accumulation of capital, seen as an historical process, employs force as a permanent weapon, not only at its genesis, but further on down to the present day. From the point of view of the primitive societies involved, it is a matter of life or death; for them there can be no other attitude than opposition and fight to the finish — complete exhaustion and extinction. Hence permanent occupation of the colonies by the military, native risings and punitive expeditions are the order of the day for any colonial regime. The method of violence, then, is the immediate consequence of the clash between capitalism and the organisations of a natural economy which would restrict accumulation. Their means of production and their labour power no less than their demand for surplus products is necessary to capitalism. Yet the latter is fully determined to undermine their independence as social units, in order to gain possession of their means of production and labour power and to convert them into commodity buyers. This method is the most profitable and gets the quickest results, and so it is also the most expedient for capital. In fact, it is invariably accompanied by a growing militarism whose importance for accumulation will be demonstrated below in another connection. British policy in India and French policy in Algeria are the classical examples of the application of these methods by capitalism.

The ancient economic organisations of the Indians — the communist village community — had been preserved in their various forms throughout thousands of years, in spite of all the political disturbances during their long history. In the sixth century B.C. the Persians invaded the Indus basin and subjected part of the country. Two centuries later the Greeks entered and left behind them colonies, founded by Alexander on the pattern of a completely alien civilisation. Then the savage Scythians invaded the country, and for centuries India remained under Arab rule. Later, the Afghans swooped down from the Iran mountains, until they, too, were expelled by the ruthless onslaught of Tartar hordes. The Mongols' path was marked by terror and destruction, by the massacre of entire villages — the peaceful countryside with the tender shoots of rice made crimson with blood. And still the Indian village community survived. For none of the successive Mahometan conquerors had ultimately violated the internal social life of the peasant masses and its traditional structure. They only set up their own governors in the provinces to supervise military organisation and to collect taxes from the population. All conquerors pursued the aim of dominating and exploiting the country, but none was interested in robbing the people of their productive forces and in destroying their social organisation. In the Moghul Empire, the peasant had to pay his annual tribute in kind to the foreign ruler, but he could live undisturbed in his village and could cultivate his rice on his *sholgura* as his father had done before him. Then came the British — and the blight of capitalist civilisation succeeded in disrupting the entire social organisation of the people; it achieved in a short time what thousands of years, what the sword of the Nogaians, had failed to accomplish. The ultimate purpose of British capital was to possess itself of the very basis of existence of the Indian community: the land.

This end was served above all by the fiction, always popular with European colonisers, that all the land of a colony belongs to the political ruler. In retrospect, the British endowed the Moghul and his governors with private ownership of the whole of India, in order to 'legalise' their succession. Economic experts of the highest repute, such as James Mill, duly supported this fiction with 'scientific' arguments, so in particular with the famous conclusion given below.[1]

As early as 1793, the British in Bengal gave landed property to all the *zemindars* (Mahometan tax collectors) or hereditary market superintendents they had found in their district so as to win native support for the campaign against the peasant masses. Later they adopted the same policy for their new conquests in the Agram province, in Oudh, and in the Central Provinces. Turbulent peasant risings followed in their wake, in the course of which tax collectors were frequently driven out. In the resulting confusion and anarchy British capitalists successfully appropriated a considerable portion of the land.

The burden of taxation, moreover, was so ruthlessly increased that it swallowed up nearly all the fruits of the people's labour. This went to such an extreme in the Delhi and Allahabad districts that, according to the official evidence of the British tax authorities in 1854, the peasants found it convenient to lease or pledge their shares in land for the bare amount of the tax levied. Under the auspices of this taxation, usury came to the Indian village, to stay and eat up the social organisation from within like a canker.[2] In order to accelerate this process the British passed a law that flew in the face of every tradition and justice known to the village community: compulsory alienation of village land for tax arrears. In vain did the old family associations try to protect themselves by options on their hereditary land and that of their kindred. There was no stopping the rot. Every day another plot of land fell under the hammer; individual members withdrew from the family unit, and the peasants got into debt and lost their land.

The British, with their wonted colonial stratagems, tried to make it appear as if their power policy, which had in fact undermined the traditional forms of landownership and brought about the collapse of the Hindu peasant economy, had been dictated by the need to protect the peasants against native oppression and exploitation and served to safeguard their own interests.[3] Britain artificially created a landed aristocracy at the expense of the ancient property-rights of the peasant communities, and then proceeded to 'protect' the peasants against these alleged oppressors, and to bring this illegally usurped land into the possession of British capitalists.

Thus large estates developed in India in a short time, while over large areas the peasants in their masses were turned into impoverished small tenants with a short-term lease.

Lastly, one more striking fact shows the typically capitalist method of colonisation. The British were the first conquerors of India who showed gross indifference to public utilities. Arabs, Afghans and Mongols had organised and maintained magnificent works of canalisation in India, they had given the country a network of roads, spanned the rivers with bridges and seen to the sinking of wells. Timur or Tamerlane, the founder of the Mongol dynasty in India, had a care for the cultivation of the soil, for irrigation, for the safety of the roads and the provision of food for travellers.[4] The primitive Indian Rajahs, the Afghan or Mongol conquerors, at any rate, in spite of occasional cruelty against individuals, made their mark with the marvellous constructions we can find to-day at every step and which seem to be the work of a giant race. 'The (East India) Company which ruled India until 1858 did not make one spring accessible, did not sink a single well, nor build a bridge for the benefit of the Indians.'[5]

Another witness, the Englishman James Wilson, says: 'In the Madras Province, no-one can help being impressed by the magnificent ancient irrigation systems, traces of which have been preserved until our time. Locks and weirs dam the rivers into great lakes, from which canals distribute the water for an area of 60 or 70 miles around. On the large rivers, there are 30 to 40 of such weirs... The rain water from the mountains was collected in artificial ponds, many of which still remain and boast circumferences of between 15 and 25 miles. Nearly all these gigantic constructions were completed before the year 1750. During the war between the Company and the Mongol rulers — and, be it said, *during the entire period of our rule in India* — they have sadly decayed.[6]

No wonder! British capital had no object in giving the Indian communities economic support or helping them to survive. Quite the reverse, it aimed to destroy them and to deprive them of their productive forces. The unbridled greed, the acquisitive instinct of accumulation must by its very nature take every advantage of the 'conditions of the market' and can have no thought for the morrow. It is incapable of seeing far enough to recognise the value of the economic monuments of an older civilisation. (Recently British engineers in Egypt feverishly tried to discover traces of an ancient irrigation system rather like the one a stupid lack of vision had allowed to decay in India, when they were charged with damming the Nile on a grand scale in furtherance of capitalist enterprise.) Not until 1867 was England able to appreciate the results of her noble efforts in this respect. In the terrible famine of that year a million people were killed in the Orissa district alone; and Parliament was shocked into investigating the causes of the emergency. The British government has now introduced administrative measures in an attempt to save the peasant from usury. The Punjab Alienation Act of 1900 made it illegal to sell or mortgage peasant lands to persons other than of the peasant caste, though exceptions can be made in individual cases, subject to the tax collector's approval.[7] Having deliberately disrupted the protecting ties of the ancient Hindu social associations, after having nurtured a system of usury where nothing is thought of a 15 per cent charge of interest, the British now entrust the ruined Indian peasant to the tender care of the Exchequer and its officials, under the 'protection', that is to say, of those draining him of his livelihood.

Next to tormented British India, Algeria under French rule claims pride of place in the annals of capitalist colonisation. When the French conquered Algeria, ancient social and economic institutions prevailed among the Arab-Kabyle population. These had been preserved until the nineteenth century, and in spite of the long and turbulent history of the country they survive in part even to the present day.

Private property may have existed no doubt in the towns, among the Moors and Jews, among merchants, artisans and usurers. Large rural areas may have been seized by the State under Turkish suzerainty — yet nearly half of the productive land is jointly held by Arab and Kabyle tribes who still keep up the ancient patriarchal customs. Many Arab families led the same kind of nomad life in the nineteenth century as they had done since time immemorial, an existence that appears restless and irregular only to the superficial observer, but one that is in fact strictly regulated and extremely monotonous. In summer they were wont, man, woman and child, to take their herds and tents and migrate to the sea-swept shores of the Tell district; and in the winter they would move back again to the protective warmth of the desert. They travelled along definite routes, and the summer and winter stations were fixed for every tribe and family. The fields of those Arabs who had settled on the land were in most cases the joint property of the clans, and the great Kabyle family associations also lived according to old traditional rules under the patriarchal guidance of their elected heads.

The women would take turns for household duties; a matriarch, again elected by the family, being in complete charge of the clan's domestic affairs, or else the women taking turns of duty. This organisation of the Kabyle clans on the fringe of the African desert bears a startling resemblance to that of the famous Southern Slavonic *Zadruga* — not only the fields but all the tools, weapons and monies, all that the members acquire or need for their work, are communal property of the clan. Personal property is confined to one suit of clothing, and in the case of a woman to the dresses and ornaments of her dowry. More valuable attire and jewels, however, are considered common property, and individuals were allowed to use them only if the whole family approved. If the clan was not too numerous, meals were taken at a common table; the women took it in turns to cook, but the eldest were entrusted with the dishing out. If a family circle was too large, the head of the family would each month ration out strictly proportionate quantities of uncooked food to the individual families who then prepared them. These communities were bound together by close ties of kinship, mutual assistance and equality, and a patriarch would implore his sons on his deathbed to remain faithful to the family.[8]

These social relations were already seriously impaired by the rule of the Turks, established in Algeria in the sixteenth century. Yet the Turkish exchequer had by no means confiscated all the land. That is a legend invented by the French at a much later date. Indeed, only a European mind is capable of such a flight of fancy which is contrary to the entire economic foundation of Islam both in theory and practice. In truth, the facts were quite different. The Turks did not touch the communal fields of the village communities. They merely confiscated a great part of uncultivated land from the clans and converted it into crownland under Turkish local administrators (*Beyliks*). The state worked these lands in part with native labour, and in part they were leased out on rent or against payment in kind. Further the Turks took advantage of every revolt of the subjected families and of every disturbance in the country to add to their possessions by large-scale confiscation of land, either for military establishments or for public auction, when most of it went to Turkish or other usurers. To escape from the burden of taxation and confiscation, many peasants placed themselves under the protection of the Church, just as they had done in medieval Germany. Hence considerable areas became Church-property. All these changes finally resulted in the following distribution of Algerian land at the time of the French conquest: crownlands occupied nearly 3,750,000 acres, and a further 7,500,000 acres of uncultivated land as common property of All the Faithful (*Bled-el-Islam*). 7,500,000 acres had been privately owned by the Berbers since Roman times, and under Turkish rule a further 3,750,000 acres had come into private ownership, a mere 12,500,000 acres remaining communal property of individual Arab clans. In the Sahara, some of the 7,500,000 acres fertile land near the Sahara Oases was communally owned by the clans and some belonged to private owners. The remaining 57,500,000,000 acres were mainly waste land.

With their conquest of Algeria, the French made a great ado about their work of civilisation, since the country, having shaken off the Turkish yoke at the beginning of the eighteenth century, was harbouring the pirates who infested the Mediterranean and trafficked in Christian slaves. Spain and the North American Union in particular, themselves at that time slave traders on no mean scale, declared relentless war on this Moslem iniquity. France, in the very throes of the Great Revolution, proclaimed a crusade against Algerian anarchy. Her subjection of that country was carried through under the slogans of 'combating slavery' and 'instituting orderly and civilised conditions'. Yet practice was soon to show what was at the bottom of it all. It is common knowledge that in the forty years following the subjection of Algeria, no European state suffered so many changes in its political system as France: the restoration of the monarchy was followed by the July Revolution and the reign of the 'Citizen King', and this was succeeded by the February Revolution, the Second Republic, the Second Empire, and finally, after the disaster of 1870, by the Third Republic. In turn, the aristocracy, high finance, petty bourgeoisie and the large middle classes in general gained political ascendancy. Yet French policy in Algeria remained undeflected by this succession of events; it pursued a single aim from beginning to end; at the fringe of the African desert, it demonstrated plainly that all the political revolutions in nineteenth-century France centred in a single basic interest: the rule of a capitalist bourgeoisie and its institutions of ownership.

'The bill submitted for your consideration', said Deputy Humbert on June 30, 1873, in the Session of the French National Assembly as spokesman for the Commission for Regulating Agrarian Conditions in Algeria, 'is but the crowning touch to an edifice well-founded on a whole series of ordinances, edicts, laws and decrees of the Senate which together and severally have as the same object: the establishment of private property among the Arabs.'

In spite of the ups and downs of internal French politics, French colonial policy preserved for fifty years in its systematic and deliberate efforts to destroy and disrupt communal property. It served two distinct purposes: The break-up of communal property was primarily intended to smash the social power of the Arab family associations and to quell their stubborn resistance against the French yoke, in the course of which there were innumerable risings so that, in spite of France's military superiority, the country was in a continual state of war.[9] Secondly, communal property had to be disrupted in order to gain the economic assets of the conquered country; the Arabs, that is to say, had to be deprived of the land they had owned for a thousand years, so that French capitalists could get it. Once again the fiction we know so well, that under Moslem law all land belongs to the ruler, was brought into play. Just as the English had done in British India, so Louis Philippe's governors in Algeria declared the existence of communal property owned by the clan to be 'impossible'. This fiction served as an excuse to claim for the state most of the uncultivated areas, and especially the commons, woods, and meadows, and to use them for purposes of colonisation. A complete system of settlement developed, the so-called *cantonments* which settled French colonists on the clan land and herded the tribes into a small area. Under the decrees of 1830, 1831, 1840, 1844, 1845 and 1846 these thefts of Arab family land were legalised. Yet this system of settlement did not actually further colonisation; it only bred wild speculation and usury. In most instances the Arabs managed to buy back the land that had been taken from them, although they were thus incurring heavy debts. French methods of oppressive taxation had the same tendency, in particular the law of June 16, 1851, proclaiming all forests to be state property, which robbed the natives of 6,000,000 acres of pasture and brushwood, and took away the prime essential for animal husbandry. This spate of laws, ordinances and regulations wrought havoc with the ownership of land in the country. Under the prevailing condition of feverish speculation in land, many natives sold their estates to the French in the hope of ultimately recovering them. Quite often they sold the same plot to two or three buyers at a time, and what is more, it was quite often inalienable family land and did not even belong to them. A company of speculators from Rouen, e.g., believed that they had bought 50,000 acres, but in fact had only acquired a disputed title to 3,425 acres. There followed an infinite number of lawsuits in which the French courts supported on principle all partitions and claims of the buyers. In these uncertain conditions, speculation, usury and anarchy were rife. But although the introduction of French colonists in large numbers among the Arab population had aimed at securing support for the French government, this scheme failed miserable. Thus, under the Second Empire, French policy tried another tack. The government, with its European lack of vision, had stubbornly denied the existence of communal property for thirty years, but it had learned better at last. By a single stroke of the pen, joint family property was officially recognised and condemned to be broken up. This is the double significance of the decree of the Senate dated April 22, 1864. General Allard declared in the Senate:

'The government does not lose sight of the fact that the general aim of its policy is to weaken the influence of the tribal chieftains and to dissolve the family associations. By this means, it will sweep away the last remnants of feudalism [*sic!*] defended by the opponents of the government bill... The surest method of accelerating the process of dissolving the family associations will be to institute private property and to settle European colonists among the Arab families.'[10]

The law of 1863 created special Commissions for cutting up the landed estates, consisting of the Chairman, either a Brigadier-General or Colonel, one *sous-préfet*, one representative of the Arab military authorities and an official bailiff. These natural experts on African economics and social conditions were faced with the threefold task, first of determining the precise boundaries of the great family estates, secondly to distribute the estates of each clan among its various branches, and finally to break up this family land into separate private allotments. This expedition of the Brigadiers into the interior of Africa duly took place. The Commissions proceeded to their destinations. They were to combine the office of judge in all land disputes with that of surveyor and land distributor, the final decision resting with the Governor-General of Algeria. Ten years' valiant efforts by the Commissions yielded the following result: between 1863 and 1873, of 700 hereditary estates, 400 were shared out among the branches of each clan, and the foundations for future inequalities between great landed estates and small allotments were thus laid. One family, in fact, might receive between 2.5 and 10 acres, while another might get as much as 250 or even 450 acres, depending on the size of the estate and the number of collaterals within the clan. Partition, however, stopped at that point. Arab customs presented unsurmountable difficulties to a further division of family land. In spite of Colonels and Brigadiers, French policy had again failed in its object to create private property for transfer to the French.

But the Third Republic, an undisguised regime of the bourgeoisie, had the courage and the cynicism to go straight for its goal and to attack the problem from the other end, disdaining the preliminaries of the Second Empire. In 1873, the National Assembly worked out a law with the avowed intention immediately to split up the entire estates of all the 700 Arab clans, and forcibly to institute private property in the shortest possible time. Desperate conditions in the colony were the pretext for this measure. It had taken the great Indian famine of 1866 to awaken the British public to the marvellous exploits of British colonial policy and to call for a parliamentary investigation; and similarly, Europe was alarmed at the end of the sixties by the crying needs of Algeria where more than forty years of French rule culminated in wide-spread famine and a disastrous mortality rate among the Arabs. A commission of inquiry was set up to recommend new legislation with which to bless the Arabs; it was unanimously resolved that there was only one life-buoy for them — the institution of private property; that alone could save the Arab from destitution, since he would then always be able to sell or mortgage his land. It was decided therefore, that the only means of alleviating the distress of the Arabs, deeply involved in debts as they were because of the French land robberies and oppressive taxation, was to deliver them completely into the hands of usurers. This farce was expounded in all seriousness before the National Assembly and was accepted with equal gravity by that worthy body. The 'victors' of the Paris Commune flaunted their brazenness.

In the National Assembly, two arguments in particular served to support the new law: those in favour of the bill emphasised over and over again that the Arabs themselves urgently desired the introduction of private property. And so they did, or rather the Algerian land speculators and usurers did, since they were vitally interested in 'liberating' their victims from the protection of the family ties. As long as Moslem law prevailed in Algeria, hereditary clan and family lands were inalienable, which laid insuperable difficulties in the way of anyone who wished to mortgage his land. The law of 1863 had merely made a breach in these obstacles, and the issue now at stake was their complete abolition so as to give a free hand to the usurers. The second argument was 'scientific', part of the same intellectual equipment from which that worthy, James Mill, had drawn for his abstruse conclusions regarding Indian relations of ownership: English classical economics. Thoroughly versed in their masters' teachings, the disciples of Smith and Ricardo impressively declaimed that private property is indispensable for the prevention of famines in Algeria, for more intensive and better cultivation of the land, since obviously no one would be prepared to invest capital or intensive labour in a piece of land which does not belong to him and whose produce is not his own to enjoy. But the facts spoke a different language. They proved that the French speculators employed the private property they had created in Algeria for anything but the more intensive and improved cultivation of the soil. In 1873, 1,000,000 acres were French property. But the capitalist companies, the Algerian and Setif Company which owned 300,000 acres, did not cultivate the land at all but leased it to the natives who tilled it in the traditional manner, nor were 25 per cent of the other French owners engaged in agriculture. It was simply impossible to conjure up capitalist investments and intensive agriculture overnight, just as capitalist conditions in general could not be created out of nothing. They existed only in the imagination of profit-seeking French speculators, and in the benighted doctrinaire visions of their scientific economists. The essential point, shorn of all pretexts and flourishes which seem to justify the law of 1873, was simply the desire to deprive the Arabs of their land, their livelihood. And although these arguments had worn threadbare and were evidently insincere, this law which was to put paid to the Algerian population and their material prosperity, was passed unanimously on July 26, 1873.

But even this master-stroke soon proved a failure. The policy of the Third Republic miscarried because of the difficulties in substituting at one stroke bourgeois private property for the ancient clan communism, just as the policy of the Second Empire had come to grief over the same issue. In 1890, when the law of July 26, 1973, supplemented by a second law on April 28, 1887, had been in force for seventeen years, 14,000,000 francs had been spent on dealing with 40,000,000 acres. It was estimated that the process would not be completed before 1950 and would require a further 60,000,000 francs. And still abolition of clan communism, the ultimate purpose, had not been accomplished. What had really been attained was all too evident: reckless speculation in land, thriving usury and the economic ruin of the natives.

Since it had been impossible to institute private property by force, a new experiment was undertaken. The laws of 1873 and 1887 had been condemned by a commission appointed for their revision by the Algerian government in 1890. It was another seven years before the legislators on the Seine made the effort to consider reforms for the ruined country. The new decree of the Senate refrained in principle from instituting private property by compulsion or administrative measures. The laws of February 2, 1897, and the edict of the Governor-General of Algeria (March 3, 1898) both provided chiefly for the introduction of private property following a voluntary application by the prospective purchaser or owner.[11] But there were clauses to permit a single owner, without the consent of the others, to claim private property; further, such a 'voluntary' application can be extorted at any convenient moment if the owner is in debt and the usurer exerts pressure. And so the new law left the doors wide open for French and native capitalists further to disrupt and exploit the hereditary and clan lands.

Of recent years, this mutilation of Algeria which had been going on for eight decades meets with even less opposition, since the Arabs, surrounded as they are by French capital following the subjection of Tunisia (1881) and the recent conquest of Morocco, have been rendered more and more helpless. The latest result of the French regime in Algeria is an Arab exodus into Turkey.[12]

The Introduction of Commodity Economy

The second condition of importance for acquiring means of production and realising the surplus value is that commodity exchange and commodity economy should be introduced in societies based on natural economy as soon as their independence has been abrogated, or rather in the course of this disrupted process. Capital requires to buy the products of, and sell its commodities to, all non-capitalist strata and societies. Here at last we seem to find the beginnings of that 'peace' and 'equality', the *do ut des*, mutual interest, 'peaceful competition' and the 'influences of civilisation'. For capital can indeed deprive alien social associations of the means of production by force, it can compel the workers to submit to capitalist exploitation, but it cannot force them to buy its commodities or to realise its surplus value. In districts where natural economy formerly prevailed, the introduction of means of transport — railways, navigation, canals — is vital for the spreading of commodity economy, a further hopeful sign. The triumphant march of commodity economy thus begins in most cases with magnificent constructions of modern transport, such as railway lines which cross primeval forests and tunnel through the mountains, telegraph wires which bridge the deserts, and ocean liners which call at the most outlying ports. But it is a mere illusion that these are peaceful changes. Under the standard of commerce, the relations between the East India Company and the spice-producing countries were quite as piratical, extortionate and blatantly fraudulent as present-day relations between American capitalists and the Red Indians of Canada whose furs they buy, or between German merchants and the Negroes of Africa. Modern China presents a classical example of the 'gentle', 'peace-loving' practices of commodity exchange with backward countries. Throughout the nineteenth century, beginning with the early forties, her history has been punctuated by wars with the object of opening her up to trade by brute force. Missionaries provoked persecutions of Christians, Europeans instigated risings, and in periodical massacres a completely helpless and peaceful agrarian population was forced to match arms with the most modern capitalist military technique of all the Great Powers of Europe. Heavy war contributions necessitated a public debt, China taking up European loans, resulting in European control over her finances and occupation of her fortifications; the opening of free ports was enforced, railway concessions to European capitalists extorted. By all these measures commodity exchange was fostered in China, from the early thirties of the last century until the beginning of the Chinese revolution.

European civilisation, that is to say commodity exchange with European capital, made its first impact on China with the Opium Wars when she was compelled to buy the drug from Indian plantations in order to make money for British capitalists. In the seventeenth century, the East India Company had introduced the cultivation of poppies in Bengal; the use of the drug was disseminated in China by its Canton branch. At the beginning of the nineteenth century, opium fell so considerably in price that it rapidly became the 'luxury of the people'. In 1821, 4,628 chests of opium were imported to China at an average price of £265; then the price fell by 50 per cent, and Chinese imports rose to 9,621 chests in 1825, and to 26,670 chests in 1830.[1] The deadly effects of the drug, especially of the cheaper kinds used by the poorer population, became a public calamity and made it necessary for China to lay an embargo on imports, as an emergency measure. Already in 1828, the viceroy of Canton had prohibited imports of opium, only to deflect the trade to other ports. One of the Peking censors commanded to investigate the question gave the following report:

'I have learnt that people who smoke opium have developed such a craving for this noxious drug that they make every effort to obtain this gratification. If they do not get their opium at the usual hour, their limbs begin to tremble, they break out in sweat, and they cannot perform the slightest tasks. But as soon as they are given the pipe, they inhale a few puffs and are cured immediately.

'Opium has therefore become a necessity for all who smoke it, and it is not surprising that under cross-examination by the local authorities they will submit to every punishment rather than reveal the names of their suppliers. Local authorities are also in some cases given presents to tolerate the evil or to delay any investigation already under way. Most merchants who bring goods for sale into Canton also deal in smuggled opium.

'I am of the opinion that opium is by far a greater evil than gambling, and that opium smokers should therefore be punished no less than gamblers.'

The censor suggested that every convicted opium smoker should be sentenced to eighty strokes of the bamboo, and anybody refusing to give the name of his supplier to a hundred strokes and three years of exile. The pigtailed Cato of Peking concludes his report with a frankness staggering to any European official: 'Apparently opium is mostly introduced from abroad by dishonest officials in connivance with profit-seeking merchants who transport it into the interior of the country. Then the first to indulge are people of good family, wealthy private persons and merchants, but ultimately the drug habit spreads among the common people. I have learnt that in all provinces opium is smoked not only in the civil service but also in the army. The officials of the various districts indeed enjoin the legal prohibition of sale by special edicts. But at the same time, their parents, families, dependants and servants simply go on smoking opium, and the merchants profit from the ban by increased prices. Even the police have been won over; they buy the stuff instead of helping to suppress it, and this is an additional reason for the disregard in which all prohibitions and ordinances are held.'[2]

Consequently, a stricter law was passed in 1833 which made every opium smoker liable to a hundred strokes and two months in the stocks, and provincial governors were ordered to report annually on their progress in the battle against opium. But there were two sequels to this campaign: on the one hand large-scale poppy plantations sprang up in the interior, particularly in the Honan, Setchuan, and Kueitchan provinces, and on the other, England declared war on China to get her to lift the embargo. These were the splendid beginnings of 'opening China' to European civilisation — by the opium pipe.

Canton was the first objective. The fortifications of the town at the main arm of the Perl estuary could not have been more primitive. Every day at sunset a barrier of iron chains was attached to wooden rafts anchored at various distances, and this was the main defence. Moreover, the Chinese guns could only fire at a certain angle and were therefore completely ineffectual. With such primitive defences, just adequate to prevent a few merchant ships from landing, did the Chinese meet the British attack. A couple of British cruisers, then, sufficed to effect an entry on September 7, 1839. The sixteen battle-junks and thirteen fire-ships which the Chinese put up for resistance were shot up or dispersed in a matter of forty-five minutes. After this initial victory, the British renewed the attack in the beginning of 1841 with a considerably reinforced fleet. This time the fleet, consisting in a number of battle-junks, and the forts were attacked simultaneously. The first incendiary rocket that was fired penetrated through the armour casing of a junk into the powder chamber and blew the ship with the entire crew sky-high. In a short time eleven junks, including the flag-ship, were destroyed, and the remainder precipitately made for safety. The action on land took a little longer. Since the Chinese guns were quite useless, the British walked right through the fortifications, climbed to a strategic position — which was not even guarded — and proceeded to slaughter the helpless Chinese from above. The casualty list of the battle was: for the Chinese 600 dead, and for the British, 1 dead and 30 wounded, more than half of the latter having been injured by the accidental explosion of a powder magazine. A few weeks later, there followed another British exploit. The forts of Anung-Hoy and North Wantong were to be taken. No less than twelve fully equipped cruisers were available for this task. What is more, the Chinese, once again forgetful of the most important thing, had omitted to fortify the island of South Wantong. Thus the British calmly landed a battery of howitzers to bombard the fort from one side, the cruisers shelling it from the other. After that, the Chinese were driven from the forts in a matter of minutes, and the landing met with no resistance. The ensuing display of inhumanity — an English report says — will be for ever deeply deplored by the British staff. The Chinese, trying to escape from the barricades, had fallen into a moat which was soon literally filled to the brim with helpless soldiers begging for mercy. Into this mass of prostrate human bodies, the sepoys — acting against orders, it is claimed — fired again and again. This is the way in which Canton was made receptive to commodity exchange.

Nor did the other ports fare better. On July 4, 1841, three British cruisers with 120 cannon appeared off the islands in the entrance to the town of Ningpo. More cruisers arrived the following day. In the evening the British admiral sent a message to the Chinese governor, demanding the capitulation of the island. The governor explained that he had no power to resist but could not surrender without orders from Peking. He therefore asked for a delay. This was refused, and at half-past two in the morning the British stormed the defenceless island. Within eight minutes, the fort and the houses on the shore were reduced to smouldering rubble. Having landed on the deserted coast littered with broken spears, sabres, shields, rifles and a few dead bodies, the troops advanced on the walls of the island town of Tinghai. With daybreak, reinforced by the crews of other ships which had meanwhile arrived, they proceeded to put scaling-ladders to the scarcely defended ramparts. A few more minutes gave them mastery of the town. This splendid victory was announced with becoming modesty in an Order of the Day: 'Fate has decreed that the morning of July 5, 1841, should be the historic date on which Her Majesty's flag was first raised over the most beautiful island of the Celestial Empire, the first European flag to try triumphantly above this lovely countryside.'[3]

On August 25, 1841, the British approached the town of Amoy, whose forts were armed with a hundred of the heaviest Chinese guns. These guns being almost useless, and the commanders lacking in resource, the capture of the harbour was child's play. Under cover of a heavy barrage, British ships drew near the walls of Kulangau, landed their marines, and after a short stand the Chinese troops were driven out. The twenty-six battle-junks with 128 guns in the harbour were also captured, their crews having fled. One battery, manned by the Tartars, heroically held out against the combined fire of three British ships, but a British landing was effected in their rear and the post wiped out.

This was the finale of the notorious Opium War. By the peace treaty of August 27, 1842, the island of Hong Kong was ceded to Britain. In addition, the towns of Canton, Amoy, Futchou, Ningpo and Shanghai were to open their ports to foreign commerce. But within fifteen years, there was a further war against China. This time, Britain had joined forces with the French. In 1857, the allied navies captured Canton with a heroism equal to that of the first war. By the peace of Tientsin (1858), the opium traffic, European commerce and Christian missions were admitted into the interior. Already in 1859, however, the British resumed hostilities and attempted to destroy the Chinese fortifications on the Peiho river, but were driven off after a fierce battle in which 464 people were wounded or killed.[4]

After that, Britain and France again joined forces. At the end of August 1860, 12,600 English and 7,500 French troops under General Cousin-Montauban first captured the Taku forts without a single shot having been fired. Then they proceeded towards Tientsin and on towards Peking. A bloody battle was joined at Palikao, and Peking fell to the European Powers. Entering the almost depopulated and completely undefended city, the victors began by pillaging the Imperial Palace, manfully helped by General Cousin himself, who was later to become field marshal and Count of Palikao. Then the Palace went up in flames, fired on Lord Elgin's order as an imposed penance.[5]

The European Powers now obtained concessions to set up embassies in Peking, and to start trading with Tientsin and other towns. The Tchi-fu Convention of 1876 guaranteed full facilities for importing opium into China — at a time when the Anti-Opium League in England agitated against the spreading of the drug habit in London, Manchester and other industrial districts, when a parliamentary commission declared the consumption of opium to be harmful in the extreme. By all treaties made at that time between China and the Great Powers any European, whether merchant or missionary, was guaranteed the right to acquire land, to which end the legitimate arguments were ably supported by deliberate fraud.

First and foremost the ambiguity of the treaty texts made a convenient excuse for European capital to encroach beyond the Treaty Ports. It used every loophole in the wording of the treaties to begin with, and subsequently blackmailed the Chinese government into permitting the missions to acquire land not alone in the Treaty Pots but in all the provinces of the realm. Their claim was based upon the notorious bare-faced distortion of the Chinese original in the Abbé Delamarre's official translation of the supplementary convention with France. French diplomacy, and the Protestant missions in particular, unanimously condemned the crafty swindle of the Catholic padre, but nevertheless they were firm that the rights of French missions obtained by this fraud should be explicitly extended to the Protestant missions as well.[6]

China's entry into commodity exchange, having begun with the Opium Wars, was finally accomplished with a series of 'leases' and the China campaign of 1900, when the commercial interests of European capital sank to a brazen international dogfight over Chinese land. The description of the Dowager Empress, who wrote to Queen Victoria after the capture of the Taku forts, subtly underlines this contrast between the initial theory and the ultimate practice of the 'agents of European civilisation':

'To your Majesty, greeting! — In all the dealings of England with the Empire of China, since first relations were established between us, there has never been any idea of territorial aggrandisement on the part of Great Britain, but only a keen desire to promote the interests of her trade. Reflecting upon the fact that our country is now plunged into a dreadful condition of warfare, we bear in mind that a large proportion of China's trade, seventy or eighty per cent, is done with England; moreover, your Customs duties are the lightest in the world, and few restrictions are made at your sea-ports in the matter of foreign importations; for these reasons our amiable relations with British merchants at our Treaty Ports have continued unbroken for the last half century, to our mutual benefit. — But a sudden change has now occurred and general suspicion has been created against us. We would therefore ask you now to consider that if, by any conceivable combination of circumstances, the independence or our Empire should be lost, and the Powers unite to carry out their long-plotted schemes to possess themselves of our territory' — (in a simultaneous message to the Emperor of Japan, the impulsive Tzu Hsi openly refers to 'The earth-hungry Powers of the West, whose tigerish eyes of greed are fixed in our direction'[7]) — 'the results to your country's interests would be disastrous and fatal to your trade. At this moment our Empire is striving to the utmost to raise an army and funds sufficient for its protection; in the meanwhile we rely on your good services to act as mediator, and now anxiously await your decision.'[8]

Both during the wars and in the interim periods, European civilisation was busy looting and thieving on a grand scale in the Chinese Imperial Palaces, in the public buildings and in the monuments of ancient civilisation, not only in 1860, when the French pillaged the Emperor's Palace with its legendary treasures, or in 1900, 'when all the nations vied with each other to steal public and private property'. Every European advance was marked not only with the progress of commodity exchange, but by the smouldering ruins of the largest and most venerable towns, by the decay of agriculture over large rural areas, and by intolerably oppressive taxation for war contributions. There are more than 40 Chinese Treaty Ports — and every one of them has been paid for with streams of blood, with massacre and ruin.

THE STRUGGLE AGAINST PEASANT ECONOMY

An important final phase in the campaign against natural economy is to separate industry from agriculture, to eradicate rural industries altogether from peasant economy. Handicraft in its historical beginnings was a subsidiary occupation, a mere appendage to agriculture in civilised and settled societies. In medieval Europe it became gradually independent of the *corvée* farm and agriculture, it developed into specialised occupations, i.e. production of commodities by urban guilds. In industrial districts, production had progressed from home craft by way of primitive manufacture to the capitalist factory of the staple industries, but in the rural areas, under peasant economy, home crafts persisted as an intrinsic part of agriculture. Every hour that could be spared from cultivating the soil was devoted to handicrafts which, as an auxiliary domestic industry, played an important part in providing for personal needs.[1]

It is a recurrent phenomenon in the development of capitalist production that one branch of industry after the other is singled out, isolated from agriculture and concentrated in factories for mass production. The textile industry provides the textbook example, but the same thing has happened, though less obviously, in the case of other rural industries. Capital must get the peasants to buy its commodities and will therefore begin by restricting peasant economy to a single sphere — that of agriculture — which will not immediately and, under European conditions of ownership, only with great difficulty submit to capitalist domination.[2] To all outward appearance, this process is quite peaceful. It is scarcely noticeable and seemingly caused by purely economic factors. There can be no doubt that mass production in the factories is technically superior to primitive peasant industry, owing to a higher degree of specialisation, scientific analysis and management of the productive process, improved machinery and access to international resources of raw materials. In reality, however, the process of separating agriculture and industry is determined by factors such as oppressive taxation, war, or squandering and monopolisation of the nation's land, and thus belongs to the spheres of political power and criminal law no less than with economics.

Nowhere has this process been brought to such perfection as in the United States. In the wake of the railways, financed by European and in particular British capital, the American farmer crossed the Union from East to West and in his progress over vast areas killed off the Red Indians with fire-arms and blood-hounds, liquor and venereal disease, pushing the survivors to the West, in order to appropriate the land they had 'vacated', to clear it and bring it under the plough. The American farmer, the 'backwoodsman' of the good old times before the War of Secession, was very different indeed from his modern counterpart. There was hardly anything he could not do, and he led a practically self-sufficient life on his isolated farm.

In the beginning of the nineties, one of the leaders of the Farmers' Alliance, Senator Peffer, wrote as follows: 'The American farmer of to-day is altogether a different sort of man from his ancestor of fifty or a hundred years ago. A great many men and women now living remember when farmers were largely manufacturers; that is to say, they made a great many implements for their own use. Every farmer had an assortment of tools with which he made wooden implements, as forks and rakes, handles for his hoes and ploughs, spokes for his wagon, and various other implements made wholly out of wood. Then the farmer produced flax and hemp and wool and cotton. These fibres were prepared upon the farm; they were spun into yarn, woven into cloth, made into garments, and worn at home. Every farm had upon it a little shop for wood and iron work, and in the dwelling were cards and looms; carpets were woven, bed-clothing of different sorts was prepared; upon every farm geese were kept, their feathers used for supplying the home demand with beds and pillows, the surplus being disposed of at the nearest market town. During the winter season wheat and flour and corn meal were carried in large wagons drawn by teams of six to eight horses a hundred or two hundred miles to the market, and traded for farm supplies for the next year — groceries and dry goods. Besides this, mechanics were scattered among the farmers. The farm wagon was in process of building a year or two; the material was found near the shop; the character of the timber to be used was stated in the contract; it had a length of time specified, so that when the material was brought together in proper form and the wagon made, both parties to the contract knew where every stick of it came from, and how long it had been in seasoning. During winter time the neighbourhood carpenter prepared sashes and blinds and doors and moulding and cornices for the next season's building. When the frosts of autumn came the shoemaker repaired to the dwellings of the farmers and there, in a corner set apart to him, he made up shoes for the family during the winter. All these things were done among the farmers, and a large part of the expense was paid with products of the farm. When winter approached, the butchering season was at hand; meat for family use during the next year was prepared and preserved in the smoke house. The orchards supplied fruit for cider, for apple butter, and for preserves of different kinds, amply sufficient to supply the wants of the family during the year, with some to spare. Wheat was threshed, a little at a time, just enough to supply the needs of the family for ready money, and not enough to make it necessary to waste one stalk of straw. Everything was saved and put to use. One of the results of that sort of economy was that comparatively a very small amount of money was required to conduct the business of farming. A hundred dollars average probably was as much as the largest farmers of that day needed in the way of cash to meet the demands of their farm work, paying for hired help, repairs of tools, and all other incidental expenses.'[3]

This Arcadian life was to come to a sudden end after the War of Secession. The war had burdened the Union with an enormous National Debt, amounting to £1,200,000, and in consequence the taxes were considerably increased. On the other hand, a feverish development of modern traffic and industry, machine-building in particular, was encouraged by the imposition of higher protective tariffs. The railway companies were endowed with public lands on an imposing scale, in order to promote railroad construction and farm-settlements: in 1867 alone, they were given more than 192,500,000 acres, and so the permanent way grew at an unprecedented rate. In 1860 it amounted to less than 31,000 miles, in 1870 it had grown to more than 53,000 miles and in 1880 to more than 93,000 miles. (During the same period — 1870-1880 — the permanent way in Europe had grown from 80,000 miles to 100,000 miles.) The railways and speculations in land made for mass emigration from Europe to the United States, and more than 4 1/2 million people immigrated in the twenty-three years from 1869 to 1892. In this way, the Union gradually became emancipated from European, and in particular from British, industry; factories were set up in the States and home industries developed for the production of textiles, iron, steel and machinery. The process of revolutionary transformation was most rapid in agriculture. The emancipation of the slaves had compelled the Southern planters to introduce the stream plough shortly after the Civil War, and new farms had sprung up in the West in the wake of the railways, which from the very beginning employed the most modern machinery and technique.

'The improvements are rapidly revolutionising the agriculture of the West, and reducing to the lowest minimum ever attained, the proportion of manual labour employed in its operations.... Coincident with this application of mechanics to agriculture, systematic and enlarged business aptitudes have also sought alliance with this noble art. Farms of thousands of acres have been managed with greater skill, a more economical adaptation of means to ends, and with a larger margin of real profit than many others of 80 acres.'[4]

During this time, direct and indirect taxation had increased enormously. On June 30, 1864, during the Civil War, a new finance bill was passed which is the basis of the present system of taxation, and which raised taxes on consumption and income to a staggering degree. This heavy war levy served as a pretext for a real orgy of protective tariffs in order to offset the tax on home production by customs duties.[5] Messrs. Morrill, Stevens and the other gentlemen who advanced the war as a lever for enforcing their protectionist programme, initiated the practice of wielding the implement of a customs policy quite openly and cynically to further private profiteering interests of all descriptions. Any home producer who appeared before the legislative assembly with a request for any kind of special tariff to fill his own pocket saw his demands readily granted, and the tariff rates were made as high as any interested party might wish.

'The war', writes the American Taussig, 'had in many ways a bracing and ennobling influence on our national life; but its immediate effect on business affairs, and on all legislation affecting moneyed interests, was demoralising. The line between public duty and private interests was often lost sight of by legislators. Great fortunes were made by changes in legislation urged and brought about by those who were benefited by them, and the country has seen with sorrow that the honour and honesty of public men did not remain undefiled.'[6]

This customs bill which completely revolutionised the country's economic life, and remained in force unchanged for twenty years, was literally pushed through Congress in three days, and through the Senate in two, without criticism, without debate, without any opposition whatever.[7] Down to the present day it forms the basis of U.S. customs legislation.

This shift in U.S. fiscal policy ushered in an era of the most brazen parliamentary log-rolling and of undisguised and unrestrained corruption of elections, of the legislature and the press to satisfy the greed of Big Business. 'Enrichissez-vous' became the catchword of public life after the 'noble war' to liberate mankind from the 'blot of slavery'. On the stock exchange, the

Yankee negro-liberator sought his fortunes in orgies of speculation; in Congress, he endowed himself with public lands, enriched himself by customs and taxes, by monopolies, fraudulent shares and theft of public funds. Industry prospered. Gone were the times when the small or medium farmer required hardly any money, when he could thresh and turn into cash his wheat reserves as the need arose. Now he was chronically in need of money, a lot of money, to pay his taxes. Soon he was forced to sell all his produce and to buy his requirements from the manufacturers in the form of ready-made goods. As Peffer puts it:

'Coming from that time to the present, we find that everything nearly has been changed. All over the West particularly the farmer threshes his wheat all at one time, he disposes of it all at one time, and in a great many instances the straw is wasted. He sells his hogs, and buys bacon and pork; he sells his cattle, and buys fresh beef and canned beef or corned beef, as the case may be; he sells his fruit, and buys it back in cans. If he raises flax at all, instead of putting it into yarn and making gowns for his children, as he did fifty years or more ago, he threshes his flax, sells the seed, and burns the straw. Not more than one farmer in fifty now keeps sheep at all; he relies upon the large sheep farmer for the wool, which is put into cloth or clothing ready for his use. Instead of having clothing made up on the farm in his own house or by a neighbour woman or country tailor a mile away, he either purchases his clothing ready made at the nearest town, or he buys the cloth and has a city tailor make it up for him. Instead of making implements which he uses about the farm — forks, rakes, etc. — he goes to town to purchase even a handle for his axe or his mallet; he purchases twine and rope and all sorts of needed material made of fibres; he buys his cloth and his clothing; he buys his canned fruit and preserved fruit; he buys hams and shoulders and mess pork and mess beef; indeed, he buys nearly everything now that he produced at one time himself, and these things all cost money. Besides all this, and what seems stranger than anything else, whereas in the earlier time the American home was a free home, unencumbered, not one case in a thousand where a home was mortgaged to secure the payment of borrowed money, and whereas but a small amount of money was then needed for actual use in conducting the business of farming, there was always enough of it among the farmers to supply the demand. Now, when at least ten times as much is needed, there is little or none to be obtained, nearly half the farms are mortgaged for as much as they are worth, and interest rates are exorbitant. As to the cause of such wonderful changes....the manufacturer came with his woollen mill, his carding mill, his broom factory, his rope factory, his wooden-ware factory, his cotton factory, his pork-packing establishment, his canning factory and fruit preserving houses; the little shop on the farm has given place to the large shop in town; the wagon-maker's shop in the neighbourhood has given way to the large establishment in the city where...a hundred or two hundred wagons are made in a week; the shoemaker's shop has given way to large establishments in the cities where most of the work is done by machines.'[8]

Finally, the agricultural labour of the farmer himself has become machine work: 'He ploughs and sows and reaps with machines. A machine cuts his wheat and puts it in a sheaf, and steam drives his threshers. He may read the morning paper while he ploughs and sit under an awning while he reaps.'[9]

Sering estimated in the middle eighties that the necessary cash 'for a very modest beginning' of the smallest farm in the North West is £240 to £280.[10]

This revolution of American agriculture after the 'Great War' was not the end. It was only the beginning of the whirlpool in which the farmer was caught. His history brings us automatically to the second phase of the development of capitalist accumulation of which it is an excellent illustration. — Natural economy, the production for personal needs and the close connection between industry and agriculture must be ousted and a simple commodity economy substituted for them. Capitalism needs the medium of commodity production for its development, as a market for its surplus value. But as soon as simple commodity production has superseded natural economy, capital must turn against it. No sooner has capital called it to life, than the two must compete for means of production, labour power, and markets. The first aim of capitalism is to isolate the producer, to sever the community ties which protect him, and the next task is to take the means of production away from the small manufacturer.

In the American Union, as we have seen, the 'Great War' inaugurated an era of large-scale seizure of public lands by monopolist capitalist companies and individual speculators. Feverish railroad building and ever more speculation in railway shares led to a mad gamble in land, where individual soldiers of fortune and companies netted immense fortunes and even entire counties. In addition a veritable swarm of agents lured the vast flow of emigrants from Europe to the U.S.A. by blatant and unscrupulous advertising, deceptions and pretences of every description. These immigrants first settled in the Eastern States along the Atlantic seaboard, and, with the growth of industry in these states, agriculture was driven westward. The 'wheat centre' which had been near Columbus, Ohio, in 1850, in the course of the subsequent fifty years shifted to a position 99 miles further North and 680 miles further West. Whereas in 1850 51.4 per cent of the total wheat crop had been supplied by the Eastern States, in 1880 they produced only 13.6 per cent,

71.7 per cent being supplied by the Northern Central and 9 per cent by the Western States.

In 1825, the Congress of the Union under Monroe had decided to transplant the Red Indians from the East to the West of the Mississippi. The redskins put up a desperate resistance; but all who survived the slaughter of forty Red Indian campaigns were swept away like so much rubbish and driven like cattle to the West to be folded in reservations like so many sheep. The Red Indian had been forced to make room for the farmer — and now the farmer in his turn was driven beyond the Mississippi to make way for capital.

Following the railway tracks, the American farmer moved West and North-West into the land of promise which the great land speculators' agents had painted for him in glowing colours. Yet the most fertile and most favourably situated lands were retained by the companies who farmed them extensively on completely capitalistic lines. All around the farmer who had been exiled into the wilderness, a dangerous competitor and deadly enemy sprang up — the 'bonanza farms', the great capitalist agricultural concerns which neither the Old World nor the New had known before. Here surplus value was produced with the application of all the resources known to modern science and technology.

'As the foremost representative of financial agriculture we may consider Oliver Dalrymple, whose name is to-day known on both sides of the Atlantic. Since 1874 he has simultaneously managed a line of steamers on the Red River and six farms owned by a company of financiers and comprising some 75,000 acres. Each one is divided into departments of 2,000 acres, and every department is again subdivided into three sections of 667 acres which are run by foremen and gangleaders. Barracks to shelter 50 men and stable as many horses and mules, are built on each section, and similarly kitchens, machine sheds and workshops for blacksmiths and locksmiths. Each section is completely equipped with 20 pairs of horses, 8 double ploughs, 12 horse-drawn drill-ploughs, 12 steel-toothed harrows, 12 cutters and binders, 2 threshers and 16 wagons. Everything is done to ensure that the machines and the living labour (men, horses and mules) are in good condition and able to do the greatest possible amount of work. There is a telephone line connecting all sections and the central management.

'The six farms of 75,000 acres are cultivated by an army of 600 workers, organised on military lines. During the harvest, the management hires another 500 to 600 auxiliary workers, assigning them to the various sections. After the work is completed in the fall, the workers are dismissed with the exception of the foreman and 10 men per section. In some farms in Dakota and Minnesota, horses and mules do not spend the winter at the place of work. As soon as the stubble has been ploughed in, they are driven in teams of a hundred or two hundred pairs 900 miles to the South, to return only the following spring.

'Mechanics on horseback follow the ploughing, sowing and harvesting machines when they are at work. If anything goes wrong, they gallop to the machine in question, repair it and get it moving again without delay. The harvested corn is carried to the threshing machines which work day and night without interruption. They are stoked with bundles of straw fed into the stokehold through pipes of sheet-iron. The corn is threshed, winnowed, weighed and filled into sacks by machinery, then it is put into railway trucks which run alongside the farm, and goes to Duluth or Buffalo. Every year, Dalrymple increases his land under seed by 5,800 acres. In 1880 it amounted to 25,000 acres.[11]

In the late seventies, there were already individual capitalists and companies who owned 35,000-45,000 acres of wheat land. Since the time of Lafargue's writing, extensive capitalist agriculture in America has made great strides in technique and the employment of machinery.[12]

The American farmer could not successfully compete with such capitalist enterprises. At a time when the general revolution in the conditions of finance, production and transport compelled him to give up production for personal needs and to produce exclusively for the market, the great spreading of agriculture caused a heavy fall in the prices of agricultural products. And at the precise moment when farming became dependent on the market, the agricultural market of the Union was suddenly turned from a local one into a world market, and became a prey to the wild speculations of a few capitalist mammoth concerns.

In 1879, a notable year for the history of agricultural conditions in Europe as well as in America, there began the mass export of wheat from the U.S.A. to Europe.[13]

Big Business was of course the only one to profit from this expanding market. The small farmer was crushed by the competition of an increasing number of extensive farms and became the prey of speculators who bought up his corn to exert pressure on the world market. Helpless in the face of the immense capitalist powers, the farmer got into debt — a phenomenon typical for a declining peasant economy. In 1890, Secretary Rusk of the U.S. Department of Agriculture sent out a circular letter with reference to the desperate position of the farmers, saying:

'The burden of mortgages upon farms, homes, and land, is unquestionably discouraging in the extreme, and while in some cases no doubt this load may have been too readily assumed, still in the majority of cases the mortgage has been the result of necessity.... These mortgages...drawing high rates of interest...have to-day, in the face of continued depression of the prices of staple products, become very irksome, and in many cases threaten the farmer with loss of home and land. It is a question of grave difficulty to all those who seek to remedy the ills from which our farmers are suffering. At present prices the farmer finds that it takes more of his products to get a dollar wherewith to buy back the dollar which he borrowed than it did when he borrowed it. The interest accumulates, while the payment of the principal seems utterly hopeless, and the very depression which we are discussing makes the renewal of the mortgage most difficult.'[14]

According to the census of May 29, 1891, 2.5 million farms were deep in debt, two-thirds of them were managed by the owners whose obligations amounted to nearly £440,000.

'The situation is this: farmers are passing through the "valley and shadow of death"; farming as a business is profitless; values of farm products have fallen 50 per cent since the great war, and farm values have depreciated 25 to 50 per cent during the last ten years; farmers are overwhelmed with debts secured by mortgages on their homes, unable in many instances to pay even the interest as it falls due, and unable to renew the loans because securities are weakening by reason of the general depression; many farmers are losing their homes under this dreadful blight, and the mortgage mill still grinds. We are in the hands of a merciless power; the people's homes are at stake.'[15]

Encumbered with debts and close to ruin, the farmer had no option but to supplement his earnings by working for a wage, or else to abandon his farm altogether. Provided it had not yet fallen into the clutches of his creditors like so many thousands of farms, he could shake from off his feet the dust of the 'land of promise' that had become an inferno for him. In the middle eighties, abandoned and decaying farms could be seen everywhere. In 1887, Sering wrote:

'If the farmer cannot pay his debts to date, the interest he has to pay is increased to 12, 15 or even 20 per cent. He is pressed by the banker, the machine salesman and the grocer who rob him of the fruits of his hard work...He can either remain on the farm as a tenant or move further West, to try his fortunes elsewhere. Nowhere in North America have I found so many indebted, disappointed and depressed farmers as in the wheat regions of the North Western prairies. I have not spoken to a single farmer in Dakota who would not have been prepared to sell his farm.[16]

'The Commissioner of Agriculture of Vermont in 1889 reported a widespread desertion of farm-lands of that state. He wrote: "...there appears to be no doubt about there being in this state large tracts of tillable unoccupied lands, which can be bought at a price approximating the price of Western lands, situated near school and church, and not far from railroad facilities. The Commissioner has not visited all of the counties in the state where these lands are reported, but he has visited enough to satisfy him that, while much of the unoccupied and formerly cultivated land is now practically worthless for cultivation, yet very much of it can be made to yield a liberal reward to intelligent labour.'''[17]

The Commissioner of the State of New Hampshire issued a pamphlet in 1890, devoting 67 pages to the description of farms for sale at the lowest figures. He describes 1442 farms with tenantable buildings, abandoned only recently. The same has happened in other districts. Thousands of acres once raising corn and wheat are left untilled and run to brush and wood.

In order to resettle the deserted land, speculators engaged in advertising campaigns and attracted crowds of new immigrants — new victims who were to suffer their predecessors' fate even more speedily.

A private letter says: 'In the neighbourhood of railroads and markets, there remains no common land. It is all in the hands of the speculators. A settler takes over vacant land and counts for a farmer; but the management of his farm hardly assures his livelihood, and he cannot possibly compete with the big farmer. He tills as much of his land as the law compels him to do, but to make a comfortable living, he must look for additional sources of income outside agriculture. In Oregon, for instance, I have met a settler who owned 160 acres for five years, but every summer, until the end of July, he worked twelve hours a day for a dollar a day at road-making. This man, of course, also counts as one of the five million farmers in the 1890 census. Again, in the County of Eldorado, I saw many farmers who cultivated their land only to feed their cattle and themselves. There would have been no profit in producing for the market, and their chief income derives from gold-digging, the felling and selling of timber, etc. These people are prosperous, but it is not agriculture which makes them so. Two years ago, we worked in Long Cañon, Eldorado County, living in a cabin on an allotment. The owner of this allotment came home only once a year for a couple of days, and worked the rest of the time on the railway in Sacramento. Some years ago, a small part of the allotment was cultivated, to comply with the law, but now it is left completely untilled. A few acres are fenced off with wire, and there is a log cabin and a shed. But during the last years all this stands empty; a neighbour has the key and he made us free of the hut. In the course of our journey, we saw many deserted allotments, where attempts at farming had been made. Three years ago I was offered a farm with dwelling house for a hundred dollars, but in a short time the unoccupied house collapsed under the snow.

In Oregon, we saw many derelict farms with small dwelling houses and vegetable gardens. One we visited was beautifully made: a sturdy block house, fashioned by a master-builder, and some equipment; but the farmer had abandoned it all. You were welcome to take it all without charge.'[18]

Where could the ruined American farmer turn? He set out on a pilgrimage to follow the wheat centre and the railways. The former had shifted in the main to Canada, the Saskatchewan and the Mackenzie River where wheat can still thrive on the 62nd parallel. A number of American farmers followed — and after some time in Canada, they suffered the old fate.[19] During recent years, Canada has entered the world market as a wheat-exporting country, but her agriculture is dominated to an even greater extent by big capital than elsewhere.[20]

In Canada, public lands were lavished upon private capitalist companies on an even more monstrous scale than in the United States. Under the Charter of the Canadian Pacific Railway Company with its grant of land, private capital perpetrated an unprecedented act of robbing the public. Not only that the company was guaranteed a twenty years' monopoly of railway-building, not only that it got a building site of about 713 miles free of charge, not only that it got a 100 years' state guarantee of the 3 per cent interest on the share capital of £m. 20 — to crown it all, the company was given the choice of 25 million acres out of the most fertile and favourably situated lands, not necessarily in the immediate vicinity of the permanent way, as a free gift. All future settlers on this vast area were thus at the mercy of railway capital from the very outset. The railway company, in its turn, immediately proceeded to sell off 5 million acres for ready cash to the North-West Land Company, an association of British capitalists under the chairmanship of the Duke of Manchester. The second group of capitalists which was liberally endowed with public lands was the Hudson Bay Company, which was given a title to no less than one-twentieth of all the lands between Lake Winnipeg, the U.S. border, the Rocky Mountains, and Northern Saskatchewan, for renouncing their privileges in the North-West. Between them, these two capitalist groups had gained possession of five-ninths of all the land that could be settled. A considerable part of the other lands was assigned by the State to 26 capitalist 'colonising companies'.[21] Thus the Canadian farmer was practically everywhere ensnared by capital and capitalist speculation. And still mass immigration continued — not only from Europe, but also from the United States!

These are the characteristics of capitalist domination on an international scale. Having evicted the peasant from his soil, it drives him from England to the East of the United States, and from there to the West, and on the ruins of the Red Indians' economy it transforms him back into a small commodity producer. Then, when he is ruined once more, he is driven from the West to the North. With the railways in the van, and ruin in the rear — capital leads the way, its passage is marked with universal destruction. The great fall of prices in the nineties is again succeeded by higher prices for agricultural products, but this is of no more avail to the small American farmer than to the European peasant.

Yet the numbers of farmers are constantly swelling. In the last decade of the nineteenth century they had grown from 4,600,000 to 5,700,000, and the following ten years still saw an absolute increase. The aggregate value of farms had during the same period risen from £150,240,000 to £330,360,000.[22] We might have expected the general increase in the price of farm produce to have helped the farmer to come into his own. But that is not so; we see that the growing numbers of tenant farmers outstrip the increase in the farming population as a whole. In 1880, the proportion of tenant farmers amounted to 25.5 per cent of the total number of farmers in the Union, in 1890 it was 28.4 per cent, in 1900 35.3 per cent, and in 1910 37.2 per cent.

Though prices for farm produce were rising, the tenant farmer was more and more rapidly stepping into the shoes of the independent farmer. And although much more than one-third of all farmers in the Union are now tenant farmers, their social status in the United States is that of the agricultural labourer in Europe. Constantly fluctuating, they are indeed wage-slaves of capital; they work very hard to create wealth for capital, getting nothing in return but a miserable and precarious existence.

In quite a different historical setting, in South Africa, the same process shows up even more clearly the 'peaceful methods' by which capital competes with the small commodity producer.

In the Cape Colony and the Boer Republics, pure peasant economy prevailed until the sixties of the last century. For a long time the Boers had led the life of animal-tending nomads; they had killed off or driven out the Hottentots and Kaffirs with a will in order to deprive them of their most valuable pastures. In the eighteenth century they were given invaluable assistance by the plague, imported by ships of the East India Company, which frequently did away with entire Hottentot tribes whose lands then fell to the Dutch immigrants. When the Boers spread further East, they came in conflict with the Bantu tribes and initiated the long period of the terrible Kaffir wars. These god-fearing Dutchmen regarded themselves as the Chosen People and took no small pride in their old-fashioned Puritan morals and their intimate knowledge of the Old Testament; yet, not content with robbing the natives of their land, they built their peasant economy like parasites on the backs of the Negroes, compelling them to do slave-labour for them and corrupting and enervating them deliberately and systematically. Liquor played such an important part in this process, that the prohibition of spirits in the Cape Colony could not be carried through by the English government because of Puritan opposition. There were no railways until 1859, and Boer economy in general and on the whole remained patriarchal and based on natural economy until the sixties. But their patriarchal attitude did not deter the Boers from extreme brutality and harshness. It is well known that Livingstone complained much more about the Boers than about the Kaffirs. The Boers considered the Negroes an object, destined by God and Nature to slave for them, and as such an indispensable foundation of their peasant economy. So much so that their answer to the abolition of slavery in the English colonies in 1836 was the 'Great Trek', although there the owners had been compensated with £3,000,000. By way of the Orange River and Vaal, the Boers emigrated from the Cape Colony, and in the process they drove the Matabele to the North, across the Limpopo, setting them against the Makalakas. Just as the American farmer had driven the Red Indian West before him under the impact of capitalist economy, so the Boer drove the Negro to the North. The 'Free Republics' between the Orange River and the Limpopo thus were created as a protest against the designs of the English bourgeoisie on the sacred right of slavery. The tiny peasant republics were in constant guerilla warfare against the Bantu Negroes. And it was on the backs of the Negroes that the battle between the Boers and the English government, which went on for decades, was fought. The Negro question, i.e. the emancipation of the Negroes, ostensibly aimed at by the English bourgeoisie, served as a pretext for the conflict between England and the republics. In fact, peasant economy and great capitalist colonial policy were here competing for the Hottentots and Kaffirs, that is to say for their land and their labour power. Both competitors had precisely the same aim: to subject, expel or destroy the coloured peoples, to appropriate their land and press them into service by the abolition of their social organisations. Only their methods of exploitation were fundamentally different. While the Boers stood for out-dated slavery on a petty scale, on which their patriarchal peasant economy was founded, the British bourgeoisie represented modern large-scale capitalist exploitation of the land and the natives. The Constitution of the Transvaal (South African) Republic declared with crude prejudice: 'The People shall not permit any equality of coloured persons with white inhabitants, neither in the Church nor in the State.'[23]

In the Orange Free State and in the Transvaal no Negro was allowed to own land, to travel without papers or to walk abroad after sunset. Bryce tells us of a case where a farmer, an Englishman as it happened, in the Eastern Cape Colony had flogged his Kaffir slave to death. When he was acquitted in open court, his neighbours escorted him home to the strains of music. The white man frequently maltreated his free native labourers after they had done their work — to such an extent that they would take to flight, thus saving the master their wages.

The British government employed precisely the opposite tactics. For a long time it appeared as protector of the natives; flattering the chieftains in particular, it supported their authority and tried to make them claim a right of disposal over their land. Wherever it was possible, it gave them ownership of tribal land, according to well-tried methods, although this flew in the face of tradition and of the actual social organisation of the Negroes. All tribes in fact held their land communally, and even the most cruel and despotic rulers such as the Matabele Chieftain Lobengula merely had the right as well as the duty to allot every family a piece of land which they could only retain so long as they cultivated it. The ultimate purpose of the British government was clear: long in advance it was preparing for land robbery on a grand scale, using the native chieftains themselves as tools. But in the beginning it was content with the 'pacification' of the Negroes by extensive military actions. Up to 1879 were fought 9 bloody Kaffir wars to break the resistance of the Bantus.

British capital revealed its real intentions only after two important events had taken place: the discovery of the Kimberley diamond fields in 1869-70, and the discovery of the gold mines in the Transvaal in 1882-5, which initiated a new epoch in the history of South Africa. Then the British South Africa Company, that is to say Cecil Rhodes, went into action. Public opinion in England rapidly swung over, and the greed for the treasures of South Africa urged the British government on to drastic measures. South Africa was suddenly flooded with immigrants who had hitherto only appeared in small numbers — immigration having been deflected to the United States. But with the discovery of the diamond and gold fields, the numbers of white people in the South African colonies grew by leaps and bounds: between 1885 and 1895, 100,000 British had immigrated into Witwatersrand alone. The modest peasant economy was forthwith pushed into the background — the mines, and thus the mining capital, coming to the fore. The policy of the British government veered round abruptly. Great Britain had recognised the Boer Republics by the Sand River Agreement and the Treaty of Bloemfontein in the fifties. Now her political might advanced upon the tiny republics from every side, occupying all neighbouring districts and cutting off all possibility of expansion. At the same time the Negroes, no longer protected favourites, were sacrificed. British capital was steadily forging ahead. In 1868, Britain took over the rule of Basutoland — only, of course, because the natives had 'repeatedly implored' her to do so.[24] In 1871, the Witwatersrand diamond fields, or West Griqualand, were seized from the Orange Free State and turned into a Crown Colony. In 1879, Zululand was subjected, later to become part of the Natal Colony; in 1885 followed the subjection of Bechuanaland, to be joined to the Cape Colony. In 1888 Britain took over Matabele and Mashonaland, and in 1889 the British South Africa Company was given a Charter for both these districts, again, of course, only to oblige the natives and at their request.[25] Between 1884 and 1887, Britain annexed St. Lucia Bay and the entire East Coast as far as the Portuguese possessions. In 1894, she subjected Tongaland. With their last strength, the Matabele and Mashona fought one more desperate battle, but the Company, with Rhodes at the head, first liquidated the rising in blood and at once proceeded to the well-tried measure for civilising and pacifying the natives: two large railways were built in the rebellious district.

The Boer Republics were feeling increasingly uncomfortable in this sudden stranglehold, and their internal affairs as well were becoming completely disorganised. The overwhelming influx of immigrants and the rising tides of the frenzied new capitalist economy now threatened to burst the barriers of the small peasant states. There was indeed a blatant conflict between agricultural and political peasant economy on the one hand, and the demands and requirements of the accumulation of capital on the other. In all respects, the republics were quite unable to cope with these new problems. The constant danger from the Kaffirs, no doubt regarded favourably by the British, the unwieldy, primitive administration, the gradual corruption of the *volksraad* in which the great capitalists got their way by bribery, lack of a police force to keep the undisciplined crowds of adventurers in some semblance of order, the absence of labour legislation for regulating and securing the exploitation of the Negroes in the mines, lack of water supplies and transport to provide for the colony of 100,000 immigrants that had suddenly sprung up, high protective tariffs which increased the cost of labour for the capitalists, and high freights for coal — all these factors combined towards the sudden and stunning bankruptcy of the peasant republics.

They tried, obstinately and unimaginatively, to defend themselves against the sudden eruption of capitalism which engulfed them, with an incredibly crude measure, such as only a stubborn and hide-bound peasant brain could have devised: they denied all civic rights to the *uitlanders* who outnumbered them by far and who stood for capital, power, and the trend of the time. In those critical times it was an ill-omened trick. The mismanagement of the peasant republics caused a considerable reduction of dividends, on no account to be put up with. Mining capital had come to the end of its tether. The British South Africa Company built railroads, put down the Kaffirs, organised revolts of the *uitlanders* and finally provoked the Boer War. The bell had tolled for peasant economy. In the United States, the economic revolution had begun with a war, in South Africa war put the period to this chapter. Yet in both instances, the outcome was the same: capital triumphed over the small peasant economy which had in its turn come into being on the ruins of natural economy, represented by the natives' primitive organisations. The domination of capital was a foregone conclusion, and it was just as hopeless for the Boer Republics to resist as it had been for the American farmer. Capital officially took over the reins in the new South African Union which replaced the small peasant republics by a great modern state, as envisaged by Cecil Rhodes' imperialist programme. The new conflict between capital and labour had superseded the old one between British and Dutch. One million white exploiters of both nations sealed their touching fraternal alliance within the Union with the civil and political disfranchisement of five million coloured workers. Not only the Negroes of the Boer Republics came away empty-handed, but the natives of the Cape Colony, whom the British government had at one time granted political equality, were also deprived of some of their rights. And this noble work, culminating under the imperialist policy of the conservatives in open oppression, was actually to be finished by the Liberal Party itself, amid frenzied applause from the 'liberal cretins of Europe' who with sentimental pride took as proof of the still continuing creative vigour and greatness of English liberalism the fact that Britain had granted complete self-government and freedom to a handful of whites in South Africa.

The ruin of independent craftsmanship by capitalist competition, no less painful for being soft-pedalled, deserves by rights a chapter to itself. The most sinister part of such a chapter would be out-work under capitalism; — but we need not dwell on these phenomena here.

The general result of the struggle between capitalism and simple commodity production is this: after substituting commodity economy for natural economy, capital takes the place of simple commodity economy. Non-capitalist organisations provide a fertile soil for capitalism; more strictly: capital feeds on the ruins of such organisations, and although this non-capitalist *milieu* is indispensable for accumulation, the latter proceeds at the cost of this medium nevertheless, by eating it up. Historically, the accumulation of capital is a kind of metabolism between capitalist economy and those pre-capitalist methods of production without which it cannot go on and which, in this light, it corrodes and assimilates. Thus capital cannot accumulate without the aid of non-capitalist organisations, nor, on the other hand, can it tolerate their continued existence side by side with itself. Only the continuous and progressive disintegration of non-capitalist organisations makes accumulation of capital possible.

The premises which are postulated in Marx's diagram of accumulation accordingly represent no more than the historical tendency of the movement of accumulation and its logical conclusion. The accumulative process endeavours everywhere to substitute simple commodity economy for natural economy. Its ultimate aim, that is to say, is to establish the exclusive and universal domination of capitalist production in all countries and for all branches of industry.

Yet this argument does not lead anywhere. As soon as this final result is achieved — in theory, of course, because it can never actually happen — accumulation must come to a stop. The realisation and capitalisation of surplus value become impossible to accomplish. Just as soon as reality begins to correspond to Marx's diagram of enlarged reproduction, the end of accumulation is in sight, it has reached its limits, and capitalist production is in extremes. For capital, the standstill of accumulation means that the development of the productive forces is arrested, and the collapse of capitalism follows inevitably, as an objective historical necessity. This is the reason for the contradictory behaviour of capitalism in the final stage of its historical career: imperialism.

Marx's diagram of enlarged reproduction thus does not conform to the conditions of an accumulation in actual progress. Progressive accumulation cannot be reduced to static interrelations and interdependence between the two great departments of social production (the departments of producer and consumer goods), as the diagram would have it. Accumulation is more than an internal relationship between the branches of capitalist economy; it is primarily a relationship between capital and a non-capitalist environment, where the two great departments of production sometimes perform the accumulative process on their own, independently of each other, but even then at every step the movements overlap and intersect. From this we get most complicated relations, divergencies in the speed and direction of accumulation for the two departments, different relations with non-capitalist modes of production as regards both material elements and elements of value, which we cannot possibly lay down in rigid formulæ. Marx's diagram of accumulation is only the theoretical reflection of the precise moment when the domination of capital has reached its limits, and thus it is no less a fiction than his diagram of simple reproduction, which gives the theoretical formulation for the point of departure of capitalist accumulation. The precise definition of capitalist accumulation and its laws lies somewhere in between these two fictions.

Production and the working class are affected alike in this way. At their expense, the accumulation of capital is raised to the highest power, by robbing the one of their productive forces and by depressing the other's standard of living. Needless to say, after a certain stage the conditions for the accumulation of capital both at home and abroad turn into their very opposite — they become conditions for the decline of capitalism.

The more ruthlessly capital sets about the destruction of non-capitalist strata at home and in the outside world, the more it lowers the standard of living for the workers as a whole, the greater also is the change in the day-to-day history of capital. It becomes a string of political and social disasters and convulsions, and under these conditions, punctuated by periodical economic catastrophes or crises, accumulation can go on no longer.

But even before this natural economic impasse of capital's own creating is properly reached it becomes a necessity for the international working class to revolt against the rule of capital.

Capitalism is the first mode of economy with the weapon of propaganda, a mode which tends to engulf the entire globe and to stamp out all other economies, tolerating no rival at its side. Yet at the same time it is also the first mode of economy which is unable to exist by itself, which needs other economic systems as a medium and soil. Although it strives to become universal, and, indeed, on account of this its tendency, it must break down — because it is immanently incapable of becoming a universal form of production. In its living history it is a contradiction in itself, and its movement of accumulation provides a solution to the conflict and aggravates it at the same time. At a certain stage of development there will be no other way out than the application of socialist principles. The aim of socialism is not accumulation but the satisfaction of toiling humanity's wants by developing the productive forces of the entire globe. And so we find that socialism is by its very nature an harmonious and universal system of economy.

ENDNOTES

The Struggle against Natural Economy

1.   Mill, in his *History of British India*, substantiates the thesis that under primitive conditions the land belongs always and everywhere to the sovereign, on evidence collected at random and quite indiscriminately from the most varied sources (Mungo Park, Herodotus, Volney, Acosta, Garcilasso de la Vega, Abbé Grosier, Barrow, Diodorus, Strabo and others). Applying this thesis to India, he goes on to say: 'From these facts only one conclusion can be drawn, that the property of the soil resided in the sovereign; for if it did not reside in him, it will be

impossible to show to whom it belonged' (James Mill, *History of British India* (4th edition, 1840), vol. i, p. 311). Mill's editor, H. H. Wilson who, as Professor of Sanskrit at Oxford University, gives an interesting commentary to this classical deduction. Already in his preface he characterises the author as a partisan who has juggled with the whole history of British India in order to justify the theories of Mr. Bentham and who, with this end, has used the most dubious means for his portrait of the Hindus which in no way resembles the original and almost outrages humanity. He appends the following footnote to our quotation: 'The greater part of the text and of the notes here is wholly irrelevant. The illustrations drawn from the Mahometan practice, supposing them to be correct, have nothing to do with the laws and rights of the Hindus. They are not, however, even accurate and Mr. Mill's guides have misled him.' Wilson then contests outright the theory of the sovereign's right of ownership in land, especially with reference to India. (Ibid., p. 305, footnote.) Henry Maine, too, is of the opinion that the British attempted to derive their claim to Indian land from the Mahometans in the first place, and he recognises this claim to be completely unjustified. 'The assumption which the English first made was one which they inherited from their Mahometan predecessors. It was that all the soil belonged in absolute property to the sovereign, — and that all private property in land existed by his sufferance. The Mahometan theory and the corresponding Mahometan practice had put out of sight the ancient view of the sovereign's rights which, though it assigned to him a far larger share of the produce of the land than any Western ruler has ever claimed, yet in nowise denied the existence of private property in land' (*Village Communities in the East and West* (5th edition, vol. 2, 1890), p. 104). Maxim Kovalevski, on the other hand, has proved thoroughly that this alleged 'Mahometan theory and practice' is an exclusively British legend. (Cf. his excellent study, written in Russian, *On the Causes, the Development and the Consequences of the Disintegration of Communal Ownership of Land* (Moscow, 1879), part i.) Incidentally, British experts and their French colleagues at the time of writing maintain an analogous legend about China, for example, asserting that all the land there had been the Emperor's property. (Cf. the refutation of this legend by Dr. O. Franke, *Die Rechtsverhältnisse am Grundeigentum in China*, 1903.)

2 'The partitions of inheritances and execution for debt levied on land are destroying the communities — this is the formula heard nowadays everywhere in India' (Henry Maine, op. cit., p. 113).

3 This view of British colonial policy, expounded e.g. by Lord Roberts of Kandahar (for many years a representative of British power in India) is typical. He can give no other explanation for the Sepoy Mutiny than mere 'misunderstandings' of the paternal intentions of the British rulers. '...The alleged unfairness of what was known in India as the land settlement, under which system the right and title of each landholder to his property was examined, and the amount of revenue to be paid by him to the paramount Power, as owner of the soil, was regulated...as peace and order were established, the system of land revenue, which had been enforced in an extremely oppressive and corrupt manner under successive

Native Rulers and dynasties, had to be investigated and revised. With this object in view, surveys were made, and inquiries instituted into the rights of ownership and occupancy, the result being that in many cases it was found that families of position and influence had either appropriated the property of their humbler neighbours, or evaded an assessment proportionate to the value of their estates. Although these inquiries were carried out with the best intentions, they were extremely distasteful to the higher classes, while they failed to conciliate the masses. The ruling families deeply resented our endeavours to introduce an equitable determination of rights and assessment of land revenue... On the other hand, although the agricultural population greatly benefited by our rule, they could not realise the benevolent intentions of a Government which tried to elevate their position and improve their prospects' (*Forty One Years in India*, London, 1901, p. 233).

4   In his *Maxims on Government* (translated from the Persian into English in 1783), Timur says: 'And I commanded that they should build places of worship, and monasteries in every city; and that they should erect structures for the reception of travellers on the high roads, and that they should make bridges across the rivers.

'And I commanded that the ruined bridges should be repaired; and that bridges should be constructed over the rivulets, and over the rivers; and that on the roads, at the distance of one stage from each other, Kauruwansarai should be erected; and that guards and watchmen should be stationed on the road, and that in every Kauruwansarai people should be appointed to reside...

'And I ordained, whoever undertook the cultivation of waste lands, or built an aqueduct, or made a canal, or planted a grove, or restored to culture a deserted district, that in the first year nothing should be taken from him, and that in the second year, whatever the subject voluntarily offered should be received, and that in the third year, duties should be collected according to the regulation'. (James Mill, op. cit., vol. ii, pp. 493, 498).

5   Count Warren, *De L'État moral de la population indigène*. Quoted by Kovalevski, op. cit., p. 164.

6   *Historical and Descriptive Account of British India* from the most remote period to the conclusion of the Afghan war by Hugh Murray, James Wilson, Greville, Professor Jameson, William Wallace and Captain Dalrymple (Edinburgh, 4th edition, 1843), vol. ii, p. 427. Quoted by Kovalevski, op. cit.

7   Victor v. Leyden, *Agrarverfassung und Grundsteuer in Britisch Ostindien. Jahrb. f. Ges., Verw. u. Volksw.*, vol. xxxvi, no. 4, p. 1855.

8   'When dying, the father of the family nearly always advises his children to live in unity, according to the example of their elders. This is his last exhortation, his dearest wish' (A. Hanotaux et A. Letournaux, *La Kabylie et les Coûtumes Kabyles*, vol. ii, 1873, 'Droit Civil', pp. 468-73). The authors, by the way, appraised this impressive description of communism in the clan with this peculiar sentence: 'Within the industrious fold of the family association, all are united in

a common purpose, all work for the general interest — but no one gives up his freedom or renounces his hereditary rights. In no other nation does the organisation approach so closely to equality, being yet so far removed from communism.'

9   'We must lose no time in dissolving the family associations, since they are the lever of all opposition against our rule' (Deputy Didier in the National Assembly of 1851).

10   Quoted by Kovalevski, op. cit., p. 217. Since the Great Revolution, of course, it had become the fashion in France to dub all opposition to the government an open or covert defence of feudalism.

11   G. Anton, *Neuere Agrarpolitik in Algerien and Tunesien. Jahrb. f. Gesetzgebung, Verwaltung und Volkwirtschaft* (1900), pp. 1341 ff.

12   On June 20, 1912, M. Albin Rozet, on behalf of the Commission for the Reform of the 'Indigenat' (Administrative Justice) in Algeria, stated in his speech to the French Chamber of Deputies that thousands of Algerians were migrating from the Setif district, and that 1,200 natives had emigrated from Tlemcen during the last year, their destination being Syria. One immigrant wrote from his new home: 'I have now settled in Damascus and am perfectly happy. There are many Algerians here in Syria who, like me, have emigrated. The government has given us land and facilities to cultivate it.' The Algerian government combats this exodus — by denying passports to prospective emigrants. (Cf. *Journal Officiel*, June 21, 1912, pp. 1594 ff.)

The Introduction of Commodity Economy

1   77,379 chests were imported in 1854. Later, the imports somewhat declined, owing to increased home production. Nevertheless, China remained the chief buyer. India produced just under 6,400,000 tons of opium in 1873/4, of which 6,100,000 tons were sold to the Chinese. To-day [1912] India still exports 4,800,000 tons, value £7,500,000,000, almost exclusively to China and the Malay Archipelago.

2   Quoted by J. Schiebert, *Der Krieg in China* (1903), vol. 2, p. 179.

3   Schiebert, op. cit., p. 207.

4   An Imperial Edict issued on the third day of the eighth moon in the tenth year of Hsien-Feng (6/9/1860) said amongst other things: 'We have never forbidden England and France to trade with China, and for long years there has been peace between them and us. But three years ago the English, for no good cause, invaded our city of Canton, and carried off our officials into captivity. We refrained at that time from taking any retaliatory measures, because we were compelled to recognise that the obstinacy of the Viceroy Yeh had been in some measure a cause of the hostilities. Two years ago, the barbarian Commander Elgin came north and we then commanded the Viceroy of Chihli, T'an Ting-hsiang, to look into matters preparatory to negotiations. But the barbarian took advantage of our unreadiness, attacking the Taku forts and pressing on to

Tientsin. Being anxious to spare our people the horrors of war, we again refrained from retaliation and ordered Kuei Liang to discuss terms of peace. Notwithstanding the outrageous nature of the barbarians' demands we subsequently ordered Kuei Liang to proceed to Shanghai in connection with the proposed Treaty of Commerce and even permitted its ratification as earnest of our good faith.

'In spite of all this, the barbarian leader Bruce again displayed intractability of the most unreasonable kind, and once more appeared off Taku with a squadron of warships in the eighth Moon. Seng Ko Lin Ch'in thereupon attacked him fiercely and compelled him to make a rapid retreat. From all these facts it is clear that China has committed no breach of faith and that the barbarians have been in the wrong. During the present year the barbarian leaders Elgin and Gros have again appeared off our coasts, but China, unwilling to resort to extreme measures, agreed to their landing and permitted them to come to Peking for the ratification of the Treaty.

'Who could have believed that all this time the barbarians have been darkly plotting, and that they had brought with them an army of soldiers and artillery with which they attacked the Taku forts form the rear, and, having driven out our forces, advanced upon Tientsin!' (I. O. Bland and E. T. Blackhouse, *China under the Empress Dowager* (London, 1910), pp. 24-5. Cf. also in this work the entire chapter, 'The Flight to Yehol'.)

5   These European exploits to make China receptive to commodity exchange, provide the setting for a charming episode of China's internal history: Straight from looting the Manchu Emperor's Summer Palace, the 'Gordon of China' went on a campaign against the revels of Taiping. In 1863 he even took over command of the Imperial fighting forces. In fact, the suppression of the revolt was the work of the British army. But while a considerable number of Europeans, among them a French admiral, gave their lives to preserve China for the Manchu dynasty, the representatives of European commerce were eagerly grasping this opportunity to make capital out of these fights, supplying arms both to their own champions and to the rebels who went to war against them. 'Moreover, the worthy merchant was tempted, by the opportunity for making some money, to supply both armies with arms and munitions, and since the revels had greater difficulties in obtaining supplies than the Emperor's men and were therefore compelled and prepared to pay higher prices, they were given priority and could thus resist not only the troops of their own government, but also those of England and France' (M. v. Brandt, *33 Jahre in Ostasien, 1911, vol. iii, China*, p. 11).

6   Dr. O. Franke, *Die Rechtsverhältnisse am Grundeigentum in China* (Leipzig, 1903), p. 82.

7   Bland and Blackhouse, op. cit., p. 338.

8   Ibid., p. 337.

The Struggle against Peasant Economy

1   Until recently, in China the domestic industries were widely practised even by
    the bourgeoisie and in such large and ancient towns as Ningpo with its 300,000
    inhabitants. 'Only a generation ago, the family's shoes, hats, shirts, etc., were
    made by the women themselves. At that time, it was practically unheard-of for a
    young woman to buy from a merchant what she could have made with the labour
    of her own hands' (Dr. Nyok-Ching Tsur, 'Forms of Industry in the Town of
    Ningpo' (*Die gewerblichen Betriebsformen der Stadt Ningpo*), Tuebingen, 1909,
    p. 51).

2   Admittedly, this relation is reversed in the last stages of the history of peasant
    economy when capitalist production has made its full impact. Once the small
    peasants are ruined, the entire work of farming frequently devolves on the
    women, old people and children, while the men are made to work for their living
    for capitalist entrepreneurs in the domestic industries or as wage-slaves in the
    factories. A typical instance is the small peasant in Wuerttemberg.

3   W. A. Peffer, *The Farmer's Side. His Troubles and Their Remedy* (New York,
    1891), Part ii, 'How We Got There', chap. i, "Changed Conditions of the
    Farmer', pp. 56-7. Cf. also A. M. Simmons, *The American Farmer*) 2nd edition,
    Chicago, 1906), pp. 74 ff.

4   Report of the U.S.A. Commissioner of Agriculture for the year 1867 (Washington,
    1868). Quoted by Lafargue: *Getreidebau und Getreidehandel in den Vereinigten
    Staaten* in *Die Neue Zeit* (1885), p. 344. This essay on grain cultivation and the
    grain trade in the U.S.A. was first published in a Russian periodical in 1883.

5   'The three Revenue Acts of June 30, 1864, practically formed one measure, and
    that probably the greatest measure of taxation which the world has seen.... The
    Internal Revenue Act was arranged, as Mr. David A. Wells has said, on the
    principle of the Irishman at Donnybrook Fair: "whenever you see a head, hit it,
    whenever you see a commodity, tax it"' (F. W. Taussig, *The Tariff History of the
    United States* (New York-London, 1888), pp. 163-4.

6   Ibid., pp. 166-7.

7   'The necessity of the situation, the critical state of the country, the urgent need of
    revenue, may have justified this haste, which, it is safe to say, is unexampled in
    the history of civilised countries' (Taussig, op. cit., p. 168).

8   Peffer, op. cit., pp. 58 ff.

9   Ibid., p. 6.

10 'Agricultural Competition in North America' (*Die landwirtschaftliche Konkurrenz
    Nordamerikas*) Leipzig, 1887, p. 431.

11 Lafargue, op. cit., p. 345.

12 The Thirteenth Annual Report of the Commissioner of Labour (Washington,
    1899) tables the advantages of machinery methods over hand methods so far
    achieved as follows:

Type of work	Labour time per unit			
	Machine		Hand	
	hrs.	min.	hrs.	min.
Planting small corn	—	32.7	10	55
Harvesting and threshing small corn	1	—	46	40
Planting corn	—	37.5	6	15
Cutting corn	3	4.5	5	—
Shelling corn	—	3.6	66	40
Planting cotton	1	3	8	48
Cultivating cotton	12	5	60	—
Mowing grass (scythe *v.* mower)	1	0.6	7	20
Harvesting and baling hay	11	3.4	35	30
Planting potatoes	1	2.5	15	—
Planting tomatoes	1	4	10	—
Cultivating and harvesting tomatoes	134	5.2	324	20

13   Wheat exports from the Union to Europe:

Year	Million bushels	Year	Million bushels
1868-9	17.9	1885-6	57.7
1874-5	71.8	1890-1	55.1
1879-80	153.2	1899-1900	101.9

(Juraschek's *Uebersichten der Weltwirtschaft*, vol. vii, part i, p.32).

Simultaneously, the price per bushel wheat *loco* farm (in cents) declined as follows:

1870-9	105	1896	73
1880-9	83	1897	81
1895	51	1898	58

Since 1899, when it had reached the low level of 58 cents per bushel, the price is moving up again:

1900	62	1903	78
1901	62	1904	92
1902	63		

(Ibid., p. 18).

According to the 'Monthly Returns on External Trade' (*Monatliche Nachweise über den Auswärtigen Handel*), the price (in *marks*) per 1,000 *kg.*, was in June 1912:

Berlin	227.82	London	170.96
New York	178.08	Odessa	173.94
Mannheim	247.93	Paris	243.69

[14] Peffer, op. cit., part i, 'Where We Are', chap. ii, 'Progress of Agriculture', pp. 30-1.

[15] Ibid., p. 4.

[16] Sering, op. cit., p. 433.

[17] Peffer, op. cit., pp. 34 f.

[18] Quoted by Nikolayon, op. cit., p. 224.

[19] 49,199 people immigrated to Canada in 1902. In 1912, the number of immigrants was more than 400,000 — 138,000 of them British, and 134,000 American. According to a report from Montreal, the influx of American farmers continued into the spring of the present year [1912].

[20] 'Travelling in the West of Canada, I have visited only one farm of less than a thousand acres. According to the census of the Dominion of Canada, in 1881, when the census was taken, no more than 9,077 farmers occupied 2,384,337 acres of land between them; accordingly, the share of an individual (farmer) amounted to no less than 2,047 acres — in no state of the Union is the average anywhere near that' (Sering, op. cit., p. 376). In the early eighties, farming on a large scale was admittedly not very widely spread in Canada. But already in 1887, Sering describes the 'Bell Farm', owned by a limited company, which comprised no fewer than 56,700 acres, and was obviously modelled on the pattern of the Dalrymple farm. In the eighties, Sering, who regarded the prospects of Canadian competition with some scepticism, put the 'fertile belt' of Western Canada at three-fifths of the entire acreage of Germany, and estimated that actually only 38,400,000 acres of this were arable land, and no more than 15,000,000 acres at best were prospective wheat land (Sering, op. cit., pp. 337-8). The *Manitoba Free Press* in June 1912, worked out that in summer, 1912, 11,200,000 acres were sown with spring wheat in Canada, as against 19,200,000 acres under spring wheat in the United States. (Cf. *Berliner Tageblatt, Handelszeitung*, No. 305, June 18, 1912.)

[21] Sering, op. cit., pp. 361 ff.

[22] Ernst Schultze, '*Das Wirtschaftsleben der Vereinigten Staaten*', *Jahrb. f. Gesetzg., Verw. u. Volkswirtschaft 1912*, no. 17, p. 1724.

[23] Article 9.

[24] 'Moshesh, the great Basuto leader, to whose courage and statesmanship the Basutos owed their very existence as a people, was still alive at the time, but

constant war with the Boers of the Orange Free State had brought him and his followers to the last stage of distress. Two thousand Basuto warriors had been killed, cattle had been carried off, native homes had been broken up and crops destroyed. The tribe was reduced to the position of starving refugees, and nothing could save them but the protection of the British government which they had repeatedly implored' (C.P. Lucas, *A Historical Geography of the British Colonies*, part ii, vol. iv (Geography of South and East Africa), Oxford, 1904, p. 39).

[25] The Eastern section of the territory is Mashonaland where, with the permission of King Lobengula, who claimed it, the British South Africa Company first established themselves' (ibid., p. 72).